THE CODE
OF THE
WARRIOR

THE CODE OF THE WARRIOR

In History, Myth, and Everyday Life

RICK FIELDS

HarperPerennial
A Division of HarperCollins*Publishers*

F O R

John Steinbeck IV, pointman
still leading the way

Passages from *Under the Mountain Wall* by Peter Matthiessen, The Viking Press, 1962; *The Iliad,* trans. by Robert Fitzgerald, Doubleday/Anchor Books, 1975; *T'ai Chi Touchstones,* trans. by Douglas Wile, Sweet Ch'i Press; and *In Search of the Primitive* by Louis Cotlow, Little, Brown, 1942, are reprinted by permission of the publishers.

FIRST EDITION

Designed by Ruth Kolbert

Library of Congress Cataloging-in-Publication Data

Fields, Rick.
  The code of the warrior : in history, myth, and everyday life / Rick Fields.—1st ed.
    p. cm.
  Includes bibliographical references and index.
  ISBN 0-06-055060-0
  ISBN 0-06-096605-X (pbk.)
  1. War—Moral and ethical aspects. 2. Soldiers—Conduct of life.
I. Title.
U22.F53 1991
172'.42—dc20   90-55986

91 92 93 94 95 CC/RRD 10 9 8 7 6 5 4 3 2 1

91 92 93 94 95 CC/RRD 10 9 8 7 6 5 4 3 2 1 (pbk.)

And above all, dedicated to Force, they are triumphant victims of the internal logic of Force, which proves itself only by surpassing boundaries—even its own boundaries and those of its raison d'être.

   –GEORGES DUMEZIL, *The Destiny of the Warrior*

For to win one hundred victories in one hundred battles is not the acme of skill. To subdue the enemy without fighting is the acme of skill.

   –SUN TZU, *The Art of War*

True victory is not defeating an enemy. True victory gives love and changes the enemy's heart.

   –MORIHEI UESHIBA, founder of aikido

CONTENTS

ILLUSTRATIONS

Page 98   Portrait of the Imperial Bodyguard Hu-erh-ch'a. Anonymous, Chinese, Ch'ing dynasty, dated 1760. Detail of a hanging scroll, ink and color on silk. The Dillon Fund Gift. Courtesy of The Metropolitan Museum of Art, New York.

Page 118   Chang San-Feng, founder of Tai Chi Chuan. Courtesy of Jou Tsung Hwa, Tai Chi Foundation, Warwick, New York.

Page 132   Godefroy IV de Bouillon, duke of Basse-Lorraine (1061–1100), French leader of the first crusade (1096–1099), proclaimed King of Jerusalem. From Tanco de Frexenall's *Libro Intulade Palinodia*, printed at Orense, 1547. Courtesy of The Bettmann Archive, New York.

Page 168   Sanjo-den youchi no emaki (Scroll with Depictions of the Night Attack on the Sanjo Palace). From the Heiji monogatari emaki (Illustrated Scrolls of the Events of the Heiji Era). Japan, Kamakura period, second half of the thirteenth century. Handscroll, ink and colors on paper. Fenollosa-Weld Collection. Courtesy of Museum of Fine Arts, Boston.

Page 206   The Bad Heart Buffalo Manuscript by Helen Bliss. A native historical record of the Ogalala Dakota. Neg. No. 336464. Courtesy of Department Library Services, American Museum of Natural History, New York.

Page 232   Photo courtesy of The Bettmann Archive, New York.

Page 250   Dahomey Palace Guard. Neg. No. 14216. Courtesy of Department Library Services, American Museum of Natural History, New York.

Page 260   Anita Roddick, founder of The Body Shop, Inc. Photo credit: Thomas L. Kelly.

Page 272   Valerie Wake, 92 feet above ground on yarder, to stop logging on Sapphire sale, Siskiyou National Forest, Oregon, 7/23/87. Photo copyright © 1989, courtesy of David J. Cross.

ACKNOWLEDGMENTS

This book could not have been written without the encouragement
and vision of literary agent Peter Livingston. It also owes a great
deal to challenging discussions with poet-playwright Sidney
Goldfarb, part of a conversation that has wandered on for
twenty-five years now. In addition, Dr. Francis Harwood generously
shared her extensive anthropological knowledge, lore, and library.
Eve Wallace read and reread drafts with a sharp and sympathetic
eye. Fellow nonfictionist Marc Barasch commiserated.
Mouser-Inanna hunted, and kept me company. John Steinbeck IV,
calling long-distance, kept me on target.

My kyudo teacher, Kanjuro Shibata Sensei, reminded me that
"mind is target," as did Ikeda Sensei, of the Boulder Aikikai, and
Bob Wing, master of the morning sword class. Jude Blitz showed
me how to blend, fall, and roll. John Milton sent me to the
mountain. Howard Bad Hand opened the way to the Pine Ridge
Sun Dance. The McClellans—John, Roz, Jethro, and
Robin—provided warmth and good cheer, along with after-dinner
insights. And the Bowen Gulch 3 A.M. Raiders proved that warriors
who refuse to give up can still save a few ancient trees for the next
generation.

THE
TARGET CALLS

High above the plains of Valltorta in Eastern Spain, there is a rock overhanging a cliff. Under the rock, on the cliff wall, facing west, is a painting in red ocher depicting two groups of archers in what seems to be a battle. Experts disagree on the date of the painting, but whatever the true age, the lithe, lively lines of the warriors are still clearly visible, though long faded from exposure to sun and rain: two groups of men, some armed with bows and carrying three or four arrows in one hand, facing each other in a loose ragged battle line. The warriors in the front lines are shooting arrows at each other; the warriors in the rear are carrying bundles of arrows. Some are advancing to the front; others appear to be retreating.

On the left about ten warriors, with two archers leading the way, are opposed by a larger group—three clusters of five or six archers, with an equal number waiting behind them, as if in reserve. Though some authorities believe this and other similar scenes may represent dances or ritual fighting, it would be hard to disagree with the painter Douglas Mazonowicz that "this is almost certainly a battle scene."[1]

In fact, this is quite possibly the earliest representation of warriors fighting in battle, if not of war. The great ice age paintings to the north, in the famous Paleolithic cathedrals, are filled with pictures of the animals of the time, the woolly rhinoceros, the horse, the saber-toothed tiger, the mastodon, and men hunting them. The exact nature of the thousands of paintings is still, after more than a hundred years of study, hotly disputed. But nowhere—not in the vast open caverns of Lascaux or in the hidden niches that can be reached only by crawling through winding passageways, and at no time during the span of perhaps twenty or so thousand years they were painted—are there any scenes of men fighting other men. It is only here, in the open-air paintings of the caves of the Spanish Levant, that the hunters of animals appear to have become hunters of men.

△△ II △△

Nobody knows when war began.

The question is more than academic for a species with the unique luxury of pondering its own extinction. If war—defined, provisionally and broadly, as an organized fight, with lethal intent, between two groups—is inherent, innate, or natural, then we must face the possibility that war is perhaps inevitable.

War may have had its uses. But not many people these days can ignore the fact that the million-armed shape-shifting creature we call war has evolved so successfully along with all the rest of our technology that no one—neither the civilian, nor the most ferocious and skillful frontline warrior, nor the technician with a finger on a button, nor, perhaps, life itself—will emerge unscathed from the fog of the next world war, whether it be nuclear, chemical, petroleum, or "conventional."

It hardly matters that the very same specialization that has enabled us to successfully conquer the environment and destroy and outbreed most other species has come to be so deeply implicated in our own potential self-destruction. Overspecialization has led many species to extinction.

Traditionally, times of crisis call forth the warrior. But today the very warrior we might call on is implicated in the problem, for are not the warriors themselves responsible for the pass we have come to? While this may be true, it may also be true that the sword the warrior holds is the key that unlocks the fortress of fear we hide within. If the warrior is responsible, then let us call on the warrior to be fully responsible. If there is a way out of our current crisis, it will not come about by turning away from the source of the crisis. We cannot destroy the warrior without entering endlessly into the very cycle we wish to break.

The warrior is by definition a fighter, a man or woman of action, a specialist in meeting and resolving conflict and challenge. In most societies, warriors have taken this role quite literally. They seek out battle; fighting is what gives meaning to their lives. In other societies, battle is only a last resort, something to be engaged in only after all other means of resolving conflict have been exhausted. And finally, there is a tradition in which the warrior sees the true battle as an inner or spiritual one, in which the fight is with the enemies of self-knowledge or realization.

Though the true warrior is a fighter, he or she does not fight out of aggression. The apparent fierceness of the warrior proceeds from a primary caring for others. Putting others before oneself is the ultimate source of the warrior's courage. Like the thorn on the rose, the warrior exists to protect others—the family, the clan, the nation. In the contemporary world, where the interdependence of all forms of people and of all forms of life is now clear, the warrior's loyalty and protection is beginning to extend to the earth itself.

The figure of the warrior is truly cross-cultural. The ancient warrior tradition is found in Africa, among the Masai; among the North and South American Indians; and among the Chinese and Japanese, to name just a few. In Europe, the figure of the warrior appeared among the Greeks, and also among the knights.

In each of these traditions, the warrior is considered an essential part of society, a protector and a source of good. And in each of these traditions, the warrior is bound by a code, a rule, a way of life. This code of the warrior embodies ways to regulate and in some cases to transform or transcend aggression. This code—which separates the true warrior from the mere mercenary—can become a path of personal and spiritual development. From a global perspective, an understanding of the way the warrior's code has functioned in different societies and at different times may help us solve the problems of war and environmental devastation. However, we can call on the warrior to meet the common crisis only by looking back to the roots of what it means to be a warrior, and looking forward to his or her continual transformation. This may sound utopian or idealistic; it may *be* utopian and idealistic. But warriors have a predilection not only for strategy but for a certain reckless and perhaps even foolhardy courage as well.

In fact, there are many signs that the alarm has gone around the earth and called forth new bands of warriors. Men and women, in both likely and unlikely places, are springing up like so many dragon's teeth to protect and defend both humanity and the earth. And it is a good thing. Today more than ever we need the fierce compassion of the warrior.

THE FIRST PEOPLE

Warriors Before War

Ancestral evolution has made us all warriors. . . .
—William James

Visions of the past are visions of the future, too.

It was a summer afternoon in 1924 in Johannesburg when Professor Raymond Dart opened a crate of fossils that had just been delivered to his study from the Taung limestone works. The first crate contained little of interest—only a few fossilized eggshells and turtle shells. But as he pried open the lid of the second crate, a thrill of excitement shot through the young anatomy professor. He was, as he would point out years later, one of the few men in the world able to recognize the importance of what he saw. It was an endocranial cast, a mold of the interior of a skull, clearly imprinted with the swirling convolutions and furrows of the primate brain. Only it was a brain that seemed considerably larger than any ape's.

Dart ransacked the mass of rock for the missing face. He came up with a block of limestone in which he thought he saw the faint outlines of part of a skull, a portion of jaw, and a tooth socket. He thought of Darwin's discredited theory that man's ancestors would probably be found in Africa, where his nearest relatives, the great apes, still lived. Standing with the skull in his hand, Dart wondered if he was to be the instrument by which the missing link between apes and man would be found.

Dart set to work, first with a hammer and chisel and then with his wife's knitting needles. On the seventy-third day, "the rock parted," and Dart found himself staring into the long-empty eyes of a baby's face.

There were a number of things that made the Taung baby, as it came to be known, a very special child. Like a proud father, Dart enumerated its virtues: It was clever, if not a genius. The high forehead housed a well-developed forebrain. It was also handsome, since its reduced canines saved it from "the truly frightful physiognomy" (as Darwin called it) that the fighting fangs gave the apes. But most impressive of all, it could stand and walk on two legs—at least that was what Dart deduced from the fact that the hole through which the nerves of the spinal column joined the brain, the *foramen magnum*, opened at the base of the skull.

Dart concluded that the Taung baby was either a man-ape or an ape-man, and that if it was not the missing link it was the nearest thing to it that had ever been found. At the very least, it was the first homonid to have been found in Africa, and the oldest in the world. Judging from the surrounding geological strata—and from the various fossils found with it—Dart estimated that the Taung baby was a million or so years old. He christened his man-ape or ape-man *Australopithecus*.

Thirty years later, his claims for his initial discovery having been alternatively rejected and acclaimed by the paleontological establishment, Professor Dart returned to the field. Excavations at Makapansgat had revealed a very early fossil baboon skull. Dart found forty-two more baboon skulls. They all exhibited depressions in their skulls, as if they had been struck with a clublike object.

But the most shocking specimen to come out of Makapansgat was, as Dart wrote, "the fractured lower jaw of a 12-year-old son of a manlike ape. The lad had been killed by a violent blow delivered with smashing accuracy on the point of the chin, either by a smashing fist or a club. The bludgeon blow was so vicious that it had shattered the jaw on both sides of the face and knocked out all the front teeth."[1]

Back in the laboratory Dart noticed that more than half the baboon skulls, twenty-seven out of forty-two, had been struck on the left side of the head—which suggested they had been struck by someone who was mostly right-handed. The finger of evidence pointed straight at *Australopithecus.*

The only evidence missing was the weapon, and Dart soon found that among the profusion of antelope bones and horns littering the cave. The leg bones were perfect clubs, with knobby ends that fit neatly into the depressions in the baboon skulls. The australopithecines, said Dart, had fashioned weapons and tools from the bones, horns, and teeth (conveniently fixed to jawbones) of the animals they hunted. The earliest humans had a culture, an osteodontokeratic (that is, bone-tooth-horn) culture that had allowed the small, defenseless hominids to survive and to triumph in a dangerous world. The use of weapons, which had opened the way to hunting and meat eating, was the behavioral missing link, the evolutionary turn in the road that explained how we had come to be who we are.

Dart published his views in a paper titled "On the Predatory Transition from Ape to Man" in 1953. "On this thesis," he wrote, "man's predecessors differed from living apes in being carnivorous creatures, that seized living quarries by violence, battered them to death, tore apart their broken bodies, dismembered them limb from limb, slaking their ravenous thirst with the hot blood of victims and greedily devouring livid writhing flesh."[2]

Dart's speculations, so far reserved for readers of obscure scientific journals, were given wide currency by the American journalist, playwright, and screenwriter Robert Ardrey in the best-selling book *African Genesis*. Before long, Dart's killer ape turned up in Hollywood. Millions of moviegoers watched as one clever ape in the opening scene of Stanley Kubrick's *2001* picked up an osteodontokeratic weapon—a jawbone—and hurled it over a water hole at an opposing group of apes, only to see it turn lazy arcs against a blue African sky, end over end, until it was transformed into an orbiting, spinning spaceship. The message was unmistakable: It was humanity's use of weapons as a means of aggression that had propelled our evolution from terrestrial ape to intergalactic engineer.

⋀⋀ II ⋀⋀

Professor Dart expounded his theory at the 1957 Pan-African Conference on Prehistory held in Livingston, Kenya. Afterward, one of the conference participants, S. E. Washburn, a social anthropologist from the University of Chicago, had gone on to the Wankie Game Reserve in southern Rhodesia to observe baboons. But while there, with Dart's theory fresh in his mind, he scrutinized the remains of antelopes and other prey killed by lions and concluded that Dart's bone-and-teeth weapons had actually been brought to the caves by scavaging hyenas. "This makes it probable," he concluded in a brief paper in the *American Anthropologist,* "that the australopithecines were themselves the game, rather than the hunters."[3]

Washburn's suggestive work was expanded and amplified by another conference participant, C. K. Brain. A specialist in taphonomy, a subbranch of paleontology that "concerns itself with what happens to animal remains between death and fossilization,"[4] Brain began by analyzing thousands of fossil fragments taken from the limestone caves.

Brain went further than Washburn, however, in identifying the hunter—or hunters—who had included australopithecines in their prey. Measuring the space between the marks at the base of an australopithecine skull—marks which Dart had attributed to blows from another australopithecine—Brain found that they exactly matched the marks that a cave leopard's canines would make while it was gripping a skull in its jaws.

Brain published the results of his research in a book which he titled, in homage to Washburn's earlier essay, "The Hunter or the Hunted?" The caves, Brain concluded, had not been the homes of the first humans, but their burial chambers. And far from being the great hunter that Dart had imagined, our first ancestors had been the hunted. It was not as predator but as prey that we had come into the world.

⋀⋀ III ⋀⋀

It now seems that our first step on the evolutionary path to humanness was taken about 3.5 million years ago. That at least is the radiocarbon date for Lucy—so called because Donald Johanson and the other young paleontologists who found her nearly complete skeleton in Afar, Ethiopia, celebrated by playing the Beatles' "Lucy in the Sky with Diamonds" all night. Lucy was only four feet tall and her brain was smaller than a chimpanzee's, but judging from her pelvis and knees, she walked very well on two feet.

Bipedalism, the ability to stand and walk upright on two feet, is considered the first sign of the hominid—of humanness. Darwin had noted that bipedalism freed the hands and so allowed or encouraged the use of tools and weapons. But there is something perhaps more basic about the bipedalism we share only with the birds. A standing creature gazes out to the distance, to the horizon. It arranges the world, the universe, the cosmos along a vertical axis—standing makes an up and a down, and four directions.

A creature standing and moving at the center of this axis must develop a wakeful alertness and balance just to keep standing. If the first step to humanness, the first victory of the ancestral warrior, was to merely and triumphantly stand, then the first worthy opponent—the first challenger—of the ancestral warrior was that constant inexorable force we would one day identify as the law of gravity. It is here, at the very beginning, that we may find the origin of the stance of readiness so characteristic of the warrior.

What, then, of the freed hands? Darwin had placed tools and weapons in the hands, a lead followed to a murderous, homicidal conclusion by Dart. But the recent paleological evidence leads in a different direction. Lucy stood, but her brain was too small to manipulate tools or weapons. In any case, the earliest known tools—Louis Leakey's small round pebble-shaped "choppers" from the Olduvai Gorge—go back a mere two million years or so.

It is much more likely, then, that the freed hands of the first hominids were busy gathering and carrying food back to some kind of home base, where it was probably divided and shared. C. J. Lovejoy, the physical anthropologist who reconstructed Lucy, locates the beginning of the monogamous human family here, with males carrying food back to their women and children. But Adrienne Zihlman and Nancy Tanner, two anthropologists with a feminist perspective, have argued that females first gathered plants (as they still do in most hunter-gatherer societies) for their children, and that the first great invention was not the club or the spear or the bow of the later male hunters, but the humble carrying basket hollowed out of gourds or woven from leaves.[5]

Gathering by females or males or both may well have been extended to include scavenged meat from large animals killed by predators or disease or accident. Louis Leakey—or Son of the Sparrow Hawk, to use the name the Kikuyu elders had given him during his initiation into the way of the hunter at the age of thirteen—was so taken with the scavenging hypothesis that he took his son Richard with him to test it out in the field. They went as Leakey supposed the first men had gone—naked and with only a few giraffe limbs and jawbones picked up along the way for protection.

They soon came upon a zebra which had been killed and half eaten by lions. "We drove off the vultures and hyenas when they came in for the kill," said Leakey. "But we couldn't drive off the lions. We watched them and the vultures watched them and the hyenas watched them, and then we rushed in."[6]

They managed to fight off the hyenas for nearly ten minutes. "Then I signaled to my son, 'Get out, it's not safe any longer. They're going to kill us now.' But we got a little zebra meat."

Leakey hypothesized that scavenging had led the early humans he called *Homo habilis* to make stone tools like the ones he had found in the Olduvai Gorge to butcher scavenged meat. But that, of course, was just one of many steps and revelations along the way—there was wild-fire to be caught before it was tamed and kindled; there were dreams, visions arising from hunger or possibly from psychotropic mushrooms that spoke with voices from other realms; there was dancing and sing-ing and coupling; there was language; there was the roar of the thunder and the jagged spear of lightning hurled down to earth—by whom or what?—from the unfathomable height of the luminous sky. There were the wheeling stars at night and the great warmth of the sun that vanquished the stars at dawn.

So it was that wonder, curiosity, intelligence, and social life devel-oped and interacted, enabling humans to create culture and occupy a unique cognitive niche all their own. The result was that by the middle Paleolithic—about seven hundred thousand years ago—the hominid prey was well on the way to becoming "the supreme predator of life on earth," in Ervin Laszlo's phrase.[7]

The first hard evidence of human hunting prowess were the charred bones of deer, wild pig, bison, rhinoceros, elephant, and monkey found in the ashes of a hearth in a cave in Choukoutien, China, in 1925. The ashes have been dated at around fifty thousand years old. The cave's inhabitant, Peking man, or *Homo erectus* (upright man) was solidly built, with a brain three-fourths the size of modern man. The long-cold ashes in Choukoutien proved that man had learned how to capture wildfire, if not tame it.

Homo erectus used fire to transform certain foods that could not otherwise be eaten, to fire-harden the points of his wooden spears, to keep warm, and to remain awake through the dark, watching the flickering flames, perhaps talking, perhaps telling stories. But, again, it was not fire, nor the spear, nor the various stone axes which now appeared that allowed *Homo erectus* to hunt large game. It was intelligence, cunning, and skill. Men tracked, snared, and ambushed their prey. Many of the big game animals—elephants, buffalos, and reindeer—were herded over cliffs or driven into marshes through the use of grass fires. Human hunters outwitted rather than overpowered their prey.[8]

Hunting in this way had an important secondary effect: it brought men together. Gathering food was a solitary or family-unit activity, but hunting favored communication, cooperation, and coordination. All of this, so the hunting hypothesis went, encouraged men to control the competition, aggression, and fighting within the male group. Thus, as Lionel Tiger theorized, hunting was the origin of the male bond that survives today in football teams, fraternity houses, board rooms, and armies.

ΛΛ I V ΛΛ

Was hunting, then, the key to human evolution? By the 1960s, many anthropologists seemed to think so. At a well-attended conference on the subject of Man the Hunter held at the University of Chicago in 1966, anthropologist William Laughlin claimed that "hunting is the master behavior pattern of the human species." Hunting, he said, involved much more than simply killing animals for food. It meant mastering a complex curriculum that included an intimate knowledge of land, plants, animal behavior, animal anatomy, strategy, and the skillful use of weapons. Hunting, as Laughlin said, "placed a premium upon inventiveness, upon problem solving." In addition, it provided strong evolutionary incentives for learning, since it was dangerous and risky—it "imposed," as Laughlin put, "a real penalty for failure to solve the problem."[9]

In a sense, the hunter had to "become" his prey in order to hunt at all. The hunter had to know what the animal ate, the terrain it favored in different seasons, when it migrated and where, when it mated and gave birth, and a hundred other details. But most important of all, he has to know how to look.

This "looking" encouraged the development of a certain kind of attention. The hunter "does not believe that he knows where the critical moment is going to occur," as hunter and philosopher Jose Ortega y Gasset noted in *Meditations on Hunting*.

> He does not look tranquilly in one determined direction, sure beforehand that the game will pass in front of him. The hunter knows that he does not know what is going to happen, and this is one of the greatest attractions of his occupation. Thus he needs to prepare an attention of a different and superior style—an attention which does not consist in riveting itself on the presumed but consists precisely in not presuming anything and in avoiding inattentiveness. It is a "universal" attention, which does not inscribe itself on any point and tries to be on all points. There is a magnificent term for this, one that still conserves all its zest of vivacity and imminence: alertness. The hunter is the alert man.[10]

Hunting was a game of chance. The hunter might throw and miss, or the spear might hit but not kill, and the animal might escape, taking the spear and the hours or days of stalking with it. Or, cornered and fighting for its life, the quarry might turn and strike out with rage and fury. It was at this moment, when life faced life, that the hunter's courage or bravery—his willingness to risk all on a throw of a spear— was called into play.

Having learned to identify with the lives of animals, and given the nearly eye-to-eye closeness necessary for killing, it is likely that hunters would also identify with the deaths of animals. The mammals killed, butchered, and eaten by human hunters were in most ways similar to human beings—indeed the red blood animals shed was indistinguishable from human blood.

Though man had become the most dangerous of predators, he was a predator who knew what he was doing. He knew, to begin with, what death was, or at the very least he knew *that* death was, at least since the arrival of the Neanderthals forty thousand or so years ago. An excavation at the cave of La-Chappelle-aux-Saints in France revealed a Neanderthal buried with a bison leg on his chest, as well as flint tools—all of which suggest the familiar practice of supplying the dead with provisions for a journey. At Shanidar, a later Neanderthal site in a cave in what is now Turkey, pollen analysis of the soil revealed that at least eight species of brightly colored wild flowers had been laid over the body, which lay on a bed of branches.

For death was, and is, the great mystery. In its simplest and most direct form, death asks, Where has the life that was present before death gone? What has become of life?

The answer, again in its simplest and most direct form, is that life has gone away; it has gone somewhere else. This held for any being with life, including the hunter's quarry.

"Every good hunter," says Ortega y Gasset, "is uneasy in the depths of his conscience when faced with the death he is about to inflict on the enchanted animal. He does not have the final and firm conviction that his conduct is correct. But neither, it should be understood, is he certain of the opposite."[11]

It is this uneasiness that is sung by the Akoa Pygmies while placing a garland around the tusks of a freshly killed elephant:

> Our spear strayed from its course.
> O Father Elephant!
> We didn't mean to kill you,
> We didn't mean to hurt you,
> O Father Elephant!
> It wasn't the warrior who took your life,
> Your hour had come,
> Don't come back to trample down our huts . . .
>
> Don't be angry with us.
> From now on your life will be better,
> You live in the land of the Spirits,
> Our fathers will go with you to renew their bond,
> You live in the land of the Spirits.[12]

△△ V △△

If the spirit of the hunted animal was honored and given safe passage, the body that remained behind was equally cared for and respected. Flesh, internal organs, hide, bones, teeth, tusks—hardly anything was discarded. The meat was divided among the hunters and the rest of the band in an orderly fashion. Among some hunters, the largest or choicest portion went to the hunter who had first spotted the prey, or to the one whose spear or arrow had struck first, or to the hunter who had delivered the final blow. Kin, children, old people were all given their portions. The details varied, but sharing and generosity were the rule, the way, among all hunter-gatherers.

The centrality of the ethics of sharing and generosity among hunters brings us back full circle to the question of whether hunting alone can be taken as "the master behavior pattern of the human species." If it is that for men, where does that leave women? Have they been left out of the "master behavior pattern"?

Richard Leakey, the second-generation hunter of human origins, has come up with what may be the closest thing to a master key or behavior pattern. It is not just hunting or just gathering that is the key, says Leakey, but sharing itself, the spear and the basket together. "The essential element of the uniquely human way of life," he writes in his book *People of the Lake,* "was the economic pact between suppliers of meat and suppliers of vegetables. . . . Sharing, not hunting or gathering as such, is what made us human."[13]

△△ VI △△

Warfare—which exists, according to Margaret Mead, "if the conflict is organized and socially sanctioned and the killing is not regarded as murder"[14]—very probably played no part in the lives of our hunter-gatherer ancestors. Certainly they would seem to have little to gain from war. They had no personal possessions except for hunting weapons and ornaments. There was no reason to capture slaves, since there were no fields or workshops for them to labor in. Human sacrifice was not part of their spiritual life, which recognized the intrinsic aliveness of rocks, mountains, rivers, forests, plants, and animals. And since there was no hierarchical political control within the band, there was neither the structure nor the desire to extend control over other bands. Food was considered a gift from the forest, as the Mbuti Pygmies say. There were no stores of grain or oil or gems, no horses or cattle or pigs either to plunder or to protect. And since meat couldn't be stored or hoarded, a good kill was celebrated by feasting, singing, gambling, and dancing.

Thomas Hobbes had characterized the life of primitive man as being one of "continuall feare, and danger of violent death . . . solitary, poore, nasty, brutish, and short." But some contemporary anthropologists have taken the opposite view. Marshall Sahlins, for example, characterized the hunter-gatherers as "the original affluent society." The hunter-gatherer, said Sahlins, had adopted "a Zen solution to the problem of scarcity and affluence" based on the premise that "human material ends are few and finite and technical means unchanging but on the whole adequate. . . . We might entertain the possibility that hunters are in business for their health, a finite objective, and bow and arrow are adequate to the end."[15]

Sahlin's notion that hunters comprised "the original affluent society" has been criticized as romantic primitivism by some. But it has also been supported by extensive research conducted by Richard Lee of Harvard among the !Kung Bushmen in 1964. Lee had found that most of the hunting and gathering was done by adults between the ages of twenty and sixty, who freely supported elders, adolescents, and children. Women spent about three hours a day working in camp. The hardest working hunter went out after game on sixteen out of twenty-eight days. Men might hunt for a week and then take a few weeks off. When they weren't hunting, they sang spontaneous mood songs, and they danced, playing the strings of their hunting bows, the sounds of which were deepened by amplifiers fashioned from hollow gourds. They danced before and after hunts, especially when they had killed a gemsbok. And sometimes they danced all night, entering into healing trances.

This is not to make the naive claim that hunter-gatherers lived in a perfectly peaceful world, whatever that might be. A world without warfare is not necessarily a world without conflict. If people disagreed, they might simply leave to join another band, or they might fight with words—"little sharp words, like the wooden splinters which I hack off with my axe," as an Eskimo song duel goes—or come to blows. Conflict might even erupt into violence and death. But the conflict was for the most part personal, familial. "Usually," says anthropologist Elman Service, "the occasion for any kind of battle or threat of battle is caused by elopement, an illegal love affair of some kind, or simply an insult."[16]

The Australian anthropologist M. J. Meggitt, who lived with the desert-dwelling Walbiri in the fifties, came to a similar conclusion. "Walbiri society did not emphasize militarism—there was no class of permanent or professional warriors; there was no hierarchy of military command. . . . Every man was (and still is) a potential warrior, always armed and ready to defend his rights; but he was also an individualist who preferred to fight independently."[17]

In *The Forest People*, Colin Turnbull provides us with an eyewitness account of the way the Mbuti Pygmies of the Ituri rain forest in central Africa handled territorial disputes. Turnbull was traveling with a band when an elder named Masisi told him that Pygmies from the other side of the forest had "invaded our territory and were stealing our honey to the east." Masisi sent his son to call the scattered bands, "so that we could all make war on the other Pygmies together."

Turnbull was beginning to worry—though Pygmy arrows are tiny, they carry a deadly poison—until a Pygmy friend took him aside to reassure him. "Old Masisi's head is unsteady," he told the anthropologist. "It has worms in it. He will fight only with words. Every year those Pygmies come into our land and we into theirs. There is plenty of food; so long as we do not meet there is no fighting. If we do meet, then those who are not in their own land run away and leave behind whatever they have stolen. That is the only way we ever fight—we are not villagers."[18]

◮◮ V I I ◮◮

The hunting-gathering way of life was based on an ethic of reciprocity, sharing, and generosity. It was hard but not mean, dangerous but not cruel, contentious but not warlike. The hunter hunted, after all, to feed his people as well as himself; he took life for life. "It is virtually a standard rule among hunters," Carlton Coon finds, "that they should never mock or otherwise insult any wild creature whose life they have brought to an end. . . . Hunters sense the unity of nature and the combination of humility and responsibility of their role in it."[19]

The hunting-gathering way of life was also extraordinarily successful in evolutionary terms. It has now been almost entirely obliterated from the face of the earth, but it is worth considering that human beings lived as hunter-gatherers for ninety-eight percent of the time that we have existed as a distinct species. From this point of view, the "progress" of the last ten thousand years or so may yet turn out to be an evolutionary dead end. The cautionary note sounded by the anthropologists who convened the conference on Man the Hunter in 1966 is even more true today: "It is still an open question whether man will be able to survive the exceedingly complex and unstable ecological conditions he has created for himself."[20]

We cannot go back to the days of the hunter-gatherers. But much of their wisdom—wisdom which we sorely need—has survived in the way of the warrior. For if, as William James says, "ancestral evolution has made us all warriors," it is because the best qualities that made a good hunter—alertness, the skillful use of weapons, courage, endurance, loyalty to the band, the willingness to take risks, to be alone, to wait in silence, to become one with the quarry—foreshadowed the best virtues of the warrior.

Hunting, not war, was the evolutionary matrix from which the code of the warrior would be forged.

A DEADLY BALANCE

The Invention of the Warrior

Warfare is just an invention
known to the majority of human societies by which
they permit their young men either to accumulate prestige
or avenge their honor or acquire loot or wives
or slaves or sago lands or cattle or appease the blood lust
of their gods or the restless souls of the recently dead.
It is just an invention,
older and more widespread than the jury system,
but none the less an invention.
—Margaret Mead

The Dani, who lived in the Baliem Valley of Central New Guinea and spent much of their time perched on tall watchtowers guarding their gardens and the women who worked in them, were rumored to be one of the few people left in the world who still practiced ritual war. Though there were a few missionary stations at either end of the valley, the northern part where the Willhibee-Willhou of the Dani lived was effectively isolated. The presence of a few steel axes, traded up from the next valley, was about the only sign that the Neolithic gardeners and warriors lived in the twentieth century.

When Robert Gardner—the advance man for the Harvard-Peabody Expedition—made contact on September 1, 1961, he was met by a party of warriors sitting with their seven-foot-long spears held high.

Like other New Guineans, the Dani prized shells that were traded from the coast, and Gardner presented a man whom he took to be a leader with a rare giant Cymbium diadema shell he had obtained from a collector in Massachusetts. The gift was accepted. In return, the Harvard-Peabody Expedition was allowed to pitch camp in an area some distance from the village. But nothing could persuade the porters, who came from the next valley, to stay. They all set out immediately, anxious to leave before nightfall.

The Dani seemed to live in a timeless world. They cultivated gardens where they grew sweet potatoes and kept pigs. Game was scarce, but they hunted on occasion, mostly for feathers from the bird of paradise; and they traded salt from pools that lay within their territories for stone axes and adzes quarried by a neighboring people. They wove their clothes from reeds. Their culture, in the parlance of archaeologists, was Neolithic, or New Stone Age.

While the shift from hunting and gathering to cultivating and domesticating now seems to have occurred gradually beginning around ten thousand or twelve thousand years ago, the Neolithic Revolution— as the prehistorian R. Gordan Childe called it—utterly transformed the relationship between human beings and their environment. The first people, the hunter-gatherers, had lived on plants and game plucked lightly *from* the forest, and had left the forest—the father and mother forest, as the Pygmies called it—as it was. But the Neolithic cultivators who burned the forest to provide space for their gardens and pigs had taken a turn toward the control and taming of their world. They did not hunt animals or harvest plants from the forest as gifts, as the hunter-gatherers did; rather, they ate the forest itself.

At the same time, the Neolithic Revolution brought an increase in social organization and control. Gardens and domestic animals had to be watched and protected against predators and human thieves, for now there was food to own and therefore food to steal as well. There was also work to be done. Land had to be cleared, seeds and cuttings planted, gardens irrigated, weeded, and fenced. Some of this stooping, backbreaking work was done by men, but much of it—such as protecting gardens and herding pigs—was done by children. Women, too, bent to work over their flat stones, pressing and crushing maize and tapioca and grains.

As Lewis Mumford remarks, the phrase "the daily grind" can be traced directly back to the Neolithic. So, too, can the first glimmers of specialization, which freed some and constricted others—and with all of it, possibly, the beginnings of frustration and resentment. The parental demand that children work may well have resulted in anger and rage, which—because it could not be safely expressed—was projected outward later in aggression, revenge, and the pervasive guilt-ridden fear of ancestral ghosts.

Mircea Eliade suggests that the tangled profusion of warlike violence—of cannibalism, head-hunting, sacrifice—that seems to sprout directly from the rich, fire-cleared soils of the first gardens may be a ritual reenactment of an archaic Neolithic origin myth. According to Eliade, the basic Neolithic origin myth describes the "ritual (that is, violent) death of a primeval giant, from whose body the worlds were made and the plants grew." This myth, he says, provides "the pattern drama from which originated every human or animal sacrifice intended to strengthen and increase the harvest."[1]

If Eliade is right, this "pattern drama" was a play with countless scenarios. The person who was to be the regenerating sacrifice may at some time have volunteered or been selected, willingly or otherwise, from the villagers whose crops were to benefit. But among the contemporary Neolithic peoples, the very unwilling victim was usually taken from another tribe. The hunters of animals thus became transformed into hunters of men—or children or women, for that matter—and the bordering tribes were dehumanized and transformed into prey, whose deaths, as Eliade says, served to "repeat the act of creation that first made grain live."[2] Life, so the basic Neolithic message went, came from death.

◬◬ II ◬◬

The members of the Harvard-Peabody Expedition had only been in the valley two days when they heard the high-pitched cries they were later to recognize as the bird-song-like challenge to fight. The Dani, the anthropologists were relieved to find, had not been distracted or deterred by the expedition's presence. Standing on the sides of the hills that overlooked the fighting field, the anthropologists were able to film and photograph the whole amazing scene.

The Dani came to the battlegrounds between their territories plumed and painted. They wore, in particular, the great bird of paradise feathers that swayed and dipped as they ran. Rain, which might ruin the feathers, was reason to call the battle off. They took their time arriving and getting set and spent much of it calling ribald insults back and forth. They fought in two great lines, either by throwing spears or shooting arrows that were strangely (given the Dani's interest in birds) unfletched and so easier to dodge. Men came and went to the front. Other men, and women, kept on working unconcernedly in nearby gardens, looking up only when a shout indicated that something exciting had happened.

Twenty-five years later the scene was still vivid for Robert Gardner as he sat in his office in the basement of Harvard's Carpenter Center for the Visual Arts. "There were these great ceremonial battles, with hundreds of Dani, flying spears, clouds of arrows like Agincourt, only the element of chivalry was not exactly pronounced," he remembered. "But there were these distinct conventions and codes, and both sides could depend on the other side to follow through. It was an incredible sort of Wagnerian scene actually happening. It was very vocal. The blood was real, the fear was real, the excitement was incredible. There was something very compelling about the behavior."

The novelist Peter Matthiessen, who, like Gardner, witnessed the action from the vantage point of a nearby hillside, has given us what will probably remain our best eyewitness account of a Neolithic ritual battle:

> The alarums and excursions fluttered and died while warriors came in across the fields. The shouted war was increasing in ferocity, and several men from each side would dance out and feign attacks, whirling and prancing to display their splendor. They were jeered and admired by both sides and were not shot at, for display and panoply were part of war, which was less war than ceremonial sport, a wild, fierce, festival. . . .
>
> Toward midmorning a flurry of arrows was exchanged, and the armies, each three or four hundred strong, withdrew once more. But soon a great shout rose up out of the distance, and the Kurelu answered it exultantly, *hoo-ah-h, hoo-ah-h, hua, hua, hua,* like a pack cry of wild dogs. From the base of the tree the advance parties ran to the hillock at the edge of the reed pool, mustered so close that the spears clashed. More companies came swiftly from the rear positions, bare feet drumming on the grass. Here and there flashed egret wands, or a ceremonial whisk; the whisk was made of the great airy feathers

of the cassowary bound tight by yellow fiber of an orchid. The wands and whisks were waved in the left hand, while the spears were borne at shoulder level in the right. . . .

Two armies of four to five hundred each were now opposed, most of the advance warriors armed with bows, a few with spears. They crouched and feinted, and the first arrows sailed lazily against the sky, increasing in speed as they whistled down and spiked the earth. Shrieks burst from the Wettaia, and a wounded Kurelu was carried back, an arrow through his thigh; he stared fearfully, both hands clenched upon a sapling, as two older men worked at the arrow and cut it out.[3]

The battle lasted, with long lulls, until late in the afternoon, when the warriors who had come from distant villages started home. A number of men had been wounded, but no one had been killed.

This is not to say that the ritual battle was entirely without danger. True, a battle always ended when a warrior was killed or seriously wounded (or when it rained or the sun set). But death, even if only a single death, was still the object of the battle. The arrows may have been unfletched and consequently less accurate and easier to dodge, but they were wound with an orchid fiber that caused an often lethal festering infection. In fact, in the battle Matthiessen and the Harvard-Peabody Expedition witnessed, one man, Ekitamalek, wounded by an arrow in the chest, did eventually die.

A death had two serious, related consequences. According to the Dani, the *etai-eken,* the "seeds of singing," which resided in the solar plexus were considered the essence of a person's strength and vitality. With death, and especially with a death caused by an enemy, the *etai-eken* of the individual were diminished, but so were the *etai-eken* of the whole group. Therefore, as Robert Gardner noted, "The Dani regard the killing of a comrade, wife or child personally as a physical and spiritual threat and as a spur to actions which will redress the unequal balance between themselves and the enemy."[4]

The most effective answer to the weakening of the seeds of singing caused by death was the cry of the bird that challenged the enemy to battle. If the death went unavenged, there would be trouble: sickness, spiritual malaise, failed crops, bad luck. It was not hard to find some pretext—a raid on a watchtower or garden, stolen sweet potatoes or pigs, an abduction or rape—for battle.

Weem—the Dani word for what we call war—seemed entirely a ritual. The Dani were not fighting about land or about protein. They were not trying to conquer the other Dani, nor were they trying to defend their homes. They were fighting, it seemed, for each other. For the winners—for those who had killed or wounded an enemy warrior— the world was once more in balance. But for the losers who had lost a warrior, the balance could only be restored by the revenge of another death. And so it went, victor and vanquished, killer and killed, back and forth, the deadly balance, the to and fro of life and death. "The war," as Robert Gardner remembered, "settled things, it brought harmony into their lives rather than disharmony. It was ironic, but war there was being used as a cultural antidote to the awful feeling of being out of joint with the cosmos."

◬ I I I ◬

Balance of a very different order was at the center of what has become one of the most influential theories of primitive warfare. For Marvin Harris of Columbia University and other cultural ecologists, the real reason the Neolithic cultivators made war was simply that it "enhanced the well-being and survivability of individuals and groups by regulating the balance between population size and crucial local and regional ecological variables."[5] And the warrior, whether he knew it or not, no matter how proud of his waving plumes, how brave or crafty in attack, had been invented in order to limit and balance his own population as well as his enemies', so that he had enough to eat.

The precise mechanism by which warfare served to balance the population with its environment was not what one might think, however. In fact, the mechanism Harris posited worked with a Malthusian starkness worthy of Jonathan Swift. Neolithic warrior societies, said Harris, limited their population by killing or neglecting a certain percentage of their female infants.

Harris argued, moreover, that population was only marginally limited by the deaths of male warriors, whose reproductive place could be easily taken by other men; the real effect of primitive warfare on limiting population was that warfare encouraged the practice of female infanticide. In *Cannibals and Kings,* Harris wrote:

> A very powerful cultural force was needed to motivate parents to neglect or kill their own children, and an especially powerful force

was needed to neglect or kill more girls than boys. Warfare supplied this force and the motivation because it made the survival of the group contingent on the rearing of combat-ready males. Males were chosen to be taught how to fight because armaments consisted of spears, clubs, bows and arrows, and other hand-held weapons. Hence military success depended upon relative numbers of brawny combatants. For this reason males became socially more valuable than females, and both men and women collaborated in "removing" daughters in order to rear a maximum number of sons.[6]

Though Harris is one of the most influential contemporary anthropologists, his war theory was by no means universally accepted. In fact, it was challenged by one of the few anthropologists with direct experience of primitive warfare.

Napoleon Chagnon, then of the University of Michigan, had spent some twenty years doing fieldwork among the Fierce People—the Yanomamo of the Amazonian rain forests. According to Chagnon, Yanomamo men fought over women, and villages fought to maintain their sovereignty, since a village that was considered weak would be attacked, its men killed, and its women stolen by a more aggressive village. Drawing from sociobiology, Chagnon thought that men fought because this was the way they increased their inclusive fitness—the most ferocious fighters got the most women and had the most children. As far as Chagnon was concerned, Harris's theory was not supported by the Yanomamo. They had more than enough to eat, and tests by a team of medical researchers had shown them to be among the healthiest of all primitive people.

But Chagnon was also speaking from hard-won experience. He had spent twenty years, off and on, with the Yanomamo, risking his life more than once. Not only had he attended the preraid ceremonies during which the warriors invite the fierce man-killing spirits into their chests, but he had even inhaled *ebene,* the hallucinogenic snuff which brought the fierce man-killing spirits into the warriors—much to the horror of the missionaries. He had witnessed the brutal chest-slapping duels and club fights which left the men with proud scars crisscrossing their heads. He had heard the warriors sing the song of the carnivorous wasp and then rush off to their huts to retch with the rotten meat of their enemies. And he had watched as they lined up in the early morning, clacking their six-foot-long cane arrows as they marched proudly off to the raid.

He did not have to depend on the field notes of other anthropologists, as Harris did, or the memories of informants who often recounted tales (quite possibly exaggerated) told by their fathers or grandfathers. Napoleon Chagnon was reporting from the front. And Napoleon Chagnon did not agree with Marvin Harris.

△△ I V △△

The showdown came at Columbia. On the eve of Chagnon's return to the Yanamamo, Chagnon and Harris debated the question. For Harris, said Chagnon, protein was the "resource par excellence in human cultural adaptations and human social behavior."[7] Chagnon therefore asked Harris how much protein the Yanomamo would have to eat for him to be convinced that the Yanomamo were not fighting about meat. Harris replied that if it could be demonstrated that the Yanomamo ate the equivalent of a Big Mac (a "paleoMac," as Chagnon joked), about forty cm of protein, he would be satisfied. A team of graduate students undertook to compile the data, and published their findings in *Science.* The Yanomamo, they said, had as much protein as anyone in the world.

But the matter did not rest there. A letter from two other researchers said that the Yanomamo studied by the researchers were not typical at all. Whereas the true Yanomamo were inland "foot" Indians, these Yanomamo lived at a fishing station with other acculturated Indians. They used gasoline engines, shotguns, and flashlights for night hunting, and they worked for money growing hay and other crops. And so it went. Articles, letters, charges, and countercharges filled the pages of the scholarly journals.

And what about the Yanomamo themselves? Chagnon had taken the liberty of trying *ebene.* He now took the liberty of asking the Yanomamo what *they* thought about the debate. "I explained Harris' theory of their warfare to the Yanomamo. 'He says you are fighting over game animals and meat, and insists that you are not fighting over women.' They laughed at first, and then dismissed Harris' view in the following way. 'Even though we do like meat, we like women a whole lot more!' "[8]

Back at Columbia, Harris was undeterred. "The point," he said, "is that successful Yanomamo warriors get both meat and women. Not having read Malthus and Darwin, the Yanomamo cannot be expected to understand that if resources were unlimited, they would have to fight for neither women nor meat."[9]

Chagnon did not retreat, however. In the last edition of his textbook *Yanomamo: The Fierce People,* he insisted that "Warfare among the Yanomamo—or any sovereign people—is an expected form of political behavior and no more requires special explanations than do religion or economy."[10]

Chagnon's conclusion that war was the natural state of things might not matter that much in itself, but Chagnon's Yanomamo had become something of an anthropological industry. *Yanomamo: The Fierce People* was required reading in many introductory anthropology classes, and the films that Chagnon's team had made of the Yanomamo—there were at least twelve—were widely shown in the same classes. The meta-war—the war about the meaning of war—between Chagnon and Harris was a war for the hearts and minds of graduate students in anthropology; it was a war for the future of anthropology. As R. Brian Ferguson, a young anthropologist who had edited a collection of essays on the cultural ecology of war, worried, "Thousands of students every year are learning that war between sovereign political groups is normal, expectable, and need not be questioned."[11]

For Harris the stakes in the meta-war were even greater. He charged that Chagnon and the sociobiologists he was allied with supported the notion that, because both warfare and the male superiority complex were so widespread in primitive cultures, they were "natural," and so part of human nature—and that in the now familiar and indeed inevitable conclusion, war itself was inevitable. But Harris insisted on the opposite position. "The fact that war and sexism have played and continue to play such prominent roles in human affairs does not mean that they must continue to do so for all future time," he insisted. "War and sexism will cease to be practiced when their productive, reproductive, and ecological functions are fulfilled by less costly alternatives." And so, he concluded with a final salvo, war is not inevitable, since "such alternatives now lie within our grasp for the first time in history."[12]

△△ V △△

Like Harris and Chagnon, the Sambia of highland New Guinea had a myth about the origins of war. It went something like this:

> Chenchi, the wife of the Nunboolyu, the first ancestor, killed her first male child. She did it because the pregnancy was very painful.

That is why we Sambia men now fight war. That is why we Sambia men have initiations and ceremonially beat our children during our initiations.

It was Numboolyu who cut open the vulva with a bamboo knife to make a passage-way for male children. For that reason, babies aren't born quickly.

And therefore men fight. Men hold initiations. And women do not fight; they have no weapons.[13]

The myth reveals a fear and fascination with the awesome sexual life-creating power of woman that is widespread throughout New Guinea in particular, but very much present in the Neolithic cultures of South America and other old planter cultures as well. Women become women without any apparent effort, at least so it seems to men. Their cycles are natural cycles, like the cycles of the moon, or the rise and fall of the tides.

But for men in New Guinea—and in many other warrior cultures as well—men are what they do, not who they are. "Manhood is never the certain result of a natural process," as anthropologist K. E. Read wrote in a classic paper in 1952, "nor is it established by his sexual maturity alone, for its supreme expression is cultural, the result of demonstrated ability in those actions which are designated male. . . . The challenge of the physiological processes of growth and sexual maturity in women is met by men's initiation rites, and thereafter, by the practice of regular self-induced bleeding and magical acts."[14]

So it was that Sambia boys were taken from their mothers at the age of seven to be initiated into the secret men's *nama* cult. The *nama* bird represented the ancestral powers that were crucial to the group's survival. The song of *nama* could be heard in the sounds of the sacred bamboo flutes that were played only in pairs, as "age-mates," in secret; women and uninitiated boys could hear the sound of the flutes, but they were forbidden—on pain of death—from seeing them, and so knowing the true source of the *nama* bird's song.

What happened to women naturally, men self-created ritually. Inside the men's house, rough leaves were inserted into the nose to produce bleeding which—in one widely accepted interpretation, at least—mimicked menstruation. Cane was swallowed to induce vomiting to purify boys and men of pollution from women.

Among the Sambia, the young boys were initiated into secret homoerotic relationships with older males. Anthropologist Gilbert Herdt lived with the Sambia for six months before he accidentally discovered that the young boys performed fellatio on older men for ten or fifteen years. It was the consumption of semen, the essence of maleness, Herdt was told, that turned Sambia boys into real Sambia men: into fierce warriors who killed other men.

And men, as Read says,

> are, ideally, aggressive, flamboyant, given to quick outbursts of anger—the warriors, guardians of custom, and repositories of knowledge on whom the continued welfare and security of the group depend Women's role is seen to be one of submission. A disproportionate share of both the drudgery and heavy work entailed in daily life falls to them, while men are free to gossip, indulge in speechmaking, and put on their brilliant decorations and seek diversion elsewhere.[15]

⋀⋀ VI ⋀⋀

The creation of such a warrior was neither easy nor "natural." Says anthropologist Walter Goldschmidt, "If a society is to have the advantages of having military personnel, the motivations for warriorhood must be established. It is a matter of great significance that these must be *created.*"[16]

L. L. Langness makes a similar point:

> If men, because of some "innate bonding propensity," naturally band together, presumably want to do so, enjoy doing so, why is it necessary for them to force the young males from the company of women and invent such elaborate rules and sanctions to keep them apart as adults? . . . Boys are naturally attracted to their mothers and must be removed from them by the community of males. Young men are naturally attracted to females and must be forcibly kept in line lest their loyalties stray. If a man, in the depths of his passion, or even in his everyday routine, came to favor his mother and wife and wanted to please her more than he wanted to please and help his fellows the foundations of the New Guinea social order would collapse.[17]

As Margaret Mead writes in *Sex and Temperament in Three Primitive Societies:*

If a society insists that warfare is the major occupation for the male sex, it is therefore insisting that all male children display bravery and pugnacity. . . . When, however, a society goes further and defines men as brave and women as timorous, when men are forbidden to show fear and women are indulged in the most flagrant display of fear, a more explicit element enters in. Bravery, hatred of any weakness, of flinching before pain and danger—this attitude which is so strong a component of some human temperaments has been selected as the key to masculine behavior.[18]

To be a man, then, was to be a particular kind of man, the warrior whose maleness was defined by those qualities that made for success in brutal hand-to-hand combat using spears and stone axes. Masculinity was shaped on and by the battlefield. Says Herdt:

Sambia values and beliefs convey a warrior's conception of manhood. . . . Men should be strong, brave, and unyielding in the face of the pursuit of all tasks; and most of all in facing the enemy. Strength had come to mean toughness on arduous, danger-filled guerilla raids to distant enemy lands. Strength meant that if cornered and ambushed by an enemy group, one stood alone, creating havoc and taking as many warriors as possible with oneself to the grave.[19]

The other pole, the far end of this ideal, was the weakling and coward: the *wasaatu,* the rubbish man, the soft man, the (literally) sweet potato man, the man who is more like a woman than a man.

△△ V I I △△

In 1949, the independent explorer and filmmaker Lewis Cotlow arrived in Quito, Ecuador, to film *Jungle Headhunters* for RKO. Picking up a copy of the local paper, *El Commercio,* at his hotel he read a report from the Upano River region he planned to film in. He found that "there had been a recent increase in the number of wars and assassinations for revenge. One man held responsible was a chief named Utitiaja, who was said to have taken fifty-eight heads. He was the most feared warrior the Jivaros had produced in many years."[20]

Lewis Cotlow and his crew went armed mainly with a copy of *Life* magazine containing color photographs of Jivaro from the Paute region taken on an earlier trip in 1945. Cotlow contacted a more or less friendly group of Jivaro, who agreed to perform the *tsa-tsa* dance for him, but it turned out to be just that: a performance. Cotlow decided that his film needed somebody who could ignite the other dancers, "a dynamic character, a real leader who can get some spirit into these people."

An envoy was dispatched with the copy of *Life* to find Utitiaja. He returned with the message that Utitiaja would dance for the film.

> I told him you could not have a successful film without the greatest warrior of the Jivaros. But he also said that Utitiaja would be joined by all the warring Jivaro groups, who had agreed to a temporary truce. As far as anyone knew, it was the first time that had happened since the Jivaro had joined together under the leader Quiruba to success- fully defeat the Spanish in 1599.

The assembled Jivaro were tense and jumpy, but the dance turned out surprisingly well. The dancers, wearing feathers and jaguar-tooth necklaces, joined hands and circled a spear with a shrunken *tsa-tsa* head on top, to the sound of small drums and long flutes. They danced with "queer shuffling steps, sideways forward, and sideways back."

After half an hour, Cotlow had what he needed. He went out on the dance clearing to shake the warriors' hands to thank them. But without warning the drums and flutes started up again, and the warriors started dancing again, with Cotlow in hand.

> I found myself emitting a hoarse grunt along with the others, and being a part of that movement, a contributor to the weird sound, made me share their feelings, somehow. A steady rhythm can do strange things to people, and for a moment it almost made a Jivaro out of me. Across the circle I watched the shrunken head as it bobbed against Juantiga's chest. I looked at Juantiga's face and saw a rapt, dedicated expression that welled up from the depths of his soul. And I felt something of that emotion myself. For a little while I was very close to experiencing the feelings of a man who has cut off another man's head, has shrunk it, and now dances around it.

Perhaps it was because of this experience that Cotlow was able to establish an immediate rapport for his interview with Utitiaja. His training as a warrior, he told Cotlow, had begun when his father had taken him hunting at the age of seven, teaching him how to use the blowgun and the lance, and to "move through the forest like a jaguar." Every morning, even before they ate, his father told him who his enemies were, who had killed his brother and his father's brother. Utitiaja said, "Each time he told me exactly how they died and who had caused their deaths, and he told me what I must do when I grew up."

His father had taken him on his first raid at the age of ten. He kept the boy beside him during the fighting, and "when he had killed his enemy with the lance, he called me to his side and gave me the lance. Then he told me to plunge it in the dead man's body so that I would come to know the feel of it and learn how hard I must thrust. He wanted me to do this, also, so I would not be afraid, so I would become accustomed to blood."

Like all would-be Jivaro warriors, Utitiaja had gone on a quest to a sacred waterfall to seek the vision and possession of the *aruntum,* or ancestral soul. The *aruntum,* which might take the form of a giant leopard fighting or a huge head or ball of fire, would add to a warrior's power; it would increase one's intelligence, make it difficult to lie or be otherwise dishonorable. And it would seize its possessor with a "tremendous desire to kill."

During the day he had walked back and forth under the cold water and drank a tea made from green tobacco. He had fasted in a lean-to—"a dream house"—in the forest for five days, drinking the hallucinogenic *maikoa.* He had dreamed the same dream over and over again: "In this dream I was lying alone in the forest resting, my lance at my side. Suddenly a jaguar charged and leaped at me. I sprang up in time to grab my lance and speared the jaguar through the heart."

The *wishnu,* the shaman, told him that "the dream of killing a jaguar was the most significant dream anyone could have. It meant that I would grow up to be a strong and brave warrior, a great hunter. If I could kill the jaguar I could kill anything and would have no troubles. When I dreamed that I jumped up so quickly that the jaguar could not kill me, that meant I would be cleverer and faster than my enemies. They could never trick me or ambush me."

He went out on his first raid at the age of seventeen. "Doing something the first time is always hard," he said, "even when you feel you will succeed. Because the enemy has spirits, too, spirits that are sometimes as strong as yours. But after the first time I learned that my good spirits were stronger than my enemies'. And I would always win."

Utitiaja's father had also been killed in a raid, and it was on this first raid that he killed the man who had killed his father. "It was four long years that his soul was restless and unhappy because I could not take blood revenge. When I killed him, I could say, 'See, my father, I have brought your soul peace.'"

Utitiaja's father had trained him well. But Utitiaja felt that the prophecies he obtained from the Old Ones through *maikoa* were responsible for his great success as a warrior. If the Old Ones said he would succeed, he went ahead with confidence, but if they said he would not succeed, he postponed his raid.

"Utitiaja, you have killed fifty-eight men," said Cotlow. "Do you think it is right to kill men like that?"

"It is right to kill your enemies, who would kill you if they could," Utitiaja replied. "Even you people know that, for I have heard of your wars."

"But do you think it is right for you to take the law in your hands and execute the man?"

"Who else would kill him?" Utitiaja asked. "I hear that you pay certain people to do that for you, in your country. I think that is wrong. I am the one who has the right and the duty to kill him. And I have always fulfilled my duties, not tried to get someone else to take care of them for me."

But headhunting was not just a matter of revenge and duty. Celebrating a *tsa-tsa* feast, said Utitiaja, was a wonderful thing. "You feel you are good, that you have done what you are supposed to do in this world. You now triumph over his evil spirit and make it a good spirit to help you more. And you tell the souls of the people you loved that they can stop wandering unhappily. These are all splendid things to feel. It seems as if you are soaring high like the condor."[21]

△△ VIII △△

Roberto Renaldo was an anthropologist working with the Ilonget, a people he *thought* were former headhunters in the Philippines.

When missionaries told him that some of his Ilonget companions had recently gone headhunting, the Ilonget denied it vehemently. One of them said, "How could you possibly think this of me? I held your wife's hand on the trail. I carried you across this bridge. I fed you.

I looked after you. How could you think I would do such a thing?"[22]

Then one day, through a casual remark, he learned that the missionaries were right. Some of his Ilonget friends had, in fact, continued the headhunting practices of their ancestors. "When I suddenly discovered that everybody took heads, that all the nice people who held my hand and fed me had taken heads," said Renaldo, "I felt completely disoriented. You can't imagine what a devastating experience it was. It confounds your categories, to say the least."

His informants' revelations were disturbing, but so was a letter he received from his draft board informing him that his deferment had been canceled. He would continue his fieldwork, it seemed, in Vietnam.

Now it was his Ilonget friends who were horrified. They remembered the Japanese occupation of the Philippines, and they remembered seeing a Japanese officer telling his brothers—that was how they put it—to move directly into the line of fire. They told Renaldo, "We would never ask our brother to sell his body. That's unspeakable; how can a human being do that?"

They implored Renaldo to stay with them where it was safe, where no soldiers would find him. "I said, 'I thought you guys were into headhunting. Don't you think I should go off to fight the war?' They said, 'War? Soldiers sell their bodies.' " It was, Renaldo remembered, "hard to describe how morally appalled they were by this. It was just unthinkable to them that anyone could do that."[23]

And that, perhaps, is the underlying message of the first warrior. He might kill for many reasons, many of them inexplicable or even reprehensible to our eyes. He might kill for revenge, or to be admired, or to take a head to gain a powerful soul, or to give his child a name; in some cases he might even kill, like us, for resources like land or "protein." But whatever the causes of his fight, whether it had to do with the mythic-psychic undergrowth of the first planters, or the ecological paleo-cybernetic balancing of people and environment, or the genetic success of the fittest and fiercest, whether brave or chivalrous or sneaky, the first warrior's fight was personal. No one fought for him and no one could order or force him to fight.

The first warrior was sown along with the first garden, was invented along with cultivation, when the clear-cutting of the earth began. He fought, strange as it may seem, to bring life from death, as the seed fallen in the earth brings the plant to the sun. He fought to restore the balance of the world, of his people, again and again, against the others, the not-quite-humans.

But he didn't sell his body, and he didn't sell the body of his brother, either. He was, to put it simply, responsible for his own actions. It was a straightforward sort of code—a good place for a warrior to start.

THE
WARRIOR-KINGS
OF SUMER

Sumer was the pioneer of the western world.
To it we can trace much of the art
and the thought of the Egyptians and Babylonians,
of the Assyrians, Phoenicians and Hebrews
and ultimately of the Greeks also.
–Sir Leonard Wooley

The first cities were magic. Rising abruptly from the plains, the walls of Eridu, Ur, Nippur, Uruk, and Kish glistened bright as copper in the morning sun. Outside, the brightly colored sails of the high-prowed trading barques glided smoothly along the latticework of canals that ran through the deep green fields of barley and wheat between the Tigris and Euphrates. Inside, within the heavy wooden gates, a maze of narrow streets crowded with metalworkers, tile makers, tanners, weavers, scribes, and courtesans converged at the center of the city, where the gods and goddesses lived.

Here, within another set of walls, in a small room at the very top of the ziggurat that towered hundreds of feet above the city, the deity who founded the city—Inanna, Enlil, Nanna, or Enki—was bathed with sesame oil and served elaborately prepared ceremonial meals every morning and evening. Within the great storehouses of the temple, the names of the donors who offered barley and wheat, sheep, goats, oxen, and cattle, as well as lapis lazuli, gold, and silver were recorded by scribes on clay tablets in the arrow-shaped cuneiform.

Though other cities are older—the earliest of the many stone and brick walls of Jericho have been carbon dated at seventy-five hundred years old—it is within the walls of Sumer that we can first find the mud-brick matrix of civilization, the beginning of that complex of characteristics identified with cities: extensive irrigation, monumental architecture, economic specialization, and writing. And it is in Sumer as well that we find the first armies, and the beginnings of "civilized war."

The men who led these armies were the warrior-kings of Sumer. Thanks to the cuneiform tablets, we know something of their names, titles, deeds, victories, and defeats. We can see the warrior-king also in the statues and friezes that have remained: curly bearded, his long black hair worn loose for battle, wearing a kilt of sheepskin, riding in a four-wheeled cart pulled by wild asses, bronze sword in hand. It is this first Sumerian warrior-king who is the archetypal forefather, the *patrix*, of the tragic warrior-hero of Greece, the chivalric knight of Europe, and even perhaps of the cultivated warrior-poet of ancient China and Japan.

⋀⋀ I I ⋀⋀

According to the Sumerians, the first war was fought between the Old Ones—Tiamat, the goddess of the salt waters, and Apu, the god of the sweet waters—and their children. It was caused by noise, by the "hilarity" the children made by their dancing and singing. This clamor, which was not unlike the clamor of the teeming new cities, disturbed the peaceful (and inert) slumber of the old gods. Tiamat, with a mother's forbearance, counseled tolerance. But Apu, goaded on by his vizier Mummon, set out to destroy his children.

In this first generational battle, Apu's son Ea, "the all-wise," made words into weapons. Using a magic incantation, he put Apu to sleep, took his tiara and halo, and killed him. He then built his house over Apu's body in Eridu, the oldest of all the Sumerian cities. Ea and his consort Damkina dwelt in their temple in splendor and gave birth to a son, Marduk.

It did not take long for Tiamat to be persuaded to avenge Apu. Calling an assembly of the gods, she gave birth to a hideous host of monsters—the Viper, the Dragon, the Sphinx, the Great-Lion, the

Mad-Dog, and the Scorpian-Man—and appointed her firstborn son, Kingu, as commander-in-chief of her army.[1]

Faced with this military crisis, Ea and the other gods called their own assembly. Opening their hearts and loosening their tongues with the customary feasting and quaffing of beer, they chose Marduk—"the loftiest and strongest of the gods"—as military leader. Armed with a mace, a bow, and a net, with lightning flashing before him and his body filled with flame, Marduk raised up a flood-storm and mounted his storm-chariot.

Marduk and Tiamat met in single combat. Raging like one possessed, in a divine fury, Tiamat cast spells and then opened her mouth to consume Marduk, who cast his net over her. As the Evil Wind that followed him entered her open mouth and distended her body, Marduk shot an arrow which tore into her bloated belly and split her heart. Tiamat's army fled in terror, but Marduk and his army captured them in nets and smashed their weapons. Kingu, the routed army's leader, was bound and taken prisoner.

Marduk then "split Tiamat like a shellfish into two parts," from which he created the ordered universe. He fixed the abodes of the gods, set up the constellations of stars with their astrological signs, and created the calendar. Kingu was then executed for inciting Tiamat to rebellion, and Marduk fashioned man from Kingu's blood.[2]

The creation of the world and of man from a slain god or giant is a recurrent motif in many archaic creation stories. But as cities and civilization rose from the muddy fields and pastures of the Neolithic, the familiar story took an unexpected turn: man was created from the slain god for a very specific purpose. "He shall be charged," as Marduk declared, "with the service of the gods, that they might be at ease!"[3] Henceforth, with men as their servants, the gods would be freed from all the backbreaking and repetitive labor of civilization—from digging and maintaining irrigation ditches and canals, from building walls out of sun-baked bricks—so that they would have the leisure to rule their divine estates under the beneficent kingship of Marduk himself. The lordly gods would be divine administrators—lords and organizers of man's labor. And men would work.

△△ III △△

The cities of Sumer were administered by the *en*, who managed the temple, along with its storehouses and lands, for the god or goddess who had founded the city. If the founding deity of the city was a god, the *en* would be female; if the founding deity was a goddess, the *en* would be male. As "priest" the *en* was the consort of the god or goddess and performed a yearly *hieros gamos,* or "sacred marriage."

During the first few thousand years of Sumerian civilization—when famine, flood, and drought were the principal concerns—the *en* and the temple ruled. But by the fourth millennium, as the Sumerians prospered, the cities—some of which had been built a scant ten or fifteen miles apart—began to expand toward their neighbors' borders, resulting in what archaeologist Ronald Cohen calls CSR—"conflict for scarce resources." Circumscribed by the sea to the west, the mountains of Turkey to the north, and the desert to the south, the cities began to fight over the borders that had been set by the gods.

Such disputes were not always easily settled. Uruk and Kish fought over boundaries for more than a hundred and fifty years without any clear victory. At the same time, nomadic raiders—"people who knew not grain"—came out of the mountains and deserts to prey on the rich cities; more civilized raiders came through the canals and reeds in their longboats.

As above, so below. Just as the assembly of the gods had elevated Marduk to military leadership to meet a military crisis, so did the Sumerians choose a warrior, called the *lu-gal,* or "big man," to lead in place of the *en*-priest during times of military crisis. Crisis, however, has a way of perpetuating itself, and the temporary war leader was pressed to extend his service into permanence. In time, the *lu-gal* took over many of the administrative peacetime functions of the *en,* until the two came together in the powerful and awesome figure of the warrior-king. And so it was during this period, as Sumerologist Thorkild Jacobsen writes, "that a new saviour-figure had come into being, the ruler: exalted above men, fearsome as a warrior, awesome in the power at his command."[4]

By the time the Sumerians themselves came to set down their version of history, as they did on the tablets of the Sumerian *King-List,* they had come to equate kingship with civilization itself. And like all the other standards and norms of civilization—the *me,* as they were called—the Sumerians considered kingship to have been bestowed on them by the gods. The warrior-king was chosen by the assembly of the gods, and then "kingship descended from heaven" on the world of men.

According to the scribes who compiled the Sumerian *King-List,* the kingship of Sumer and Akkad (the northern Semetic-speaking area) was held by one city at a time. Though this seems to be an idealized oversimplification, it was in fact the case, at least when any one city-state was powerful enough to make it so—when, for example, kingship descended from heaven on Etna of Kish, "he who stabilized all the land." How he did this is indicated by the phrase that is repeated in the list each time the gods decide to bestow the kingship on another city: "Uruk was smitten with weapons; its kingship to Ur was carried."[5]

△△ IV △△

The man the gods picked was likely, therefore, to be powerful and skilled in the use of the sword and mace. But the warrior-king was not only a strong man; he was also the foremost servant of the gods from whom kingship descended. Though he might often come to the attention of the gods through his martial deeds, the gods also expected the warrior-king to care for and protect both the city and its citizens, who were also the servants of the gods. The warrior-king, as we hear for the first but not last time in history, is the "shepherd" of the people. As Assurnasupal II sang to the goddess Inanna:

> *"Thou didst take me from among the mountains.*
> *Thou didst call me the shepherd of men*
> *Thou didst grant me the sceptre of justice."*[6]

The warrior-king also "waged peace," then. It was his duty to oversee the building and upkeep of canals, irrigation ditches, walls, and temples, and to trade with other cities. And it was his duty, as well, to protect the city from internal danger—to dispense justice ("straightforwardness," in Sumerian), and to protect the weak—particularly orphans and widows—against the strong.

A vivid portrait of the ideal Sumerian warrior-king has come down to us in a series of "Self-Laudatory Hymns" written by Shulgi of Ur during the third dynasty, which lasted from around 2094 to 2047 B.C. The son of a king, Shulgi received an aristocratic education. He learned to write cuneiform on tablets and to do arithmetic—he mentions "adding, subtracting, counting, and accounting."[7] He was also, as he tells us in one of his hymns, a master musician, possessed of a "clear and sweet voice," able to tune and play every musical instrument. His music, he says, brought joy to others, including his divine mother, Ninsun.

In addition, he was an ideal administrator and a righteous judge, who could speak in all five languages of the Sumerian empire, whose eloquence could "promote peace and harmony in the land." Finally, he knew best how to serve the gods and make them happy. An expert diviner, he was able to discern the will of the gods and to "read divine instructions concerning the whole universe in the entrails of a single sheep." He was, therefore, "most competent to pray for the life of all mankind."[8]

But Shulgi also possessed great physical prowess. He hunted the lions that were reserved for royalty in special parks in close combat, rather than using nets or hurling his ax from a safe distance. He was a superior athlete, running between Nippur to Ur in one day in time to attend the eses-feast in both cities. "Like a fierce lion I gnashed my teeth," he sang in a poem. "Like a wild ass I galloped / With my heart full of joy, I ran onward / Racing like a wild donkey." And, of course, he learned to master all the weapons—the bow, the net, the mace, the bronze sword, and the lance.

Shulgi then led his army against the Gutians, who had invaded his kingdom from the mountains. He made the god of their city withdraw, caused weeds to grow in the barley fields, tore up the date palms by their crowns, uprooted the orchards, ruined the walls, and "dispersed the seed of the Gutians like seed-grain." Then he loaded "the pure lapis-lazuli of the foreign land into leather-sacks, heaped up all its treasures," and sacrificed the fattened oxen and sheep of the Gutians to Enlil.

Having thus pacified the frontier, Shulgi sailed to Nippur in his royal barge, taking his ease while his court singers sang victory songs to him. In Nippur, he brought spoils and offerings to the temple of Enlil, as he had promised, and then continued his triumphal procession to Uruk, where he brought lavish animal offerings to Inanna (or perhaps we should say the priestess representing Inanna), who greeted Shulgi with a spontaneous love song detailing the pleasures of the sacred yearly marriage rite, which joined warrior and goddess, male and female, and ensured the continued fertility of the lands and flocks:

> *"In the Lofty Palace of Ninegal, on the holy*
> *dais, he has taken his seat,*
>
> *For the land he renders firm judgement.*
> *For the land he obtains firms decisions;*
> *(So that) the strong does not oppress the weak,*
> *The mother says pleasing words to her son,*
> *The son speaks truth to his father.*

Under him Sumer is filled with abundance,
Ur abounds in prosperity."[9]

△△ V △△

Inanna, Queen of Heaven, was the most important goddess of the Sumerian pantheon. Like the Paleolithic goddesses from whom she was descended, Inanna was not just a "fertility" goddess. She was a radiant reminder that birth and death are inextricably intertwined as two aspects of the unfathomable, mysterious power that manifests itself as life. Inanna the goddess of love was also Inanna the goddess of war; and therefore the Sumerians called battle, the place where life and death are held in precarious balance, "the dance of Inanna." As she herself proudly sings:

> *When I stand in the front (line) of battle,*
> *I am the leader of all the lands,*
> *When I stand at the opening of the battle,*
> *I am the quiver ready to hand,*
> *When I stand in the midst of the battle*
> *I am the heart of the battle,*
> *the arm of the warriors,*
> *when I begin moving at the end of the battle,*
> *I am an evilly rising flood*
> *when I follow in the wake of the battle*
> *I am the woman (exhorting the stragglers)*
> *"Get going! Close (with the enemy)!"*

As goddess of both wars and thunderstorms, she sings:

> *My father gave me the heavens,*
> *gave me the earth,*
> *I am Inanna!*
> *. . . waging of battle he gave me,*
> *the attack he gave me*
> *the floodstorm he gave me,*
> *the hurricane he gave me!*[10]

Inanna's masculine counterpart was her brother Ninurta. Ninurta was originally the force and power imminent in the great thunderstorms that gathered in the mountains to the north to bring the spring floods or, all too often, to sweep away the dikes and flood the fields men had worked so hard to protect. It was, to begin with, this double-edged force of the thunderstorm, the violent force whose power releases the raging storms that bring the flood both of destruction and creation, that made Ninurta the warrior-god.

The great black wings of the thundercloud gave rise to the early image of Ninurta as a black thunderbird whose wings spread across the sky and whose lion's head roared with the sound of the thunder, while the bolts of lightning were Ninurta's arrows. Finally, the rolling sound of the thunder became the sound of Ninurta's chariot thundering across the sky, flinging thunderbolts in battle—just as Thor would wield his great hammer in the warrior's paradise of Valhalla, just as Zeus would hurl his thunderbolts from Mount Olympus, and just as Indra would do battle with his thunderbolt, the magic vajra, on Mount Meru.

△△ VI △△

As far as we can tell, the armies led by Inanna, Ninurta, and warrior-kings like Shulgi were not composed of a warrior class. Aside from the palace guard, the Sumerian army was a citizen army subject to being called up in times of military need. Unlike the tribal warriors, who fought more or less on their own, the Sumerian citizen-soldiers were organized and trained to fight under the leadership of the warrior-king and his officers. The individual tribal warrior had become transformed and diminished into the individual citizen-soldier. He no longer picked his own fight. He no longer chose his own opponent.

Unlike the warriors on the cave walls at Valltorta, or the Dani of New Guinea, the Sumerian soldiers pictured on the Stela of the Vulture, which commemorates the victory of King Eannatum of Langesh over nearby Umma, are marching in ranks. Each soldier is a part, arms and legs, of a phalanx, marching together to the *tingli* drums as warriors had once danced together to the tribal drums, one organism—a wall of leather-plaited armor, spears bristling like the quills of a porcupine or the stingers of bees, their tiny legs and feet moving beneath the wall of shields like the marching feet of a many-footed scorpion. It was this disciplined infantry phalanx, combined with the chariot carts, that made the first army so deadly and effective.

It is here, with the advent of civilized war, that we also come upon true savagery. The men, women, and children of a defeated city were either killed and left for the birds of prey—as we can see in the Stela of the Vulture—or taken captive. Slavery now appears for the first time: in fact, the Sumerian word for "slave" is derived from the word for "foreigner." Neolithic prisoners might have been sacrificed to ensure the fertility of the land in archaic rites; the prisoners the Sumerians took were bound and blinded to prevent their escape, and given to the temple as slaves or put to work on labor gangs. The magical had become practical; the mythical was transformed into the economic.

This was the way war would be fought for thousands of years. There would of course be advances of technology and scale. The Akkadian Semite Sargon the Great, who brought the defeated king Lugalzaggisi to the gate of Enlil in a dog collar, would forge the world's first empire by destroying the walls of the cities he conquered, leaving a garrison of his own troops behind. The Indo-European Mittani would triumph with a lighter, faster, spoke-wheel chariot, and the Assyrians would recognize the military value of both iron weapons and terror, leaving no one alive and wearing the heads they took as ornaments or garden decorations—an Assyrian frieze shows a king and his queen dining placidly in their garden under a tree from which hangs a head. But all these advances were only changes rung on the basic Sumerian theme of organization which submerged and transformed the individual warrior into the mass soldier, a necessary but still expendable part of a deadly and efficient killing machine.

ΔΔ V I I ΔΔ

By reducing warriors to soldiers, the Sumerians elevated the war leader to a near divine status. But such power was not without its dangers. As the Sumerologist Leo Oppenheim tells us, the warrior-king's power in battle depended, in part, on his *melammu*, or "awe-inspiring luminosity." "This *melammu* terrifies and overwhelms the enemies of the king," Oppenheim says, "but is said to be taken away from him if he loses divine support."[11] Clearly the kingship that descended from heaven could also be taken back if the king became too arrogant in his pride.

When the gods seemed to withdraw their favor from his city, for example, Namin-Sin, king of Ur and grandson of Sargon the Great, accepted their decree for seven years by wearing sackcloth and piously humbling himself. But when his repeated request to visit the oracle at the temple of Ekur in Nippur was twice ignored, he lost his temper, and ordered his troops

> *To destroy the Ekur like a huge boat*
> *To turn it into dust like a mountain mined for silver*
> *To cut it into pieces like a mountain of lapis lazuli.*[12]

His soldiers burned all the precious wood brought from the far-off mountains—the cedars from Lebanon, cypress and boxwood—pulverized the gold, carried off the silver, and piled up the copper grain on the quays to be carried off in ships. Finally, Namin-Sin broke down the famed Gate of Peace with a pickax.

This last act was especially sacrilegious. Nippur was the city holy to Enlil, and it stood aloof from the usual battles among cities. It was a neutral place, a kind of Sumerian Geneva, where cities came to resolve and negotiate their disputes. And it was precisely under the Gate of Peace that such meetings took place.

The sacking of his temple so angered Enlil that he brought the scourge of the Gutians down on the people of Ur. A barbarous mountain people who "knew not grain," they destroyed the all-important canals and irrigation ditches and plunged Sumer into a dark age of famine and anarchy. "In the wide streets where feasting crowds would gather, scattered they lay," went *The Lamentation over the Destruction of Ur.* "In open fields that used to fill with dancers, they lay in heaps."[13]

◭◭ V I I I ◭◭

We might say that the Sumerians were the first people to recognize—at least in writing—that intoxication with his own powers could become the warrior's chief temptation and most dangerous enemy. This, in any case, was one of the main themes of the story of Gilgamesh, the first and perhaps most profound of all warrior epics. The Gilgamesh story was probably sung to the sounds of the Sumerian harp in the courts of the warrior-kings long before it was written down on the tablets that were uncovered in the ruins of the Assyrian king Assurbanipal's library in 1876. Reading the story today, we seem to glimpse the very moment the warrior begins to turn from the outer to the inner world. But this turning, so the story suggests, can only take place after the warrior's arrogance has been shattered by the gods.

Gilgamesh was the lord of Uruk and the proud builder of the copper-colored walls (said to have been the first walls of any Sumerian city).[14] He was as strong as "a wild ox," and "the onslaught of his weapons verily [had] no equal." And though the code of the Sumerian warrior-king stated that he was to act as the shepherd of the people, in actuality he oppressed them. Outrageous and unrestrained, he took what he wanted: "His arrogance knew no bounds by day or night," as the tablets tell us. "His lust leaves no virgin to her lover, neither the warrior's daughter, nor the wife of the noble,"[15] while the young men are forced to work day and night building walls and digging canals. He was, in short, a bully and a tyrant, who lorded it over the very people he was meant to shepherd.

Being Sumerians, the aggrieved citizens of Uruk lamented and complained to the gods—"Day and night is unbridled his arrogance. Is this the shepherd of ramparted Uruk?"—and the gods responded by creating Enkidu, Gilgamesh's equal and, we might say, worthy opponent, so that they could "strive together and leave Uruk in quiet."

Enkidu was a wild man, the original noble savage, his body covered with matted hair, a man who "knew nothing of cultivated land." He ate grass and drank at water holes with the gazelles and lions; and in order to protect his animal friends, he destroyed the traps set by hunters.

Enkidu's acts of environmental protection (of eco-terrorism, one might say) caught the attention of a hunter, who set a trap of his own. Acting on the advice of Gilgamesh, the hunter secured the services of a courtesan, who undressed, "laying bare her ripeness," by the lake where Enkidu came to drink every evening. Enkidu's "love was drawn unto her," and he lay with her for six days and seven nights. When at last he rose, "sated with her charms," he found that "the gazelles ran off, the wild beasts of the steppe drew away from his body," and he no longer had the strength to keep pace with them.

The courtesan comforted him by teaching him the ways of civilization—how to eat bread, drink wine, wear clothes. After she anointed his hairy body with oil, "he arose as a man," and turned on the animals he had lived with. "He took his weapon to chase the lion, that shepherds might rest at night. He caught wolves, he captured lions [that] cattlemen could lie down."[16]

Entering the city of Uruk, Enkidu encountered Gilgamesh in the marketplace and barred his way with his foot. "I have come to change the old order, for I am the strongest here," he cried, and the two began to fight, not with weapons, but wrestling in hand-to-hand combat. "They grappled, holding each other like bulls. They broke the doorposts and the walls shook, they snorted like bulls locked together."[17] Finally Gilgamesh bent his knee, planted his foot firmly on the ground, and threw Enkidu—which apparently meant that Gilgamesh had won, since "immediately his fury died." But oddly enough, Gilgamesh did not use his victory to oppress Enkidu as he had oppressed the citizens of Uruk. He won the contest—the first duel or martial arts match ever recorded—and with it he won something he had never had, a friend, someone he had affection for rather than power over. ("They kissed one another, and formed a friendship,"[18] say the tablets.) Enkidu, who was his match, became his equal, and so Gilgamesh was no longer the lone warrior and tyrant.

With time Enkidu grew bored with civilized life, and so Gilgamesh proposed that they strike out on an adventure—"to travel an unknown road and fight a strange battle" with the monster Humbaba, who guarded the cedar forest which Gilgamesh planned to cut down and bring back for the walls and gates of Uruk.

Enkidu, who knew the forests Humbaba guarded, did his best to discourage Gilgamesh. He warned the leader that the keeper of the cedar forests "is a great warrior, a battering ram. He is mighty, never resting—his roaring is the storm-flood, his mouth is fire, his breath is death."[19]

But Gilgamesh would not be deterred. He roused Enkidu with the warrior's call for glory and fame—for "a name that endures."

> "Who, my friend, can scale heaven?
> Only the gods live for forever under the sun.
> As for mankind, numbered are their days;
> Whatever they achieve is but the wind!
> Even here thou art afraid of death.
> What of thy heroic might?
> Let me go then before thee,
> Let thy mouth call to me, 'Advance, fear not!'
> Should I fall, I shall have made me a name:
> 'Gilgamesh'—they will say—'against fierce Humbaba
> Has fallen!' Long after
> My offspring has been born in my house."[20]

They began, as so many warriors after them have, by visiting a master smith who cast "mighty axes and swords" for them. With the help of Shamash, the god of the sun, who summoned the winds—"the north wind, the storm wind, the chill wind, the tempestuous wind, the hot wind"—they subdued Humbaba, who pleaded for his life. If Gilgamesh let him go, he said, he would be his servant, he would cut down the cedars so that Gilgamesh could build houses. Gilgamesh was inclined to mercy, but Enkidu convinced him it was safer to kill Humbaba—which Gilgamesh did with "a thrust of his sword to the neck."

Gilgamesh washed his grimy hair, cleaned and polished his sword, and put on clean clothes. Returning to Uruk in triumph, he wrapped himself in a fringe cloak, fastened a sash around his waist, and put on his tiara. Overcome with his beauty and splendor, the goddess Inanna offered herself.

> "Come, Gilgamesh, be thou my lover!
> Do but grant me of thy fruit.
> Thou shalt be my husband and I will be thy wife.
> I will harness for thee a chariot of lapis and gold . . .
> Thou shalt have storm-demons to hitch on for mighty mules.
> In the fragrance of cedars thou shalt enter our house."[21]

But Gilgamesh was wary. "Which lover didst thou love forever? Which of thy shepherds pleased thee for all time?" he asked, reminding the goddess of the unfortunate fate that her other lovers had met. Of course, it was true that Inanna was hot-tempered and fickle, but it was also true that the *hieros gamos,* or yearly sacred marriage with Inanna, was one of the major responsibilities of the warrior-king. By refusing her love, Gilgamesh also refused one of his most sacred and ancient ritual duties. By denying the *hieros gamos,* that is, Gilgamesh denied the place of the feminine, both in his own psyche and in the city he ruled. By relying completely on his outer, purely physical strength, by exaggerating his masculine side, he abandoned his role as Inanna's counterpart and his responsibility for the abundance and fertility of his city, which only Inanna could bestow. The warrior-king was in this instance perhaps more warrior than king.

Enraged, Inanna convinced the gods to send the Bull of Heaven against Gilgamesh. When the Bull of Heaven descended to earth, he snorted and a hole opened up, into which two hundred men fell. Then he turned on Enkidu, who parried and leapt up, grabbing his horns (like the bullfighters of Crete) and then grabbing his tail while Gilgamesh thrust his sword between the bull's shoulder blades. When the still unvanquished warriors tore out the bull's heart and presented it to Shamash, Inanna mounted the wall and cursed Gilgamesh—whereupon Enkidu, in a final insult, "tore loose the right thigh of the Bull of Heaven and tossed it in her face."

Gilgamesh and Enkidu were now, it would seem, at the height of their powers. Gilgamesh filled the great horns of the Bull of Heaven with six measures of oil, which he offered to his titular diety, Lugalbanda, and he then hung them in his palace bedchamber. He and Enkidu washed their hands in the purifying waters of the Euphrates and embraced as the people of Uruk gathered to gaze at the two heroes in the marketplace. Turning to the lyre girls of Uruk, Gilgamesh boasted:

> *"Who is most splendid among the heroes?*
> *Who is the most glorious among men?*
> *Gilgamesh is most splendid among the heroes.*
> *Gilgamesh is most glorious among the men."*[22]

But that night, after a celebration in the palace, Enkidu had an ominous dream. "The great gods met in Assembly," he told Gilgamesh, "and Anu said to Enlil, 'because the Bull of Heaven they have slain, and Humbaba, the one of them who stripped the forests of cedar must die.' But Enlil said, 'Enkidu must die; Gilgamesh, however, shall not die.'"

So it was that Enkidu was stricken with sickness and died—not gloriously and suddenly, "like one who falls in battle," as Gilgamesh had promised—but slowly, in sickness, "in disgrace." Enkidu was dying because the gods had judged him guilty of goading Gilgamesh into killing Humbaba, and also of killing the Bull of Heaven. But these two acts are only the most flagrant examples of the warrior's trap, which is pride. Both Enkidu and Gilgamesh had fallen into a fatal and arrogant overreliance on their own strength and power.

▲▲ IX ▲▲

The death of Enkidu was one of those events that utterly reverses the world by revealing something that has been hidden within or below the surface: Enkidu's death ripped away the veil of life; it revealed the death that lurks just below the surface.

Gilgamesh did his best to deny the revelation. He would not let Enkidu be buried, but kept watch over the body for seven days and nights until "a worm fell out of his nose" and the brutal reality of Enkidu's decaying body made avoidance impossible. Earlier Gilgamesh had roused Enkidu to courage with the martial notion that, live or die, the two warriors would win immortality and glory by their brave deeds. But Enkidu's death revealed the futility of Gilgamesh's attempt to meet death by winning glory. The power and strength of the warrior is no defense against death. Killing is no defense against death.

"When I die, shall I not be like Enkidu?" cried Gilgamesh. "Woe has entered my belly. Fearing death, I roam over the steppe." So Gilgamesh set out on a very different sort of journey; he was driven now not by a swaggering quest for fame: his enemies were no longer Humbaba or the Bull of Heaven. Now death, his own death, was the enemy he stalked. Stripped of his fine clothes, reduced to wearing rags and the skins of wild animals, hair grown long and wild as Enkidu's, Gilgamesh wandered over the steppes and across great mountains in search of the one man who had achieved immortality, Utmapishtim.

Roaming like a wild man over the steppes and crossing the great mountains guarded by the scorpion-men, half mad with grief and fear, Gilgamesh came to Sindura, the ale-woman and mysterious wise old crone so familiar to fairy tales. Drinking Sumerian beer (we may imagine) at her tavern at the end of the world, Gilgamesh confided his woes:

> "Enkidu, whom I loved dearly,
> Who with me underwent all hardships—
> Has now gone to the fate of mankind!
> Day and night I have wept over him.
> I would not give him up for burial—
> In case my friend should rise at my plaint—
> Seven days and seven nights,
> Until a worm fell out of his nose.
> Since his passing I have not found life,
> I have roamed like a hunter in the midst of the steppe.
> O ale-wife, now that I have seen thy face,
> Let me not see the death which I ever dread."

To which the ale-wife replied:

> "Gilgamesh, whither rovest thou?
> The life thou pursuest thou shalt not find.
> When the gods created mankind,
> Death for mankind they set aside,
> Life in their own hands retaining.
> Thou, Gilgamesh, let full be thy belly,
> Make thou merry by day and night.
> Of each day make thou a feast of rejoicing.
> Day and night dance thou and play!
> Let thy garments be sparkling fresh,
> Thy head be washed; bathe thou in water.
> Pay heed to the little one that holds on to thy hand,
> Let thy spouse delight in thy bosom!
> For this is the task of mankind!"[23]

The lines telling us what Gilgamesh thought of this advice are either missing or never existed. We do know, however, that Gilgamesh pressed on with his quest, convincing a reluctant ferryman to take him to Utmapishtim's home across the Waters of Death. Like the biblical Noah, Utmapishtim had survived a great flood, though in this case it had been sent by the gods to destroy man because—as in the creation tale—he had been making too much noise.

Gilgamesh had expected to find an extraordinary man, a man "resolved to do battle" with death. But he found that Utmapishtim was a very ordinary man who was content to lie "indolent on [his] back." The reason, as Utmapishtim confided to Gilgamesh, was that his immortality had been granted by the assembly of the gods as a reward for building the ark; it was a unique boon which had no relevance to Gilgamesh's search. Nevertheless, Utmapishtim set Gilgamesh a challenge, which was somehow related to his quest: Gilgamesh was to remain "up, and lie not down to sleep for six days and seven nights."

Perhaps the test was meant to show Gilgamesh that if he couldn't master sleep, the little sister of death, he could hardly expect to overcome the greater adversary. Or perhaps the test was symbolic of an inner battle between forces within Gilgamesh. To fight sleep is to fight ignorance; to keep the vigil of wakefulness is to resist the sleepy forces of the unconscious; to remain aware is the task of the warrior who would begin the journey into the enemy land of his own death.

ᐯᐯ X ᐯᐯ

But Gilgamesh was still fighting with the sword and the ax of the heroic monster-slaying warrior—weapons that are useless in this unfamiliar inner battleground—and so he fell soundly asleep for the full six days and seven nights as soon as Utmapishtim issued the challenge. "Sleep," as the tablets say, "fans him like a mist." But all was still not lost. Utmapishtim's wife persuaded her husband to tell Gilgamesh a secret about a thorny plant that had the power to restore youth. Tying stones around his legs for weight, Gilgamesh then succeeded in bringing the plant up from the depths of the sea. But once more an all-too-human moment of careless forgetfulness, of unawareness, defeated him. Drawn to the cool, refreshing waters of a pool, Gilgamesh set the plant on the bank, where a snake, attracted by its sweet fragrance, swallowed it. And so it is that the snake and not man sloughs his skin and renews his life.

Disappointed and disillusioned—"his tears running down his

face"—Gilgamesh returned, finally, to the starting point, the ramparts of Uruk, and invited the ferryman to admire the copper-colored walls that both glorify and limit the civilized world of the human. Neither the power over others, nor the gaining of glory, nor the inner search for immortality had brought success. Power for its own sake or glory for the sake of the future are without meaning, for the "gods have set aside death for mankind, and retained life in their own hands."

But in Gilgamesh's realization that death cannot be conquered by death—by killing and war—and that the true enemy is his own death, or his own fear of death, the tale of Gilgamesh reveals a new dimension for the warrior. Entering through the wound of his own vulnerability, Gilgamesh shows us the warrior beginning to turn from the outer to the inner world. The tale of Gilgamesh is the tale of the warrior's coming of age with his acceptance that he is an ordinary man—for death is the great equalizer. "Do they not draw a picture of death," says Gilgamesh, "the commoner and the noble, once they are near to their fate?"[24]

We do not know, but we may well imagine that the Gilgamesh who returned to Uruk was to be a very different warrior-king than the Gilgamesh who left the walls for the glorious adventure with Enkidu. There is no extant code of the Sumerian warrior, but the Gilgamesh story suggests something of the warrior-king's true task.

First, the Sumerian warrior-king is fully human. He faces and makes his peace with death, as all who are not gods must do. By recognizing the impermanence of human existence, he also makes the best of life—he makes every day a feast, as Sindura, the ale-woman, advised Gilgamesh. "He pays heed to the little one that holds his hand, and delights in his spouse, for this is the task of mankind."

Second, he is the servant of the gods and the consort of the goddess Inanna. He is the intermediary between humans and gods. Like Inanna, the stars are his tiara and the earth his sandals.

And finally, he is the shepherd of the city. It is his task to build the copper-colored wall that protects and encircles the people, to lead in battle, both by the strength of his arms and his *melammu,* his awe-inspiring luminosity, and to rule with justice, with straightforwardness.

When the true warrior-king thus joins heaven and earth, then it is as Inanna sings:

> *"Sumer is filled with abundance*
> *Ur abounds in prosperity."*

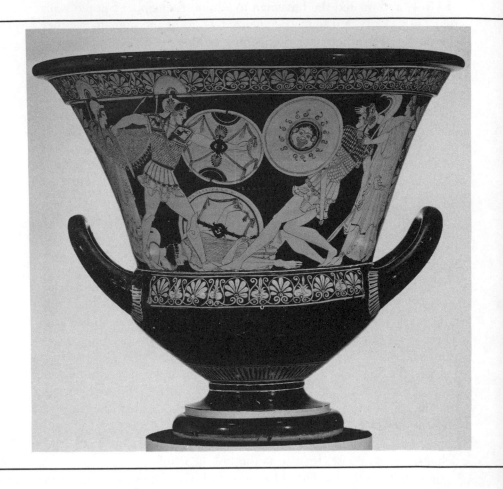

THE WARRIOR'S DILEMMA

The Indo-Europeans

And so they are transfigured,
made strangers in the society
they protect.
—Georges Dumezil

They were sackers of cities and breakers of horses. They came riding out of the east from the grassy steppes of the Eurasian heartland, strange and terrifying, with four feet and two arms, hooves thundering, battle-axes flashing, boar's teeth strung around their necks, driving cattle and horses before them, women, children, and elders following in lumbering four-wheeled carts pulled by oxen.

They came first in small bands, then in waves. They reached the farms and villages of the Balkans and the Danube around the first half of the fourth millennium B.C. Five hundred years later, a second wave headed east and broke over Transcaucasia, Iran, and Anatolia. By 2500 B.C. raiding parties appeared on the shores of the Aegean and Adriatic, on into Syria and Palestine, and possibly Egypt. A thousand years later, they rode out of the mountains of the Near East in their light spoke-wheeled chariots, setting off movements of peoples that led to the destruction of the first great archaic civilizations of Sumer and Akkad. A closely related eastern branch, the Aryas, used the same chariots to sweep down into the plains of the Ganges, subjugating the city-dwellers and peasants of Mohenjo-daro and Harrapa.

We do not know if they were originally one people or a group of related peoples, or even where they came from. The Central Asian steppes, Central or Eastern Europe, Scandinavia, Siberia, and the Balkans (as well as the North Pole) have all been suggested, though today the forested steppes of south Russia are generally considered their likeliest homeland. But wherever they originated, we do know that they spoke a language linguists call "proto-Indo-European" (or PIE, in academic shorthand), which later developed into Greek, Iranian, Celtic, Latin, German, Scandinavian, Slavic, Armenian, and Sanskrit—to name just a few.

Many details of the original proto-Indo-European language and culture remain elusive, for the original Indo-European people did not leave many traces. But by correlating common elements in the far-flung Indo-European languages with archaeological sites, archaeologists and linguists have been able to reconstruct the outlines of the proto-Indo-European culture.[1]

They were not builders of cities, like the Mesopotamians, nor of great tombs, like the Egyptians or the megalith builders of Stonehenge. The original Indo-Europeans, according to this reconstruction, were semi-nomadic pastoralists who lived part of the year in subterranean huts whose upper walls and roofs were covered with timber and skins. The climate was considerably warmer then—five or six thousand years ago, that is—and the rivers and streams of southern Russia watered forests of fir, birch, oak, aspen, apple, and cherry. They grew a little grain, probably a kind of millet, but most of their time was spent following their herds of cattle and horses from pasture to pasture. They hunted as well, as they had always done: the great wild cattle, the aurochs, elk, deer, beaver, wolves, and the fierce boar, taking salmon and other fish from the teeming rivers. And they gathered wild honey, which they fermented into mead.

They buried their dead at the bottom of a deep shaft or in a timber-house covered with great mounds of earth, making barrows or *kurgans*, to use the Slavic and Turkish term. The earliest of these kurgans, from the fifth millennium B.C., contained combination hammer-and-hoes made from elk antlers (possibly the prototypes of the later stone and copper battle-axes), bone and obsidian knives and daggers, and a lethal-looking swordlike bone dagger inset with sharpened obsidian like teeth along the blade, as well as ceremonial battle-axes of shining, polished black jade and horsehead "scepters," which were probably emblems of authority and power. By 2500 B.C. the kurgans reveal that the Indo-European warriors were using bronze, probably traded from Sumer and Anatolia, to fashion slashing swords particularly suitable for use from horseback; this last weapon may well have been an Indo-European invention.

Differences in grave furnishings suggest that proto-Indo-European society was patriarchal and hierarchical. One group, presumably farmers and herders, was buried with only a single piece of pottery and a flint tool each. But another group, presumably warriors and nobility, was buried with their weapons, as well as the sort of portable luxuries suitable for nomadic people—gold and silver vases, rings, small figurines depicting the ram, bull, and lion, and amber, turquoise, and carnelian beads.

These first Indo-European warriors did not go to death alone. The kurgans contained the bones of sacrificed horses, as well as human beings, often (according to archaeologist Marija Gimbutas) members of the dead warrior's family—early evidence, says Gimbutas, of "the old Indo-European custom that the housemaster had unrestricted right of property over his wife and children and that the wife should die with her husband."[2]

Their religion, as far as it can be reconstructed, was sky oriented. The primary deity was probably a thunder god represented by stone stelae carved in the shape of a man holding a battle-ax, as well as by the many ceremonial battle-axes found in kurgans. The god's power and virility could be heard in the thunder and seen in the lightning, in the heavenly battle which brought rain to the pastures of the steppes and—by a simple extension—victory to men in battle. His signs—which ornamented weapons—were of the sky: swirling swastika sun disks and lightning zigzags. His original name, according to the some linguists, was Dyeus; later he became Zeus in Greece, Deus in India, Jupiter in Rome.

Their gods were not enclosed within the walls of sanctuaries or temples. They were worshiped outside, in sacred spaces open to the vast sky: in groves, or inexhaustible streams, or on top of cloud-gathering mountains. They were reached by the word—spoken, sung, or chanted—and by the sacrifices consumed in the sacred fire kindled by the thunder god's lightning bolt.

The thunder god could also be reached by blood. After a victorious battle, for instance, the Scythians took one out of every hundred of their captives, poured wine over his head, cut his throat, collecting the blood in a bucket and then pouring it over a short sword, an *akinake*, which—stuck in the bare earth or simply on a pile of brush—was all that was needed to represent the god of war.

◮◮ I I ◮◮

The actual source of the Indo-European's power, though—at least on earth—was the horse, which they seem to have been the first to break, tame, and domesticate. Marija Gimbutas, judging from antler cheek bridles she found in kurgans in the Volga steppes, believes that the Indo-Europeans were riding horses "as early as 5000 to 4500 B.C."

The taming of the horse was both the means and the cause for the first great Indo-European migrations. Wild horses, which were hunted by men and other predators, did not overgraze their pastures. But when human hunters began protecting their horses from other predators, the herds grew far beyond their previous "natural" populations. Not even the thunder god could bring enough rain to keep the multiplying herds in pasture. And so the young men who had spent their lives on horse-back guarding their herds from wolves (and probably other bands of men as well) gathered—like bees swarming—and rode off in search of new pastures.

They found these pastures to the west, along with herds of fat cattle and sheep, stores of grain, deep forests with wood for carts and houses, and villages centered around buildings with one floor on top of the other. Within the buildings were long rooms, with platforms and niches holding odd, brightly painted ceramics decorated with curving lines instead of the black jagged lightning zigzags of the rough Indo-European pots, and strange figures of women with the heads of birds or holding snakes. Stranger still, these people seemed to have no weapons, no battle-axes or swords, but only a few stone-tipped spears and arrows for hunting. And though they had domesticated many animals—cattle, sheep, pigs, and dogs—they did not seem to know about the most powerful animal of all. They had no horses.

◮◮ I I I ◮◮

The distinguished Oxford archaeologist Stuart Piggott introduced his standard survey, *Ancient Europe,* with the contention that "so far as inference can reasonably be made from archeological evidence there is nothing to suggest that the desire for domination by force and if necessary killing is not as deeply seated a human emotion and urge as any other." And he goes on to claim, referring specifically to ancient Europe, that "warfare and everything connected with it were inseparable from the life of prehistoric village civilisation."[3]

But Marija Gimbutas, who, like Piggott, has done extensive fieldwork in Eastern Europe, draws a very different conclusion from the same archaeological period. To begin with, Gimbutas argues that the graves and living quarters of Old Europe—her name for the Europe before the Indo-European invasions—reveal a society that was "unstratified and egalitarian." According to her, this society was organized around the worship of a goddess and her male consorts and was largely peaceful.

"There was no interest in weapon production; instead sculptural and ceramic arts flourished. There was no horse nor fighting from horseback, no thrusting weapons, nor daggers or swords or spears," she writes, "except at the very end of this civilization in areas where horse-riding Kurgan people first appeared. . . . Weapons are nonexistent in Old European imagery."[4] She concludes that "the characteristic absence of heavy fortifications and of weapons speaks for the peaceful character of most of these art-loving peoples," though she does admit that "some defensive measures were taken to protect the villages from animal or human intruders, or—in the marginal areas in the east—from possibly hostile neighbors."[5]

Peaceful or not, the people who lived in the northernmost extension of Old Europe, in the Cucutenci culture which extended as far as the middle Dnieper to what is now Kiev, somehow managed to placate the first bands who arrived around 4400 B.C. Perhaps they gave the invaders what they wanted without a fight; perhaps the invaders were too few and the Cucutenci too many. In any case, the two cultures managed to coexist alongside each other, perhaps for hundreds of years.

But that was hardly to be the rule. Between 3400 and 3200 B.C. a second wave from the steppes completely overran the Old Europeans of the Dnieper and Danube. A massive third wave followed between 3000 and 2800 B.C., and this time the invaders were clearly the conquerors. The Kurgans (as Gimbutas named the various groups of Indo-European peoples from the steppes) "built hill-forts in inaccessible locations and frequently surrounded them with cyclopean stone walls." They did not destroy the Old Europeans (except for those few who may have resisted), but they clearly dominated them.

"The new ideology," as Gimbutas puts it, "was an apotheosis of the horseman and warrior." The gods now "carry weapons and ride horses or chariots; they are figures of inexhaustible energy, physical power, and fecundity."[6] Once the initial resistance had been broken by the mounted warrior bands wielding the slashing sword and the skull-crushing battle-ax, they deposed or sent the goddess underground, replacing her with the shining ax-wielding thunder god. The rudimentary sacred script of the Old Europeans was lost, as were their richly decorated pottery and other arts.

Many of the Old Europeans, however, went on farming, tending their cattle, pigs, and sheep and growing their grains. The Kurgan conquerors took what they wanted, ate the Old Europeans' food, and sired children by their daughters. They controlled the conquered Old Europeans just as they controlled their herds of horses and cattle, watching over them and making good use of them. In short, the Kurgans "domesticated" the Old Europeans.

△△ I V △△

Marija Gimbutas, now retired from her post as the head of the Department of Slavic Studies at UCLA, responds with a bemused shrug when asked to provide a description of the warrior Kurgans. "It is very difficult to say," she says in her Lithuanian accent. "We are talking seven, five thousand years ago." But when pressed, she looks out across the tall tops of the eucalyptus trees that surround the deck of her book-lined house in Topanga Canyon. "But let me try. I see a very strong warrior prototype—horse riding, carrying weapons, dagger in one hand, bow and arrow in other. Very fast, very quick.

It was the male mastery of the horse, Gimbutas thinks, "which was the primary cause why patriarchy became established." For finally, she says, "the men had the power to do it, the strength that led to the powers of the horse. It was quite impressive. They were stealing cattle. More and more raiding became a way of life. It continued until late history, this trait was going through millennia.

"Stealing, fighting, fighting at night. That was how they succeeded in conquering Europe. By spreading fear. They terrorized them."[7]

△△ V △△

Indeed they did. The shadowy figures of the Indo-European *manner-bund*, the warrior bands, howling, painted, tattooed, wrapped in the pelts of bear and wolf, can be glimpsed in myths and tales from Ireland to India. In the Near East they were the chariot-fighting *mariannu*, who spread terror in the second millennium B.C.; in India they were the storm-cloud Maruts, who accompanied the thunderbolt-wielding Indra; in Ireland they were the outlaw Finnians led by the warrior-poet Finn McCool; in Scandinavia they were the berserkirs and the wolf-coat men as well as the *Eihenjahr,* whose brave death in battle transported them to Valhalla, where they battled happily, their wounds magically healed by Odin, day after day; and in Greece they were Achilles' Myrmidons, who fought "like wolves, carnivorous and fierce and tireless, who rend a great stag on a mountainside and feed on him, their jaws reddened with blood."[8]

In Germany, they were the terrifying Harii. "Fierce in nature," as Tacitus described them, they "trick out this natural ferocity by the help of art and season: they blacken their shields and dye their bodies, they choose pitchy nights for their battles; by sheer panic and darkness they strike terror like an army of ghosts. No enemy," as he says, "can face this novel, and as it were, phantasmal vision: in every battle after all the eye is conquered first."[9]

The *mannerbund* were the shock troops of the conquering Indo-Europeans. But they were not just military in nature. They also served as male initiatory groups, whose main function was to turn boys into adult men.

Among hunters the ultimate test that confirmed initiation often involved stalking and killing a particularly ferocious or dangerous animal. But within what the African anthropologist Ali Mazrui calls "a combat culture of the spear"—where "killing is a confrontation between individuals, and a man tests his manliness within a spear-throw of another"—to be a warrior is to be man. "The martial and sexual qualities," as Mazrui says, "become virtually indistinguishable."[10]

In such a culture, initiation into male adulthood sometimes involved a ritual battle or the actual killing of an enemy in a face-to-face confrontation which tested to the fullest all those qualities the young warrior will need: strength, agility, bravery, as well as the readiness or at least willingness to kill.

Among the Indo-Europeans, according to Mircea Eliade, "The essential part of the military initiation consisted in ritually transforming the young warrior into some species of predatory wild animal. It was not only a matter of courage, physical strength, or endurance, but of a magico-religious experience that radically changed the young warrior's mode of being. He had to transmute his humanity by an access of aggressive and terrifying fury that made him like a raging carni-vore."[11]

The identification of warrior with predator is so nearly universal that we may reasonably characterize it as archetypal, for the warrior, as Eliade says, "is the preeminent example of the hunter; like the hunter he has his model in the behavior of the carnivore."

The Indo-Europeans, who came from the northern steppes, trans-formed themselves into two predators in particular: the bear and the wolf. Thus the members of the secret German and Scandinavian socie-ties were known variously as *berserkirs* (*ber* = "bear"; *serkr* = "body-covering") and *uldhedhnar,* or "wolf-skin men." (Originally the bear may have stood for the solitary warrior, with the wolf standing for warriors in bands. But that distinction, if it was ever made, does not appear in the sagas, where berserkirs and wolf-coat men seem to be used interchangeably.)

Both bear and wolf played a central role in Indo-European mythol-ogy. But the cult of the bear, in particular, went back to the northern Paleolithic hunters who were ancestral to the Indo-Europeans. The huge (nine-foot-long) cave bear was hunted by the Neanderthals and was apparently treated with ritual respect: a famous cache of seven cave bear skulls and bones in a stone crypt with a limestone cover, uncovered at Drachenloch, a cave in the German Alps, has been carbon-dated to fifty thousand B.C.; a painting in the cave of Pechialet, in the Dor-dogne, depicts two men dancing beside a bear.

Of all the northern European animals, the bear is the one most like the human being. Like humans, bears are omnivorous and opportunis-tic eaters, wide-ranging and curious, and they are two-legged when they stand to fight. And the body of a skinned bear is said to be strikingly similar to a human being.

Unlike humans, however, bears possess the mysterious power to withdraw into hibernation in the winter and then emerge reborn in the spring. The hunter who killed a bear with spear or knife, therefore, not only gained something of the bear's ferocity and fighting spirit, but he may also have gained something of the bear's mysterious ability to die and be reborn.[12]

△△ V I △△

The initiatic metamorphosis of the warrior into bear or wolf was achieved by magical techniques which may have been borrowed (or held in common with) the Siberian shamans who lived in close proximity to the original Indo-Europeans.

Like the shamans, the young warriors learned to be "shape-shifters"—to send forth their bear spirit to fight while they lay in a trance; like the shamans, they danced themselves into identity with bear and wolf, shambling, loping, wrapping themselves in fur, wearing masks, wrapping themselves in pelts, howling, grunting, growling. And like the shamans, they may also have danced while sharing the magic and secret drink of the spirits of the other worlds—perhaps an extract pressed from the fly agaric mushrooms the Siberian shamans used for their otherworldly flights, or mead fermented from honey mixed with herbs and flowers (perhaps as many as a hundred and twenty different flowers, judging from pollen found in the tomb of a warrior from the Celtic Hallstadt culture), or honey mixed with blood and saliva, as a legend about the creation of mead in the Norse sagas describes it.

Very probably they practiced ritual pederasty, like some of the warriors in New Guinea. The custom was known among warrior societies in Sparta and Crete, where young boys were "captured" by older warriors as part of initiation. It was also found among the Celts and the Germans.[13] To complete the initiation, the warrior usually had to kill or capture a fierce animal. But often the warrior fought other warriors. A warrior wanting to become one of the Finnians had to strip naked and fight nine men armed only with a spear. And Chu Chulainn's initiation, reflecting a widespread triadic Indo-European theme, set him against three brothers, whom he dispatched and beheaded (also a venerable Indo-European tradition) one after the other.

The fully initiated warrior was thus also the fully metamorphosed warrior. He had entered an altered or extraordinary state of consciousness which freed him from the inhibitions (or fear or reluctance) against killing another human being. He underwent, as Eliade says, "a radical change of behavior. As long as he was wrapped in the animal's skin, he ceased to be a man, he was the carnivore itself: not only was he a ferocious and invincible warrior, possessed by the *furor heroicus*, he had cast off all humanity; in short, he no longer felt bound by the laws and customs of men."[14]

In Scandinavia, the metamorphosed warrior was one of Odin's bereserkirs who "went to battle without armour, were as mad as dogs or wolves, bit their shields, and were as strong as bears or wild bulls, and killed people at a blow, but neither fire nor iron told upon themselves. This was called the Berserk fury."[15]

The warrior in his battle frenzy was thus transported beyond himself and filled with a sacred force. The proof of this new state was the generation of a fiery heat that went back to what Eliade called "the most archaic strata of magic and universal religion." Shamans had demonstrated their "magico-religious power" by perspiring with an inner fire or by walking on fire or handling hot coals with impunity. This same sacred force burned in warriors, too—sometimes making them immune to fire and sometimes filling them with the terrible raging battle fire of the berserkir.

◬ VII ◬

The problem was how to turn the mad beast of the berserkir or wolf-man back into a normal human being. Unfortunately, the very rage that made the berserkir such an effective killer was also a blind rage, a rage which struck indiscriminately at anyone who was unlucky enough to fall within his range. The warrior overcome by his rage was in danger of losing the ability to discriminate between friend and foe.

The old Irish epic *The Tain* (or "Cattle-Raid") tells how Chu Chulainn, the great Irish warrior, still boiling with this martial heat, his hero-halo like a ring of fire around his head, returned to Ulster from his first battle with the bloody heads of the three brothers he had just killed hanging from his chariot.

Seeing that he was still in his battle frenzy, the watchman cried out, "If he comes on us with his anger still upon him, the best men of Ulster will fall by his hand." Then the people of Ulster took quick council and agreed "to send out three fifties of the women of Emain red-naked to meet him."

Taken aback, Chu Chulainn "hid his countenance. Immediately the warriors of Emain seized him and plunged him in a vat of cold water. That vat burst asunder about him. Then he was seized and thrust in another vat and it boiled with bubbles the size of fists. He was at last placed in a third vat and warmed it till its heat and cold were equal. Only then was he cooled enough to return safely to the world."[16]

The dilemma was given a civic and patriotic twist in the Roman legend about a fight between three Roman champions, the Horatians, and three Albans. Two of the Horatian brothers and all of the Albans were killed in the ferocious fight, but the one surviving brother returned from his victory still in such a rage that when he found his sister weeping for her dead Alban lover, he killed her as well. He justified the killing with the rationalization that "her body was Roman but her heart was Alban," but the Romans themselves treated the killing as a simple case of the battle frenzy gone too far. "And so," as Livy writes, "that the flagrant murder might yet be cleansed away by some kind of expiatory rite," Horace's father offered sacrifices and "erecting a beam across the street, to typify a yoke, he made his son pass under it with covered head."[17] The Roman solution was ceremonial and formal. The triumphal arch under which armies pass is thus a rite not so much of victory as of return from the exalted state of battle frenzy to the ordinary human state of civil society.

The ministrations of women, cold showers, and parades are only some of the rites used to purify and cool the raging heat of the warrior so that he can return with safety to society. But the rites must be repeated, and even then they do not always work. The berserk frenzy threatens to burst into a raging all-consuming fire every time the warrior goes to battle.

The double-bladed ambiguity of the warrior's position is inescapable. The force by which the warrior protects society is the same force which threatens that society. As Georges Dumezil, the Indo-European mythologist, writes in *The Destiny of the Warrior:*

> They [the Indo-European warriors] cannot ignore order, since their function is to guard it against the thousand and one demonic or hostile endeavors that oppose it. But in order to assure this office they must first possess and entertain qualities of their own which bear a strong resemblance to the blemishes of their adversaries. . . . Drunk or exalted, they must put themselves into a state of nervous tension, of muscular and mental preparedness, multiplying and amplifying their powers. And so they are transfigured, made strangers in the society they protect. And above all, dedicated to Force, they are triumphant victims of the internal logic of Force, which proves itself only by surpassing boundries—even its own boundaries and those of its raison d'être.[18]

According to Dumezil, this Indo-European warrior's dilemma generated a proto-myth called "The Three Sins of the Warrior," in which the Indo-European warrior-hero committed three "sins" or transgressions against the three functions—sovereignty, force, and fecundity—which Dumezil believed constituted the basic structure of Indo-European society.

In the first sin, against sovereignty, the warrior-hero usually murdered a ruler or committed an act of sacrilege against a priest; in the second sin, against force, he behaved in a cowardly "unwarriorlike" fashion or won a battle by trickery and deceit; and in the third sin, against fecundity, he acted out of greed or lust, raping or committing adultery, often in disguise. As a result of these three sins the warrior lost his powers or was punished. Finally, he performed a difficult expiation, which led either to a restoration of his powers or to a sacrificial death, after which he achieved a final apotheosis in the realm of the gods.

It is worth considering at this point how far this version of the warrior-hero diverges from the current vogue of seeing the "hero's journey" as a psychological analogue of the ordinary everyman's journey through archetypal "stages of life." The most popular exponent of this approach is Joseph Campbell, who drew heavily on the comparative work of Lord Raglan, Otto Rank, and C. G. Jung, to identify a universal "mono-myth." The nucleus of this myth, as Campbell gives it, is simple: "A hero ventures forth from the world of common day into a region of supernatural wonder; fabulous forces are there encountered and decisive victory is won; the hero comes back from this mysterious adventure with the power to bestow boons on his fellow man."[19]

Though common structures can and have been identified in widely divergent myths, Campbell's search for a monomyth may be—to mix mythological metaphors—a little like searching for the Holy Grail in the Minotaur's Labyrinth. Since myths are by their nature "multivalent," interpretations of myths could hardly be otherwise. Compared to Campbell's rather benign view of the monomythical and universal boon-granting culture hero, Dumezil's distinctive Indo-European warrior-hero is a volatile and stormy figure who represents an opposition inherent in the very structure of Indo-European society, as well as an interior opposition within the warrior between "dark" and "light" or brutal and chivalrous aspects of the warrior himself. From this point of view, the development of the warrior's code, though it necessarily takes different forms in different cultural epochs, is at bottom a reflection of the need for society to protect itself from the darker berserkir aspects of the warrior—while the code itself serves to define, express, and further the "light" or chivalrous aspects of the warrior. In any case, the thread left by Dumezil is well worth picking up, especially for those hunting the true nature of the warrior, be it Grail or Minotaur, or a little of both.

△△ VIII △△

Let us pick up the trail, then, in the heart of the expanding Indo-European sphere of influence, during the second millennium B.C., the period Stuart Piggott calls the High Barbarian Age of Europe. During this period of consolidation and assimilation, the descendants of the old nomadic Indo-European warrior bands settled down and became a landed nobility or a noble retinue gathered around a warrior-chieftain in a court which became the center for the development of the new aristocratic warrior's code. And though the old shamanic berserkir seemed to have faded from view, he continued to hibernate in his cave, ready to emerge in all his fury the moment he sniffed the hot blood of battle.

The warrior's estates provided the new nobility with wealth—land, cattle, and tenants (or slaves in some places) to work the land—which enabled the warriors to obtain expensive bronze armor, weapons, horses, and chariots. The landed estates also granted the aristocratic warriors the time and the leisure to learn their art—to practice riding, charioteering, archery, swordsmanship, and—in Germany and Greece, at least—to dance. Tacitus described "naked youths, jumping and bounding between swords and upturned spears."[20] Philostatos, in a treatise on gymnastics, remarked on how "the Lakedaimonians danced in such a way as though about to dodge a missile or to hurl one, or to leap from the ground, and to handle a shield skillfully." In the end, as Socrates said, "Whoso honour the gods best with dances are best in war."[21]

The wealth derived from the great estates also supported craftsmen and swordsmiths as well as the wandering bards who sang the praises of the warriors, sometimes accompanying the warriors into battle so they could observe firsthand the great deeds they would later celebrate in their songs at court. And below them all, in the fields and villages were the houses and huts of the farmers and stockmen—possibly the descendants of the Old European inhabitants—whose grain and cattle sustained the whole enterprise.

Raids and wars were indistinguishable in this world of petty kingdoms and independent estates. The warriors were like Thucydides' "leading pirates, powerful men, acting both out of self-interest and in order to support the weak among their own people. They would descend upon cities which were unprotected by walls and indeed consisted only of scattered settlements; and by plundering such places would gain most of their livelihood. At this time," as Thucydides said, "such a profession, so far from being regarded as disgraceful, was considered quite honorable."[22]

△△ I X △△

The "honorable profession" came also to be considered a necessary profession. Warriors who plundered had to be ready to protect their treasures; warriors who attacked other towns had to be ready to defend their towns.

The problem has been nicely identified by the classical scholar James Redfield in his study of *The Iliad*. "As the community's need of warriors generates a social organization," he writes, "it generates also a paradox. War is initially an unhappy necessity, the precondition of protected community. But as the warriors become a class or caste, the advantages—and more important the prestige—of the warrior become themselves desirable."

The warriors' qualities thus come to be valued for themselves, and not only as a means to success in battle. But in order to prove that they were worthy of their status, warriors had to find ways to display their skills, most usually on the battlefield. "And so it happens," as Redfield says, "that the community's need for security and defensive warfare generates a warrior ethic, which then gives rise to aggressive warfare which is a threat to security."[23]

An aristocratic warrior's code, then, was generated by the warrior's paradox. Just as it was necessary to find a way to contain the powers of the berserkir's frenzy, so it was necessary for aristocratic warriors to develop and demonstrate their powers in a way which did not destroy society or decimate their own ranks. The aristocratic warrior's code was the human version of the biological code which sets the rules for the competition between males of the same species. It turned the battle between males of the same warrior aristocracy into a contest—a deadly contest at times, but a contest nonetheless.

This code called on each warrior "to be best [*aristos*] always"—as Achilles' father had admonished him before he left for Troy. Or, as Sarpedon's father had told *him,* in a phrase that would come to be the classical formulation of the aristocrat's code, "to be always the bravest and to hold my head always above all others."[24]

For the Bronze Age warrior, "to be best" was very specific: it meant being the best in hand-to-hand combat. Bronze Age swordplay had very little to do with strategy or finesse. The most frequent strokes, according to one scholar's analysis, were the downward cut through the head or the sideways slash severing head or arms or legs at one stroke.[25] These cuts demanded sheer physical strength and the brawn needed to carry bronze armor, as well as a certain agility. As Hector boasted at the beginning of a duel:

> . . . I know
> and know well how to fight and how to kill,
> how to take blows upon the right or left,
> shifting my guard of tough oxhide in battle,
> how to charge in a din of chariots,
> or hand to hand with a sword or pike to use
> timing and footwork in the dance of war.[26]

△△ X △△

The inexorable logic of the heroic code is the logic of competition. There can be no best, no heroes, without worthy opponents to defeat. "The hero's whole life and efforts," as Werner Jaeger says, "are a race for the first prize, an unceasing strife for supremacy over his peers."[27]

This supremacy was established in battle—"the test that brings men honor,"[28] as Homer calls it. Given this, battle took the form of a contest or duel between peers and was fought according to certain rules. A typical duel, therefore, was a ritualized display of prowess. The warriors in *The Iliad* were conveyed to the field of battle in their chariots, which functioned purely as status symbols. They wore shining bronze armor, bright as the sun; helmets were sometimes of sleek bronze, with nose and cheek guards, or (in older models) made of rows of overlapping boar's teeth, and always crested, usually with long horse-tail plumes; bronze greaves were fitted tightly over the warrior's shins, and breastplates were molded to follow the contour of their chests. Weapons as well were elaborately decorated, inlaid with gold, silver, and precious stones. The whole cosmos, in fact, was painted on the famous shield which the smith of the gods, Hephaestus, had fashioned for Achilles.

The duel began with a recitation of each warrior's lineage, both as a boast and as a confirmation that the participants were indeed members of the same warrior aristocracy. Having established the fact that they were worthy opponents, they moved in. They were armed with two spears and a sword—bows, which were not suitable for hand-to-hand combat, were considered the weapons of cowards. First one, then the other warrior threw his spear with—he hoped—enough force to pierce his opponent's shield. Next they moved closer still to attack with their second, shorter spears. Only then did they close with their swords, though they did not necessarily fight to the death. Hector and Aias, for example, fought and gave no quarter until nightfall, until the heralds proclaimed that "the Lord Zeus cares for you both. Both are great spearmen," and they exchanged gifts and parted friends.

More often, however, duels ended in serious wounds or death. But even that did not end the contest. The Greek word for honor—*time*—meant "value" or "price." Honor was thus the visible and concrete proof of the victorious warrior's prowess as reflected in the trophies of battle. These had a certain value, bronze weapons and armor being expensive, but they were worth more as visible proof of the victorious warrior's superior prowess, in much the same way that a head or scalp was proof of prowess for Scythians and Celts.

The successful warrior thus stripped his fallen opponent of his valuable armor and weapons, while warriors on the other side tried to recover the body of their fallen comrade with his armor intact. The heroic warrior was much more concerned with his own honor than with the outcome of the battle, and so he often took precious time out from the battle to fight over trophies.

But even when the battle or war was won, the warrior's honor was measured by the trophies which the leader of the expedition awarded him. The more cattle, the more "tawny-headed horses," the more bronze armor and silver caldrons and gold tripods, and the best and the "hottest" women (as *The Iliad* has it), the more honor. Modesty was not one of the virtues of the heroic warrior.

Yet the heroic warrior was no mere materialist, no merchant or trader. Success in battle—prowess—not wealth, was the final measure of the warrior. Greater even than honor counted in plunder was the public recognition the warrior won when the bards sang of his great deeds—his *aristeia*. When that happened the warrior's honor was transformed and extended into the future as *kleos*, fame and glory sung by the wandering court bards to future generations of warriors. This glory justified and fulfilled his existence, since it demonstrated that he had proven himself worthy of his ancestors, that he continued his heroic lineage and bequeathed it to his descendants.

Thus, though Hector knew that Achilles would almost certainly kill him—and that the Greeks would therefore sack Troy, slaughter its inhabitants, including his child, and carry off his wife—he still performed the *aristeia*, the great deed, of meeting Achilles face-to-face: "Better we duel now, at once, and see to whom the Olympian awards the glory," for he was determined not to "die ingloriously, but in some action memorable to men in days to come." And thus Achilles, knowing that it was his fate to die "but gain unfading glory" if he fought on, headed straight for Hector.[29]

△△ X I △△

Achilles was the greatest of all the Achaeans, the exemplary Greek warrior who became the exemplary warrior for the whole Western world. But he was still caught in the "knot of war," as Homer calls it, and in his grief and rage at the death of his closest companion, Patrocles, the old Indo-European battle frenzy overtook him. The smell of blood brought the bear out of the cave, and Achilles became as possessed and unstoppable as any of the old berserkirs. Raging like a forest fire whipped by winds, "so Achilles flashed to right and left, like a wild god, trampling the men he killed, and black earth ran with blood."[30] Cutting a bloody swath through the ranks, running down all who fled from him, Achilles refused to take prisoners, even when his victims flung their arms around his knees, begging for mercy.

Achilles finally met and killed Hector, spearing him through his neck, outside the walls of Troy. But Achilles' rage was so great, so out of control, that he refused to honor Hector's dying request that Achilles return his body to the Trojans, threatening—in what James Redfield calls the poem's greatest moment of terror—"Would god, my passion drove me to slaughter you and eat you raw, you've caused such agony to me!" Achilles then passed a thong through Hector's ankles and dragged his naked body through the dust behind his chariot around the walls of Troy and around Patrocles' funeral pyre.

In his battle rage, Achilles revealed how fragile the heroic warrior's code really was. For even half-divine Achilles, the greatest and noblest of all warriors, could be turned into a raging beast.

And though he did not actually turn into that most frightening of human predators, the cannibal, whose frenzy toward his enemy extended even beyond his enemy's death, Achilles had become a mere instrument of death and decay, a scavenger, a predator of the dead. In his rage, he had violated the most sacred tenet of the heroic warrior's code: that the worthy opponent must be treated with respect in death as well as in life.

It was fitting, then, that it was only through acknowledgment of just this aspect of the heroic warrior's code—namely the proper respect and treatment for the dead—that the berserk Achilles regained his honor as a chivalrous warrior. For if the berserkir is blind with rage, then the chivalrous warrior, who lives by the code, is the warrior who *sees* his opponent with empathy, clearly, as a worthy opponent.

And so when Priam, king of Troy and Hector's father, was led by the gods safely to Achilles' camp, where he pleaded for his son's body, Achilles thought of the grief his own death would cause his father and was moved to see his father in Priam. By opening his heart and allowing himself to feel Priam's grief, Achilles allowed the chivalrous warrior to come forth, like the tentative slender crescent of a new moon. In returning Hector's body to his father, Achilles returned to himself, like a berserkir laying aside his bearskin, or like Chu Chulainn when his furor was extinguished in the vats of cold water. Priam wept for Hector, and Achilles wept for his own father and Patrocles. Sorrow replaced rage, and, as Homer says, "sobbing filled the room."

◭◭ X I I ◭◭

If battle was the test of honor, if battle was a contest, it was nevertheless a deadly contest. The game in which honor was won was a zero-sum game. For honor was recognition of the warrior's prowess in battle, and that prowess depended on force—the pure, frenzied force of the berserkir come raging out of the cave—and this "force," like any force exercised against another, is finally, as Simone Weil so succinctly defined it in her 1938 essay on *The Iliad* "that x that turns anybody who is subjected to it into a *thing.* Exercised to the limit, it turns man into a thing in the most literal sense: it makes a corpse out of him."[31]

The inexorable logic of the heroic code, the logic of competition, is that there can be no heroes without worthy opponents to defeat.

And indeed, every warrior who lived by the heroic code, no matter how great his prowess, had to face the fact that sooner or later a worthier opponent, or sickness, or old age, or if that be his destiny, a poison arrow shot by an unworthy treacherous opponent, will find the one soft vulnerable spot of mortality that no one, not even the bravest warrior, can hide.

Achilles knew the value of life, he knew that the warrior's "life's breath cannot be hunted back or be recaptured once it pass his lips."

But he also knew that all must die, that "not even Hercules escaped that terror," and so he went forth to "confront the dark drear spirit of death at any hour Zeus and the other gods may wish to make an end."[32] For finally Achilles, like any warrior who sought honor before all else, could win only by sacrificing himself in the old Indo-European way: death in battle.

For most people, death is the great terror, the great enemy, the invincible enemy. But for the truly heroic warrior, death—his own death—is also the worthiest opponent. The noble warrior fights other men and takes their lives with his own hand, but the noblest of the noble warriors, the best—the *aristoi*—demonstrate bravery in the unequal contest with their own death, and this, finally, is what allows him to "hold his head above all others." Achilles achieved the highest honor; he became "the best of the Acheans," not just because he thrust his spear through Hector's throat or because he won honor and glory, but because he did so even at the cost of his own life.

And so Achilles' death, as the gods had foretold, followed Hector's death. He was killed by that least heroic of weapons, the bow. The arrow, loosed by the cowardly Paris from a hidden place of ambush, lodged in his heel, the one place his goddess mother had held when she dipped him in the waters of Lethe, which she hoped would make him invulnerable.

In the end, according to Homer, Odysseus found Achilles a somewhat cynical shade in the dark underworld of Hades, rather disillusioned with the heroic honor and fame he had traded his life for. It would be better, he told Odysseus, "to break sod as a farm hand for some poor country man than lord it over all the exhausted dead."[33]

But there was another Achilles, a pre-Homeric Achilles, an Achilles whose roots lay closer to the Indo-European origins of the Greek warriors. This Achilles' bones were buried in a great barrow that was raised overlooking the tempestuous Hellespont. Here Achilles was apotheosized as a hero—a great warrior, whose deeds had made him more than a mortal man, though less than an immortal god—who could be called on to help and protect the young men who poured blood and wine into the ground where he lay like the great ancestors, the warrior-chieftains who had led the Indo-European ancestors of the Greeks out of the steppes so many thousand forgotten years ago. The hero lived on in that Greek version of Valhalla described by Hesiod as the place reserved only for the heroic chosen warriors to whom the thunderbolt-wielding Zeus "gave a living and an abode apart from men, and made them dwell at the ends of the earth. And they lived untouched by sorrow in the islands of the blessed along the shore of the deep swirling Ocean, happy heroes for whom the grain-giving earth bears honey-sweet fruit flourishing twice a year."[34]

△△ X I I I △△

The heroic code which Achilles and other heroes exemplified lived on as well. It continued to inspire and structure warfare during the sixth and fifth centuries of the Greek city-states, even as the urban *hoplite* supplanted the landed aristocrats of the Homeric world.

During the period of the city-states, power shifted from the warrior-aristocrats to the free land-owning citizens of the *polis*. As first expressed by the seventh century Spartan poet Tyrtaeus, the citizen-warrior was exhorted to defend the city-state to which he owed all the advantages of a free—that is, a land-owning—citizen. "Make up your minds that happiness depends on being free," as Pericles says, "and freedom depends on being courageous. Let there be no relaxation in the face of war."[35] In militaristic Sparta, the ruling class devoted itself entirely to a military way of life, while the second-class helots worked the fields and tended the flocks. The military training of Spartan rulers began at birth: weak or deformed boys were left to die by exposure at the foot of Mount Taygetus. The others entered a period of austere training at the age of seven; they went barefoot, slept on a bed of reeds, and learned to obey as well as to steal without being caught. Their literary education was supposedly limited to the works of poets who extolled the virtues of the warrior. This first phrase of training ended with an initiation period—the *krypteia*—during which they lived like wolves in the old Indo-European *mannerbund* way. They hid out during the day, emerging only at night to forage, steal, and occasionally murder a helot. At the end of this period they became adults and warriors, living in the warrior barracks and eating at the common mess.

The Athenians, in contrast, began a two-year period of training in the *ephebiea* at the age of eighteen. Each trainee took an oath "not to dishonour his arms, not to desert his post, to extend the territory of his homeland, and to defend and respect its laws and religious cults."[36] In Athens, and most of the other Greek cities, the gymnasium was the center of the men's life, and athletics provided the basic military training. In addition to the usual races, gymnastics, wrestling, and javelin and discus throws, there were races in full armor, including shield and weapons. Warrior dances performed naked—except for greaves, shield, spear, and helmet—developed agility and movement. Finally, the trainee spent a year out in the field guarding the borders.

At the end of his two-year period of training, the Athenian warrior was considered an adult and a citizen-soldier—a *hoplite*—a word deriving from the round shield he carried. The rest of the panoply was similar to the Homeric warrior's: a bronze helmet, greaves, breastplate, short sword (of iron, by this time), and spear. The hoplites were supported by the city during their two-year period of training, but once they became citizens they had to provide their own armor and weapons. Fighting was thus both the prerogative and responsibility of the well-to-do middle and upper classes; slaves and other second-class citizens, like the Spartan helots, accompanied the citizen-warriors as servants or pages. They were not allowed to fight, except in exceptional circumstances.

◬ X I V ◬

The Greeks fought, at least some of the time, according to an unwritten law. This code was based on a recognition that while it was the natural condition of the Greek city-states to be always at war, there was still a Panhellenic commonality based on a common language, customs, and a shared apprehension of the sacred. Thus the unwritten law included respect for treaties, truces, and religious festivals; the right of the vanquished to recover their dead for burial; and the inviolability of heralds, priests, pilgrims, and sacred sites. The use of the "nonheroic" projectiles like slings were also limited on occasion. During the eighth- or seventh-century Lelantine War, Eretria and Chacis agreed not to use missiles and slings. At one point the Delphic oracles even attempted to extend the principles to siege warfare: they prohibited the use of projectiles and the cutting off of water. The whole enterprise was summarized by the Greek historian Polybius:

> The ancients would not consent to get the better of their enemies by fraud, regarding no success as brilliant or secure unless they crushed the spirit of their adversaries in open battle. For this reason they entered into a convention amongst themselves to use against each other neither secret missiles nor those discharged from a distance, and considered it was only hand to hand battle at close quarters

which was truly decisive. Hence they preceded war by a declaration, and when they intended to do battle gave notice of the fact and of the spot to which they would proceed and array their army.[37]

Greek wars, as Walter Burkert says, "may almost appear like one great sacrificial action."[38] They were fought in summer, so they would not interfere with the harvests, and not during sacred festivals and the Panhellenic games held at Olympus, Delphi, Corinth, and other sites sacred to all Greeks. The city-states generally fought over disputed border areas or about matters of honor, real or imagined insults, and obligations to allies.

War was never undertaken without the advice and consent of the oracle seeresses at Delphi or at other sacred sites, even though their advice was well known to be dangerously ambiguous. Cyrus, for example, was told by the oracle at Python that if he fought the Persians, he would put to end a great kingdom. He assumed, wrongly as it turned out, that the kingdom the oracle referred to was the Persians'. The Spartans, on the other hand, were especially conservative. In addition to the usual oracles, they would not go to war unless the sacrifices they performed were received favorably by the gods—sacrifices to Zeus inside Sparta, and to Athena at the border of Sparta.

The city-state united large numbers of men in a common purpose. In the same way, the citizen-warriors fought together in a phalanx which was only as effective as the sum of its individual members working together with discipline. Unlike the Homeric warriors, the hoplites did not use horses or chariots, either to fight or to reach the field of battle. Instead they marched together, eight rows deep, sometimes running, and sometimes moving slowly to the sound of flutes. As they approached the battlefield they sang the deep low dirge of the paean, the war song. Just before the battle began, more sacrifices were made; the Spartans sacrificed a goat on the field of battle. Then, to the sounds of the war cry—the *Alala*—the phalanxes moved toward each other until they met like two great rams colliding, shields clashing with shields, and one side broke through and the battle turned in the *trope*, or "turning."

It was at this point, in the melee that followed the initial clash of the phalanx, that the new collective way of fighting gave way to the old heroic mode as individual hoplites fought hand-to-hand with sword and spear. The temptation to turn and run must have been very great, especially when it seemed that the tide of battle was with the other side. "Abide then, O young men, shoulder to shoulder and fight," sang

Tyrtaeus, the Spartans' favorite poet, "but make the heart in your breasts both great and stout, and never shrink when you fight the foe."[39]

The fighting could be bloody enough, but in general—that is, when the unwritten law was followed—fleeing warriors were not pursued beyond the battlefield. "The shield I left because I must, poor blameless armament! beside a bush gives joy now to some Saian, but myself I have saved. What care I for the shield!"[40] sang the un-Spartanlike poet-soldier Archilochus. When prisoners were taken, they were not executed but held for ransom or exchange; those not ransomed or exchanged might be sent to work in mines or to languish in prisons.

The victors then gathered their dead, stripped the armor from their fallen opponents, and built a *trophaion* at the place where the battle had turned. This was either a pile of captured armor and arms or a wooden post which was hung with the armor of a fallen enemy warrior—a kind of scarecrow or effigy offered to the gods.

Finally, the heralds of the defeated army would appear on the field to request a truce, which could not be refused, and which would allow them to gather their dead for proper burial.

The victors then returned in triumph to their city for feasts and celebrations. The dead were honored in funeral games which reenacted the feats of warriors: footraces in full armor, chariot and horse races, javelin throwing, archery, and wrestling. The living who had acted like heroes, who had fought bravely in hand-to-hand combat, were honored with *aristeia* which now included crowns and laurel wreaths. A tenth of the booty was dedicated to the gods—the temples were filled with gleaming armor and weapons. There were more sacrifices. Sometimes the plunder was used to finance the restoration of temples or the building of new temples. And finally there were the poems or funeral orations honoring the brave heroes. The fact that the hoplites fought for their city and not only for their own honor, as Achilles had, was merely an addition to and not a diminishment of the old heroic ideal. As Pericles said of the Athenian dead in his famous funeral oration: "They gave their lives to her [to Athens] and to all of us, and for their own selves they won praises that never grow old."[41]

⋀⋀ X V ⋀⋀

The same code and spirit survived, as well, in the great empire forged by the last of the great Greek hero-warriors, Alexander of the Macedonians.

The Macedonians were great horsemen and hunters in the old Indo-European tradition, whose military success was based partly on their adaptation of the phalanx equipped with a six- or seven-meter-long pike, a *sarissa*, along with their use of cavalry. But none of it would have worked without the heroic ambition and self-confidence of Alexander himself. Surrounding himself with a hand-picked warrior band, the Companions, all of whom were of the landed nobility, Alexander slept with a dagger and a copy of *The Iliad*, annotated by his tutor Aristotle, beneath his pillow, saying that he "esteemed it a perfect portable treasure of all military virtue and knowledge." And he began his campaign against the Persians by worshiping at Achilles' shrine at Troy, where, as Plutarch tells us, he poured libations, "and with his friends, as the ancient custom is, ran naked about his sepulcre, and crowned it with garlands."[42]

Alexander was, perhaps, the last of the great Indo-European conquerers, as well as the last of the heroic warriors. He led his men by risk and example, always at the forefront. All in all, he was wounded no less than eight times—"wounded by sword, shot with arrows, struck from a catapult, smitten many times with stones and clubs."[43] When his advisors urged him to launch a surprise night attack against a superior Persian force, Alexander replied with heroic disdain that "darkness belongs to robbers and waylayers. But my glory shall not be diminished by stealing a victory. . . . I am determined to attack openly by daylight; I prefer to regret my fortune rather than be ashamed of my victory."[44] And so he charged recklessly into the midst of the enemy on his great charger, Bucephalus, plainly visible with his snowy white plumes streaming from his shining silver helmet, and won the battle.

When Alexander reached Gordium, a town in eastern Phrygia strategically placed on the trade route to Asia Minor, he faced his own personal warrior's dilemma. Ahead lay the remaining Persian army, still commanded by their king, and India. Behind lay the considerable Persian territory he had already conquered, and Greece itself, which was still threatened by the Persian navy as well as by Greek revolts against Macedonian rule. If he went ahead, he risked losing everything. If we went back, he gave up the whole heroic enterprise, the great dream of uniting Europe and Asia in one harmonious empire.

The town of Gordium, as it happened, contained a shrine with an oxcart tied to a yoke by a rawhide knot. The man who could unravel this knot, it was said, would become lord of all Asia.

The knot was a tangled "Turk's head" knot, its ends and beginnings hidden and covered within the knot itself. It was an impossible knot to unravel, an insoluble problem. Alexander struggled for some time without success, watched carefully by warriors and priests alike. He tried everything Aristotle had taught him—analysis, intuition, and prayer. He was patient and reasonable. All to no avail. His whole life and his whole empire were tied in the knot which would not yield its secret. Then, finally at his wit's end, fighting for survival, he cried out, "What difference does it make *how* I loose it?"[45] The old Indo-European battle rage rose, and Alexander cut through the knot with one great stroke of his sword.

There were some, perhaps even Alexander himself, who had their doubts about this drastic solution. But that night the old Indo-European storm god sent rain, thunder, and lightning, and Alexander and the seers declared themselves convinced that Zeus himself had shown his approval. And so Alexander turned toward India.

CHAPTER FIVE

THE BED
OF ARROWS

The Aryans from Arjuna to Asoka

How can we be happy if we kill our own people?
–Arjuna to Krishna

When Alexander reached India in 326 B.C., he was met by the majestic figure of King Porus commanding his troops from a throne on top of an elephant. The Indian army was large and well equipped—forty thousand cavalry, three hundred chariots, two hundred elephants, and thirty thousand infantry—but Alexander, displaying his customary boldness, won the battle by charging across a swollen river under cover of a fierce storm. Porus refused to surrender until his troops were scattered and he himself was wounded in the shoulder. Impressed by the Indian king's courage, Alexander asked Porus how he would like to be treated. When Porus answered simply and proudly, "Treat me, O Alexander, as befits a king," Alexander appointed Porus the ruler of the kingdom he had just lost.

Though he had no way of knowing it, Alexander's Indo-European ancestors had already conquered India two millennia earlier—the earliest date is estimated at around 2000 B.C.—when the Indo-Iranians or Aryans, as they called themselves, crossed the Khyber Pass with their bronze swords, battle-axes, and bows, and with their horses, chariots, oxcarts, and cattle.

The Aryans (the "noble," or "free," according to one etymology) were an Indo-European warrior society, fierce and nomadic, "a wild turbulent people, with few of the taboos of later India," in A. L. Basham's words.[1] There is some evidence that early Aryan women were considerably freer than their Hindu descendants. The *Rig-Veda*, the oldest collection of Aryan hymns, recounts the story of a renowned woman warrior, Idrasena Mudgala, "the long-haired charioteer," who drove her husband's chariot in a great cattle raid, "becoming the very army of Indra," sings the *Rig-Veda*. "She gambled and won the spoils."[2]

The Aryans had no interest in cities or trade. They measured their wealth in cows, whose skins they wore and whose flesh they happily ate. They raided cattle, raced horses and chariots, hunted, and gambled for high stakes with dice. And they drank the juice of the sacred soma, the exact nature of which remains one of the great unsolved mysteries of Vedic studies. Some have argued that soma was a drink made from cannabis or some kind of alcoholic beverage. The mycologist R. Gordon Wasson believed that soma was the *Amanita muscaria*, the fly agaric mushroom of the Siberian shamans. More recently, another scholar has nominated an Iranian desert weed, *Peganum harmala*, for the honor.[3]

Whatever its botanical classification or origin, soma was what ethnobotanists call an "entheogen," a plant that bestowed a vision of the "other" or sacred realm. But like most substances of this sort, it was risky and unpredictable. As one of the hymns in the *Rig-Veda* complains, "This restless Soma—you try to grab him but he breaks away and overpowers everything."[4]

The soma ecstasy could open up vast spaces of bliss and freedom and of poetic inspiration. But it could also "stir up passion and fury," filling warriors with strength and courage. And most powerfully, it could reveal Indra's heaven in the midst of battle, thus granting a preview of immortality. As one of the hymns in the *Rig-Veda* goes:

> *We have drunk Soma; we have become immortal,*
> *We have gone to the light; we have found the gods.*
> *What can hatred and the malice of a mortal do to us now,*
> *O immortal one?*[5]

Aryan society provided a textbook example of that tripartite structure—sovereignty/force/fecundity—which the French Indo-Euro-
peanist Georges Dumezil considered the basic structure of Indo-European society. In Aryan India, sovereignty was represented by the priests
or Brahmans, force by the warriors or the Kshatriyas, and fecundity by
the herders and cultivators. The *Rig-Veda* explained the origin of this
threefold division of society as the result of the self-sacrifice of the giant
Purusha: "His mouth became the Brahmin; his arms were made into
the Warrior, his thighs the People."[6]

The tripartite society of the Aryans was an analogue of the cosmos
itself, with each group playing an essential but interdependent role, just
as the various parts of the body have essential and interdependent roles.

The Brahmans were the rulers who performed the sacrifices that
daily recreated the world. Their "sovereignty" was based on their
knowledge of hymns, mantras, prayers, and rituals needed to effectively
communicate with the gods through sacrifice. But it was the Kshatriyas
who held both arms and actual power. The warriors fought for "land,
light, and space," as the *Rig-Veda* said, and warriors' raids supplied the
cattle and horses needed for sacrifice. And finally, it was from the ranks
of the warriors that secular rulers, the kings or rajas, were drawn.

The Brahmans and the Kshatriyas, the two noble classes, were thus
joined in an uneasy but generally effective alliance, both against the
non-Aryan indigenous people and the Aryan commoners. One attempt
to neutralize this opposition appears in the *Laws of Manu*, where the
Kshatriyas are instructed to practice "noninvolvement in the [other]
spheres of activity"—that is, to interfere with neither the sovereignty
of the Brahmans nor the livelihood of the commoners.[7] But the need
for such a prohibition only underscores the fact that the old Indo-
European warrior's dilemma still remained: there was always the frightening possibility that the warriors might use their force to dominate
rather than protect the Brahmans. It is hardly surprising, then, that the
Vedic seers who compiled the law codes were careful to make Brah-
manicide the most heinous of all crimes.

∆∆ I I I ∆∆

Indra was the king of the gods, and the patron of the Kshatriyas. Like
the other Indo-European warrior storm gods, Zeus and Thor, Indra
wielded the thunderbolt—in this case the five-pronged lotus-blossom-

shaped indestructible *vajra*. "Autonomous, audacious is your spirit, slaying at a single stroke," he was the leader of the Maruts, the celestial warrior band of wind gods.[8] He was also known as the greatest soma drinker of all.

Indra's greatest exploit was his battle with the demon/dragon Vrta. In the earliest version of the story, which appears in the *Rig-Veda*, the virile—"of a thousand-testicles"—and powerful Indra gained the strength for his battle against the demon Vrta by drinking the soma extract. Then, intoxicated and ecstatic from the soma, "wildly excited like a bull, Indra the Generous seized his thunderbolt to hurl as a weapon; he killed the first-born of dragons."[9]

The battle between Indra and Vrta is the old, familiar battle of the warrior-hero against the dragon of chaos. But the battle between Indra and Vrta may also represent the battles the Aryans fought against the people who inhabited the great cities of the archaic Indus River Valley civilization. If so, the victory over Vrta, which "released the seven streams so that they could flow," may refer to the destruction of the great city walls which released the floodwaters from the rivers the city-dwellers had dammed.

Though little is known of their civilization, the cities of the Indus River Valley were very likely related to the first cities of Mesopotamia, possibly by colonization, certainly through trade: a cylinder seal picturing the Sumerian warrior-king Gilgamesh fighting two lions has been found at Mohenjadaro. But there was much that was indigenous to the vast Indian subcontinent. The writing of the Indus River Valley remains undeciphered to this day, but bronze statues and pictures on cylinder seals suggest that both dancing goddesses and phallic male deities were worshiped by the pre-Aryan Indians. The most famous of these gods is the so-called "proto-Shiva," depicted as sitting with his legs crossed, in the posture which we now associate with yoga and meditation, naked, penis erect. He is crowned with a three-horned headdress and is surrounded by animals—a pair of snakes in one example, two kneeling antelope in another.

The existence of this "proto-Shiva"—as well as many other dark-skinned goddesses and gods—has led many scholars to conclude that most of the beliefs and practices we call Hinduism grew from the soil of aboriginal India, and not from the imported Vedas of the Aryans, which mention only one goddess, Dawn, and make no mention at all of reincarnation or yoga.

The conservative Brahmans held themselves aloof from the powerful goddesses, yogis, and phallic worshipers of the dark-skinned natives.

The Kshatriyas, however, came into close contact with the indigenous dark-skinned Indians through battle, and eventually—since they were not bound by the ritual purity of the Brahmans—through intermarriage. Some of the more adventurous warriors were drawn to the austerities of the indigenous shamans and magicians, perhaps because they were looking for new techniques to replace the powerful but unreliable soma, or perhaps because they simply wanted to pursue a path based on direct, individual experience.

In any case, the Aryan warriors did not simply absorb pre-Aryan beliefs and practices. They also seem to have contributed a great deal to the development of the system we now call yoga, beginning with the word itself. *Yoga* was cognate with the Indo-European verb *yuj*, which means to yoke or harness and was used to describe the charioteer's harnessing of horses to the chariot.[10] In time, yoga came to stand for the methods used to yoke or join the *atman*—the individual self—with the Brahman, the absolute self that pervaded and permeated the entire universe. The original meaning of *yoga* continued to be used as a metaphor for the yogic path. "Know the Self as the lord of the chariot," advised the *Katha Upanishad*, "and the body as the chariot. Know the intellect as the charioteer and the mind the reins. . . . He who has understanding for the driver of the chariot and controls the rein of his mind, he reaches the end of his journey, the supreme abode of the all-pervading."[11]

The new teaching—or perhaps we should say the *old* teaching—of the identity of *atman* and Brahman had far-reaching implications for warriors who were duty-bound to face death bravely. As a verse in the *Katha Upanishad* said:

> The soul never dies and never born is he,
> came not into being and never comes to be,
> primeval, in the body's death unslain,
> unborn, eternal, everlastingly.
>
> But he who thinks this soul can kill
> and who thinks that it is killed
> has never truly understood,
> it does not kill and is never killed.[12]

∆∆ IV ∆∆

The Aryan warrior drank from the stream of two great traditions—that of the old soma-intoxicated Indo-European warrior bands, and that of the indigenous inward-looking forest ascetics. So it was that when Arjuna, the hero of the great Indian epic the *Mahabharata,* set out alone on a journey to the Himalayas to ask the old Aryan war god Indra to initiate him into the "secret of all weapons," Indra replied that he would grant Arjuna's request only after Arjuna had put aside his weapons and practiced austerities. Following Indra's instructions, Arjuna went into the solitude of the forest, where he devoted himself to meditative exercises, subsisting first on fruit, then on fallen leaves, until finally he "lived on wind alone, with arms raised, without support, balanced on the tips of his toes."[13]

Having passed this initiatory ordeal, Indra's charioteer conducted Arjuna to Amaravati, the Aryan Valhalla and heavenly abode of the great warrior-god himself. There Indra wrapped Arjuna in his great arms and made him sit beside him on his throne. Indra then presented Arjuna with his own weapon, the indestructible diamond-hard lotus-blossom-shaped *vajra,* and instructed him further in both yoga and martial prowess.

Arjuna spent five years in Indra's heaven. When he returned to the world, he found that his cousins, the Kauravas, led by the evil and jealous Duryodhana, had arrogantly refused to grant Arjuna and his four brothers—the Pandavas—even a single village of the kingdom that should rightfully have been shared between them.

Due to Duryodhana's intransigence and treachery, war seemed inevitable, and the two sides met in council to review the rules of the great battle that would decide the succession to the kingdom. According to *dharmavijaya* (literally "dharma conquest," or conquest by righteousness) Brahmans were considered exempt from battle unless they attacked first, and armies desisted from battle when a Brahman "desirous of peace goes between two contending armies."[14] Farmers and other noncombatant citizens were also considered exempt.

Ideally, *dharmavijaya* was a great tournament. As with the Greeks, Indian battles took place at a prearranged time, on an open plain suitable for chariots. The battle itself was a series of duels in which "only equals should fight each other." This meant, in particular, that "elephants should oppose only elephants; and so the chariots, cavalry, and infantry should attack only their opposite number. A king should fight only with a king, and a commoner should not strike a monarch.

Similarly, a Kshatriya should fight an equal in battle, a man of his own order. Those indulging in wordy warfare should be fought only with words."[15]

The rules of *dharmavijaya* went far beyond the notion of equality, however, to concern and responsibility toward weaker or disabled opponents and innocent noncombatants. "Those who leave the ranks should never be slain. One should strike another only after giving due notice, and only when justified in so doing by considerations of fitness, daring, and might. No one should strike another who is confiding or unprepared or panic-stricken. A foe engaged with another should never be struck, as also one without armour, or whose weapon is rendered useless. Chariot drivers and draught-animals, men engaged in transport of weapons, and drummers and buglers, should not be attacked. A kshatriya should not strike one who is fatigued and frightened, weeping and unwilling to fight; one who is ill and cries for quarter, or one of tender years or advanced age."[16]

Carried to its logical conclusion, the Kshatriya's fastidious concern for his opponent could even end in a paradoxical reversal of battle altogether: "If entreated with joined hands," the texts say, "a kshatriya should defend even his enemy."[17] It is difficult to say how often such high ideals were actually followed, or even to what extent they reflected a purely literary idealization. But we do have two reasonably reliable eyewitness accounts. Megasthenes, the Greek ambassador to the Mauryan emperor, observed in 300 B.C. that "at the very time when a battle was going on, the neighboring cultivators might be seen quietly cultivating their work—perhaps ploughing, gathering in their corps, pruning trees, or reaping the harvest."[18] And the Chinese Buddhist pilgrim Huan Tsang reported from the Deccan in the fourteenth century that "when they have an injury to avenge they never fail to give warning to their enemy, after which each puts on his cuirass and grasps spear in hand. In battle they pursue the fugitives but do not slay them who give themselves up."[19] In any case, scholar A. L. Basham, author of *The Wonder That Was India,* is surely justified in his contention that "it is doubtful if any other ancient civilization set such humane ideals for warfare."[20]

△△ V △△

It would seem, then, that Arjuna had good reason to object to the war between the Pandavas and the Kauravas, for as he looked out at the great army arrayed for battle at Kurukshestra he was filled with horror at the thought of killing his revered teachers and his relatives, especially his beloved grand-uncle Bhisma.

Turning to Krishna, who was serving as his charioteer, Arjuna asked, "How can we be happy if we kill our own people? It would be better for me if the Kauravas slayed me while I remained unresisting and unarmed. . . . It is better to live in this world even by begging than to slay these honored teachers. By slaying them I would only enjoy delights smeared with blood. I will not fight."[21]

It was the charioteer's role to encourage and inspire his warrior, as well as to give advice. But Krishna was not only a charioteer—he was also a god, a kind of cosmic recruiting officer, who marshaled every argument at his disposal to convince Arjuna to fight. He began with a blunt appeal to Arjuna's masculine Aryan pride. Arjuna's dejection at this hour of crisis, he said, was decidedly "un-Aryan" *(anaryajustam)*. It "does not lead to heaven on earth, and causes disgrace." Therefore, he exhorted, "Yield not to this unmanliness. Cast off this petty faint-heartedness and arise."[22]

Arjuna held his ground, however, and so Krishna turned to a more subtle argument, which was the real subject of the *Bhagavad-Gita,* the sixteenth book of the *Mahabharata.*

Krishna explained to Arjuna that his refusal to fight was based on a confusion between appearance and reality. The individual self, the *atman,* Krishna said, was actually identical to the immutable, indestructible Brahman. "Weapons do not cleave this self," Krishna said, "fire does not burn him, waters do not make him wet; nor does the wind make him dry. . . . The dweller in the body of everyone, O Bharata, is eternal and can never be slain. Therefore you should not grieve for any creature."[23] (This same verse, thousands of years later, became the battle song Gandhi's nonviolent warriors sang to give them courage to endure attacks and beatings.)

But this transcendental view, Krishna warned, should not be taken as an excuse for the warrior to renounce the world to practice yoga in the forest. Even he, Krishna, acted in order to sustain the world. In the same way, said Krishna, all men should act in the world according to their birth, their nature, their *dharma* or duty. "Heroism, vigour, steadiness, resourcefulness, not fleeing even in a battle, generosity and leadership," said Krishna, "these are the duties of a Kshatriya born of his nature." In fact, the warrior who did his duty could not lose. If he was killed in battle, he went to heaven, and if victorious, he "will enjoy the earth: therefore arise, O Arjuna, resolved on battle."[24]

This might have been a good enough argument for the old Aryan warrior, who followed the Aryan tradition that the warrior had to act according to his nature and role in the divinely ordered society. But according to the yogic tradition which Arjuna and the Kshatriyas also followed, every action (or "karma") always led to further entanglement in the world of cause and effect, leading to a ceaseless round of birth and death. The solution to this apparent contradiction, according to Krishna, was to act without attachment to the result or fruit of the action. By acting without attachment, the warrior could have the best of both the relative and absolute world. The way of the warrior would thus be transformed into a method for liberation.

This yoga led full circle, however, back to the Vedic rites of sacrifice. Krishna revealed that he was actually Vishnu, the Creator and Sustainer of All, and the warrior who offered him the fruits of his actions, victory or defeat, was actually making an inner sacrifice to Krishna. "Resigning all your works to Me, with your mind fixed in the Self, being free from desire and egoism, fight the battle delivered from thy fever without being in any way agitated,"[25] Krishna instructed Arjuna—for it was, finally, Krishna and not Arjuna who decided the fate of the warrior in battle. Arjuna was merely the instrument of Krishna. And battles fought in this way were, for Kshatriyas, the supreme sacrifice.

And then Krishna revealed his supreme and divine form: "Of many mouths and eyes, of many divine ornaments, of many divine uplifted weapons, resplendent, boundless, as if the light of a thousand suns were to blaze forth all at once in the sky."[26] (It was this verse that Robert Oppenheimer, Sanskritist as well as nuclear physicist, found himself repeating as he watched the first atomic bomb explode with "the light of a thousand suns" over the desert at Los Alamos.)

Trembling, his hair standing on end, Arjuna saw the chief warriors of both the Pandavas and the Kauravas plunge into Krishna's "mouths terrible with their Tusks like Time's devouring flame, as moths rush swiftly into a blazing fire."

Then Krishna told Arjuna:

Whenever there is a decline of *dharma* and a rise in unrighteousness (*adharma*) I send forth myself. For the protection of the good, for the destruction of the wicked, for the establishment of *dharma,* I am born in *yuga* (time cycle) after *yuga.*

I am Time itself. Even without your effort all the opposing warriors shall cease to exist. Therefore arise and win great glory, conquor your enemies and enjoy a glorious kingdom.[27]

Arjuna—and who could blame him?—abandoned his objections, and so, with the sound of conches and drums, roaring like lions so that the earth and sky shook with their war cries, the armies began the terrible battle. Thousands of single combats took place between chariot warriors, horsemen, and foot soldiers. Protected by five chariots, the noble Bishma, the beloved grand-uncle, penetrated the lines of the Pandavas, shooting a continuous stream of arrows in all directions, like a circle of fire, calling out the names of the warriors he killed. Arjuna met Bishma on the battlefield many times, but because he still revered the old man, he held back. The result was that Bishma slaughtered thousands of Pandavas "like a fire in the midst of a forest."[28]

At twilight on the eight day of the battle, the Pandavas retreated in despair. But Bishma, as Krishna knew, believed in the Pandavas' cause and fought only because it was his duty as a Kshatriya. Urged on by Krishna, the Pandavas implored Bishma to tell them how he could be killed. Bishma replied that he was indeed invincible in a fair battle, but that as a Kshatriya who followed the rules of *dharmavijaya* he would not fight against a weaponless man, an unhorsed warrior, a chariot without a banner, a coward, a terror-stricken warrior, or a woman.

That night the Pandavas held a council with Krishna, who convinced Arjuna to attack Bishma while hiding behind Sikhandan, whom Bishma would presumably not attack, since he, or she—Sikhandan, that is—had been a woman in a previous life. Remembering how his beloved grand-uncle Bishma used to hold him on his lap, Arjuna argued against the plan. But Krishna was adamant: it was Arjuna's duty as a warrior to kill Bishma.

The next day, safely hidden behind Sikhandan—whom the noble Bishma did indeed refuse to attack—Arjuna shot a steady stream of arrows at Bishma until the old warrior fell from his chariot, with "so many arrows sticking in his body on all sides that he did not touch the ground in his fall, but rested on a bed of arrows."[29]

The next day Drona took Bishma's place as leader of the Kauravas, and once again Krishna pursuaded Arjuna to use trickery, in this case lying that Drona's beloved son had been killed, which caused Drona to drop his weapon in despair. Next Krishna urged Arjuna to kill Karna while Karna was extricating his chariot wheel from the mud, a clear violation of the rules of battle. And finally, Krishna encouraged Bhima, Arjuna's brother, to kill Duryodhana by striking him below the belt (specifically on the thigh) during a duel with clubs, a cowardly blow specifically forbidden by the rules of club fighting.

Arjuna and the Pandavas were now victorious, but only because they had violated the code of the warrior by resorting to trickery. They had won, paradoxically, by becoming like their enemies, and their enemies had become as the Pandavas had supposed themselves to be. And so, as he fell, Duryodhana bitterly reminded Krishna that he and the greatest warriors of the Kauravas had all been struck down unfairly. He himself, he said, was destined to join the war god Indra in heaven because he had died in battle. "Glory is all that one should acquire here, and it can be obtained by battle, and by no other means," he declared. "The death that a kshatriya meets with at home is censurable. Death on one's bed is a sin. I have obtained that end which kshatriyas observant of the duty of their own order look forward to, death in battle. With all my well wishers, and my younger brothers, I am going to heaven!"[30]

The Pandavas were stricken with remorse. But not Krishna. The god-charioteer who had instructed Arjuna to fight without attachment to victory or defeat now rationalized his trickery with the most expedient and practical of arguments: it was the only way to win. "The Kauravas were great chariot warriors," he explained. "All your bravery could not have defeated them . . . so I used my powers of *maya* in many ways on the battle-field. If you had not followed my deceitful ways, you would never have been victorious. When one is outnumbered by his enemies, then destruction should be brought about by stratagem. The gods themselves, in killing the *asuras* [titans] have followed the same methods. The way that was followed by the celestials may be followed by all."[31]

In fact, Krishna had a point. He stood on firm mythological, if not moral, ground. In the battles between gods and monstrous demons, neither strength nor virtue alone sufficed. The gods had to use trickery, spells, and magic weapons because the demonic forces—be they dragons or giants—*were* more powerful than the most powerful gods or heroes. The demon monsters were more powerful than the gods who opposed them because they were incarnations of chaos which was always prior to order—for it was from chaos that the world of plants, humanity, and society was created.

The gods won through various subterfuges, then, but their victory could never be complete. If it were, if they utterly annihilated the enemy—if they made the world safe for order, so to speak—it would be disastrous because there would then be no more chaos with which to re-create the world. And so the demon was cast out into the darkness, exiled to the bottom of the ocean, or sprang up once again from the dragon's teeth, or—as in the *Mahabharata*—the roles of the combatants were reversed. The "virtuous" Pandavas won by deceit; the "deceitful" Kauravas lost by the rules. Both sides, it turned out, were merely playing a role in a cosmic drama that had no end.

This drama can be seen as an Aryan version of the old Indo-European drama, in which the cosmic battle between the forces of order and chaos begin with a golden age when virtue or *dharma* is in the ascendent, and then run down until the forces of chaos or evil are nearly victorious—at which point the world must be purified in a great sacrificial bloodletting. The mythologist Jaan Puhvel, for one, finds other Indo-European versions of this "cataclysmic holocaust" in the Old Iranian struggle between divine and demonic forces, at the end of which the world is purified and transfigured in molten metal, and in the Old Norse war between the Aesir and Vanir at the battle of Ragnarok.[32]

The great battle of Kurukshestra is the first act of this great purification. As Krishna-Vishnu says, "In every cycle, I take birth in various forms in order to protect Virtue and establish it. I am the creator of all objects that exist. Knowing no change in myself, I am also the destroyer of all creatures that live in sinfulness."[33]

But whatever Krishna or anyone else says, one thing is clear. Once the rules governing the sacred battle are abandoned by both sides, nothing can stop the demonic escalation of violence. And so the few surviving Kauravas—who now felt justified in ignoring the warrior's code just as their opponents had done—launched a surprise night attack and massacred the sleeping Pandava troops.

With the code now broken by both parties, the righteous war was reduced to nothing more than a field of blood and carnage. The precarious balance of the sacred war had been destroyed. The chivalrous code of the Kshatriyas had given way to the blood thirst of the berserkir and the slippery deceit of the warrior-trickster. The field of battle became a dancing ground for the terrible black goddess Kali, who appeared with bloody mouth and disheveled hair to lead the dead away by her noose. Only Arjuna and his four brothers, having been warned just in time by Krishna, survived.

From Krishna's cosmic perspective, the Kshatriyas who died gloriously in the great battle of Kurukshestra were merely acting as his instruments, and so both Pandavas and Kauravas were rewarded, like good Aryan warriors, by ascending to the throne of Indra. And so the wheel of life and death turned. But down below, here in our world, the

Kali Yuga, the last and the most degenerate of the four great cycles of time, had only just begun.

◬ VII ◬

Was there—*is* there—then no way out?

That, to put it simply, was the question that pierced the heart of a young Kshatriya, prince Siddhartha, on the day he left his father's luxurious palace for the first time.

When Siddhartha was born in a kingdom in northwest India in 567 B.C., the astrologers had predicted he would become either a world conqueror or a world renouncer. His father, therefore, did his best to keep his son within the palace walls. He provided him with hundreds of dancing girls for his pleasure; he ordered the most learned Brahmans to teach him philosophy, the greatest warriors to instruct him in archery, charioteering, and horsemanship. And finally, he found Siddhartha a wife, with whom he had a son.

Not all these pleasures, however, could stop Siddhartha's curiosity about life outside the palace, and so one day he called his charioteer and secretly rode out into the city. There he encountered four sights he had never seen: first, a man walking along with a cane—old, his charioteer told him, as all beings were subject to old age; then a man shaking with fever—sick, his charioteer told him, as all were subject to disease; next, a woman lying lifeless by the side of the road—dead, his charioteer told him, as all beings were subject to death; and finally, he encountered a forest dweller and ascetic, walking calmly and slowly, like an elephant, along the road—a man, Siddhartha's charioteer told him, who had renounced the world and sought liberation from sickness, old age, and death in the forest. And at that very moment Siddhartha determined to leave the palace and follow the path of the forest-dwelling ascetic.

He left the palace at night on his great white horse, Katanka, and when he had reached the edge of the forest, he dismounted and cut off the long black hair of a Kshatriya with one cut of his sword. Then he freed Katanka, as the old Kshatriya-kings freed a horse for the great horse sacrifice, and disappeared into the forest.

For the next seven years he wandered among the forest sages and yogis, many of whom had abandoned their duties as Brahmans or Kshatriyas. This was exactly what Krishna had convinced Arjuna not to do—and for good reason. The new seekers who had taken to the forests during Siddhartha's time insisted on the primacy of the search for liberation. Their ascetic withdrawal from society threatened to undermine its whole structure.

After seven years of austerities and meditation—of great heroic effort, of *virya*—Siddhartha sat down under the Bodhi tree on a mat of grass. "Skin, sinew and bone may dry up; my flesh and blood may dry in my body," he vowed, "but I will not leave this seat until I attain complete enlightenment."[34]

Siddhartha had not gone in search of dragons, monsters, or demons. But because he had stayed put, doing battle with his own delusions and ignorance, the demons came to him. Siddhartha's vow to attain complete enlightenment was taken as a direct challenge by Mara, the Destroyer, the Master of Illusion, the Enemy of the Good Law.

Arming himself with his flower-made bow and his five infatuating arrows, Mara conjured up a monstrous army. Some had the faces of boars, or fish, or tigers and bears; some were one-eyed, some were many-faced; some had protuberant and speckled bellies. They all swarmed around Mara waving arrows, trees, darts, clubs, and swords.

Like one great warrior challenging another, Mara challenged Siddhartha. "Difficult is the way of exertion, difficult to pass, difficult to enter upon," he taunted him.

Siddhartha lifted his eyes to look directly at Mara and the armies he commanded. He called out the names of Mara's armies as a Kshatriya called out the names of the opponents he has challenged on the field of battle. The first army he called Lust, the second Discontent, the third Hunger and Thirst, the fourth Desire. He called the fifth army Sloth and Drowsiness, the sixth Cowardice, the seventh Doubt, and the eighth Hypocrisy and Stupor.

"These armies of yours, which the world of men and gods cannot conquer," said Siddhartha, "I will crush with understanding as one crushes an unbaked earthen pot with a stone."

Mara then commanded his troops to attack. But Siddhartha remained firm in his meditation, neither retreating nor advancing, and all the deadly poison-tipped missiles hurled by Mara turned into flowers.

Left without weapons, Mara demanded that Siddhartha provide a witness who could vouch for his spiritual efforts and attainments throughout all his innumerable past lives. "There is none to witness for you even with a single word," Mara exulted. "You are conquered!"

But there was one. Siddhartha let his right hand fall to the earth, which he touched with all his fingers in what has come to be called the "earth-witnessing mudra."

"I appeal to this mother of all creatures, O Mara," Siddhartha declared. And as soon as his fingers touched the ground, the earth trembled and split apart, and the earth goddess Sthavara appeared with all her ornaments. Bowing to Siddhartha, the earth goddess said, "It is so, great being, it is as you have declared."

The way was now clear. Describing the undescribable hundreds of years later, the *Dhammapada* quoted Siddhartha, now known as the Buddha, the Awakened One: "I have conquered all, I know all; in all conditions of life I am free from taint; I have left all, and through the destruction of thirst I am free; having by myself attained supernatural knowledge, to whom can I point as my teacher?"[35]

Siddhartha had conquered Mara with the weapon of understanding. He had fought without weapons, without moving, without retreating or advancing. He had ridden and tamed his mind with the daring of the first Indo-European warriors; he had attacked the fortress of self with the strength of city-destroying Indra; and he had faced the death of the self by himself. He had challenged the armies of Mara in a fair duel, with no trickery, and he had won. He had destroyed in one stroke the illusion of self that divided the world into "I" and "other."

The teachings of Siddhartha represented a radical reinterpretation and transformation of the warrior's code. Recognizing that the final enemy, the worthiest enemy, was within, the world renouncer became the conqueror. From that time on—in India, at least—the term *Vira*, or hero, was reserved for those who became what, for want of a better term, we might call "spiritual warriors."

The knot of war is the cosmic knot of Krishna, but it is also the knot of self—the wrath and pride of Achilles, the envy and greed of Duryodhana, the sacrifice of Arjuna, the Gordian knot of Alexander—and it must be untied, again and again, by every warrior, in every place and in every cycle of time. "If one man conquer in battle a thousand times a thousand men," as Siddhartha said, "and if another conquers himself, he is the greatest of conquerors."[36]

ᴧᴧ V I I I ᴧᴧ

But the knot of war is not only the knot of self. It is also the knot that millions of selves tie together.

Though the Buddha had turned the warrior's code outside in, so to speak, the nonviolent teachings of the Buddha were to have a profound effect on Indian society. Recognizing that "all men tremble at punishment and fear death, remembering that you are like them," he taught his followers, "Do not strike or slay." When the Sakyas and Koliyas were about to go to war in a dispute about water rights, the Buddha stepped between the two armies and stopped the war. "Victory breeds hatred, for the conquered is unhappy," he said. "He who has given up both victory and defeat, he, the contented, is happy."[37]

No doubt many, then as now, judged the Buddha's teaching as unworldly and impractical. But scarcely two hundred years after his death, the Buddha's message had a profound effect on a world conqueror by the name of King Asoka.

Asoka's grandfather, Chadragupta, was the founder of the Maurya Empire, which he controlled through a tight network of spies, informers, and secret police. In the beginning, Asoka—who may have murdered his own father to gain the throne—seemed destined to follow in his grandfather's footsteps. But in the eighth year of his reign, after a bloody victory over the Kalingas, Asoka had a complete change of heart. As he himself recounted on Rock Edict XIII, which he had carved on stone throughout his kingdom:

> One hundred fifty thousand persons were carried away captive, one hundred thousand were slain, and many times that number died. Immediately after the Kalingas had been conquered, King Asoka became intensely devoted to the study of Dharma, to the love of Dharma, and to the inculcation of Dharma. The Beloved of the Gods, conqueror of the Kalingas, is moved to remorse now. For he has felt profound sorrow and regret because the conquest of a people previously unconquered involved slaughter, death, and deportation.[38]

As a result of his conversion, Asoka transformed the old Aryan idea of *dharmavijaya*, or "righteous conquest." Under his rule, righteous conquest was no longer conquest fought to uphold the *dharma* or order of things, nor was it a war fought according to a particular code of warfare. It was now reinterpreted with a meaning much closer to its literal etymology: conquest by *dharma* or the nonviolent treachings of the Buddha. "Because of King Asoka's practice of Dharma," as he proclaimed in Rock Edict IV, "the sound of war-drums has become the call to Dharma."[39]

Asoka came to be regarded throughout Asia as the model of the enlightened warrior-king. Though he did not renounce the use of force entirely, his regime was remarkably humane, even by present standards. In Rock Edict XIII, Asoka announced that he desired "security, self control, impartiality, and cheerfulness for all living creatures," and adopted the principle that "even a person who wrongs him must be forgiven for wrongs that can be forgiven."[40]

Asoka put his principles into practice with all the qualities of the Kshatriya which Krishna had given to Arjuna: "heroism, vigour, steadfastness, resourcefulness, bravery, generosity and leadership." Considering himself the servant of his people, Asoka made himself available at any time, even when he was engaged in meditation or in his harem. He built rest houses, planted shade trees, established hospitals, imported medicinal plants and herbs, and gave prisoners leave every twenty-five days. He promoted toleration for all religious groups and teachers, and taught respect for teachers and the elderly.

Asoka's concern extended also to the animals in his kingdom. He ended the practice of animal sacrifice in his capital and placed many species of animals under royal protection. He also did his best to end the killing of animals for food. Formerly, he said, "many hundreds of creatures were slaughtered every day for the curries in the kitchens of his Majesty. But at present only three living creatures are killed daily: two peacocks and a deer, and the deer is not slaughtered regularly. In the future not even these three animals shall be slaughtered."[41]

Pursuing *dharmavijaya* with an energy and ambition as great as Chadragupta or Alexander had pursued their worldly conquests, Asoka dispatched missionaries to the ends of the earth, from Sri Lanka to Greece. His literal attempt at *dharmavijaya* thus had far-reaching consequences, though his kingdom did not survive the rule of his incompetent and dissolute heirs. When satraps appointed by Alexander threatened to invade from the northwest, an army general usurped the throne, defeated the invaders, and so brought both the Maurya dynasty and the Asokian experiment to an end—just as one would expect in the Kali Yuga.

But that does not necessarily count as defeat, especially according to the rules of *dharmavijaya*—or the code of the spiritual warrior, for that matter. As Robert Thurman, a recent translator of Asoka, asks:

> How can we say that his "Truth Conquest" *(dharmavijaya)* failed, when, without military expansion at all, all of Asia accepted and put into practice the Dharma as best they could over the next millennium . . . and although Europe did conquer India finally rather than the other way around, the game of evolution is not yet over. In a transnational planet, such as we must surely have within decades, there will be no ancient ruler other than Asoka to point to as a visionary predecessor of the rule of Dharma replacing the rule of force.[42]

頭等侍衛呼爾
查巴圖魯占音
保

赤手長鯨俘衛
諾賊級纍纍注之
一韨捧橛闢展達
巴里坤馬不刷騣
還報軍門

乾隆庚辰春
勒恭賛

THE TAOIST SOLUTION

You do not use good iron to make a nail,
or a good man to make a soldier.
—Chinese proverb

The Chinese saw things differently.

They had, to be sure, their share of war, bloodshed, and brutality. Vast China was the real world, with all the problems that came with a large and ever-growing population dependent on the heavenly rains for millet and rice, surrounded by fierce, nomadic horse-riding barbarians. And, as always, there were those all too ready to solve those problems with arms.

But there were also many who were willing to put forth another approach, an approach based on government in accord with the Tao or the way of nature. "I have heard of gaining the support of one's people through virtue," as one minister said in the *Spring and Autumn Annals* in the fourth century B.C., "but I have never heard of doing so through violence. To try to do so through violence is like trying to straighten out threads by further tangling them. . . . Military force is like fire—if not kept in check, it will end by consuming the user."[1]

From this point of view, warfare was to be pursued only as a last resort—either for self-defense or to restore order or punish the tyrannous. The Taoist warriors who followed this code sought to solve conflict first of all by peaceful means; but at the same time the Taoist warriors recognized that since most men had forgotten—or not yet learned—how to live in accordance with the Way, it was necessary to study and master the martial arts as well as the Way. The Taoist martial artists and strategists thus developed a warrior's code which struck a unique balance between extremes of aggressive conquest and pacifistic surrender.

The wise man, the warrior-sage, was a strategist who did not fight out of greed or anger or to prove his bravery. He knew the limits of violence. "Military action is a perverse affair, used by the civilized only when unavoidable," went one proverb. "Putting on armour," said another, "is not the way to promote a country's welfare; it is for eliminating violence."[2]

For those who knew the Tao, the true purpose of war could be deconstructed from the etymology of the word itself. The warrior-scholar, the king of Ch'u, said, "The character for prowess is formed by those of 'to stay' and 'a spear.' . . . Thus military prowess is seen in the repression of cruelty, the calling in of weapons of war, the preservation of the great appointment, the firm establishment of one's merit, the giving of repose to the people, the harmonizing of all [the States], and the enlargement of the general wealth."[3]

"Weapons are instruments of ill omen, war is immoral," as Liu Ji said. "Really they are only to be resorted to when there is no other choice. It is not right to pursue aggressive warfare because one's country is large and prosperous, for this ultimately ends in defeat and destruction."[4]

△△ II △△

The Chinese had lived in the center of the world, at the pivot of the four directions, in the Middle Kingdom, from the very beginning. The first sage-emperors and kings had shown the people how to live in accord with Heaven: how to hunt and fish with nets, how to make fire, how to plant millet and rice, and how to fix the calendar so that millet and rice could be planted at the right time. They taught the people how to dig channels instead of dams, so that the floodwaters would follow their natural course to the sea, and how to celebrate the rites and make the proper sacrifices to the ancestors.

Perhaps the greatest of them, Huang Ti, the Yellow Emperor, had taught the arts of medicine and longevity, how to move the heavenly energy of the breath, the *ch'i,* through the body, how to use sexual pleasure to balance the complementary energies of yin and yang. He had also, so it was said, defeated the barbarians by means of magical weapons, and then won their allegiance simply by the power of his *te*—his "virtue" or nature, which was, as the *History Classic* said, "reverent, accomplished, and thoughtful—naturally and without effort."[5] Ruling simply by facing south, arranging his robes, and composing his mind, he set an example of harmony with Heaven.

The sage-emperors ruled, then, because they brought benefits to the people. As *The Counsels of the Great Yu* put it, "The virtue of the ruler is seen in good government, and government is tested in nourishing of the people."[6] The sage-emperor had only to "attend harmoniously" to the five elements—water, fire, metal, wood, and earth—to care for the altars of grain and soil, and to "caution the people with gentleness of words, correct them with the majesty of law, and stimulate them with the Songs."[7] Modest and obedient to Heaven, like a good son, the relationship between the sage-emperor and Heaven was the model for the relationship between ruler and minister, husband and wife, father and son, elder son and younger son.

Even in battle the power of virtue was known to be greater than the power of arms. When Yu, the digger of channels and the founder of the Hsia Dynasty, the first of the ancient Three Dynasties, set out to subjugate the "rebellious and insolent" Lord of Miao, he fought for three decades without success—until reminded by the wise Minister Yi that "it is virtue that moves Heaven." Returning promptly to his capital, Yu promptly set about promoting "the virtuous influences of peace on a grand scale" according to the customary rites. The stone and jade chimes and bronze bells and drums were played in the proper way, and "there was dancing with shield and feather between the two staircases in the courtyard." This expression of virtue accomplished what three decades of warfare had not been able to. "In seventy days," says the *History Classic,* "the lord of Miao came to make his submission."[8]

The Mandate of Heaven, however, was not constant. Rulers and dynasties had a way of running out of virtue, and so in 1766 B.C. Lord T'ang, bowing to the command of Heaven, punished the king of Hsia "for his many crimes" and founded the Shang Dynasty—the dynasty that was, as the archaeologist H. G. Creel says, "the ancestor of the civilization of most of the Far East."9

△△ I I I △△

Except for a few literary references in ancient chronicles, almost nothing was known of the Shang Dynasty until 1928, when archaeologists uncovered a deep pit grave on the site of An-yang, the legendary last capital of the dynasty. At the very bottom of the grave, which was reached by four earthen ramps, inside a timber-supported lower chamber, they found the remains of a coffin, with the Shang king or noble facedown, head pointing north.

The archaeologists also found hundreds of pieces of ox and cattle scapulae and turtle carapaces, which the Shang had used as an oracle to ask their ancestral spirits all sorts of questions—questions about the weather and crops, war and health, to give just a few examples. These "oracle bones" had been heated with a red-hot poker—the answer was obtained by reading the pattern of the resulting cracks—and often the question and answer, as well as the name of the person who had asked the question, had been written on the shell or bone.

In addition to the oracle bones, the grave pits contained the remains of chariots and bronze weapons—daggers, arrow- and spear heads, battle-axes, and most frequently, the ko or halberd. There was also a particular kind of half-moon-shaped dagger which some archaeologists say is found only among Mongolians, Eskimos, and American Indians—among people, that is, whose origin may be traced to an archaic circumpolar culture.

The most spectacular finds, however, were not weapons but hundreds of different ritual vessels—graceful three-legged caldrons, called ting, fluted wine beakers and cups, spherical and square containers decorated with intricately intertwined and twirling geometric designs and twisting and twirling animals—tigers, rhinoceroses, lions, dragons—and a grinning toothsome mask, the t'ien tien. These bronzes, no less than the weapons, were also the symbols and means of Shang power, for it was by the offerings served in these vessels that the Shang nobles supplicated their ancestors—the only ones who could communicate with Shang Ti, the Ruler Above, who in turn controlled the fortunes of men and nature.

But Shang power was also expressed in another, more familiar way. Archaeologists found evidence of human sacrifice everywhere—under the great post which had supported the thatched roofs of the great earth and bamboo houses and ancestral halls of the nobles; in the great tamped-earth walls that protected the cities from surprise attack; and, of course, in the tombs themselves. Some of the victims seemed to have been sacrificed to accompany their masters on their final journeys; others seemed to have been offered as gifts to the ancestral spirits, or possibly to Shang Ti himself.

The Shang king derived his authority from his close kin relationship to Shang Ti, sitting, as K. C. Chang says, "over a hierarchy of government, economy, and religion, with himself at both top and center."[10] But power also radiated out from this center—to his closest relatives, and then to other members of the nobility.

The Shang nobility led a privileged life in their thatched houses and ancestral lives, at the center of the cities. They spent much of their time celebrating the ancestral rites—ceremonies which called for the proper music from stone chimes, bronze bells, drums, and flutes; warriors dancing with spears, in their long-sleeved silk robes; and much feasting and drinking wine. And they hunted tiger, boar, elephant, rhinoceros, and deer from their chariots in the royal sanctuaries.

Hunting served as training for warfare, which was also a favorite pastime of the Shang nobility. Even aristocratic women seem to have been involved. One of the few unplundered tombs discovered by archaeologists (in 1951) belonged to Fa Hui, one of the sixty-four consorts of the king Wing Wang, and the first Chinese woman warrior we know of. Her grave contained—in part—sixteen sacrificed humans and six dogs, two hundred bronze ritual vessels, seven thousand cowrie shells, ninety-five jade objects, seventy stone sculptures, four hundred and ninety bone hairpieces, and more than a hundred and thirty bronze weapons, as well as twenty bone arrowheads.

Fa Hui most likely administered her own walled city some distance from the capital, and she oversaw both peasants and troops. According to inscriptions found in her grave, she commanded troops on more than one occasion. Other inscriptions indicate that other consorts very likely did the same.

The Shang kings (and their consorts) seem to have gone to war very much the way they went hunting. Certainly they considered the border tribes less than human. Though they returned from their expeditions with cattle, sheep, and horses, they were mainly after human prey. Skilled prisoners of war may have been employed as craftsmen and artisans; others became fresh recruits to the *jen*—the multitudes—who fueled the labor-intensive Shang economy as indentured agricultural laborers or outright slaves.

These were the lucky ones. The rest were sacrificed to the ancestors and deities. For some reason the Ch'iang people from the West seem to have been especially favored—one scholar has counted at least 7,426 Ch'iang individuals contemplated for sacrifice on oracle bone inscriptions.

The Shang use of the Ch'iang seems to have been a classical example of what Erik Erikson called "pseudospeciation"—the perceptual trick of seeing other people as another species rather than as other people, thus overriding cultural (or perhaps even biological) taboos against killing members of the same species.[11] The ideogram for many of the barbarian tribes used the radical sign for animal. Expeditions against the barbarians were spoken of as hunting expeditions, and the barbarians were referred to as animals. The relative value of a Ch'iang life and a cow can be seen from one oracle inscription: "Inquired: The following day Yi-Wei, perform the *yu* ritual to Tsu Yu [and sacrifice] Ch'iang, fifteen persons? Perform the *yu* ritual and use one cow?"[12]

△△ I V △△

Given the use the Shang made of them, it is hardly surprising that in 1154 B.C. the Ch'iang and other border states joined Lord Wu, the warrior chief of the half-barbarian western kingdom of Chou, in a revolt against the Shang kings. Wu was the very model of the enlightened Chinese warrior who wins without bloodshed—if we can believe the account given by the T'ang Dynasty historian Ssu-ma Chi'en. He first humbly requested that the Shang king reform—that he stop drinking and building extravagant pleasure palaces, and that he appoint competent officials instead of incompetent relatives to office. Only then, when his good counsel went unheeded, did Wu heed Heaven's command to punish the Shang king and assume the Mandate of Heaven himself. He challenged the vastly superior Shang force of seven hundred thousand men at the battle of Mu with only fifty thousand trusted men. As Ssu-ma Chi'en writes, "Wu ordered his general Shang-fu with only a hundred of his most daring warriors to dash forward at the head of a large body of foot soldiers. The opposing army, knowing full well the Shang dynasty's lack of virtue and thus the inevitability of its own defeat, inverted its lances and surrendered without suffering a casualty."[13]

The victorious King Wu turned from war to peace and demonstrated the virtue that had made Heaven choose him. He generously granted the surviving Shang heirs their own small state, so that they could continue their ancestral sacrifices. There would be no angry Shang ghosts loose in the new dynasty of Chou. Taking up his writing brush, Wu composed a poem on a bamboo slip:

> *"Then put away your shields and axes,*
> *Then case your arrows and bows;*
> *I have store enough of good power*
> *To spread over all the lands of Hsia."*[14]

King Wu then set about reestablishing the ancient harmony, realizing—as the sages taught—that without good administration conquest meant nothing. He gave office only to the worthy, taught the people the five relations of society, took measures to ensure a proper supply of food, and saw to the rites of mourning and of sacrifice. He honored virtue and rewarded merit. He established the tablets of his father, King Wen, in the most honored position in the ancestral hall. He established his kin and allies on estates, where they could defend the frontiers against the barbarians. Remembering the profligate drunkenness of the Shang kings, he made it an offense, punishable by death, for men to drink wine together in groups, except when engaged in sacrifices.

And then—or so the *History Classic* says—"he had only to let his robes fall down, fold his hands, and the kingdom was orderly ruled."[15]

△△ V △△

King Wu ordered the Chou kingdom as a father orders his family. He arranged the nobles in five orders—ranks usually translated as duke, marquis, earl, count, and baron. Those who were relatives he addressed as paternal uncles; those who were not, he addressed as maternal uncles. As in a family, where no one is equal but each one is either superior or inferior to the other, depending on age and sex, the nobles were all either superior or inferior to each other. The king, for example, was inferior to Heaven, for he was the elder son of Heaven; the dukes were inferior to the king but superior to the marquis; and so on.

The relationship between superior and inferior was reciprocal. "A good leader will reward the virtuous and punish the wicked," as one text states. "He will nourish his people as his children, overshadowing them as heaven, and supporting them as earth. Then the people will maintain their ruler, love him as a parent, look up to him as the sun and moon, revere him as they do spiritual beings, and stand in awe of him as thunder."[16]

It was because of this ideal and reciprocal relationship, we are told, that the kings of Chou were able to establish peace and prosperity within their kingdom for five hundred years. Five great classics were written down on bamboo slips and silk—the *I Ching* (with commentaries written by King Wen), the *Book of Songs,* the *History Classic,* the *Book of Rituals,* and the *Book of Music.* Human sacrifice was first limited to servants accompanying their masters to the grave, and then it was abandoned altogether. Once a year the great lords came to wait on the king in the capital. The rest of the time they watched over their lands, helping the king's armies guard the borders.

The Chou kings held The Mandate of Heaven for five hundred years or so. Inexorably, however, the population increased, estates were divided, and the loyalties of the feudal lords to the weakened Chou kings grew progressively tenuous—until there were more than seven hundred fairly independent feudal principalities. It was during this Spring and Autumn period (named after a chronicle of that time), which lasted about two hundred years, from 766 to 577 B.C., that Chinese chivalry reached its fullest flowering—a thousand or so years before it would reappear as the code of the samurai in Japan, and fifteen hundred years before it would appear independently in Europe.

The Chinese code of chivalry was based on the fixed familial relationships developed by the Chou nobles, especially the *shih,* the lowest and broadest rank of nobles, who functioned as retainers and advisors of the great lords. The *shih* or "knights" were skilled fighters—they were trained both in archery and charioteering. But they were not just military men. The ideal *shih* was a gentleman as well. He acted more as part of a family than as an individual; he knew his place. He was sincere and respectful to his superiors, and considerate and tolerant with his inferiors. He respected tradition, for it was tradition that preserved and transmitted the virtuous lessons of the venerable ancestors. And of course he was loyal—though he considered it his duty to speak his mind, even if what he had to say displeased his lord. ("Do not deceive him, but when necessary withstand him to his face," was how Confucius put it.)[17] Finally, he was modest, with no interest in glory or fame. He was brave without being heroic; he did not exceed the limits of proper conduct.

He was, in short, a well-rounded and cultivated man. The traditional training of the *shih* thus included the Six Arts: *li* or rites (rituals, customs, manners); writing (including the study of the classics); arithmetic; music (including dance and singing); and the two martial arts of charioteering and archery.

The powerful composite bow was the preferred weapon of the Chinese knight. But the bow, which took a great deal of practice to master, was more than a weapon. It was also considered an instrument of aristocratic self-cultivation, since it did not depend on brute strength, but on elegance of movement, sureness of hand, accuracy, timing, balance, and composure. As the knight-scholar Confucius said in the *Analects,* "By the drawing of the bow, one can know the virtue and conduct of men."[18]

Aristocratic archery matches were structured in accord with the cooperative and noncompetitive ideals of the Chinese knight. During the Spring and Autumn period, aristocratic archers dressed in long embroidered silk robes and high peaked hats and shot from a raised platform set under the mulberry trees at a target with a square bull's-eye. The archers shot in teams of two, one to a target on the left and one to a target on the right. So that no one was unduly shamed or praised, the winning score was averaged from both left and right. As a further precaution, the master of archery stood behind the archers, ready to help them adjust their form and aim. Finally, the losing team served wine to the winners, and the contest ended in convivial feasting and drinking.

The lesson, as Confucius pointed out, was that "even in archery gentlemen never compete. They bow and make way for one another when they are going up to the archery-ground, when they are coming down, and at the subsequent drinking bout. Thus when competing, they still remain gentlemen."[19]

Similar behavior was expected of gentlemen engaged in the game of war. In 632 B.C., on the morning of one of the most important battles of the period, the Ch'u commander sent a message to the Marquis of Chin, "Will your Excellency permit our knights and yours to play a game? Your Lordship may lean on the cross-board of your carriage and look on, and I too will observe."[20]

Chinese knights did not ride horses. (Only barbarians willing to wear the un-Chinese and ungentlemanly short jackets and trousers did that.) Instead, they rode to battle in richly decorated chariots, each pulled by four horses. Each chariot carried three knights wearing red-lacquered rhinoceros-hide armor, one knight holding the reins, one carrying a halberd, and one wielding a bow. Vividly colored pennants and banners flew from the chariots, identifying the ranks of the participants and signaling different maneuvers.

Wars began, as most important events did, in the ancestral hall. Sacrifices were offered, prayers made, and the *I Ching* oracle consulted by tossing stalks of yarrow. Oaths were sealed by smearing blood drawn from sacrificial animals (or an occasional prisoner of war) over war drums, brass bells, or stone chimes.

The conditions under which states could attack were closely regulated. It was not considered proper, for example, to attack a state in mourning for its ruler, or one suffering from internal disorders. "Wars" were usually decided by a single day-long battle, which took place at an agreed-upon time and location, most often in the spring, so as not to interfere with planting or harvesting. Certain days—like the last day of the month, when the yin force predominated—were avoided as inauspicious for battle.

The true gentleman knight, the *chuan tzu,* fought less to win than to demonstrate his composure and good manners under the pressure of combat. The gentleman warrior fought without anger, like a parent disciplining his children. "To attack the rebellious is an act of punishment," says the *Tso chuan.* "To be gentle with the submissive an act of virtue."[21]

The well-mannered warrior pursued modesty with as much fervor as the Greek hero-warrior pursued honor and glory. Confucius praised Meng-Chih-fan, who fought against Ch'i outside the capital of Lu in 484 B.C., saying he was "no boaster. When his people were routed he was the last to flee; but when they neared the city-gate, he whipped up his horses, saying, It was not courage that kept me behind. My horses were slow."[22]

When the Chin army returned home, the commander Shih Hsieh entered the capital after the others. His father Shih Hui said, "Surely you knew how anxiously I was waiting for your return, didn't you."

Shih Hsieh replied, "The army had won a victory and the people of the state were greeting it with joy. If I had entered ahead of the rest, I would have necessarily cut a very conspicuous figure. It would have looked as though I were trying to steal renown from the other commanders. Therefore I did not dare go first."[23]

Death itself was an occasion for the display of modesty. It was neither courted nor avoided, but when the final moment arrived, the gentleman knight accepted his fate with a kind of ironic equanimity. The cords holding Tzu-lu's hat were severed in battle. He noted,

"When a gentleman dies, his hat does not fall off!" He retied the cords before he died.[24]

A company commander by the name of Lin Pu-niu faced death with equal aplomb. Finding that they were trapped in the rear, his men asked, "Should we make a dash for it?"

"Who is there to run from?" said Lin Pu-niu.

"Then should we take a stand here?"

"What would be so admirable about that?" said Lin Pu-niu. He then proceeded on his way in a leisurely fashion and was killed in the fighting.[25]

The epitome of the gentleman warrior was a man like the Duke of Sung—a descendant of the vanquished Shang dynasty—who refused to take the slightest advantage of his opponents, no matter what the consequences. A story from the *Tso chuan,* a commentary on the *Spring and Autumn Annals,* recounts that in 683 B.C., when an army from Ch'u invaded Sung, the Sung defenders were drawn up in battle lines while the Ch'u troops were fording the river:

> The Minister of War said to the Duke, "They are many and we are few. I request permission to attack them before they have all crossed over." The Duke replied, "It may not be done."
>
> After they had crossed over, but not yet formed their ranks, the Minister once again asked leave to attack, but the Duke replied, "Not yet." The attack was not begun until the enemy was fully deployed.
>
> The army of Sung was disastrously defeated. The Duke himself was wounded in the thigh, and the guards of the palace were all killed. The people of the state all blamed the Duke, but he said: "The gentleman does not inflict a second wound, or take the grey-haired prisoner. When the ancients fought, they did not attack an enemy when he was in defile. Though I am but the unworthy remnant of a fallen dynasty, I would not sound my drums to attack an enemy who had not completed the formation of his ranks."[26]

But others would. The destruction of the chivalrous Duke of Sung's army was the merest hint of the horror that was to come. The impossibly high ideals of Chinese chivalry may well have been broken more often than they were honored—we simply do not know—but even if they were only ideals, they were ideals that lasted only for the briefest Spring and Autumn. The mutual trust and precarious network of alliances began to fall apart. Rivers were poisoned, countries invaded without warning, allies betrayed, solemn treaties broken.

By 475 B.C. only twenty-two states remained; then there were seven, and so the feudal Spring and Autumn period collapsed into the time of anarchy and unceasing war known as the Warring States period. As one contemporary chronicle put it, "Usurpers set themselves up as lords and kings, states run by pretenders and plotters set up armies to make themselves superpowers, filling the fields with bloodshed. . . . Fathers and sons were not close to each other, brothers were not secure with each other, husbands and wives separated—no one could safeguard his or her life. Virtue disappeared."[27]

⋀⋀ VI ⋀⋀

While the blood flowed, the sages and philosophers of the Hundred Schools wandered from state to state, arguing and searching for rulers who would take their advice. The Confucians advocated education, individual moral responsibility, and a return to the good old days of King Wu and the Chou Dynasty; the Moists preached the ideal of universal love and volunteered to defend the weak against the powerful; the Logicians worried about the existence of abstract qualities; and the Legalists insisted that only "agriculture and warfare" were of importance and that these should be directed by a leader with absolute power to reward and punish.

A few men took the opposite course and withdrew from society to the mountains. There they sought the Tao—the Way—in the contemplation of original nature, sitting quietly, emptying their minds of all artificial and "civilized" notions.

Taoists were this-worldly mystics who found the Way everywhere. They found it, as Chuang Tzu said when he was challenged to be more specific, "in this ant, in this grass, in tiles"; they found it even in "ordure and urine." It was the unity of all things, and the man who realized the Tao attained a remarkable and joyous serenity, free from worries about life and death. "The Great Mass gives me the support of my bodily form, my toil in life, my ease in old age, my rest in death," Chuang Tzu said. "Thus what makes my life good also makes my death good. . . . Therefore the sage man roams with light heart through the universe, in which nothing can ever be lost because all is preserved."[28]

The Taoists were at peace with men and nature. They were at peace with men because they made do with little and had no interest in positions of official power, and they were at peace with nature because they were merely, and sublimely, a part of nature. Like their spiritual descendants, the contemporary deep ecologists, they were "antianthropocentric"—that is, they did not place man (or God, for that matter) at the center of the world. They did not believe, as one Confucian said, that "Heaven makes the five kinds of grain to grow, and brings forth the finny and feathered tribes, especially for our benefit."

They believed instead, as a shockingly disrespectful twelve-year-old Taoist youth told a Confucian, that "The ten thousand things and we belong in the same category, that of living things, and in this category there is nothing noble and nothing mean. It is only by reason of size, strength, or cunning, that one particular species gains the mastery over another. . . . Mosquitoes and gnats suck his skin; tigers and wolves devour his flesh—but we do not therefore assert that Heaven produced man for the benefit of mosquitoes and gnats, or to provide food for tigers and wolves."[29]

Or, as Chuang Tzu said, "To have attained to the human form is a source of joy. But, in the infinite evolution, there are thousands of other forms that are equally good. What an incomparable bliss it is to undergo these countless transitions!"[30]

For Chuang Tzu and the others, the Tao was best left alone. The Taoists thus advocated a kind of anarchic acceptance, which was summed up in the phrase *wu-wei,* literally "not-doing." But this not-doing did not imply—as some thought—a passive resignation. It meant, rather, living fully and spontaneously in accord with the Tao—"not doing anything that went against nature." As Huai Nan Tzu commented, "What is meant by *wu wei* is that no personal prejudice interferes with the universal Tao and that no desires and obsessions lead the true course of techniques astray. Non-action does not mean doing nothing and keeping silent. Let everything be allowed to do what it naturally does, so that its nature will be satisfied."[31]

The Taoist sage who practiced not-doing by yielding to nature partook of the greatest power of nature itself. This power, for the Taoist, was not expressed by fire (as it was for the Indo-European) or by stone or metal (as it was for the Sumerians) or even by wind, but by water, the one element that could overcome all the rest. "Nothing under heaven," as the *Tao Te Ching* said, "is softer or more yielding than water; but when it attacks things hard and resistant there is not one that can prevail. . . . That the yielding conquers the resistant and the soft conquers the hard is a fact known by all men, yet utilized by none."[32]

Left alone—left to the power and wisdom of the Tao, that is—the Taoists believed that society would pattern itself along natural and self-fulfilling lines of pre–Bronze Age village society, just as everything else in nature.

But—and it was a big *but*—human beings had not and seemingly would not join the Tao in its natural unceasing transformations. Men did make laws and distinctions. The forces of change let loose by the technological marvels of the Bronze Age were—for the time being, at least—in the ascendant. So the Taoists turned their attention (as all Chinese philosophers did, sooner or later) to the very real problems of power and government during a time of social disintegration and ceaseless civil war.

They pointed out, first of all, that violence based on weaponry and armies was not a natural state of affairs, but the result of civilization— "the great turning-point," as Joseph Needham says, being in fact "the introduction of bronze metallurgy, in which a complex technique was associated with the making of superior weapons"—which had created unnatural divisions among men based on greed for material wealth, status, and rank.[33] This "civilized" man was the very opposite of the true man of Tao, who was at ease and peaceful in the contemplation of the inexhaustible riches of the Tao. And so, as the *Tao Te Ching* advised:

> *He who by Tao proposes to help a ruler of men*
> *Will oppose all conquest by force of arm;*
> *For such things are wont to rebound.*
> *Where armies are, thorns and brambles grow.*
> *The raising of a great host*
> *is followed by a year of dearth.*[34]

But the Taoists were also realists, adapting to the ever-changing conditions of the world. Violence violated the Tao and led only to further violence; it was therefore to be avoided. But *not* at all costs. If they were pacifists, the Taoists were provisional pacifists, pacifists who recognized the right to self-defense. "Weapons," the *Tao Te Ching* says, "are inauspicious instruments, not the tools of the enlightened."[35] But the *Tao Te Ching* also recognized that there might be times when the wise man would indeed have to take up arms.

As a verse from the *Tao Te Ching* says, "When there is no choice but to use them, it is best to be calm and free from greed, and not celebrate victory. Those who celebrate victory are bloodthirsty, and the bloodthirsty cannot have their way in the world."[36]

⋀⋀ V I I ⋀⋀

The most realistic and practical of the Taoists was a general by the name of Sun Tzu, the author of a ruthlessly objective field manual for war which was nevertheless firmly grounded in the traditional Taoist repugnance to violence.

The Warring States period was one of the bloodiest and most anarchic periods of Chinese history. War was no longer considered a game or contest or ritual for gentleman knights. The composite bow, which had once been restricted to gentlemen knights, had been replaced by the even more powerful crossbow, a weapon which could be used by conscripts after only minimal training. At the same time, expensive bronze weapons were giving way to cheaper iron swords and lances. Skilled generals and infantry replaced hereditary nobility in chariots. All these technological and social transformations combined to make war a deadly serious business—"the ground of death and life, the path of survival and destruction," as Sun Tzu put it in the very first maxim of *The Art of War*. Which was why, after all, "it is imperative to examine it."[37]

Sun Tzu's examination of war led him also to see its cost very clearly. Sun Tzu pointed out that war brought inflation, famine, and pestilence to both sides, while victory only created a more determined and revengeful future enemy.

But the greatest cost, as Sun Tzu knew, the cost which could not be measured, was very simply the irreversible loss of life. Unlike the Indo-Europeans, the Chinese had no conception of a Valhalla or warrior's heaven for those who died in battle, no conception of an eternal soul transmigrating over lifetimes from body to body. Death was simply the irreversible and final end of life. "Anger can revert to joy," Sun Tzu said, "and wrath can revert to delight. But a nation destroyed cannot be returned to existence, and the dead cannot be restored to life."[38]

The bald simplicity of this statement should not mislead us. From it followed the conviction that since war caused loss of life, war was always to be avoided if at all possible. The good Taoist general tried his best, then, to end his war before it began. He did this by fighting first on the political and diplomatic front, and then by exhausting all possible nonmilitary actions, from trade wars to seduction. A more or less complete catalogue of these dirty tricks was given by the commentator Wang Hsi: "Sometimes entice [the enemy's] wise and virtuous men away so that he has no counsellors. Or send treacherous people to wreck his administration. Sometimes use cunning deceptions to alienate his ministers from the sovereign. Or send skilled craftsmen to encourage his people to exhaust their wealth. Or present him with licentious musicians and dancers to change his customs. Or give him beautiful women to bewilder him."[39]

Only after all these nonmilitary options had failed, said Sun Tzu, should war be considered. But even then, it should never be undertaken lightly or under the influence of emotions—"a government should not mobilize an army out of anger, military leaders should not provoke war out of wrath."[40]

The wise leader should, instead, meet with his advisors and staff to consider which side has the advantage in the Five Things: The Way, the weather, terrain, leadership, and discipline. The first of these, the Way or Tao, which referred to the relationship between the people and the leadership, was considered the most important condition. A government that did not support its people did not have the support of its people—and therefore did not have the Mandate of Heaven.

The wise general, therefore, undertook war only as a last resort and only when he had thoroughly and rationally analyzed his chances for victory. The responsibility was his alone. It was up to the legitimate rulers of the civil government to decide to go to war. But with the army in the field, only the general could be trusted to make a realistic on-the-spot assessment of the true situation. If he thought he could win by attacking immediately, he could not wait for orders from the distant capital. And if he did not think he could win, there was no point in fighting, "even if the government orders war."[41]

Once the decision was made, the strategist's aim was to win as quickly as possible, with the minimum of bloodshed and destruction. This was accomplished, as Sun Tzu bluntly says, by deceit. "Even though you are competent, appear to be incompetent," Sun Tzu said. "Though effective, appear to be ineffective. When you are going to attack nearby make it look like you are going to go a long way; when you are going far away, make it look as if you are going just a short distance."[42]

In this sense, strategy was the very opposite of chivalry. If the gentleman knight fought to demonstrate his aristocratic superiority— his prowess, virtue, or manner—the strategist fought to win. The knight never took advantage, while the strategist took every advantage he could.

But even though Chinese chivalry and strategy were opposites, both had a common underlying purpose. They were both attempts to minimize, contain, or control the violence of warfare. Their differences were the results of different social structures. The chivalric code arose from a stratified feudal society in which all the members of the same rank, the fighting nobility, monopolized the most powerful weapons, and all recognized and honored the same code.

Strategy, on the other hand, grew out of a society of warring states fighting for supremacy with force, without any agreed-upon code. Wars were fought by large armies of soldiers armed with the crossbow and the new iron swords, which were not only cheaper but also stronger than the old bronze swords. In these conditions, the best—indeed, the only—way to minimize bloodshed was to use strategy to win as quickly and as bloodlessly as possible.

In the context of chivalry, deception and trickery were betrayals of trust. They were deliberate and dastardly—ignoble, that is—violations of an agreed-upon code. Their very use demonstrated defeat. The warrior who resorted to trickery was admitting that he could not win by the rules of the game and that he had therefore decided to violate the very basis of the code itself. He had decided that winning was all-important, no matter how he won.

In the context of the warring states, there were no agreed-upon norms, and trickery and deception were not betrayals but contests of wit, dependent on superior intelligence and knowledge. Doing the unexpected, surprising the enemy, keeping plans secret, gathering intelligence by the use of agents and spies, treating prisoners well so that they would join your forces—all these deceptive tricks were, at bottom, strategies to bring a speedy end to violence.

Knowledge was the most powerful weapon of the Taoist warrior. The outer knowledge of the terrain and his opponent's position and morale was obtained by careful observation and the liberal use of intelligence gained from spies and double agents. But the true secret weapon of the Taoist warrior was self-knowledge. The warrior who knew both the enemy and himself could fight a hundred battles without peril, said Sun Tzu. And for the warrior who knew the Tao as well, who knew "sky and earth, victory is inexhaustible."[43]

The warrior who knew himself had made a realistic appraisal of his own inner condition by taking a kind of psychological inventory. He had to have the Five Strengths of the good leader: intelligence, trustworthiness, humaneness, courage, and sternness. These in turn had to be correctly balanced; overreliance on any one quality would be disastrous. This emphasis on balance and moderation was detailed further in the Five Traits Dangerous in Generals: those who are ready to die can be killed; those who are intent on living can be captured; those who are quick to anger can be shamed; those who are puritanical can be disgraced; and those who love people can be troubled.

"What is essential in the temperament of a general," the commentator Wang Hsi said, "is steadiness." The Taoist warrior thus sought to "settle" his mind by the inner training of sitting still in contemplation, in order to make his mind calm, firm, stable, orderly, and "undisturbed by events, not deluded by prospects of gain." Such a mind freed the warrior from the clouded bias and prejudice of his own emotionality. As Sun Tzu said, "Using order to deal with the disorderly, using calm to deal with the clamorous, is mastering the heart."[44]

At the same time, the skillful strategist had to be inscrutable, for strategy in war, as Sun Tzu insists, depends throughout on deception. The strategist kept his plans hidden from the enemy to be effective, of course, but the truly inscrutable warrior remained hidden and mysterious in a much more fundamental way, for his actions were not based on plans fixed in advance, but on the movements and conditions of the enemy. The enemy, it could be said, determined his strategy for him. Having no fixed plans, he was a master of adaptability, immediately responsive to changing conditions and circumstances. When the enemy attacked, he withdrew; when the enemy retreated, he attacked. When the enemies' force was smaller than his, he surrounded; when more numerous, he divided. He struck where the enemy was weak. For the most part, he considered a direct head-on clash to be a failure of strategy.

If the Mesopotamians fought with the rigidity of the phalanx and the hardness of metal, and if the Indo-Europeans fought with the raging fury of fire, then the Taoists fought with the fluidity and adaptability of water—the one element that could quench the hottest fire and wear down the hardest stone. "Military formation is like water," Sun Tzu said. "The form of water is to avoid the high and go to the low, the form of a military force is to avoid the full and attack the empty; the flow of water is determined by the earth, the victory of a military force is determined by the opponent. So a military force has no constant formation, water has no constant shape: the ability to gain victory by changing and adapting to the opponent is called genius."[45]

A Taoist victory, however, always involved the minimum amount of bloodshed. If weapons had to be used, it was best to capture the entire state and take "All-under-Heaven intact." If that was not possible, the next best thing was to take the army. To lay siege to cities was the worst of all, for that resulted in the greatest number of casualties for both soldiers and civilians.

Sun Tzu did not equate victory with the annihilation, domination, or subjugation of the enemy. He warned that a surrounded force must be given an opening, for troops with no way out would fight to the death. Similarly, it was dangerous to subject an enemy to rape, excessive pillage, or despoilation of their ancestors' graves, for then "rage will multiply their strength by ten." And finally, "it is important to treat captives well, and care for them," for such captives can often be induced to join your force, and this, says Sun Tzu, "is called winning a battle and becoming stronger."

But victories in battle, as far as Sun Tzu was concerned, brought the warrior "neither reputation for wisdom nor merit for valour."[46] For even the merely good general, fighting according to the way of strategy, would have made his victory seem easy, while the truly great warrior, the warrior who lived according to the Way, won without fighting at all.

EVERY OPEN HAND A SWORD

The Martial Arts in China

Be still as a mountain,
Move like a great river.
–Wu Yu-hsiang

The Bodhidharma who brought Zen Buddhism from India to China sometime in the sixth century B.C. was a fierce, scowling, wild-eyed, and uncompromising sort of fellow. When Emperor Wu had asked him how much merit he had gained by building thousands of Buddhist temples throughout China, Bodhidharma had shocked the court by replying, "None." And when the emperor had asked him who he was to speak to the son of heaven with such impudence, he had answered, "Don't know."

After that, he sat in a cave staring at the wall, eyebrows bristling, for nine years. He refused to speak to anyone until his first Chinese warrior disciple, Hui Ko, cut off his hand with his own sword and presented it to Bodhidharma as proof of his determination. "What do you want," growled Bodhidharma. "I want you to pacify my mind," said Hui Ko. "Show me this mind you want to pacify," said Bodhidharma. "I can't," said Hui Ko. "There," said Bodhidharma, "I have already pacified it."[1]

Bodhidharma went on to found the Shaolin Temple on Song Mountain in Henan Province. This was an event of great importance not only for Zen Buddhism but for the martial arts as well, for it was in Shaolin Temple—so the legend goes—that the martial arts for which the Chinese are so celebrated had their beginnings.

It may seem strange that a Buddhist temple became the center of Chinese boxing and remained so for thousands of years. But from another point of view, the development of unarmed martial arts was a logical response to the Buddhist prohibition against monks carrying weapons, as well as to the Taoist injunction that weapons were to be avoided except as a last resort.

In any case, neither the vow not to harm living beings nor the related rule prohibiting monks from carrying weapons solved the primordial problem of self-defense (or defense of others, for that matter). Nor could the Buddhist monks depend on the protection of a dedicated warrior class, as could the Brahmans, druids, and other militarily exempt priests of the Indo-Europeans.

Chinese Buddhist monks were, in fact, in a very precarious situation. Brought to China by missionaries from India, Buddhism was considered a foreign religion, dangerous to Chinese society on two counts. First, Buddhist monks had taken refuge in the purely spiritual Three Jewels: the Buddha, the Dharma (law) and the Sangha (community), and not in the Son of Heaven. Even more shocking to the Chinese, however, was the fact that Buddhist monks "left home," as they expressed it, and practiced celibacy. Figuratively and literally, they were thus no longer a part of the family, and their names were often removed from the family tablets.

They were open to attack from both bandits and, at various times, the very government that might have protected them from bandits. (In A.D. 910, for example, the government burned more than fourteen thousand Buddhist monasteries; similar episodes have taken place throughout Chinese history.)

The Zen koan (or question) faced by the first Chinese Buddhist monks, then, may have gone something like this: How do you defend yourself without using a weapon? And the answer was, as was the answer to so many koans, obvious: Turn the body itself into a weapon. In the words of an unknown Shaolin monk, "We may not have knives, so make every finger a dagger; without spears, every arm must be a spear, and every open hand a sword."[2]

Bodhidharma's teachings were based on the "still sitting" meditation of the Ch'an school. But he also, apparently, brought a series of exercises with him from India to the Shaolin monastery. These exercises, called variously the 108 Monk Exercises or the 108 Lohan Exercises (after the 108 Buddhist Saints) were designed to invigorate and strengthen the monks, who were becoming so enervated by their long hours of sitting that they were unable to perform manual labor or defend themselves against attacks by bandits.

Joseph Needham, author of the monumental *Science and Civilization in China*, suggests that Taoist gymnastics may have been "derived from the dances of the rain-bringing shaman. The fact that some of the exercises are described in terms of animal movements—Chuang Tzu mentions the bear and the bird—may also indicate a possible origin in the shaman's and hunter's dance."[3] The point of the Taoist gymnastics in any case was not to build up muscular strength, but to open the inner channels of the body so that the pure, light air inhaled during the simultaneous breathing exercises could circulate freely throughout the body. As Chuang Tzu describes it, "He breathes with every part of him right down to the heels."[4]

The early Taoists combined breathing and gymnastic exercises to achieve strength and long life through softness and flexibility. The breathing exercises played an important part in developing *ch'i*—a word which has been variously translated as "breath," "spirit," or "life-force," and which is analogous to the Indian concept of *prana*. There were many types of breathing exercises, but the basic principle was, as the Taoists said, that "the breathing of a sage had to become like that of an infant before birth. This 'womb-breathing' is the essence of 'breath-control.' "[5]

Mastery of these Taoist exercises was said to lead to an invulnerability strikingly similar to that of the Indo-European berserkirs. Lieh Tzu said that the Taoist "Man of Extreme Power . . . can tread on fire without being burnt. Walk on the top of the whole world and not stagger."[6] But whereas the Indo-European berserkirs achieved invincibility through the heat and fury of their battle rage, the Taoist warrior depended on the cool and soft "embryonic" breathing of the infant, and the watery yielding of the completely relaxed man. "He is protected," as Kuan told Lieh Tzu, "by the purity of his breath. Knowledge and skill, determination and courage could never lead to this."[7]

Whatever the influence of Taoism on Bodhidharma's exercises may have been, Shaolin Temple soon became, as martial arts historians Donn Draeger and Robert Smith write, "not only a repository of boxing knowledge and a rigorous training academy, but, as important, a stimulus for other boxing styles."[8] Originally, according to Draeger and Smith, Shaolin boxing was made up of eighteen forms. In the tenth century, a royal martial arts enthusiast, the Emperor T'ai Tsu, expanded the basic repertoire to thirty-two forms of long boxing. Then, during the Yuan Dynasty, (A.D. 1260–1368) a wealthy young man who had been a master swordsman before he became a monk by the name of Chueh Yuan further expanded the Shaolin boxing until it included seventy-two different styles.

Like so many martial artists after him, Monk Chueh traveled extensively in order to perfect and test his skill against other martial artists. One day he happened to see an old peddler of sixty defend himself against the kicks of a much younger and larger bandit. After doing his best to dodge the bandit's kicks, the peddler knocked the bandit into unconsciousness simply by touching his foot with two fingers.

The old peddler, of course, professed utter ignorance of martial arts. But he did introduce Monk Chueh to his friend Pai Yu-feng of Shansi, reputedly the best martial artist in Shansi, Honan, and Hopei, a man of fifty who was "of a medium build, and radiated with spirit."[9] Impressed with Monk Chueh's dedication, Pai and the peddler accompanied him back to Shaolin Temple, where they worked together to consolidate the original 18 monk boxing exercises with the 72 movements into 170 actions. These they further classified in another series of five, the Five Styles, each of which developed one of the Five Essences: Dragon developed spirit; Tiger developed bone; Leopard developed strength; Snake developed ch'i; and Crane developed sinew.

Monk Chueh, however, was still concerned that undisciplined martial artists might use the new, improved Shaolin boxing techniques for their own advantage. He therefore drew up a code, which probably included many tenets that had been passed on by word of mouth from master to novice in the earlier days.

The so-called "Ten Commandments of Shaolin Boxing" were distinctly Buddhist in character. They stipulated that students must practice without interruption; use boxing only for legitimate self-defense; be forever kind, honest, and friendly to all colleagues; refrain from showing their art to the common people, even if that meant they had to refuse challenges; never be bellicose; never taste wine and meat; be celibate; not teach boxing to non-Buddhists, lest it produce harm; transmit the teachings only to those who are gentle and merciful; and finally, eschew aggressiveness, greed, and boasting.[10]

⋀⋀ I V ⋀⋀

Promoted and guided by Monk Chueh, Shaolin boxing "thundered throughout China," eventually giving birth to hundreds of different schools and styles. But sometime in the fourteenth century—according to legend—a Taoist Immortal by the name of Chang San-feng of Wu-tang Mountain felt that Shaolin boxing had strayed too far from its original purpose; it had become too rigid, hard, and offensive.

As Yang Ch'eng-fu, the great nineteenth century master, describes him, Chang San-feng was "seven feet tall with the bones of a crane and the posture of a pine tree. His face was like an ancient moon with kind brows and generous eyes. His whiskers were shaped like a spear and in winter and summer he wore the same wide bamboo hat. Carrying a horse-hair duster, he could cover a thousand miles in one day."[11]

One day, while Chang San-feng was sitting in his room reciting the classics, a bird landed in the courtyard, singing with a song that sounded like the notes of a zither. In the words of Master Yang Ch'eng-fu:

> The bird peered down like an eagle at a snake coiled on the ground. The snake gazed up at the bird and the two commenced to fight. With a cry the bird swooped down, spreading its wings and beating like a fan. The long snake shook its head, darting hither and thither to evade the bird's wings. The bird flew back up to the tree top, very frustrated and disconcerted. Again the bird swooped down beating with its wings, and again the snake wriggled and darted out of harm's way, all from a coiled position. This went on for a long time without a decisive strike.
>
> After a time the Immortal came out and the bird and snake disappeared. From this combat the Immortal received a revelation. The coiled form was like the symbol of T'ai-chi and contained the principle of the soft overcoming the hard. Based on the transformations of the T'ai Chi [The Great Ultimate] he developed T'ai-chi ch'uan to cultivate sexual energy, *ch'i*, and spirit, movement and stillness, waxing and waning and to embody the principles of the *I Ching.*[12]

Chang San-feng was a typical eccentric Taoist hermit type. He loved to sword-dance in moonlight (which brought him energy); to play t'ai chi ch'uan on a dark night (which brought him vigor); to climb mountains on windy nights (which lengthened his breath); to read classics on rainy nights (which cleansed his mind); and to meditate at midnight (which brightened his nature). He discussed philosophy and the classics with the local people. His body was so light that when he walked on snow he left no footprints. He protected himself against tigers and pythons with his bare hands. His closest companions were a crane and an ape, whom he taught to do t'ai chi ch'uan.

Once, when he was picking medicinal herbs in the mountains, he encountered a hunting party made up of the royal family of the Yuan Dynasty. The Mongols contemptuously ordered the ragged beggar to step out of the way, but Chang San-feng only smiled. "Your Highness hunts with bow and arrow; I use my bare hands," he said. Just then, two hawks flew overhead, and Chang San-feng leapt up and caught them. "I have mercy on living creatures; I do not want to hurt the birds," he said, and let the birds fly away. This so angered one of the prince's retainers that he shot an arrow at San-feng, who opened his mouth and caught it with his teeth. "I have no need of violent weapons," he said, and taking it between his fingers, he threw the arrow with such force that it stuck deep in a tree. Realizing that they had encountered an Immortal, the hunting party let San-feng go on about his business.[13]

T'ai chi ch'uan was based on the peaceful civil or cultural realm of *wen,* the realm of self-cultivation and philosophical or spiritual understanding. T'ai chi ch'uan was informed by the Taoist arts of Ch'i Kung or breathing exercises, and the changing relationships and transformations of yin and yang as elucidated in the *I Ching.* As Chang San-feng himself said in the *T'ai Chi Chuan Ching,* a classic work attributed to him, "He desired the whole world to attain longevity, and not only the martial techniques."[14]

The t'ai chi martial artist (or player, as he or she was sometimes called) began his exercise standing naturally erect, his body completely relaxed, knees slightly bent, feet rooted to the earth, which was the source of all strength, the spine straight but not rigid, and the head held upright, as if suspended by a skyhook, so that the *shen* or spirit was drawn up to heaven. The mind or intention directed the *ch'i* to the *tan-t'ien,* the center of gravity, a spot located just below the navel between the stomach and the backbone.

Standing in this way, the t'ai chi player was in touch with the Three

Powers—the upright head connected him with the power of heaven, the rooted feet with the power of the earth, and the *ch'i* in the *tan-t'ien* connected both these in the center of man. A contemporary t'ai chi teacher, Jou Tsung Hwa, says that "the idea of the three powers is very important in that it shows humanity living between earth and sky. When one practices Tai-Chi Chuan for years, gradually one will feel that every movement of the Tai-Chi Chuan is the movement of the universe. One's body may be perceived as moving like the branch of a tree, blown every which way by the wind. One's breathing will be part of the universe as well. The awareness of the environment being engaged in a gigantic cosmic dance will suddenly dawn on you."[15]

The "cosmic dance" of t'ai chi was originally performed in a continuous series of thirteen slow, circular, flowing movements. "In motion all parts of the body must be light and strung together," as Chang San-feng described it. "The motion should be rooted in the feet, released through the legs, controlled by the waist, and manifested through the arms. All parts of the body are strung together without the slightest break—T'ai Chi Ch'uan is like a great river rolling on unceasingly."[16]

T'ai chi ch'uan is lovely to behold, as well as being life-enhancing and rejuvenating to perform, but for all its calm beauty and elegance, it was one of the most effective and deadliest of the martial arts. Each one of the movements had a specific martial application: there were blocks; strikes with fist, open hand, elbow, and shoulder; grabs; and kicks. The spiraling circularity of all the movements also had a martial function, enabling the t'ai chi master to deflect a powerful straight attack with ease.

The t'ai chi master was a master of change. Basing his strategy on the apparently simple but endlessly various law of complementarity—of responding to yang with yin, and to yin with yang—the t'ai chi player-warrior pushed when his opponent pulled, and pulled when his opponent pushed; he advanced when his opponent retreated, and retreated when his opponent advanced; he was soft and yielding when his opponent was hard and aggressive; and hard when his opponent was soft. Sinking most of his weight—seventy percent, to be exact—on one leg, he could move the other "empty" side freely and quickly to "steal" his opponent's balance, "sever the root and topple the object."[17]

The master of change knew, however, that yin and yang were not merely polar opposites. They were two aspects of the t'ai chi—the great ultimate—and each was always changing into the other. Just as day began to turn into night at its highest point, at noon, and night began to turn into day at its lowest point, at midnight so yin turned into yang and yang turned into yin at their extremities—"in this way," as master Yang said, "yin and yang mutually change and aid each other."[18]

The t'ai chi master thus balanced the yin and yang—the soft and hard—within himself and against his opponent. He was relaxed in his body and calm and concentrated in mind, "like a hawk or a cat watching a mouse." His body was relaxed and empty, without blockages or obstructions, so that it could be filled with *ch'i* or vital energy. When he retreated or "rolled back," he merely turned his body, like a matador letting a bull roar past, waiting for the chance to attack. As master Jou said, "Just as the tree dropping its leaves in winter waits for spring to leaf and grow again, one must utilize the character of Yin to cultivate a turning point for progress. When one reaches the extreme of Yin, one will find the beginning of Yang and have the chance to counter the opponent. . . . This ability to attack while withdrawing is known as the Yang among the Yin."[19]

For the t'ai chi player-warrior, the greatest transformation of all was the transformation of soft into hard. ("When you are extremely soft," the *Tai Chi Classics* said, "then you become extremely hard and strong.")[20] This transformation was accomplished, as Chang San-feng had said, by "using mind not strength." The mind (known as the ruler in t'ai chi) directed the *ch'i* "like a general leading his troops." The whole body—sinews, bones, and blood vessels—was completely relaxed so that the *ch'i* could flow as freely as water. "Don't let one ounce of force remain in the blood vessels, bones, and ligaments to tie yourself up," advised the *Tai Chi Classics.* "In this way," as master Yang Ch'eng-fu commented, "if the *ch'i* flows unobstructed, daily penetrating all the passages in the entire body without interruption, then after long practice we will have achieved true internal power."[21]

It was this reliance on inner power—of mind, *ch'i,* and spirit—which set t'ai chi and the other "internal" schools of martial art apart from the more common, "external" forms of martial arts. The accumulated power of *ch'i* was like the power of water, which conquered with yielding and softness. "Did not Lao Tzu say, 'Concentrate your *ch'i* and develop softness. Can you be like a child?' " the contemporary master Chang Man-Ch'ing exorted his students. "This is the watchword for T'ai Chi Ch'uan. Students should begin their study with this."[22]

T'ai chi thus made it possible for individual warriors to reverse or transcend the hitherto "natural" tyranny of the bigger and stronger. The inner approach of t'ai chi (and other related inner martial arts) made it possible for the small to win over the large, the weak over the strong, the old over the young; it even made it possible for women, so long at a disadvantage because of their generally smaller size, to win over men. "In boxing there are many teachings about combat," as Wang Tsung Yeuh said in the *Tai Chi Classics*. "Although they differ with respect to postures, they can never go beyond reliance on the stronger defeating those who are weaker, or the swifter conquering those who are slower. . . . The strong and the quick, however, cannot explain nor implement the deflection of a thousand pounds momentum with a force of four ounces, or an old man's defeating a great number of men."[23]

Many stories refer to the great powers of *ch'i*. The *Yang Family Secret Transmissions* recount how Yang-Lu-chu'an, who brought the old style of t'ai chi to Peking in the nineteenth century, was sitting in meditation when a powerfully built monk, "more than six feet tall," came to pay his respects. "Master was about to humbly reply when the monk flew at him, attacking with his fists. Master slightly depressed his chest and with his right palm patted the monk's fist. As if struck by a bolt of lightning, the monk was thrown behind a screen, his body still in the attitude of attacking."[24]

Ch'en Wei-ming, a student of Yang's, described how the power of *ch'i* felt to a master: "With real *tai chi* your arm is like iron wrapped with cotton. It is very soft and yet feels heavy to someone trying to support it. . . . When you touch your opponent, your hands are soft and light, but they cannot get rid of them. When you attack it is like a bullet penetrating neatly, without recourse to force. When he is pushed ten feet away, he feels a little movement but no strength. And he feels no pain. . . . If he tries to use force to control or push you, it is like catching the wind or shadows. Everywhere is empty."[25]

△△ V △△

Such weaponless or "empty-handed" techniques represented, it may be argued, the perfect application of Taoist principles to the martial arts. But weapons such as the sword or spear are, after all, only extensions of the hand, and it is true that, in time, nearly all martial arts schools, including t'ai chi, included weapons in their training.

Taoists, in any case, were not prohibited, as Buddhist monks were, from using weapons, and the sword in particular became a specialty of many Taoist martial artists, some of whom were women. The Lady of Yueh, for example, was clearly Taoist in spirit and practice.

"I grew up in a deep forest, in the wilderness away from men," she told the king of Yueh (in the first-century *Annals of the Kingdoms of Wu and Yueh*). "I have not studied properly and I am unknown to the feudal lords. However, I am fond of swordsmanship and I practiced incessantly. I did not receive it from anyone; I just suddenly got it."[26] (This last phrase was used in later times as a metaphor for poetic inspiration.)

Not satisfied with such laconic modesty, the king begged her to explain her skill in greater detail. She replied, in the Taoist manner, "The way of swordsmanship is very subtle yet easy, its meaning very obscure and profound; it involves the principles of *yin* and *yang;* a good swordsman should appear perfectly calm like a fine lady, but capable of quick action like a surprised tiger."

The king, as we might expect, implored her to instruct his troops.[27]

Many martial artists did, no doubt, serve the rulers and lords of the empire. But many more were independent, free-lance *hsien* (literally "wandering-force") knight-errants, who lived, like the Lady of Yueh, hidden in seclusion, "unknown to the feudal lords."

These men and women were not supporters of the feudal order, like the gentlemen-knights of the Spring and Autumn period. Rather, they were commoners, or perhaps nobles who had lost their positions. Some of them were touchy and quick to take offense and seek revenge at the slightest insult; but some were generous and altruistic knights who protected and defended the poor and unfortunate in a time when law and order had broken down or was used solely to protect the rich and powerful.

A number of the knight-errants were practiced Taoists; most of them, in any case, were connected with the Taoists by virtue of their unpretentious, unconventional behavior. Like the poet Li Po—"keen on swordplay at fifteen"—many of them combined the occasional chivalrous deed with wine, women, and song. They gave away money, when they had it, and refused rewards for their services. And, most unusually, they valued loyalty to their friends more than to their families.

Taoist and Buddhist martial artists were also active in many of the populist secret societies which resisted corrupt and foreign dynasties throughout Chinese history. T'ai chi had been preserved and cultivated both for self-defense and health by the simple villagers of the Chen family long before it was introduced to the royal court of the Mongols in the seventeenth century. The Taoist Yellow Turbans, for example, fought against the Confucian and legalist Han Dynasty in the second century A.D. The White Lotus Buddhists resisted the Mongols of the Yuan Dynasty. In the seventeenth century, 128 volunteer monks from the Fukien Shaolin Temple responded to the emperor's call for volunteers. They defeated marauding bands in the border areas with such ease that the emperor was persuaded to burn the temple on a trumped-up charge of sedition; the surviving monks are said to have then formed the nucleus of the anti-Manchu Triad Society. More recently, at the end of the nineteenth century, the Society of the Harmonious and Righteous Fist (better known to the West as the Boxers) rose in rebellion against Manchu and British troops, believing that their ritual boxing, inner power, and magic amulets would protect them from the bullets that mowed them down. It was a mistake that inscrutable and wily old general Sun Tzu would never have made.

ᴧᴧ V I ᴧᴧ

The art and strategy of the Taoist warrior was hardly limited to the martial realm. War and fighting were, in any case, simply a gross and extreme example of what happened when one of the two universal complementary opposite forces was allowed to overwhelm the other. But these two forces were actually one—or one continually transforming into the other—in the yin and yang that swirled within the great circle of the Tao.

"The essence of the principles of warriors," as Liu Ji said, "is responding to change."[28] And since the Tao is made up of change, of birth and death, living and dying, the arts of the Taoist warrior led to a full life in the Tao—one which included death but was not ruled or obsessed with it; which was a part of nature, and not at war with it; which included both *wen* and *wu,* the life-affirming cultural and the life-preserving martial—in short, a whole life. From a very early time, the principles of Taoism as well as of the Taoist-influenced school of strategy were generalized into a general theory of action or practice— what sociologists call praxis, as opposed to theory—applied to various spheres.

Knowing this, the Taoist warrior could apply the strategic principles of the Tao—whether of the art of war or of t'ai chi—to the arts of peace as well as war. He could, for example, apply the strategic principles of Sun Tzu to business, as a merchant by the name of Bo Gui did in the fifth century B.C.; to calligraphy and painting, as Wang Xizhi did in the fourth century, when he wrote that "paper is a military battle-order; the brush is a weapon; the mind is a general; composition of lines is imagining strategic plans"; and even to the "flowery battle" between the sexes.[29] R. H. Van Gulik, the leading European scholar of Chinese erotica, found two fundamental principles common to the arts of war and love: "First, that one must utilize his own force while utilizing that of the opponent; and second, that one must begin by yielding to him in order to catch him unawares thereafter." And Li Yu, author of the seventeenth century erotic classic *Prayer Mat of Flesh,* echoed Sun Tzu when he wrote, "In sexual encounter, the man's first curiosity is about the hills and valleys of the woman, and hers about the size and fire-power of his armaments. Which of them has to advance and which to retreat? As in war to know yourself is as important as to know the enemy."[30]

The way of the warrior was thus applied to and nourished by the civil arts, the arts of life, whence it originally arose. The ideal Chinese warrior was not a professional or specialized man of arms, but a cultivated man of spirit and culture who was trained in martial arts and strategy, who manifested as a warrior only when it became necessary. The Chinese had no warrior class or caste separate from the rest of society. The Chinese warrior was never just a warrior; he was a warrior-scholar, a warrior-administrator, a warrior-monk; he was a warrior-sage. "Enjoy social amenities and music," Zhuge Liang advised would-be generals, "familiarize yourself with poetry and prose. Put humanity and justice before wit and bravery."[31]

"The civil is the essence and the martial is the function," wrote t'ai chi master Yang. "A single hand cannot make a clapping sound. This is not only true of civil essence and martial practice but of all things in the world. . . . Whether for practical pursuits or simply the way of being a human being, how dare we neglect the two words—*wen* and *wu,* civil and martial?"[32]

In certain ways, we might say that the paradoxical reversals of the Chinese Taoist warrior, who gives both precedence and essence to the arts of peace, suggests a winding watercourse way, a Tao, out of the deadly dilemma posed by the Indo-European warrior, whose reliance on brute strength and fiery fury led only to the glories of heroic death in battle. Borrowing for a moment the style of the *Tao Te Ching,* we might contrast the Indo-European warrior with his Taoist counterpart:

> Instead of the outer, the inner.
> Instead of hardness, softness.

Instead of fire, water.

Instead of chivalry, strategy.

Instead of deception, inscrutability.

Instead of the folly of heroism, the reason of moderation.

Instead of fame, modesty.

Instead of the glories of youthful death, the pleasures of a
   long full life.

Or, as old Lao Tzu himself summed it up: "A man or woman with outward courage dares to die. A man or woman with inward courage dares to live."

IN SHINING ARMOR

Of Knights and Chivalry

> *Behold! without renouncing our rich garments,*
> *our station in life, courtesy,*
> *and all that pleases and charms*
> *we can obtain honor here and joy in Paradise.*
> *–Aimeric de Pegulhan*

In the end, it was the knights' insistence on their peculiar mode of fighting that ensured their obsolescence. But the ideals of chivalry have continued to exist long past the feudal modes and military means that gave birth to them. The chivalric inheritance includes the basic warrior virtues of the Indo-European bands, the humane ideals of Christianity, and the romanticism of courtly love, but it also includes the idea of holy war. The chivalric code thus contains both positive and negative elements. And since it is this code that more than any other is the heritage of the West, it is especially important that we comprehend it, for even today, the Western warrior whose heir we all are has yet to wake from the spell that chivalry still casts.

*　*　*

The word *chivalry* derives from the French word for a horseman, *chevalier,* a mounted warrior, whose effectiveness depended on certain expensive and difficult-to-use equipment: an extremely large charger, called a *dressier,* trained to kick and butt in battle; stirrups, adapted from Asia sometime around the eighth century, which made it possible for the warrior to keep his saddle in battle and support his weaponry, the battle-ax, the sword and especially the lance. (The English word *knight* is derived from an Anglo-Saxon word which first meant "servant," and then "armed servant.")

The physical characteristics of the mounted warrior were thus the basis for chivalry, and so it is that we first hear the word as a description of strength in the oldest of the French epic *chansons de geste* (songs of deeds), the *Song of Roland.* Written during the late eleventh or early twelfth century, this song deals with the battle of Charlemagne and his nephew Roland against the Saracens (though historians say Basques) on the fifteenth of August in 778: "Malprimes is right chivalrous; he is big and strong and worthy of his ancestors."[1]

Roland is the model of chivalry. In this, he is similar to Achilles and the other Indo-European ancestors. His onslaught is compared to lion and leopard. He is fearless and reckless; his blow cleaves the enemy from helm to horse. He will not bring shame or disgrace on his ancestors. "God forbid that my parents be blamed, or that fair France fall in disgrace through any deed of mine. Mighty blows will I smite with Durendal, my good sword, which girt at my side; you shall see the blade all covered with blood. It is an evil day for the felon pagans who are now assembled; I pledge you, all are doomed to die."[2]

Like most warriors, Roland was fighting for "great booty . . . greater than that won by any kind of France," but he was also fighting for his lord, who happened to be the king of the realm, Charles the Great. "A man must," as Roland said, "endure great hardship for his lord; for him he must suffer both cold and heat; for him he must sacrifice both flesh and blood. Strike with thy lance and I will smite with Durendal, my good sword which the emperor gave me. If I die, he who shall inherit it will say: it was the sword of a noble vassal."[3]

But he fought also in defense of Christendom. Addressing the knights, the fighting Bishop Turpin said, "Barons, Charles gave us this task; we must die for our king. Christendom is in peril, lend it your aid. You will now have battle, for you see the Saracens before you. Confess your sins and ask God for pardon. I will absolve you to save your souls; if you die you will be holy martyrs and will win a place in Paradise the Great."[4]

Roland's death—to say nothing of the hundreds or thousands of men who followed his lead—made no military sense. (Sun Tzu would have shaken his head.) But it demonstrated and proved Roland's disdain for his enemy, his bravery, and his loyalty, both to his lord and Church. Lying under a pine with his face turned toward Spain, so that it would be clear he died a "conqueror" rather than a coward, he thought of Charlemagne, who supported and trained him in his court, and of his companions-in-arms. He tried to break his sword, Durendal, which contained holy relics, a patch of cloth from the Virgin Mary's cloak among them, lest it fall into the hands of the heathens.

Then, turning to the sovereign lord, he struck his breast, prayed for forgiveness, and held his hand aloft. At which point Gabriel, the leader of the hosts of heaven against the devil, and Michael, the knight's patron angel, descended to bear his soul to heaven.

ᐃᐃ I I ᐃᐃ

Roland was a Christian because his Frankish ancestor, Clovis, had converted to Christianity in 496, during a battle with the Alamanni. Seeing his warriors "swept to utter ruin," Clovis had turned to the God of his Burgundian wife, Clothild, since the gods "have withdrawn from helping me; wherefore I believe that they have no power." And so he lifted his eyes up to heaven, wept, and called on "Jesus Christ, Thou that art proclaimed by Clothild Son of the Living God. . . . If Thou grant me victory over these enemies, and experience confirm that power which the people dedicated to Thy name claimeth to have proved, then will I also believe on Thee and be baptized in Thy name."

"And as he said this," reported Gregory of Tours, "lo, the Alamanni turned their backs, and began to flee."

Clovis was baptized along with three thousand of his warriors by the bishop of Reims. "The streets were overshadowed with coloured hangings, the churches adorned with white hangings, the baptistery was set in order, smoke of incense spread in clouds, perfumed tapers gleamed, the whole church about the place of baptism was filled with the divine fragrance."[5]

Clovis was called a "second Constantine" by Gregory of Tours. The reference was to the Roman emperor whose own conversion had also been provoked by a military crisis, in his case a battle for the empire against the tyrant Maxentius. Like Clovis, Constantine had doubted both his own military power and the power of the old gods, when he saw "with his own eyes the trophy of a cross of light in the heavens, above the sun, and bearing the inscription, CONQUER BY THIS."[6]

Both conversions marked the beginning of an alliance and accommodation between the spiritual power of the new religion and the military pagan power which had opposed it. The Holy Catholic Church now bestowed its spiritual authority (and Church organization) on the emperor and king, while the rulers, in turn, lent their military powers to the Church.

By the beginning of the eighth century, the greatest threat to the Franks, as well as the Church, came from Islam. Muhammad himself, who had received the Koran by divine dictation in 646, considered Islam to be the culmination of Judaism and Christianity—he himself was simply the most recent prophet of Allah, the one God. Pagans were generally forced to convert, but People of the Book—which included Jews, Christians, and Zoroastrians—were permitted to live as "protected minorities," as long as they paid a tax and did not interfere with Islam.

But those foolish enough to resist the spread of the prophet's message or the plundering raids of the Arabs met with the sword. Muhammad himself had led raids against the caravans of the pagan Arabs from Mecca, and one of his best generals, Khalid ibn al-Walid, was given the name Sword of Islam for leading his troops in an orderly retreat from the Byzantines. Accustomed to living by raids and plunder, hardened by their nomadic desert life, unafraid to die, since *jihad* or "great effort" in the service of Islam would be rewarded by eternal life in a lush and verdant oasis of a paradise, the Bedouins quickly conquered Syria, Persia, Egypt, Turkey, and Byzantium.

The West was caught by surprise. The Saracens—as the medieval West called all Arabs—were mounted on swift Arabian horses; camels, able to endure long periods of thirst and hunger, served as superior transport. Unlike the knights, the Saracens were adept at archery as well as the scimitar and lance. The combination was particularly effective in the harassing warfare of *karr wa farr*, "charging and fleeing."

The Saracens overran the Gothic kingdom of Spain in 711, reaching Nimes in 725. The Arab cavalry was finally stopped by the heavy infantry of the Frankish king Charles—the Hammer—Martel at Poitiers in 733. "The nations of the North," reported a chronicler, "standing firm as a wall, and impenetrable as a zone of ice, utterly slay the Arabs with the edge of the sword."[7]

Under the leadership of Charlemagne, the Franks extended their kingdom into Germany and Italy. They took the offensive against the Saracens in 785; it was this campaign which immortalized Roland, the brave, loyal, and stubbornly arrogant warrior who refused to blow his ivory horn for help when he was ambushed by a superior Saracen force.

Charlemagne was crowned emperor of the the Holy Roman Empire by the Pope on Christmas Day in the year 800. He not only led in war, just as the old German chieftain had led the tribe's warrior bands in their plundering expeditions every spring, but it was also his responsibility, as a *holy* emperor, to keep the king's peace—to defend the poor, orphans, widows and the Church.

When Charlemagne died in 814, The Holy Roman Empire was divided among his three sons. It soon devolved into its constituents— warring baronies, principalities, fiefdoms, kingdoms. Weakened and fragmented, Europe once more became easy prey for raiders—Arab corsairs plundered the coasts of the Mediterranean and Italy; mounted Magyars from Hungary rode into Germany, and the Northmen appeared off the coasts of Ireland and England.

These were the most serious threat. The Northmen were still possessed by the fierceness of the old Indo-European warrior bands. They fought with the terrifying battle frenzy of berserkirs, unafraid of death in battle, which won Valhalla. Sailing forth in their sleek, shallow-bottomed boats, they raided coastal towns and followed rivers far inland. Leaving their boats, they rode forth on stolen horses in search of the silver, gold, and jewels that had been conveniently assembled, for the glory of God, inside unprotected churches and monasteries. Swinging great battle-axes at the end of five-foot handles, wielding sword, spear, and bow with equal dexterity, they hit England in 787 and sacked London three years later; they burned and sacked the abbeys of Lindesfarne of the Irish coast in 795. They sailed up the Seine to the isle of Paris, where they were appeased with ransom and a safe winter refuge instead of battle. In 765, a Viking warrior chieftain by the name of Rollo received Normandie. From there, three hundred years later, his descendent William the Bastard would set out across the English Channel on the last and most successful of all the Viking raids.

The defense against the Vikings fell to the local lords, who built fortified castles for protection, and who sent out mounted warriors to pursue and harry the raiders. Such a warrior was costly to outfit and maintain. A helmet cost six cows; a coat of mail, twelve; a sword with scabbard, seven; leg armor, six; lance with shield, two; and a horse, twelve—for a total of forty-seven cows. He also had to undergo a lengthy training to be able to handle charger, armor, sword, and lance in battle. "You can make a horseman of a lad at puberty," went one Carolingian maxim; "after that, never."[8]

Many of these mounted warriors were nobles supported by peasants, who worked their lands. But others were retainers who exchanged their military skill and equipment for support at the lord's manor, or for lands their lord granted them. The warrior pledged his fealty, his faithful service to his lord, kneeling before him with folded hands; his lord, in turn, promised to "bear him succor," sealing the bargain with a kiss as proof of friendship. The result was feudalism, a system in which most power was held in a decentralized, though intricately interrelated way by local noble strongmen: barons, dukes, counts, and knights.

In the absence of a strong king or emperor the power and privileges of the nobles increased, as did the power of their retainers, the armed horsemen, who protected and took advantage of the unarmed peasants whose ceaseless labor supported them. And the Church, supported by the plunder of lords and warriors and the sweat of peasants, fought with the weapon of a newly added prayer: "From the fury of the Norsemen, God deliver us."

◮◮ III ◮◮

By the first millennium—"the year one thousand of the passion of our Lord"—their prayers had been answered. The Christian empire was more or less secure, if fragmented. The Vikings had been turned back or bought with new lands, as Rollo was with Normandie. The Saracens had been driven back over the Pyrenees to Spain, and the Magyars returned to Hungary. Many of these, moreover, had become converted to Christianity themselves. The great oak of the Saxons was cut down by Bishop Xerold in 743 and made into a sacristy, and a church was erected in the grove of Uppsala, where, it was said, various sacrifices, including human ones, had been made.

But within, all was not well. Charles the Great had unified a great deal of Europe, with the notable exception of England, but his empire could not survive its division among his three sons, and the power of the great lords and barons, which was based on manors, castles, and their own mounted warriors, had rivaled if not surpassed the power of any king.

Such men pledged loyalty only to their lords and each other. Their battles against Saracens, Norsemen, and Magyars had left them with a monopoly on military power consisting of horses, armor, and strongholds. But they were not, if some contemporary witnesses are to be believed, all that different from their Indo-European ancestors or the "pagans" and "barbarians" they fought against; certainly they were far less civilized than the Spanish Saracens, some of whom were translating Aristotle. "In their savage outbursts of anger," M. Flach writes in *Les Origines de l'Ancienne France,* "or in their cold ferocity, nothing restrained them; neither regard for weakness nor religious fear had any influence over them; they killed unarmed men without mercy; they burned nuns in their convents."[9]

In 978, at the Council of Charroux, the bishops of Aquitaine met in an effort to protect its property and clergy—as well as the widows, orphans, and poor who were under its protection—from the violence of warriors. By the time of the millennium, the bishops and abbots of Aquitaine called for the prelates and princes of all countries to assemble "for the purpose of reforming the peace and the institution of the holy faith" in an open field near the abbey of Cluny. The response for the Peace of God movement, as it was called, was overwhelming. The assembled throngs—monks, clerics, nobles, warriors, and peasants— fasted and prayed before "the bodies of many saints and countless shrines of relics" that were displayed and carried in procession, and many people, it was said, were healed.

The Peace of God movement was strengthened by the penitential atmosphere of the millennium. All three orders of society—clerics, warriors, and peasants—were encouraged to acts of renunciation and purification. Clerics were urged to live like monks—to be chaste, embrace poverty, and give up arms. The *milites,* the warriors, were now asked to give up *their* greatest pleasure—fighting and pillage, just as all Christians were asked to give up meat for Lent.

As the strength of the movement grew, and as the millennium of Christ's crucifixion neared, the Peace of God movement was extended and made more specific. Such was the power of the spiritual sword of the Church—and the belief in God as dreadful judge in the world to come—that warriors who had fought, pillaged, and plundered now took a solemn oath to limit their violence:

> I will not force my way into a church in any manner since it is under God's protection; nor into the storerooms in the precinct of the church. I will not attack a monk or churchman if he be unarmed with earthly weapons, nor any of his company if he be without lance or buckler. I will not carry off his ox, cows, pig, sheep, goats, mare or unbroken colt, nor the faggot he is carrying. I will not lay hands on any peasant, man or woman, sergeant or merchant; nor take away

their money or constrain them to pay ransom. I will not mistreat them by extorting their possessions on the ground that their lord is making war.[10]

In 1027, the bishop of Vichy proposed a Truce of God which would limit warfare on the Sabbath. Soon Good Friday, Holy Saturday, and Ascension Day were added, as well as other feast days and holy days. The Truce of God was gradually extended until it lasted for four days, from Wednesday sundown to Monday sunrise. In 1054, the great Council of Narbonne threatened Christians who broke either the Peace or the Truce of God with excommunication, finally declaring, "Let no Christian kill another Christian, for there is no doubt that he who kills a Christian spills the blood of Christ."[11]

Many of the knights accepted the spirit of the Peace, even if they did not always follow the letter. The result was that the knights were brought into the Church. They were now accepted as a legitimate *ordo* of Christian society which God had divided—so it was said—into three ranks: the clerics, who prayed for the salvation of the world; the warriors, who protected the world; and the unarmed peasants, whose labor supported those who prayed for and protected them. The peasants, it was said, were like the knight's horse: "For above the people must sit the knight. And just as one controls a horse and he who sits above leads it where he will, so the knight must lead the people at his will."[12]

The knight's position within the Church bestowed a new respectability and status. The mounted warriors had not necessarily been counted among the hereditary nobility—many of them had received their fiefs or offices only while they rendered military service, or for their lifetime at most. But now—between 1130 and 1250—the boundaries between the mounted warrior who traded military service for support and the nobles who traded support for military service began to blur. The nobles sought the new sanctified status of the knight, and the knights began to act like nobility—which is to say they began to pass on their lands and fiefs, and even their title, if that was all they had, to their sons. In France, the royal court decreed that no one could be ordained a knight unless his grandfather had also been a knight.

The knight's status was also reflected by the Church's involvement in the ceremonies of knighthood. In the earliest and simplest ceremonies of knighthood, the candidate was simply girded with sword and belt, and sometimes given spurs by his father or another knight. This ceremony closely resembled the old German initiations in which a young man of twelve or fourteen was presented with spear and shield by his father or a kinsman as a sign that he was qualified to bear arms as part of the war band.

By the eleventh century, however, the Church had gained complete control of the ceremony. Knights were no longer "made" but "ordained." Knighthood became a sacrament administered by the Church. In the more elaborate versions of the ceremony, the would-be knight purified himself by bathing and fasting. He kept vigil through the night. The sword itself was placed on the altar, where the priest prayed—to give one of many variants—that God would "deign to bless with the right hand of Thy majesty this sword with which this Thy servant desires to be girded, that it may be a defence of churches, widows, orphans and all Thy servants against the scourge of the pagans, that it may be the terror and dread of all other evildoers, and that it may be just both in attack and defence."[13]

The knight was then girded with his sword and given his spurs. The binding moment of the ceremony was the "dubbing" (from an old German word for "to strike") or the *colee* (or "blow"), as the French called it—a blow which was (according to Raymond Lull's handbook on chivalry) the last blow which the knight could "receive and not return." The newly made knight then demonstrated his new status by mounting his horse and attacking a suit of armor attached to a post.

The obligations of the knight who had been ordained in the order of chivalry—"the highest order that God had made and willed"—were elaborated in prayers and handbooks, such as the French *Ordene de Chivalrie,* an imaginary dialogue between a captured knight and Saladin, and various other romances.

The knight first of all had certain religious obligations. He was supposed to attend Mass every day and fast frequently. (One story tells of a knight who stopped to say Mass even though he was late for a tournament; his piety was rewarded when the Virgin helped him achieve victory.)

He was pledged to use his sword to defend the Holy Church, particularly against infidels; to defend the widow, the orphan, and the poor; not to kill a vanquished or helpless enemy in battle; not to take part in a false judgment or an act of treason (or to withdraw if these could not be prevented); not to give evil counsel to a lady; and to give help, "if possible," to a fellow being in distress.

The Church's attitude was carved in stone, literally, in the church at Chartres: "Most Holy Lord, Almighty Father . . . thou who hast permitted on earth the use of the sword to repress the malice of the wicked and defend justice; who for the protection of thy people hast thought to institute the order of chivalry . . . cause thy servant here before thee, by disposing his heart to goodness, never to use this sword or another to injure anyone unjustly; but let him use it always to defend the Just and the Right."[14]

△△ I V △△

The Holy Catholic Church had thus tamed, chastened, and uplifted the knights. They had come to believe, more or less, that they ought not kill fellow Christians—or at least that to do so put their souls in mortal peril, calling for penitence and absolution. But their conversion was far from complete. They were still warriors whose whole way of life was based on their prowess with arms and courage in battle.

Who, then, were they to fight, now that the pagans had been beaten back or converted? The answer came from Pope Urban II, whose call for a *bellum peregrini*—a pilgrim's war—preached from a throne set up on a platform in an open field in November 1095, transformed the knight into an aggressive instrument for the Church.

The Pope began by urging the crowd of clerics and laypeople to go to the aid of their brethren in the East. The Turks, he said, were attacking Christians in Constantinople, desecrating shrines and churches. They had also made it unsafe for Christian pilgrims to travel to Jerusalem, the holiest city of Christendom, which was in the hands of infidels. Rich and poor alike should go, he said. Those who fought this righteous war would be led to victory by God.

In fact, the problem was not quite as serious as the Holy Father made out. Moslems and Christians had coexisted for many years in the Holy Land. Though disorders in the East had made it difficult for pilgrims to travel, they were nonetheless welcomed as a source of revenue. But the western wing of the Holy Catholic Church had been trying for some time to harness the warriors' energies for the Church. Even though Islam had been checked, it still remained a powerful force and serious threat. The burning of the Church of the Holy Sepulchre by the mad caliph, whether or not it was temporary, was a useful excuse. Christ, said the Pope, commanded that "the land of our brethren" be rescued from the pagans. Christians should stop fighting each other at home: "Let those who have hitherto been robbers now become soldiers of Christ. Let hatred depart from among you, let your quarrels end, let wars cease, and let all dissensions and controversies slumber," Urban II said at Clermont. "Enter upon the road to the Holy Sepulchre; wrest that land from the wicked race and subject it to yourselves."[15]

Urban's appropriation of Saint Paul's "soldiers of Christ" makes clear the distance the Church had come since its early days. Saint Paul had used the term (in his letter to Timothy) as an encouragement to stand steadfastly in faith. "Endure hardship with us," he said, "like a good soldier of Christ," so that "if we died with Him, we will also live with Him." This kind of "spiritual warfare" gave the Christian the strength to resist the might of the Roman Empire, which considered the Christian's refusal to serve in the Roman army—and worship the pagan gods of the empire—as a threat to Roman power.

But Saint Paul's notion of spiritual warfare was also active, in that the soldier of Christ wielded the sword of the spirit against the temptations sent against him by devils or demons. "Put on the full armor of God so that you can take your stand against the devil's schemes," he wrote the Ephesians. "For our struggle is not against flesh and blood, but against the authorities, against the powers of his dark world and against the spiritual forces of evil in the heavenly realms. . . . In addition to all this, take up the shield of faith, from which you can extinguish all the flaming arrows of the evil one. Take the helmet of salvation and the sword of the Spirit, which is the word of God."

It did not take much to identify this spiritual warfare against the devil with real warfare. All that was required was to identify the enemies of the Christian West with the spiritual enemies of Christ. The Church already supported warriors defending Christian nations against pagans. Bishops consecrated weapons, carried blessed banners with holy images into battle, and even granted certain indulgences to Christians killed in righteous battle—though these had always depended on the purity of the warrior's soul. Pope Gregory VII extended the Church's support to include aggressive warfare, both against pagans as well as for the political aims of the Pope. He also suggested that Christian warriors who died fighting for the Church could receive automatic absolution for all their sins.

So it was that Pope Urban, who was Gregory's successor, enlisted the knights in an "army of the Lord," to fight against "God's enemies and ours."[16]

The sword wielded by Pope Urban's soldiers of Christ was a very real sword, a sword which would win the Crusaders (as they came to be called) new fiefs and plunder, both welcome inducements for knights living in an increasingly crowded and orderly Europe. But the sword was at the same time a spiritual sword, since the knights who killed pagans were also killing "slaves of demons" who were the enemies of the Church.

Christians in the eleventh century were concerned—we might say obsessed—with the need to absolve themselves of their sins before their death. Death did not bring annihilation; it brought either eternal salvation or eternal hell. The souls of knights who lived by bloodshed and rapine were especially in peril. They might be able to save themselves, if they were rich, by building monasteries; or they could entrust themselves to God as unarmed pilgrims; or end their lives performing austerities as monks.

Pope Urban now declared that the pilgrim's war of the Crusaders was itself a penance that purified the Crusader's soul and absolved him of sin, thus transforming worldly warfare into spiritual warfare. The result was a holy war—a new kind of war which combined the advantages of both worldly and spiritual warfare. Christian knights could now win absolution without having to give up their knightly way of life. "Behold!" sang Aimeric de Pegulhan,

> without renouncing our rich garments, our station in life, courtesy, and all that pleases and charms we can obtain honor here and joy in Paradise. To conquer glory by fine deeds and escape hell; what count or king could ask more? No more is there need to be tonsured or shaved and lead a hard life in the most strict order if we can revenge the shame which the Turks have done us. Is this not truly to conquer at once land and sky, reputation in the world and with God?[17]

The forces set loose by Pope Urban's call were difficult to control. Urban and the knights who had taken the crusading pledge had set August 15 as the date for departure. But Peter the Hermit, a barefoot and charismatic lay preacher who rode a donkey, set off in April with a motley crew of twenty thousand. There were a few German monks, but most of them were poor laypeople hoping to find a "New Jerusalem," where—as the Scriptures said—milk and honey flowed.

The People's Crusade began by attacking and murdering Jews in Germany; then they plundered their way through the newly Christianized kingdom of Hungary, sacking towns and killing Christians as well. In Constantinople, they skirmished with imperial troops sent to watch over them; the Byzantine Emperor Alexius warned them to wait for the main army, but they insisted on continuing—right into a Turkish ambush. The few who were not killed were sold into slavery.

The Crusaders who followed were better prepared and more numerous—estimates range from sixty thousand to a hundred thousand. They were accompanied by a smaller army of camp followers: wives, children, traders, and what one Arab observer called "licentious harlots, full of youth and beauty," for it was considered harmful for knights to abstain from women on a long campaign, holy war or not.

Four major groups of Crusaders rendezvoused in Constantinople. They went on to take the town of Nicaea with the help of Byzantine ships. They fought off Turkish counterattacks, lost many of their horses crossing the steep and slippery Anti-Taurus mountains, and captured a number of towns and provinces, some of which the Crusaders appropriated as their own fiefs. In October 1098, they took Antioch, only to be besieged themselves in a matter of days. All seemed lost until a peasant by the name of Peter Bartholomew revealed that Saint Andrew had revealed to him in a vision that the Holy Lance which had pierced the side of Jesus Christ was buried in Antioch's St. Peter's Cathedral; and indeed, when they excavated the spot, they did find a piece of iron.

There were those, including the papal legate, who had their doubts, but seeing the effect the finding of the Lance had on the Crusaders, they wisely held their peace. On the morning of June 28 the knights rode out in all their tattered panoply, the Normans, French, Flemish, Provencals, Toulousians, and the Normans from Italy. Raymond of Aiguilers, who was later to write a history of the Crusades, carried the Lance into battle, and the Turks were routed.

The armed pilgrimage continued on its way, led by a barefoot Count Raymond of Toulouse on the final march to Jerusalem. Once more, the Crusaders faced a long and difficult siege, with food running out, water scarce (the wells had been poisoned), and the hot sun beating down on their armor. When they learned that a large force was on its way from Egypt to relieve Jerusalem, morale sank and many deserted. But once more they were saved by a vision. This time it was the papal legate, who had died in Antioch of typhoid, who appeared to the priest Peter Desiderius to order the Crusaders to give up their selfish arguments about plunder, to fast, and to walk in procession around the walls of Jerusalem with repentant hearts.

This time there were no doubts. The fast lasted for three days. Then they all removed their shoes, and the bishops and priests, carrying the cross and the holy relics, led the knights and all the others in a great procession around the city, while the Moslems jeered from the walls. Afterward, they climbed the Mount of Olives, where Peter the Hermit and others preached to them.

For the next two days the Crusaders worked feverishly to complete two great siege towers. The first to gain the wall were the Flemish knights Litold and Gilbert of Turnai. "As soon as he was there," according to one chronicle, "the defenders fled along the walls and down into the city, and we followed them, slaying them and cutting them down as far as the Temple of Solomon, where there was such slaughter that our men waded in blood up to their ankles."[18] When it was over, all the Moslems (as well as the Jews, who were burned in their temple) were slaughtered, including old men, women, and children. Afterward, the Crusaders gathered in the Church of the Holy Sepulcher to give thanks to God.

Most of the Crusaders returned to Europe loaded down with booty and sanctity. But others stayed to rule and protect the new Christian kingdom of Jerusalem and to help defend the pilgrims. One of these, Hugh De Payens, lord of a castle in Burgundy, took an oath of chastity, poverty, and obedience, along with seven other knights. King Baldwin II, the new Christian ruler of Jerusalem, gave the dedicated Poor Knights, as they were called, living quarters in a part of a mosque which was said to have once been the Temple of Solomon.

In 1127, Hugh returned to Europe to ask Saint Bernard, the founder of the Cistercian monastery of Clairvaux, to preach a new Crusade. Saint Bernard was so taken with the saintly knight that he agreed to create a rule for a new kind of order which would combine Christianized knights and militarized monks. This was something entirely new and controversial. The orders of clerics and knights had been entirely separated up to this point. Combining the two *ordos* was a revolutionary act. In *de laude novae militae (In Praise of the New Knighthood)*, he wrote that "We have heard that a new sort of chivalry has appeared on earth. . . . A new sort of chivalry that tirelessly wages . . . war against both flesh and blood and against the spiritual forces of evil." These new knights, said Bernard, were at once "meeker than lambs and fiercer than lions."[19]

The preaching of the Crusades had created a holy war. The rule of the Templars created a holy warrior. The Templar did not go to war, as the normal feudal knight did, out of anger, greed, or an "appetite for inane glory," said Bernard, but to win victory for Christ. Like a monk, the Templar or Poor Knight lived in holy poverty, a state symbolized by the standard showing two knights riding one horse. As Saint Bernard described them, they wore beards, their hair was cropped short, they were dusty and sunburned. Skilled in arms, the Templar was loyal to the Church first, as exemplified by the master, who was both spiritual and military commander.

Of course, monks dedicated to prayer were not supposed to shed blood. But Bernard was not deterred by this. The Templars did not commit homicide, he said, but malecide. They killed not men (or women) but evil.

"The soldier of Christ kills safely," wrote Saint Bernard; "he dies the more safely. He serves his own interests in dying, and Christ's interests in killing! Not without cause does he bear the sword! He is the instrument of God for the punishment of malefactors and the punishment of the unjust"; therefore, "to kill a pagan is to win glory for it gives glory for Christ." If the Templars themselves were killed, of course, they achieved martyrdom. They were not allowed to ask for ransom, as other knights commonly did, and so could expect to be killed if captured. Therefore, they asked and gave no quarter in battle. "Rejoice, brave warrior, if you live and conquer in the Lord," Saint Bernard exhorted them, "but rejoice still more and give thanks if you die and go to join the Lord. This life can be fruitful and victory is glorious yet a holy death for righteousness is worth more. Certainly 'blessed are they who die *in* the Lord' but how much more so are those who die *for* Him."[20]

Ironically, Bernard's conflation of monks and knights led to the reinstatement of one of the major tenants of the old Indo-European warrior's code. Killing, instead of being a sin, became redemptive. Woden was transformed into Saint Michael, the warrior-angel who led the hosts of heaven. Valhalla, in turn, was transformed into heaven. The Christian knights and warriors of Woden turned out to have much in common.

⋀⋀ V ⋀⋀

Ideally, as we have seen, Christian chivalry held that it was sinful to kill fellow Christians, since to do so "was to spill the blood of Christ."

But the Church also recognized that there were times when it was necessary for Christians to fight other Christians. According to Saint Augustine, righteous men might be forced to wage war against the wicked in order to fight for peace. For Saint Augustine, these occasions were classified as "just wars," which had four different criteria. A just war had to be declared by a legitimate authority; there had to be a reasonable and morally acceptable excuse for the war; there had to be no other way of achieving the war's objective; and it had to be fought by acceptable means.

Just wars, however, did not take the place of penances or bestow redemption, as holy wars did. Rather, the warrior who killed or wounded a fellow Christian in a just war had to undertake penance to absolve himself. Knights who killed fellow Christian knights during William the Conqueror's invasion of England, for example, were not rewarded with paradise or absolution of sins, even though William's attack had been approved by the Pope.

More important still than the fact that Christians should not kill Christians, it would seem, was the conviction that knights should not kill knights, if it could be at all avoided. The chivalric code was, by now, reserved for knights who had become nobles; in fact, adherence to the chivalric code served to draw the line between the nobles and commoners. Foot soldiers might be Christians, but neither their safety nor their deaths seem to have troubled knights overmuch. Thus the unknighted and unarmored foot soldiers who died in battle, as well as the unfortunate citizens of towns that were sacked because they had held out past the time set for a peaceful surrender, were hardly noticed and certainly not lamented by the jongleurs who wept many lines over the glorious deaths of Roland and other knightly heroes. Chivalry was reserved for fellow knights.

There was, in any case, little reason for knights to kill other knights. Knights did not have to kill each other to settle questions of succession. They were not fighting against rampaging Vikings or raiding Saracens, as their ancestors had; nor were they fighting pagans as soldiers of Christ in a holy war. They were fighting, when they came right down to it, for their livelihood. "Do you not know," remarked Sir John Hawkwood of Essex, "that I live by war, and that peace would be my undoing?"[21]

The chivalric wars of the Christian knights, then, were governed by a very different code than the holy wars of the soldiers of Christ. Instead of exalting death, as the holy wars did, they were fought according to a code which minimized the possibility of death or serious injury, at least for the knights. While the Indo-Europeans and Romans had either killed their captives or sold them into slavery, captured knights were held for ransom. The arrangement seemed to suit both victor and vanquished. The captured knight surrendered formally by handing over his gauntlet and giving his word of honor. Once this was done, he would not attempt to escape. Indeed, some knights were freed to raise their own ransom.

The amount of ransom reflected the rank of the knight—a king, for example, commanded a king's ransom. On the other hand, ransom was not supposed to be set so high that it exhausted the knight's resources. But in any case, the practice of ransom meant that knights were literally worth more alive than dead. War was dangerous, no doubt, but most knights agreed with the troubadour Bertron de Born: "The loss will be great, but the winning will be greater."[22]

Feudal war was therefore an entrepeneurial enterprise, a monopoly reserved for knights, a kind of chivalric cabal. Knights fought for glory, to be sure, but it was a glory that paid dividends. They won fiefs—as the nobles who accompanied William the Conqueror to England in 1066 did—or they won booty from sacked cities; and they won ransom. The chivalric code that governed battle was no doubt influenced by the humane considerations of the Church, as well as the knight's own conception of glory and fame, but the bottom line, so to speak, was that the chivalric code which governed knightly warfare was in many ways a commercial code.

Yet a knight was no mere tradesman who hoarded, saved, or invested; neither was he a usurer who loaned out his money at interest, profiting from the misfortunes of the poor. Rather, the successful knight plundered and ransomed to spend freely, to give away, to demonstrate his generosity—his openhanded largesse, to use the exact chivalric term. Thus when William Marshall won horses and ransoms at tournaments, he entertained his fellow knight-errants that very night at the nearest tavern, taking great pleasure and winning great renown for spending all he had won in one night—feasting on haunches of venison, drinking great tankards of ale, entertaining the company with the songs and antics of jongleurs, and wenching.

A good lord, after all, was measured not so much by how much he had as by how much he gave away. "I shall make over to you all my chattels," boasted a Norman duke to his retainers, "brassards, sword-belts, breastplates, helmets, leggings, horses, battleaxes and those fine richly adorned swords. Always when dwelling in my house shall you enjoy my benefactions and the glory won by chivalrous exploits if you devote yourself with a good heart to my service."[23]

The delicate balance between chivalry and commercializing is illustrated by the story of Bertrand du Guesclin, who was captured by the Black Prince, Edward, Prince of Wales, in the fourteenth century. Edward asked Bertrand what he thought his ransom should be. Bertrand suggested a hundred thousand florins. Edward, who knew that his captive had fallen on hard times and who was following the chivalric rule that ransoms should not ruin the captive, suggested a lower price. Bertrand, who considered that his honor was at stake, said he would go down to seventy thousand florins but that he would "not abate a farthing."

With his ransom settled, Edward promptly paroled Bertrand to raise the amount, the rule being that he could neither escape nor fight during this period. If he failed to raise the prerequisite amount, he was honor-bound to return to captivity. For Bertrand, as it turned out, there was no problem. Edward's own wife, Joan of Kent, contributed thirty thousand florins, while two other knights put in another thirty thousand. They and Bertrand, and Edward, too, had all sworn long ago to be brothers-in-arms who would help raise each other's ransoms.

The knight was thus thrice protected. He was protected by the bounds of *courtesie*, which bound members of his elite class together, even if the changing fortunes of feudal warfare meant that they fought against each other. He was protected by his ransom. And, finally, he was protected by his armor, for even though defense and offense tend to coevolve, for the long moment of the medieval ages, the defensive/offensive ratio remained in the knight's favor. The defensive mail, plate, and helmet of the knight's armor was more than a match for the offensive power of swords and lances. When new armor-threatening weapons such as the crossbow did appear, both Church and nobles attempted to ban them. In 1139, for example, the Lateran Council decreed that "the deadly art, hated of God, of crossbow-men and archers against Christians and Catholics is prohibited on pain of anathema."[24] And in 1215, the barons who forced the king to sign the Magna Carta demanded that he disband his crossbow companies.

⋀⋀ VI ⋀⋀

By the twelfth century good wars were getting hard to find. Europe was now nearly completely divided into fiefs, and the tendency toward centralization of power in the hands of kings had discouraged the private wars fought between barons. There were still Crusades, though the enthusiasm for them was waning as the Crusaders suffered one defeat after another. Some said it was because the Crusaders were not pure enough, but after the saintly King Louis was captured in 1067, even that excuse could no longer hold.

There were, however, the tournaments, the mock battles which were hardly distinguishable from chivalric warfare, since they supplied the same possibilities for glory and profit.

The earliest tournaments were battles in which groups of knights fought each other in great melees over large areas. Sometimes they fought in companies under the banner of one lord, or by region. They often (though not always) were armed with blunted swords and lances; they could also withdraw to the protection of lists in order to rest. As in battle, the object was not to kill or even wound your opponent, but to take a prize. Knights who won—that is, who unhorsed or otherwise captured their opponents—won the horse, with all its trappings. They also could hold the captured knight for ransom (some knights formed a brotherhood-in-arms, agreeing to pool their profits if they won, or pay each other's ransom if they lost).

Of course, tournaments (as with wars) were not without their dangers. Sometimes there were accidents, or the melees got out of hand—they "took an ill-turn,"—and knights were killed or seriously wounded. Deploring the waste of his vassals' lives and money, King Henry II of England banned tournaments from England; later English kings such as Richard I limited them to specific areas, required participants to pay entry fees, and required them to observe strict rules and vow to preserve the peace. The Church, meanwhile, opposed tournaments, preaching that the knight's energy would be better spent on Crusades. In addition, the Church deplored the "pagan" revelries of dances, fairs, and feasting that accompanied tournaments. The official lawbook of the Church, the *Decretals* of Gregory IX, prohibited tournaments altogehter, while knights who died in tournaments were denied Church burial, even if they had repented before their deaths.

None of this stopped the companies of young knights who were the main enthusiasts. English knights simply journeyed to France. Indeed, the adventures of the young wandering knights-errant provided a solution for the younger bachelor sons who had to cede to the eldest brother when it came time to inherit the family fief. For just as the eldest son was encouraged to marry in order to keep the fief intact, the younger sons were discouraged, if not forbidden, to marry, lest they weaken the family's fortune by division.

Some of these disinherited sons might find positions in the Church. But the others were sent off, often to the court of their family's lord, where they began to learn their vocation by serving as squires. Together with other young men of the same age group they formed an especially close bond, the bond of brothers-in-arms. They learned to care for horses and weapons and armor by attending the older knights; they practiced swordplay with great broadswords and tilted at wooden dummies with lances. They also learned the rudiments of *courtesie*—the manners of the court or assembly of knights. This part of the code of chivalry, which developed in the French courts of the twelfth century, included the nonmartial virtues of the knight: truthfulness, fairness, gentleness. They sang and they listened to the tales of the jongleurs who traveled from castle to castle; they attended Mass. But they were not taught to read or write, as clerics were. There was no need of it, and it might in any case distract them from their main business, which was to fight.

The culmination of their training came when they were girded with the sword and invested as knights. Then they rode off—sometimes alone or with a squire and a more experienced mentor, but most often with their fellow newly made knights, to take part in the tournaments in which they would win riches, honor, and glory.

In fact, these wandering groups of knights-errant had much in common with the Indo-European bands of earlier times. "Companies of youths like these formed the spearhead of feudal aggression," writes French medievalist Georges Duby. "Always on the lookout for adventure from which 'honour' and 'reward' could be gained and aiming, if possible, 'to come back rich,' they were mobile and ready for action with their emotions at a pitch of warlike frenzy."[25]

◬ V I I ◬

The knight-errants' youthful martial ardor was channeled, as we have seen, in a number of ways. The Church directed it toward the Crusades. The knights themselves found their own outlet in the extravagances of the tournaments; and there were still occasional private wars or plunderings available from time to time.

But there appeared as well, at first in the south of France, a new channel which would direct their youthful energies. This was the channel of courtly love—which, as Marc Bloch, the great historian of feudalism says, "was certainly one of the most curious products of the code of chivalry."

The cult of courtly love is, in fact, the most mysterious and unique of the chivalries that make up the threefold strand of the concept of chivalry. The object of the knight's devotion was neither lord nor king, as in feudal chivalry, nor Church nor Christ as in Christian chivalry, but a lady. She was usually of a higher station than her admirer, and often the manager of the castle. She was usually married, though not to her knight, for courtly love had to be freely given. The love which the lady evoked transported the lover—"when I see her, when I consider her eyes, her face, her complexion, I tremble with fear like a leaf in the wind; a child has more sense than I retain in the violence of my transports,"[26] Bernard de Ventadour sang. It also tamed and refined him. At court—in the presence of ladies, at least—the courtly knight was encouraged to clean his teeth and nails, to wear stylish clothes, to be amusing and clever, and to sing and recite poetry rather than argue and brawl.

More important, however, courtly love for a lady made the knight braver. Sang Guileme de Cabestanh, "For the ladies always make valiant the most cowardly and the wickedest felons; for however free and gracious a man is, if he did not love a lady, he would be disagreeable to everyone."[27]

Both courtly and Christian chivalry agreed that knights were duty-bound to protect ladies. But Christian chivalry, inasmuch as it was Christian, had inherited Saint Paul's view of the matter: woman were the source of the temptations of the flesh; sex was licit only in marriage, which could not be broken, and then only for the purposes of procreation (or to save one partner from the even more damning sin of illicit sex).

This view ran directly counter to the practical pagan morals of the old knights, who married for political reasons and seemed to have no moral compunctions about producing numerous bastards with their concubines. While women were definitely subservient to men in chivalric society, they were not without certain rights and strengths. Women were not sequestered in harems, as they were in parts of the East. They inherited property and ran the feudal domains; and when their husbands were absent, they directed the defense of the castle in case of siege. Some, like Eleanor of Aquitaine, accompanied their husbands on Crusades. And we know of at least one lady, Sigelgaita of Salerno, who bore arms with her Norman husband in Italy at a siege in 1081.[28]

The lady in courtly chivalry preferred to witness knights joust in her honor rather than to bear her own arms. But she was hardly without power. As the object of the knight's devotion, the lady was the source of the courtly knight's power. All his prowess came from her. She usurped the place of both the feudal lord and the Christian Lord. It was in order to win her admiration that a knight fought bravely in war and demonstrated his prowess in tournaments and jousts.

The true nature of this love continues to puzzle historians, who are at a loss to separate literary conceits and fashion from the real behavior of men and women hidden safely from view within closed chambers. On one hand, courtly love is celebrated as unattainable, as a love that proves its fidelity by its ability to endure and even relish longing, pain, separation. On the other hand, there are times when courtly love leads to an adulterous affair. Meanwhile, there is the whole range of in-between possibilities—all the things lovers can do without crossing the line of consummation, such as sleeping chastely together with a sword between them, à la Tristan and Isolde.

There is a huge scholarly industry devoted to solving the riddle. But before we consider any of this, we would do well to return to the sociology of the situation, as given by Georges Duby. Duby reminds us that most of the women considered suitable for the young knights were already married: "And when these women enjoyed adulterous love, their partners were not youths but married men. What, therefore, the love songs of the second half of the twelfth century suggest is a new kind of erotic relationship. . . . For the triangle 'husband-wife-married lover,' the poets of the 'youthful band' wanted to substitute another triangle, 'husband-lady-young courtly servant.' They wanted to break into the erotic circle to the advantage of 'youth.' "[29]

Following this line, we might add a further possibility. The existence of the *juvenes* depended, of course, on the existence of seniors, who were often married to women much younger then themselves. But the average life span of a knight, who was exposed to the dangers both of martial exploits and the indulgence of constant feasting, was no more than fifty. The unattainable lady of an older lord, then, who was courted from a chaste distance, may have been wooed with an eye to her availability in a not-so-distant future. Courtly love was, in short, a code aimed at what the anthropologists call hypergamy—the practice of marrying up.

This "sociology" of courtly love, while it may well lay bare the structure beneath the phenomena, does not tell us why courtly love burst forth in its particular form when and where it did—namely in the heartland of chivalry, the south of France, at the beginning of the twelfth century.

Perhaps the most intriguing solution is supplied by Denis de Rougement's masterpiece of historical detective work, *Love in the Western World.* De Rougemont makes a compelling case that courtly love was the result of "one of the most extraordinary confluences of history."[30] He identifies two main streams that flowed into the idea of courtly love:

the erotic mystical poetry of the Arab Sufis (itself a product of Neo-Platonism and Persian Manichaeanism) and the Gnostic heresy of the Cathars. They, too, though Christians, were Manichaeans who believed at once in the absolute purity and love of the world of the spirit, and the absolute evil and hopelessness of a material world in which the soul, seduced by Lucifer, has become imprisoned.

The Cathar communities were divided into two main groups: the *parfait*, or the perfect or good men, and the lay community. The perfects lived a life of apostolic purity and chastity. They did not eat meat (though fish was permitted) and they underwent periodic forty-day fasts. The rest of the believers, however, were permitted to marry and perhaps indulge in licentious behavior, for—so they reasoned—since the body could not be redeemed, neither could its sin.

Because so many of their records went up in the fires of the Crusades and the Inquisition, and because some of their practices may have been secret, the Cathars provide a particularly rich field for conjecture. They saw themselves not as heretics, but as the true Christians, and the *parfaits* of good men as the legitimate representatives of the apostolic life. Others were scandalized by the degree of equality, both of class and of sex, and accused them of sexual license; still others (especially more recently) have seen them as the repositories of hidden Eastern or Gnostic mysteries; while some believe that the Holy Grail was kept at Montsegurt and buried before the final assault. The list goes on and on.

With this caveat, it seems fair enough to investigate one more possibility. Cathar women were in a much better position than their Catholic counterparts—they could, for example, become perfects. The lady sung of by the troubadours was higher than any Lord. The cult of Mary, which some scholars consider to be a Catholic cooption of Cathar spiritually, came to prominence during this period. It is admittedly conjectural, but not altogether fanciful, to recognize that the Cathars represented or opened the way for the return of the feminine aspect that—to refer back to Marija Gimbutas's work—had been prevalent before the Indo-European invasions brought the masculine gods and patriarchal social structure to Europe.

This impression is born out by the investigations of the French historian Emmanuel Le Roy Ladurie, whose close examination of Inquisition records in the Cathar village of Montaillou has yielded the best record of what ordinary Cathar men and women actually believed. "The atmosphere of mental contestation created by the goodmen undermined the Catholic monopoly and opened the way to the emergence of pre-existing folklore elements, pre-Christian, non-Christian or anti-Christian," he writes in *Montaillou.* "Undoubtedly, in the Pays d'Aillon and upper Ariege in general, the Virgin Mother was of the earth. Fertility cults both human and agricultural, which were at first sight conspicuous by their absence, were unspoken rather than non-existent, and, in fact, incorporated in the cult of the Virgin." Feast days, he says, "often involved some folkloric or even pagan elements."[31]

The connection of the troubadours with all this is also a matter of conjecture. One school goes so far as to read their poetry as coded Catharism; de Rougemont argues that Catharism may have provided the inspiration for the troubadours' poetry, but need not have been a constant element or even interest of subsequent troubadours. At the very least, we can say that the position of woman in troubadour poetry and in courtly love reflects the generally higher position of women in both the south and the Cathar Church. Whatever their actual connection might be, the poetry of the troubadours, the chivalry of courtly love, and the Cathar heresy all sprang from and flourished in the fertile soil of the south at the same time.

It was the Cathars, however, who attracted the attention of the Church. The same Bernard of Clairvaux who had given the Templars their rule opened the campaign by preaching against the Cathars in the south in 1145. Despite his immense prestige and eloquence, he had very little success. Dominican missionaries were just as ineffective. In 1207, Saint Dominic, father of the Inquisition, had to listen to "heretics," has he called the Cathars, argue that the "the Roman Church is the devil's church and her doctrines are those of demons, she is the Babylon whom St. John called the mother of fornication and abomination, drunk with the blood of Saints and martyrs . . . neither Christ nor the apostles has established the existing order of the mass." Even more frustrating, perhaps, was the fact that the judges—two knights and two burgesses—decided to leave it to the listeners to make up their own minds.[32]

The decision to wage a holy war against the Cathars (known as the Albigensian Crusade) was made by Pope Innocent III in 1209. This turning of holy war against "heretics" (and Christians who were political enemies of the Church) was to have grave consequences for both the Roman Church and the western secular state. Joseph R. Strayer, the author of a standard work on the subject, considers the holy wars against heretics "to be one of the worst mistakes in the history of the papacy." Politically, it resulted in crystallizing opposition to the papacy in both Italy and Germany, where it set the stage for the Reformation. Spiritually, it cut the Church off from intellectual dialogue or internal growth or reform. The Church not only killed heretics, but it also killed its own source of creativity and renewal.

The holy war against heretics also affected secular governments, who learned, as Strayer also notes, "how easy it was to suppress opposition to their policies." There were hundreds of thousands of Cathars in the south, and hundreds of thousands of sympathizers. Yet they were destroyed by a relatively small number of well-organized and dedicated men using force, torture, "and a nicely graded set of penalties that encouraged the weak to betray the strong in return for immunity or token punishments. . . . Modern totalitarian governments have made few innovations," concludes Strayer; "they have simply been more efficient."[33]

Pope Innocent did everything he could to make the Albigensian Crusade as attractive as possible. Crusaders to the Holy Land were costly and time-consuming—it was not unusual for men to be away for years—as well as dangerous. The Albigensian Crusade, on the other hand, required very little travel, and Crusaders only had to serve for forty days. And yet Crusaders against the Cathars enjoyed all the advantages of Crusaders in the Holy Land. They were granted dispensation of all their sins, the right to plunder, and the right to acquire fiefs from "disobedient" lords. The holy war against the heretics had all of the advantages, and few of the disadvantages, of a holy war against the Saracens.

The Crusade began with a siege of the city of Beziers. When a group of citizens made a sortie against them, they were able to force their way through a gate. The massacre that followed was very similar to the massacre of Jerusalem. "All were killed," reported one chronicler, "even those who took refuge in the church. Nothing could save them, neither crucifix nor altar. Women and children were killed, the clergy were killed. . . . No one escaped. . . . I do not believe that such an enormous and savage massacre took place before, even in the time of the Saracens."[34]

There were some who thought the massacre had been planned deliberately to terrorize the south into submission; if so, it was successful. A number of villages promptly capitulated, and the stronghold of Carcassone surrendered. The inhabitants were allowed to escape with their lives, but all their possessions were taken as booty. Their leader, the viscount Raymond Roger, died in captivity. Other massacres followed, however. In 1211, the fortress of Lavaur was taken. The lady of the castle, Geralda, a Cathar well known for her charity, was thrown into a well, which was then filled with stones. Four hundred Cathar perfects were burned.

The southern counterattack was launched by Count Raymond of Toulouse, who had taken refuge in England in 1216. He entered Toulouse, overpowering the small French garrison, and the citizens took to preparing for the inevitable siege: "Everyone began to rebuild the walls. Knights and burgesses, ladies and squires, boys and girls, great and small carried up the hewn stones singing ballads and songs." In the siege which followed, Simon de Montfort, commander of the besieging forces, was killed when a stone thrown from a catapult crushed his skull. Whatever one thinks about the place of the lady in the south, it is perhaps not without meaning that the catapult which killed the leader of the Crusade was operated, according to local legend, by the women of Beziers.

For a time, it seemed as if the southerners had won. But in 1226 a new Crusade led by Louis VIII of France set out. This one was much larger and better financed than any of the previous Crusades. The final battle was fought for the mountain stronghold of Montseguir in the Pyrenees, the administrative center of the Cathar Church. The siege went on for a year. When Montseguir finally surrendered, the inhabitants were not killed, and the perfects were given the choice of being burned or recanting. Two hundred men and women perfects demonstrated the depth of their faith by entering the flames calmly and joyfully.

The Crusaders were followed by the Inquisitors, who went about their work with bureaucratic thoroughness. An Inquisitor's handbook was compiled. Suspected heretics were questioned and tortured with great patience. The names of other heretics were gathered by making it clear that only those who revealed the names of other heretics could be considered to have truly repented. Heretics who cooperated fully and quickly were let off lightly; they might only have to perform penances, such as going on pilgrimages; others might have to wear a yellow cross on their cloaks; those who resisted had their property confiscated and were imprisoned, often for life. Those who did not cooperate or who refused to recant—and there were many of these among the Cathar perfects—were "relaxed to the secular arm," a euphemism for being burned at the stake. In this way, the priests of the Church managed to avoid the shedding of blood.

△△ V I I I △△

But heresies cannot be so easily expunged. The Cathars and the troubadours who managed to escape the wrath of the Church went underground and scattered throughout Europe. The tales and spirit of courtly love, meanwhile, found a refuge in Poitiers, at the court of the pleasure-loving and free-spirited Eleanor of Aquitaine, where Andeas Capellanus composed the *Art of Courtly Love*. When Eleanor divorced Louis of France to marry Henry II of England, she moved her court with her across the channel. At the same time bilingual Breton poets had brought Celtic tales of the hero King Arthur to the French courts. As a result, both the chivalry of courtly love and its rival, Christian chivalry, found expression in the great cycles of romances and tales which developed around the figure of Arthur, king of Britain, and the knights gathered around his Round Table. Arthur himself was most likely a fifth or sixth century hero of the Romanized British resistance to the Saxons, while the stories that surround him seem to be recastings and transformations of old Celtic myths. In any case, Arthur and his knights were supplied with all the trappings and rhetoric of medieval chivalry.

Arthur is the ideal warrior-king who has gathered an international elite of the best knights of the realm to sit at his Round Table (a detail that first appears in the Wace's French translation of Mounmouth in 1155). The Round Table is both practical, in that it prevents quarrels over precedence, and symbolic, in that it represents the round earth and sky.

The adventures of Arthur's knights encompass the whole range of chivalry. The pre-Christian heroes of the Celts form the basis. Merlin the trickster harks back to Druid priests. The Lady of the Lake who presents Arthur with his magic sword, Excalibur, reminds us of the ancient Celtic goddesses and of the warrior-women, like Saceth, who instructed many of the Irish heroes.

Courtly love was represented by Lancelot's love for Guinevere, who was none other than the wife of his Lord, King Arthur. (Her independence recalls the Celtic warrior-queens who took lovers.) In any case, Lancelot's version of courtly love went well beyond the "ideal," a situation which eventually divided the knights of the Round Table.

The French Lancelot was introduced to the Arthurian world by Chretien de Troyes, who told his story—so he said—at the request of Marie de Champagne, the daughter of Eleanor of Aquitaine, in *La Chevalier de la Charette (The Knight of the Cart)*. In Chretien's twelfth century tale, Lancelot has ridden off to rescue Guinevere, when his horse dies. Offered a ride in a cart, he hesitates for just a moment, an understandable reaction for a proud class-conscious knight but not for a courtly lover. After a series of adventures, which include crossing a bridge made of swords, Lancelot reaches the castle where Guinevere has been taken, and faces her abductor. But he is so transfixed by the sight of his lady watching from a window that he cannot keep his mind on the fight or his eye on his opponent. Luckily, however, one of Guinevere's maids suggests that he face her while fighting, and as soon as he does so he is so filled with strength that he easily defeats his opponent. Guinevere withholds her love, however, because he had hesitated to ride in the cart, and she will not forgive him until he demonstrates his loyalty by deliberately losing a subsequent tournament. Only then does she relent and allow him to win both her and the tournament.

Christian chivalry, on the other hand, was represented by the quest for the Holy Grail, the wonder-working chalice which had held Christ's wine at the Last Supper and his blood at the Crucifixion. There were a number of Grail stories, the earliest of which was Chretien's *Conte del Grail (Grail Quest),* in which the foolish and literal-minded Parsifal, told that "knights do not ask too many questions," neglects to ask the one crucial question which would have healed the wounded Grail-keeper and restored the Waste Land. Chretien's story was left unfinished, but the authors of the French *Quest del Saint Graal (The Quest for the Holy Grail)* finished the tale by introducing a new character, Galahad, supposedly the son of Lancelot and the Grail-keeper's daughter. (Lancelot had been tricked—that is, drugged—into thinking she was Guinevere.) In the story, Sir Galahad is the perfect Christian knight. He is a virgin raised in a nunnery, equal in prowess and purity, "greater in virtue and knightly skills than all the fellowship of the Round Table." When he appears at the Round Table, the Grail too appears, and all the knights pledge themselves to go on a quest to find it.

Here, then, the circle closes. With the quest for the Grail, the Round Table is revealed as the table of the Last Supper, the knights of the Round Table become the knights of Christ. The Grail knights' quest includes both "real" and symbolic adventures, but the end of the quest is a purely spiritual experience available only to three of the most pure knights. Reaching the Grail castle, Galahad, Lancelot, and Bors see Christ "appear from out of the Holy Vessel, unclothed, and bleeding from his hand and feet and side," and receive the host from Him, and so they are "filled with the grace of the holy Vessel."[35]

But only Galahad, the virginal knight of perfect purity, is finally permitted to look into the Holy Vessel. "He had but glanced within when a violent trembling seized his mortal flesh at the contemplation of the spiritual mysteries." Lifting up his hands to heaven, he gives thanks that he can at last "see revealed what tongue could not relate nor heart conceive. Here is the source of valour undismayed, the spring-head of endeavour; here I see the wonder that passes every other."[36]

But no mortal man can see the face of God and live. Galahad is too pure and perfect for this world, and he therefore dies as soon as he succeeds in his quest, "borne to heaven by angels making jubilation and blessing the name of Our Lord." The Grail, as well, leaves this world, since "the inhabitants of this country neither serve nor honour it as its due . . . despite the fact that they have ever been sustained by the grace of the Holy Vessel."[37]

The fulfillment of the quest and the withdrawal of the Grail is followed shortly by the departure of King Arthur as well. Wounded in his last battle against the usurper Mordraid, he returns his sword to the Lady of the Lake and departs to the isle of Avalon, "where his wounds would be cured" to return sometime in the future.

△△ IX △△

The English kings made use of Arthur to support their own positions, as well as to bolster the new English nationalism. Edward I established a Round Table for his knights to sit at after they fought in the tournaments he loved. On Eastertide of 1271, Edward had a painted coffin opened inside the chapel of St. Mary in Glastonbury, where it had been found. Believing that it held the remains of Arthur and Guinevere, he housed them in a specially built marble monument.

In 1343, Edward III swore in the Chapel of St. George in Windsor that "he would follow in the footsteps of King Arthur and create a Round Table for his knights," and established the Order of the Garter in the restored Windsor Castle, "the which was begun by King Arthur; and there first began the Table Round, whereby sprang the fame of so many noble knights throughout all the world."[38]

Edward III's admiration for Arthurian chivalry did not prevent him from taking certain unchivalric steps to his fight for the French crown, which he claimed through his mother. Edward chivalrously challenged the French King Philip to a trial by battle, either in single combat between the two kings or between a hundred of their best knights. But he used the time gained by his challenge to raise and move into position a very un-Arthurian army. It included large numbers of paid soldiers who could be counted on to spend more than the usual forty-day service required of knights to lay siege to towns, as well as many criminals, who may have constituted as much as a tenth of the force. But most important of all, his force included large numbers of Welsh longbowmen.

In fact, Edward opened his campaign with the most unchivalrous of tactics, a *chevauchée,* or raid aimed at forcing the French to meet his army in the field by devastating the countryside. Edward's army lived off the land, taking food where they found it. They plundered and robbed, burning villages and churches, and hundreds of noncombatants, including priests and women and children, were killed; meanwhile, thousands fled to fortified towns.

The tactics did indeed force the French to meet Edward. The climactic battle took place at Crécy in 1346. Instead of leading the battle, like the old warrior-kings, Edward directed his army from the top of a windmill. He placed the longbowmen on the flanks of the dismounted knights and waited.

The French were surprised to find the English, whom they had been pursuing, arrayed for battle. Philip decided to postpone battle until the next day, to rest his troops and wait for his reserve infantry and cavalry to arrive. But the French knights were impatient. "They that were foremost tarried," Froissart wrote in his *Chronicles,* "but they that were behind would not tarry, but rode forth, and said how they would in no wise abide till they were as far forward as the foremost: and when they before saw them come on behind, then they rode forward again, so that the king nor his marshalls could not rule them. So they rode without order or good array, till they came in sight of their enemies," at which point "they took their swords and cried, 'Down with them, let us slay them all!' "[39]

The French king, realizing he had lost control of his knights, sent the Genoese crossbowmen in. The Genoese were mercenaries, and they at first hung back with the excuse that they were too fatigued from the day's march to fight. When finally they did advance, their bolts fell short. The English longbows, which had a longer range and the advantage of a downhill flight, decimated the crossbowmen, who beat a hasty retreat.

The proudest leading French knights took this as a signal to charge directly into the retreating mercenaries, crying, "Away with these faint-hearted rabble." Tangled up in their own retreating men, the French horses fell in the hail of English arrows, and the knights fell with them. So it went with a dozen or so reckless, disorganized charges. To make matters worse, those knights who did reach the English lines ignored the longbowmen (who were doing the most harm) because they were mere commoners, and concentrated on the dismounted English knights, since they, at least, could win the French knights honor—and ransom.

The English, meanwhile, held their defensive lines. Even when envoys from Edward's son, the Black Prince, arrived to ask for help, Edward refused to break the English lines. "Is my son dead or hurt or on the field felled?" the king asked. When told that he was only "sorely pressed," Edward made his famous reply, "Tell him this day to win his spurs."

And so he did. The day after the battle, two knights and three heralds were sent to count the dead. They reported to Edward that they had seen "eleven great princes dead, fourscore banners, twelve hundred knights, and more than thirty thousand other."

Philip escaped with only four lords in attendance. Edward instructed that "no man should be proud or make boast, but every man humbly to thank God."[40]

The same drama would be repeated, in different forms, for the next hundred years. Its cause was the knight's "tragic dilemma," which historian A. T. Hatto identified in 1940 in his classic article, "Archery and Chivalry: A Noble Prejudice." According to Hatto, the "tragic dilemma in the knightly caste with regard to archery" was this: "as military specialists they could either perfect a weapon which, if turned against them, inevitably threatened their cavalry and hence their supremacy as a caste, or they could repress its development to the utmost of their powers and in their neglect of it lay themselves open to those who succeeded in defying their repressive measures."[41]

At bottom, of course, this "noble prejudice" was inextricably related to all the other prejudices of the knight—"their enthusiasm for quick and showy results, their lack of self-control, and their passion for the charge," to quote Hatto again. But the knight was also the victim of his own "nobility"—won, we may remember, sometime in the eleventh century—which brought with it an arrogant disdain and scorn for the common foot soldier, no matter how great his skill with bow or pike.

Finally, we might suggest, he was victimized by his regard for his own safety, by his preference for defense over offense. No knight could add archery to his arsenal, for archers wearing mail, let alone plate, were at a disadvantage.

It was not archery that was the problem, but the knight, for sometimes the defending infantry would be Scottish spearmen, or Swiss pikemen. Nor was it that the knight was suddenly rendered useless. He could still be a deadly and effective force, but only when he submitted—against all his training, instincts, and prejudices—to discipline, reduced to one element among others, cavalry working with infantry and archers, directed from afar by an all-seeing, nonfighting commander in a tower. No longer the individual champion, the knight was doomed to play his part in an increasingly regimented and professionalized army.

$$\wedge\!\!\wedge \quad X \quad \wedge\!\!\wedge$$

In hindsight, the victories of the combined forces of bowmen and knights at Crécy and later at Agincourt marked the beginning of the end for the knight, for he was no longer the preeminent military specialist of his society but a part of a force which had to be deployed and directed by a central commander. But chivalry was hardly dead. In 1348, Edward III commemorated his decisive victory at Crécy by instituting the Arthurian Order of the Garter he had vowed to found before his war with France. According to legend, the order derived its name in true chivalrous fashion from an incident at a ball held in Calais. Edward was dancing with Joan of Salisbury when her garter fell to the floor. The chivalrous and gallant Edward quickly picked it up and placed it above his own knee. Noticing the shocked smiles of the onlookers, he is said to have remarked, *"Honi soit qui mal y pense"*— "Evil to him who thinks it evil"—which became the motto of the Order of the Garter.

The first members of the order were made up of the twelve knights chosen to represent the king and the twelve knights chosen to represent his son, the Black Prince, at the jousts at Eltham in 1348. Limited to twenty-six knights (two groups of twelve, plus the king and his son), the order was both secular and nationalistic, "a Society, Fellowship, College of Knights in which all were equal to represent how they aught to be united in all Chances and various Turns of Fortune; copartners both in Peace and War, assistent to one another in all serious and dangerous Exploits; and through the course of their lives to shew

Fidelity and Friendliness the one towards the other."[42]

In fact, the chivalric code underwent something of a revival in the fourteenth century. This paradox can perhaps be explained by the idea that the code of chivalry served to reinforce the solidarity of the knights as an elite international military caste, with their own values and code. The founding of the Order of the Garter was in fact followed by the Burgundian Order of the Golden Fleece and the French Order of the Star.

Tournaments and jousts continued to reinforce the values of the international military elite. In 1383 the English granted safe conduct to all foreign knights attending jousts at Windsor; even captive French knights competed. These tournaments tended now to take the form of jousts in which two individual knights, their horses separated by a wooden barrier, charged at each other. The object was to hit your opponent's shield straight on, splintering your lance; his fall brought instant victory. Armor had by now changed from mail to plate, while helmets were huge, visored and beaked, the better to deflect the lance.

The tournaments of the twelfth century had been mock wars; and like wars they had been sources of revenue. But the jousts of the fourteenth century were much more occasions of display, pitting individual knights against one another before the watchful eyes of an admiring audience, many of whom were ladies. There was thus an increase in pageantry, splendor, and finery. Hidden behind his visor, the knight was adorned with the signs and symbols of heraldry—with the colors of his house, his lady, or his lord. He fought now more for honor and display—armed like a stag or ram, plumed like a bird of paradise—than for booty or ransom.

Still, charging straight at another knight was dangerous, even if the contestants were armored, shielded, and separated by a wooden barrier. In 1532, the king of France was killed when his opponent neglected to lower his lance after it had shattered. As they galloped past each other, a splinter entered the visor of the king's helmet and killed him. The accident marked the end of the French tournaments.

The final blow, of course, came from the gun, which appeared—seemingly out of nowhere—in Europe and China in the middle of the fourteenth century. The earliest depictions, in Europe in 1326 and China in 1332, were nearly identical: a pipe holding a great bolt of an arrow. For quite a while the gun was ineffective, inefficient, impossible to use in rain, hard to load, aim, and light. Some took two men, and all, the jest went, took a man with at least three hands. But there was something about them—the thunderous explosion, lightning flash, and thrilling release of pent-up power—that made men feel that *they* now held the thunderbolt hammer of Thor, Zeus, Indra, and all the old stormy war gods.

So experiments continued. By the fifteenth century gunsmiths, adopting the metal casting techniques of Church bellmakers, had produced brass and cast-iron cannons; gunpowder was more powerful and reliable. By the beginning of the sixteenth century the musket or harquebus came into use. It took longer to fire than a crossbow, and it could not be used in the rain, but it still had certain advantages. It could shoot farther—250 feet compared to the crossbow's 150—and most important, its bullet could penetrate the heaviest armor. Accuracy was improved by resting the gun on a fork. It was used by the French in Italy in 1495, by the Swiss in 1499, and in a battle between the French and the Spanish in 1503.

There was resistance, for the gun—even more than the bow—threatened the presumptions of the knights. As one critic complained, "Hardly a man and bravery in war are of use any longer because guile, betrayal, treachery together with the gruesome artillery pieces have taken over so much that fencing, fighting, hitting and armor, weapons, physical strength or courage are not of much use any more. Because it happens often and frequently that a virile brave hero is killed by some forsaken knave with a gun."[43]

The knights themselves could disdain to use the new weapons. But they did not have the power to make others do so. In 1523, the English Parliament had limited gun ownership to those who had incomes of more than a hundred pounds a year. But Europe was now a nest of competing nations, and the pressure to use a new and powerful offensive weapon was too strong to be resisted. When King Henry VIII declared war on France in 1543, he lifted the ban so that "his loving subjects" could be "practiced and exercised in the feat of shooting handguns and hackbuts . . . for the anoyence of his majesty's enemies in times of war and hostility."[44]

∆∆ XI ∆∆

The knights thus became obsolete, both as warriors and as a class. Kingdoms replaced fiefs and baronies; nation-states replaced kingdoms. The Holy Catholic Church lost its claim as the only universal Church.

And the chivalric knight's lady, whoever she might have been, descended from her exalted distant heights.

But the image remains—the knight in shining armor, gleaming, protected, hidden, isolated behind helm; yet gallant, courtly, protector of the weak, of maidens, orphans, widows; dedicated to God, devoted to the distant lady, never turning back from the challenge of a joust, brave and gentle, proud and courteous, forever riding off in search of adventure, in quest of Holy Grail or holy war.

The idea of the Crusade that pits the pure against the evil in a drama of redemption and death is still our controlling image for dealing with difficult problems of otherness and conflict. We have crusades against drugs, crime, and poverty, among other things. This image (like that of war in general) may have the advantage of rousing a dulled and apathetic "public" to pay attention to the news, if nothing else. But it carries the deeper disadvantage of fogging the causes of a problem by reducing its complexities to simple demons. The virtues of chivalry are various enough for anyone to find much of value, especially in what a late nineteenth century writer calls its "purified and ideal form." But neither the practice nor the principle of holy war is one of them.

And so it is that soldiers are urged to fight for "God and country" and the "officer and gentleman" has replaced the courteous knight, while ideological warfare has replaced holy war, at least in some quarters. But the enemy is still the infidel, the other, the projection of all evil against which the noble knight fights bravely. And even when we are momentarily deprived of our enemy—of the Russians, for example—it does not take long before we ride out in quest of other holy wars, while the "inner" search for the Grail beckons with an impossible other worldly demand for purity and perfection.

In fact, the chivalric code itself, in all its contradictory complexity, remains the ideal and operative code of the heirs of the Western warrior. It is, now more than ever, a heady inheritance—a dreamy and dangerous mix of power and innocence.

因寅刻く信西うけ給り諏西洞院乃五官府避捕
志く火を放川こ七三四年ハ兵伎禁却なと
あつそ三テ静證ありつふまに事ら乱せ
弟く禁中を宣中ず軍兵もちく大里こ
ちけも ゐつまね ゑふか〜と貴賤うふこ〜あつり

THE
LIFE-GIVING
SWORD

The Samurai and Bushido

Bushido, I have found out, lies in dying.
—The Hegakure

Japan was created by a weapon. Standing in heaven, Izanagi and Izanami, the Male-who-invites and the Female-who-invites, dipped a coral-jeweled spear into the wide sea below. When they lifted the spear, four drops fell into the sea to form the four islands of Japan. The spear then became the center pole of the house of the gods on earth.

The two gods also created the sun goddess Amaterasu, whose grandson, Jimmu Tenno, the first emperor of Japan, descended from heaven to the top of Mount Takachiko with the Imperial Regalia of the Jewel, Mirror, and Sword on the eleventh of February, 660 B.C.

In fact, archaeologists say this is the date, give or take a few hundred years, on which the people we now know as the Japanese first arrived, speaking a unique language, either from the Asian mainland, or Korea, or the South Pacific, or some combination of these. Composed of seven major clans, riding small ponies, they gradually drove the aboriginal bear-worshiping Ainu to the north. Eventually the strongest of these clans, the Yamato, established their chieftain as the direct descendant of the sun goddess, and as *tenno* or emperor.

The Imperial House established a capital at Nara in 826; in 976, they moved to Heian-kyo, present-day Kyoto. Coming under the influence of Chinese culture, the country (or at least those who lived in the capital) experienced an unprecedented age of peace and tranquility. Courtiers studied the abstruse Buddhist philosophy of the Tendai school and performed esoteric Shingon rituals; they wrote love poems filled with allusions to Chinese verses; they held cherry-blossom and moon-viewing parties; they wore embroidered silk robes; they powdered their faces white, painting on thick black eyebrows and blackening their teeth for contrast; they played the bamboo flute and the koto; and they hardly ever removed their swords from their jeweled scabbards, except to polish them. For two hundred years there were no executions, the severest punishment being exile or banishment to the provinces.

In the seventh century the emperor reformed the whole country along Chinese lines, giving each farmer a plot of rice land. In return, the farmer was to supply the Imperial House with a rice tax and periodic military service. The Taisho Reform, as it was called, turned out to be singularly unsuccessful, for the court soon allowed a number of exemptions—temple lands and newly cleared lands which had been won in the north by warriors displacing the aboriginal Ainu. In addition, young princes and other nobility, sent out to guard court and temple lands or to fight against bandits, rebels, or pirates, began to lose touch with the capital and joined forces with the old clan chieftains.

It was in the provinces, therefore, that the ancient virtues of the old clan warriors were maintained. The first of these was loyalty to the clan and its chieftain; the second was an aggressive and reckless valor which led the warrior to attack with no thought of retreat—"to face the flying arrows and never turn thy back towards them," as on old saying went. Taken together, these two—absolute loyalty to the clan and reckless bravery in the face of death—created the samurai, a warrior who would willingly die for his clan or lord. As early as the eighth century, a warrior-poet's willingness to sacrifice his life for his lord (the emperor himself, in this case) was recorded in the *Manyoshu (The Hundred Thousand Verses)*: "When I go to the seas, a corpse soaked with water. When I go to the mountains, a corpse covered with grass. I will die beside the Sovereign Lord without regard for myself."[1]

In the first years of the twelfth century—1102, to be exact—two of the most powerful of the provincial warrior clans—the Taira and the Minamoto—were drawn into a succession dispute in the capital. Two rival factions of the Fujiwara regents who had gained control of the Imperial House through marriage and intrigue sought help from the provincial warriors of the Tairas and the Minamotos. The result was not quite what the courtiers had expected, for the victorious Tairas replaced the Fujiwaras in the capital. Twenty years later, the Minamotos rose in revolt, with the backing of an imperial prince who had been passed over in yet another succession dispute.

The samurai who fought in the war between the Taira and the Minamoto never turned back from battle. But they also possessed—and this is one of the samurai's unique characteristics—a highly refined aesthetic sense. Samurai wrote poems before they died, or stopped in the middle of battle to cut a bamboo to use as a flower vase in the tearoom, and their favorite instrument was neither the drum nor the trumpet but the melancholy bamboo flute. Something of the samurai's sense of beauty can be seen in the splendor of his battle dress. The Taira samurai Ashikaga no Tadatsuna, for example (as the thirteenth century *Tale of the Heike* tells us),

> wore a lattice-patterned orange brocade battle robe and over it armor laced with red leather. From the crown of his helmet curved two long ox horns, and the straps were tied tightly under his chin. In the sash around his waist was a gold studded sword, and in the quiver on his back were arrows with black and white spotted hawk feathers. He gripped a bow bound thickly with lacquered rattan and rode a dapple grey. His saddle was of gold and stamped with his crest: an owl on an oak bow.[2]

Ashikaga's elaborate dress also represented, however, the samurai's pride in his ancestral lineage. Thus the young warrior, the *Heike* continues, rose in his stirrups and

> cried out in a thunderous voice, "Men in the distance, hear—hear me! Men near at hand—behold me! I am Matataro Tadatsuna, aged seventeen, the son of Ashikaga no Taro Toshitsuna, tenth-generation descendent of Tawara no Tota Toshitsuna, the warrior who long ago won great fame and rewards for destroying the enemies of the em-

peror. . . . Here I stand, ready to meet any among the men of the third court rank. . . . Who dare to face me? Come forward and fight!"

The warrior who answered such a challenge had to fight with both ferocity and finesse. Tsutiji no Jomyo, for example,

> loosed twenty-three arrows in the twinkling of an eye. He killed twelve of his enemies and wounded eleven more. [Unlike knights, the samurai had no prejudice against archery.] With his long sickle-bladed halberd he mowed down five of his opponents, but when he encountered the sixth, the shaft of his halberd snapped in two. Enclosed on all sides, he wielded his sword like spider's legs, like twisted candy, then in the form of a cross, and finally like a somersault and waterwheel. In an instant he had cut down eight men, but when he laid a mighty stroke upon the helmet of the ninth man, the blade snapped at the hilt. . . . Now only his short sword remained. He fought as one in a death frenzy.[3]

The most important thing was to attack no matter what. Yoshitsune Minamoto, the half brother of the leader of the Minamoto, was famous for refusing to outfit his boats with "reverse oars" in the climactic naval battle of Danemara. "What an inauspicious thing to suggest at the beginning of a fight!" exclaimed Yoshitsune. "A soldier enters battle with the intention of never retreating. . . . The way to win a battle is to push forward and attack the enemy."[4]

The warrior, therefore, had two choices: he could kill or be killed. If he killed, he took his enemy's head—which he then carried back to his lord both as proof of his deed and so that he could receive the proper reward. In case *he* was killed, however, he took care great care to make himself look presentable even in death. Before going into battle, he burned incense in his helmet, so that his hair would have a pleasing scent, and he rouged his cheeks so that they would keep their color.

Unlike the knight, the samurai took no prisoners, unless he wished to show his contempt for his opponent. But neither would he allow himself to be taken. There are a number of stories about samurai spurning their opponents' offers to spare their lives and demanding to be killed. If the samurai did find himself alive and defeated, or if he was in danger of capture, he kept a third option in reserve: he could take his own life. The warrior who committed seppuku (commonly known as hara-kiri, belly-cutting) demonstrated his bravery and resolution even in defeat, since he took his life in an especially painful manner.

The *Heike* approvingly recounts the episode of Yotrimasa: "Seventy years old though he was, Yotrimasa had fought gallantly. But his left knee had been struck by an arrow, and the wound was grave. He calmly decided to kill himself." Turning to the west, the direction of the Buddhist Pure Land, he joined his palms and chanted "Hail Amida Buddha" ten times in a loud voice. Then he composed this poem:

> *Like a fossil tree*
> *Which has borne not one blossom*
> *Sad has been my life . . .*

"Having spoken these lines, he thrust the point of his sword into his belly, bowed his face to the ground as the blade pierced him through, and died. No ordinary man," as the *Heike* remarks, "could compose a poem at such a moment."[5]

◭◭ I I I ◭◭

In the end, the Minamotos won the war. But Yoritomo, the leader of the Minamotos, did not move to Kyoto, as the Taira had done. Instead, Yoritomo established his own capital in Kamakura, setting up the *bakufu* (literally "tent" or camp government) far from the corrupting influence of the court.

Though Yoritomo and the *bakufu* held the real power, he did not attempt set up a new dynasty, like so many victorious Chinese generals, but insisted that he governed in the name of the emperor. The emperor, for his part, granted Yoritomo the office of *sei-i tai-shogun*, the "Great General Who Subdues the Barbarians." The title had been used before, though always as a temporary military commission to be returned to the crown after the military crisis had passed. But Yoritomo succeeded in making the office both permanent and hereditary. In doing so, he founded a shogunate—a government of the warriors, by the warriors, and for the warriors—which would rule Japan for the next seven hundred years.

The founding of the shogunate was an important step in the development of Bushido, the code of the warrior. Yoritomo reaffirmed the basic martial ethic of the samurai in the traditional way by rewarding the bravest samurai with land taken from the defeated Taira. But he broadened the definition of loyalty to more accurately reflect the samurai's new role, as well as his own.

"Samurai warriors should take responsibility for safeguarding the Ruler and the country in the same devoted way as Buddhist priests obey the Buddha's precepts," the new shogun proclaimed. "Seeing that the country is now under the civil and military rule of the Kamakura shogun, all the shogun's retainers, irrespective of the relative extent of the fiefs granted to them, should serve their supreme lord with the uniform spirit of devotion and at any moment be prepared to lay down their lives in repayment of the favours received. They should not regard their lives as their own."[6]

Yoritomo thus strengthened his position, while weakening the court's. But he had no intention of interfering with the traditional clan loyalty that was the very foundation of Japanese society. Once, when a samurai killed his own lord and offered the head to Yoritomo, Yoritomo explained that "anyone who is so unprincipled as to harbor treacherous intentions against his own hereditary lord is not deserving of an award," and had *him* beheaded.[7]

Finally, Yoritomo encouraged the old samurai virtue of frugality. This humble virtue, so unlike the largesse of the knights, had its origins in the limited amount of land which was available for rice cultivation. Living in an agrarian economy that amounted to a steady-state system, the virtue of thriving within set limits had taken hold of the rural samurai class very early.

When the samurai took control of the government, however, they were in danger of succumbing to the ostentation and luxury of the court. It therefore became necessary to reinforce the virtues of frugality and simplicity. The first shogun was very clear about it. Once, a retainer appeared before him wearing an expensive, fashionable, many-layered skirt of expensive silks; the shogun borrowed the man's sword and cut the skirt off. "You are a very gifted man, but why are you not more thrifty and simple," he scolded. "You should use your wealth to support your retainers, who will then be enjoined to perform acts of loyalty."[8]

◮◮ IV ◮◮

Yoritomo was succeeded by his two sons, though they proved unequal to their father. The *bakufu*, however, kept the shogunate in power, while Yoritomo's wife, the so-called "Nun-Shogun," ruled from the behind the scenes. She then passed on power to the regents of her own Hojo family. It was during this period of relative stability that Kamakura samurai began to study with the Chinese Zen masters who greatly influenced the development of Bushido.

There are many reasons for the association of Zen Buddhism with the samurai. Politically, Zen offered the new samurai elite an alternative to the the earlier Tendai and Shingon Buddhism, which had been identified with the nobility, and to the militant Pure Land and Nichirin Buddhists, whose armed monasteries were considered dangerous by the shoguns. However, many samurai were adherents of Pure Land and Nichirin—and even, in the fifteenth century, of Christianity.

Yet for the samurai elite the direct and practical method of Zen training offered the warrior both spiritual and martial benefits. Zen meditation helps to develop discipline, stoicism, concentration, wakefulness, awareness, calm, and imperturbability, as well as other qualities useful for warriors. According to D. T. Suzuki, the great interpreter of Zen to the West, the samurai "finds a congenial spirit in Zen" because the

> military mind . . . is comparatively simple and not at all addicted to philosophizing. . . . Zen discipline is simple, direct, self-reliant, self-denying; its ascetic spirit goes well with the fighting spirit. The fighter is to be always single-minded with one object in mind: to fight, looking neither backward nor sidewise. To go straight forward in order to crush the enemy is all that is necessary for him. He is therefore not to be encumbered in any possible way, be it physical, emotional, or intellectual.[9]

But all these "congenial" qualities were secondary compared to the aim of Zen meditation. This was nothing less than *satori* or enlightenment. By penetrating into the actual nature of existence through the insight of meditation, the Zen Buddhist experienced the illusory nature of the self. With the death of the illusory "I" or ego, he was released "from the bondage of birth and death."

This was of great spiritual benefit. All human beings must face death, of course, but very few are willing or ready to admit that unassailable fact. Samurai, however, had no choice, since they faced death and the fear of death as a matter of course. They were therefore highly motivated to make good Zen students, since they could not deny the fear of death as easily as most people.

"The worst enemy of our life is cowardice, and how can I escape it?" the young Hojo regent, Tokimune, asked the Chinese Zen master Bukko.

"Cut off the source whence cowardice comes," Bukko responded.

"Where does it come from?"

"It comes from Tokimune himself," said Bukko.

"Above all things, cowardice is what I hate most," said Tokimune. "How can it come out of myself?"

"See how you feel when you throw overboard your cherished self known as Tokimune," said Bukko. "I will see you again when you have done that."

"How can this be done?" asked Tokimune.

"Sit cross-legged in meditation and see into the source of all your thoughts which you imagine as belonging to Tokimune."

"I have so much of worldly affairs to look after and it is difficult to find spare moments for meditation," said Tokimune.

"What ever worldly affairs you are engaged in, take them up as occasions for your inner reflection," Bukko responded, "and some day you will find out who this beloved Tokimune of yours is."[10]

When Mongol ships were sighted off the coast of Japan, Tokimune, dressed in full armor, hurried in to see his teacher.

"The great thing has come," he said.

"Can you avoid it?" Bukko asked calmly.

Tokimune stamped his feet and gave a tremendous *"Katsu!"* the great Zen shout which destroyed ignorance.

"A real lion cub, a real lion roar," said Bukko, granting his approval. "Dash straight forward and don't look round."[11]

The Mongol fleet landed first on Shigara and Iki Island. The samurai fought bravely, but were overwhelmed by the superior numbers; the force that had quickly assembled to meet them on the mainland was shocked to hear that the Mongols had not only killed the warriors who had opposed them—that was to be expected—but had also massacred old men, women, and children. This was something that samurai would never do.

Instead of waiting for reinforcements from Kamakura, the samurai defenders rode out to challenge the bravest Mongols individually. But the Mongols simply opened their close, disciplined ranks and engulfed each lone samurai. The samurai horses, moreover, were frightened by the sound of the Mongol kettledrums, while the samurai themselves did not know what to make of the "exploding rocks" the Mongols flung from their catapults. Nevertheless, the samurai rallied and fought so fiercely that the Mongols were only able to march a short distance inland when night fell. For some reason—perhaps fearing a night attack—the Mongols returned to their ships, setting fire to the coastal towns they had taken. In the morning, they sailed away.

The Japanese prepared for their return in two ways. First, the *bakufu* ordered the different lords to help build a wall along the coast. Second, Buddhist and Shinto temples held great prayer vigils and recitations.

This time, when the Mongols landed with an army of thirty thousand, the gods sent a typhoon, a *kamikaze* or divine wind, which ripped up trees and destroyed the Mongol fleet. Tokimune, however, thanked both gods and Buddhas by establishing Engakakuji monastery, installing his Zen master, Bukko, as abbot. He then held a memorial service for the souls of those who had fallen on both sides, for unlike the Crusaders, who believed that Saracens had lost their souls, Tokimune recognized that the Mongols too possessed Buddha-nature, and that warriors who fought bravely, no matter what side they were on, deserved to be honored as well.

When Tokimune himself died soon after, at the age of thirty-three, Bukko memorialized him as a bodhisattva—a Buddha who has taken a vow to postpone his own enlightenment while he works for the enlightenment of all sentient beings. "For nearly twenty years he ruled without showing joy or anger," Bukko said. "When the victory came he showed no elation; he sought for the truth of Zen and found it."[12]

△△ V △△

By the beginning of the fourteenth century, the Hojo regents were in trouble. The defense of the country against the Mongols had been a military victory but a financial defeat. Samurai expected to be rewarded, especially when they were on the winning side. When they were fighting each other, this had never been a problem: the winners had simply confiscated the lands of the losers. But the defeated Mongols had no land, and though the *bakufu* tried its best to reward warriors for their services, most of the samurai were dissatisfied. Furthermore, the *bakufu* had exhausted its resources by continuing to build coastal defenses for thirty years, preparing for a third Mongol attack which never came. And finally, the ruling Hojo regent was very different from his ancestor who had realized the truth of Zen and stopped the Mongols. Hojo Takatori was interested, it was said, only in three things: dancing, sex, and dog-fighting.

It was the perfect time for an ambitious emperor, Godaigo, to attack the upstart shoguns and restore the imperial rule. The emperor was supported by Kusunoke Masashige, who was both brave and dedicated, as well as a brilliant strategist who had studied Sun Tzu carefully. Kusunoke defended his stronghold with a handful of warriors against the combined might of the shogunate using life-sized puppets as decoys. He constructed false walls which collapsed when the enemy sought to scale them. He escaped after leading his enemies to believe that he had perished in flames. "Being the first warrior in the land to enlist himself in His Majesty's great cause," Kusunoke told his followers, "I am not likely to begrudge my life when virtue and honor are at stake. Nevertheless, it is said that in the face of danger the courageous man chooses to exercise caution and to devise stratagems."[13]

Ordered to defend an untenable position against the samurai Ashikaga Takauji's vastly superior forces at the Battle of Minato River, Kusunoke suggested an alternative plan. But when the emperor insisted, Kusunoke loyally took up his hopeless position on the beach. The battle proceeded just as Kusunoke had predicted—his small band was caught in an unprotected position on the beach between a sea and a land attack mounted by Ashikaga. Kusunoke fought valiantly until evening. Then, knowing without a doubt that the emperor's cause was lost, bleeding from no less than eleven wounds, he retreated with his brother to a small farmhouse.

When Kusunoke asked his brother for his last wish, he responded, laughing, "I should like to be reborn seven times into this world of men so that I might destroy the enemies of the Court." Kusunoke seconded the thought, and the two brothers then cut open their stomachs and finished each other off with their swords.

Kusunoke failed completely in his mission, but he became one of Japan's most popular heroes. (When the writer Yukio Mishima committed seppuku in 1970 as a protest against the Westernization of Japan, his headband bore the slogan, "Seven Lives for the Emperor.") Kusunoke's career, as Ivan Morris points out in his illuminating study of Japanese heroes, *The Nobility of Failure,* "most perfectly exemplified the Japanese heroic parabola: wholehearted effort on the behalf of a hopeless cause, leading to initial achievement and success but ending in glorious failure and a brave, poignant death."[14]

Failure thus became the occasion for the warrior to demonstrate and prove his *makoto* or sincerity. Sincerity was, of course, one of the chief Confucian virtues. For the Chinese, it denoted honesty, both with oneself and with others. But for the Japanese, sincerity was a virtue "denoting purity of motive, a rejection of self-serving, 'practical' objectives, and complete moral fastidiousness."[15]

The sincere warrior always placed means before ends. He was spontaneous instead of calculating, romantic instead of realistic, daring instead of cautious. The merits of the cause the warrior died for were of no importance. He could fight for the Taira or Minamoto, the shogun or the emperor. All that mattered was that he acted out of a selfless purity of principle.

The noble failure was thus a solitary, lone figure in a society that placed the group over the individual. The feeling evoked by this tragic hero was known as *hoganbiiki,* partiality or sympathy for the loser or underdog, and was first expressed in a poem that compared defeat to the scattering of flower blossoms.

△△ VI △△

Ashikaga, whose troops defeated Kusunoke's brave band at the Battle of Minato River, received in 1345 the office of shogun from an emperor he had placed in office. Ashikaga's victory did not bring peace, however. The Emperor Godaigo escaped with the Imperial Regalia—the Jewel, Mirror, and Sword—to the mountains in the north, where he set up his own court, thus leaving Japan with two rival courts. Ashikaga, meanwhile, moved the capital of the *bakufu* from Kamakura to Kyoto.

The proximity of the Ashikaga shoguns to the old court nobles resulted in a flowering of culture and art in the midst of the uncertainties of chronic civil war. The period of the Ashikaga shoguns saw the development of what would come to be one of the most essential principles of Bushido—the dual way of the brush and sword.

One of the most important factors in this new courtly life was the central place now occupied by the Zen monasteries and the revival of trade with China. The Japanese sent copper and silver, lacquer and fans, swords and other weapons; the Chinese sent copper coins, some of their greatest paintings, and Confucian, Taoist, and Buddhist books, as well as scholars. The Ashikaga shoguns established a university to teach the Chinese classics while the monks of the Zen monasteries promoted Confucian studies and established schools which made it possible for many people to learn to read.

The third Ashikaga shogun, Yoshimitsu, was a cultivated and dedicated aesthete, who built a villa called the Golden Pavilion (from the gold leafing on the walls). The villa was carefully set in a great garden, designed according to Chinese principles, in which every rock and tree was arranged for the fullest effect. The shogun hosted events in which courtiers, samurai, and Zen masters amused themselves with *renga* or linked-verse parties, incense-smelling contests, and cherry-blossom or maple-leaf viewing.

These arts had been adapted from the court. But the Noh drama, which Yoshimitsu was the first to promote, was a genuinely samurai art—or at least an art which owed its existence to the patronage of the samurai. Yoshimitsu was much taken by the acting of a rustic Shinto priest, Kwanami, who is usually credited with creating the Noh drama; but he was even more taken with the priest's young son, Zeami, whose writings gave full development to the Noh aesthetic. In fact, it seems that Yoshimitsu brought Zeami into the Golden Pavilion, even though he was a mere actor and provincial, as his lover. (This, in itself, was not unusual. It was common for samurai to indulge in love affairs with young pages; these relationships were generally accepted and approved, with the older warrior often acting as a mentor to the younger.)

The other major samurai art of the time was the tea ceremony, which had been developed as the embodiment of the true Zen spirit. The samurai approached the rustic grass-thatched tea house through a leaf-strewn garden path, washed his hands in a stone basin, and then removed both his swords along with his shoes. Inside, he encountered an atmosphere of *wabi,* of calm simplicity and emptiness: tatami mats, a simple flower arrangement, a scroll with a calligraphed poem in an alcove; the tea utensils, ceramic tea bowls, iron teapot, bamboo dipper; and conversation with the tea master.

But it is perhaps best not to make too much out of the simplicity of tea. We will content ourselves with a single statement by D. T. Suzuki:

> The Japanese fighting man in those old days of strife and unrest, when he most strenuously engaged in the business of war, realized that he could not go on always with nerves at the highest pitch of vigilance and that he ought to have a way of escape sometime and somewhere. The tea must have given him exactly this. He retreated for a while into a quiet corner of his Unconscious, symbolized by the tearoom no more than ten feet square. And when he came out of it, not only did he feel refreshed in mind and body, but very likely his memory was renewed of things of more permanent value than fighting.[16]

One would hope so, for he would very likely be returning to battle. There was fighting in the streets of the capital itself; in 1467 Kyoto burned. By 1477 the Ashikaga shoguns were without power, and the Imperial House was bankrupt—so much so that the emperor waited twenty years for his investiture and was reduced to selling samples of his calligraphy. As the sixteenth century began, the entire country was at war.

This era was characterized as *ge-koku-jo,* a phrase from the *Book of Changes* which meant "the overturning of those on top by those below." In the absence of any powerful centralized authority, the great lords and other strongmen raised armies made up of *ashigaru,* lightly armed foot soldiers; *ji-samurai,* armed farmers conscripted in times of emergency; as well as other mercenaries. Though these new fighters were no match for samurai, their effectiveness was increasing as generals learned to make use of the matchlocks which had been introduced by shipwrecked Portuguese traders in 1543.

The matchlock was, in fact, responsible for the crucial victory which a powerful upstart by the name of Oda Nobunaga won against the elite Takeda cavalry in 1575. Nobunaga placed ten thousand men armed with matchlocks behind breastworks on the other side of the Taki River. The matchlocks were protected from rain by little lacquer boxes—a Japanese improvement which the Europeans never hit upon—and the matchlock men themselves were lined up in three ranks. The first rank was instructed to hold their fire until the cavalry was well within range, while the second and third ranks were to hold their fire, so that the first ranks would have a chance to reload while the second and then the third ranks fired in turn.

Just as Nobunaga had planned, the Takeda cavalry charged straight on across the shallow river, and twelve thousand of the finest Takeda samurai were cut down. Nobunaga's tactics at the Battle of Nagashino transformed warfare in the same way that the English tactics at Crécy had: by using masses of disciplined infantrymen in a defensive position against the cavalry charges of a proud warrior elite.

By the time Nobunaga was assassinated by one of his own retainers at the age of forty-eight, he had brought most of the militant monasteries and a third of Japan's warring provinces under his control. His work was completed by one of his closest allies, Toyotomi Hideyoshi, the son of a farmer.

Hideyoshi did something that no Japanese ruler had ever tried to do before: he moved to disarm the population, particularly the farmers, who had become a dangerous new force. In 1588, he posted the famous Sword-Hunt Edict throughout the land: "The farmers of the various provinces are strictly forbidden to possess long swords, short swords, bows, spears, muskets, or any other form of weapon." Hideyoshi tried to soften the blow by melting down the confiscated weapons to build a great Buddha in Kyoto—an act, he said, "by which the farmers will be saved in this life and the life to come."[17]

Hideyoshi's Sword-Hunt Edict was only the first step. Hideyoshi followed up with a series of edicts that effectively froze society in place. Those who were farmers, he declared, were to remain farmers and were not allowed to move from their farms; townspeople were to remain townspeople.

Hideyoshi's edicts placed warriors at the apex of society, but it also gave the feudal lords, the *daimyo,* control of the warriors. On one hand, warriors were granted the exclusive privilege of bearing arms. On the other hand, they could no longer farm or own land—which had been their principal reward in the past; nor could they pursue any other professions. Military men under arms as of 1590—from the lowliest porters and handlers of the dead to the most exalted mounted retainers—were forbidden to return to their former places.

Cut off from their villages or farms, they were effectively turned into wards of their local *daimyo,* who owed allegiance to Hideyoshi but maintained their independance in their own *han* (district). All the warriors registered by Hideyoshi's census were now defined solely by their subordinate relationship to their lord and their function in society. Furthermore, they themselves were divided into two main groups: the upper samurai, who could ride horses, and the lower samurai, who could not.

What, then, was the warrior's function, now that the great civil wars seemed to be over? Hideyoshi had a familiar answer. In 1591, he announced his intention to rule India, the Philippines, and China. A year later an estimated 160,000 Japanese invaded Korea. The samurai carried their traditional two swords, plus spears or bows. Nonsamurai, one quarter of the force, carried matchlocks. They reached the Korean capital in a mere eighteen days. But they were stopped and then driven back at the Yalu River by Chinese and Korean troops. Refusing to admit defeat, Hideyoshi launched a second invasion a few years later, with similar results.

As Hideyoshi's health deteriorated, he extracted pledges of loyalty to his son, Hideyori, from his five most powerful *daimyo.* His old friend Ieyasu Tokugawa was especially reassuring, it was said, vowing with tears in his eyes to defend Hideyoshi's heir. Soon after Hideyoshi's death in 1591, Ieyasu Tokugawa began quietly to gather allies. In 1596, the Battle of Seighara brought the supporters of Hideyori Hideyoshi and Ieyasu Tokugawa together in a final, bloody battle. Fighting in rain and mud, the outnumbered Tokugawas seemed at first to be in a strategically weak position. But halfway through the battle the wily old general pulled his trump card when a number of *daimyo* who were allied with Hideyori suddenly switched sides. In 1603, the emperor granted Ieyasu Tokugawa the title of shogun.

⋀⋀ V I I I ⋀⋀

Nobunaga had conquered a third of the country and brought the samurai under control. Hideyoshi had finished Nobunaga's military work, putting the samurai firmly in control of the farmers and merchants, and putting the *daimyo* in control of the samurai. Now—in order to prevent the *daimyo* from seizing power, as he had himself done—Ieyasu Tokugawa did his best to bring the *daimyo* under the control of the shogunate.

Ieyasu used Confucianism, which he made the official creed of the Tokugawa shoguns, to justify and support the rigid class structure of the Tokugawa shogunate. But unlike the Chinese Confucians, he did not open the *bakufu* bureaucracy to those who had demonstrated their merit by means of competitive examinations. Instead the Tokugawas continued to rely on family and clan, as the Japanese had always done. The higher ranks of Tokugawa society were all hereditary, though the shogun did reserve the right to occasionally raise deserving men to a higher status.

The most powerful lords, the *daimyo*, were free to govern their provinces as they saw fit, as long as they did nothing that threatened the Tokugawas. The *daimyo* who had fought with the Tokugawas were given the best *han* and positions close to the new capital of Edo (present-day Tokyo). The so-called "outside" *daimyo*, whose *han* tended to be located farther from Edo, were compelled to keep a second residence in the capital. The *daimyo* himself was required to attend the shogun's court in Edo at least once a year; his wife and heirs were required to be in residence year-round. The arrangement served two purposes. The wife and heirs served as hostages, while the expense of keeping two houses, and traveling back and forth between them with large retinues, kept the *daimyo* financially weak.

In 1645, the Tokugawas managed to crush the Shimbara Christian revolt, the last serious threat to their power. In the wake of this victory, the Tokugawas closed the country to all foreigners, with the exception of a small Dutch trading mission. In addition, they made it a crime, punishable by death, for any Japanese to leave the country.

With the establishment of peace, however despotic, the Tokugawa warriors found themselves faced with a familiar, if infrequent, problem: what to do with warriors who had neither war nor enemy to fight. Hideyoshi had answered this question by mounting an expedition against Korea and China. The Tokugawas adapted the traditional Chinese ideal of the dual way. According to *The Laws Governing the Military Households,* issued a year before Ieyasu Tokugawa's death, "From of old the rule has been to practice the arts of peace on the left and the arts of war on the right: both must be mastered."[18]

The arts of peace for the Tokugawa shogunate consisted largely of the study of Chu Hsu Confucianism, which aimed at preparing the Tokugawa samurai for his new role as an administrator. Boys at the age of seven or eight learned calligraphy and studied the Confucian classics, the Four Books, the Five Classics, and the Seven Texts. Older samurai, of course, were expected to be able to write a decent verse and to to know at least the rudiments of the tea ceremony.

The study of the arts of war began at fourteen or fifteen, the age when the pre-Tokugawa samurai had gone off to war. Boys practiced archery, horsemanship, sword, spear, swimming, jujitsu, and a number of minor martial arts as well. Education took place either in provincial clan schools or at a Tokugawa academy in the capital of Edo.

While the Tokugawas encouraged military training, they were careful to keep samurai under control. Ieyasu prohibited the ancient practice of *junshi,* by which loyal retainers followed their lord in death, on the grounds that true loyalty called for the retainer to transfer his services to his lord's successor. Duels between members of the palace guard were forbidden, and revenge matches and vendettas required permission from the authorities. (But commoners could be—and sometimes were—cut down by samurai for any "crime," including disrespect.) The prohibition which was to have the greatest effect, however, was unofficial: the Tokugawas gradually phased the gun out of existence.

Noel Perrin, author of *Giving Up the Gun,* points out that this is one of the few examples we have of a country voluntarily disarming and turning its back on a technologically superior weapon. Perrin suggests that the Japanese were able to give up their guns precisely because they were ruled by warriors who recognized that the gun took away their very reason for existence. The samurai considered the gun a lower-class weapon which took neither courage nor skill to use. While this had been precisely the attitude of the European knights, the samurai were in a much better position to influence what weapons should be used than the knights had been. For one thing, the samurai made up between seven and ten percent of the population, while the knights never made up more than one percent of the population of any European country. Furthermore, the samurai were in charge.

Then, too, the various clans of Japan were at peace, while the new European nation-states continued to fight with each other. Japan was also isolated and unthreatened by foreign invasion. In addition, the well-deserved Japanese reputation for ferocity discouraged would-be invaders. Spanish captains, for example, were ordered "not to risk the reputation of our arms and state" against Japanese warriors.[19]

Then there was the exalted position of the sword itself. Unlike a European knight's, the Japanese sword was an imperial symbol. It was a work of art and the sharpest- and strongest-bladed weapon in the world. Japanese swordsmiths purified themselves before folding the blade as many as forty thousand times.

In the end, though, guns were simply not needed for protection in Tokugawa Japan. And as long as one avoided insulting a samurai, neither were other weapons. The result, as martial arts historian Donn Draeger succinctly puts it, was that "the desire for self-protection gave way to one of self-perfection."[20] The technique of the martial art began to become transformed into a *way.*

This same transformation had taken place in China, of course, but because of the close connection between samurai and Zen, it reached its greatest heights in Japan. Kyujitsu, the technique of the bow, was transformed into kyudo, the way of the bow. And kenjitsu, the deadly art of the sword, was transformed into kendo, the way of the sword.

The way of the sword evolved from the Shinkage—or "New Shade"—school of swordsmanship. Unlike some of the older schools, the New Shade school emphasized mental training in which the swordsman kept his mind receptive and hidden—hence the "shade"— in order to become aware of his opponent's mind. In a famous episode, Kamiizumi Hidetsuna, the founder of the school, had once freed a child hostage from a sword-wielding madman by disguising himself as a Buddhist monk. Offering rice cakes to the child, he then casually tossed one to the hungry swordsman; when the man reached out for it, the unarmed Hidetsuna was on him in a flash. The monk whose robes Hidetsuna had borrowed was so impressed that he asked Hidetsuna to keep them as a symbol of his attainment of *kenzen itchi*—the oneness of swordsmanship and Zen.

Hidetsuna was also known as the inventor of the *shinai-bokken,* a practice sword made of slats of wood padded with cloth and encased in leather, which he used instead of the usual practice sword, the hard wooden *bokken,* which could break bones or even kill. In 1563 Hidetsuna used his *shinai* in a duel in which he easily defeated a *bokken*-wielding warrior by the name of Yagyu Muneyoshi. In one account, Muneyoshi had been beaten first by the master's student; when he faced the master himself he found himself unable to move when faced with Hidetsuna's unwavering mind; in another, Hidetsuna managed to take Muneyoshi's sword from him. In any case, Muneyoshi bowed with his forehead in the dust and requested to become Hidetsuna's student.

Hidetsuna stayed with Muneyoshi in the isolated Yagyu family village all winter; when he left he instructed his disciple to perfect the *muto* or "no-sword" technique. After a year of practice, Muneyoshi succeeded, and Hidetsuna bestowed the *inka* or certificate of transmission. Headed with the admonition, *You must train even harder than before,* the certificate stated, "I have transmitted to you all I have learned in this one school and the state of mind to be achieved through it, leaving out nothing."[21]

The New Shade school recognized two kinds of swords—the death-dealing sword and the life-giving sword. The ordinary swordsman used the death-dealing sword to further his own ends or to prove his prowess. The New Shade school, however, taught that the death-dealing blade should be used only for good. As Yagyu Muneyoshi wrote in the *Family-Transmitted Book on Swordsmanship,* "At times, because of one man's evil, thousands of people suffer. So you kill that one man in order to let the thousands live." When the sword was used in this way, said Muneyoshi, it became transformed. "Here, truly, the blade that deals death could be the sword that gives life."[22]

In 1594 the Tokugawa shogun summoned Yagyu Muneyoshi and his son, Munemori, to demonstrate the no-sword technique. After watching father and son, Ieyasu Tokugawa decided to try for himself. Taking a wooden sword, he brought his sword forcefully down, aiming straight for Munemori's forehead. "At just that second," according to the *Records of the New Shade School,* "Muneyoshi dodged and deflected the sword by grabbing the hilt. The very next moment saw the sword flying through the air. Holding Ieyasu with his left hand, Muneyoshi lightly hit Ieyasu's chest with his right fist. Ieyasu staggered backwards. Frowning, he said, 'Admirable! You win!' "[23]

As a result of this match, Yagyu Muneyoshi's son, Munemori, became the instructor of swordsmanship to the shogun. He was especially close to the third Tokugawa shogun. Both men, shogun and master swordsman, eventually became students of the great Zen master Takuan, who greatly influenced the development of the Zen school of swordsmanship.

In the *Divine Record of Immovable Wisdom*—a letter written to Munemori—the Zen master Takuan used the image of the ferocious muscular bodhisattva-guardian Fudo to symbolize the "immovable mind" of the Zen swordsman. This "immovable mind," wrote Takuan, was the very opposite of "the mind that stops," which was the mind of attachment, or ignorance itself. The truly immovable mind, said Takuan, was completely free. The immovable mind of Fudo did not abide anywhere:

> "Suppose you see the opponent's sword come, but do not allow your mind to stay with it," wrote Takuan. "Suppose instead, that in response to the coming sword, you do not think of striking back or form any idea of judgement, but the moment you see the sword raised you move in, your mind not tarrying, and grasp the sword. Then you should be able to wrest from the opponent the sword intended to slash you, and turn it into one with which to slash him."[24]

Takuan's teaching strongly influenced Munemori's final summing up of the teachings of the New Shade school. In this book the Yagyu swordmaster reiterated the Zen teachings on keeping a mind free from thoughts, including the thought of being free of thoughts. Practicing in this way, he said, would help the swordsman to rid his mind of the "six diseases": the desire for victory, the desire to psychologically overwhelm the opponent, the desire to rely on technique and cunning, the desire to show off, the desire to remain passive in order to await for an opening, and finally, the desire to become free of these diseases.

"After seeing all the principles, do not let any of them stay in your mind," Munemori concluded. "Slash them away, one after another, and keep your mind empty so that you may conduct yourself with a natural mind."[25]

△△ IX △△

Such was the Zen solution: individual and transcendent. But there were broader social problems. The question, as the Confucian scholar-samurai Yamaga Soko saw it, was simple: "The samurai eats food without growing it, uses utensils without manufacturing them, and profits without buying or selling. What is the justification for this?"

Soko's answer led to the first formulation of the systematic exposition of Bushido, the way of the warrior. "The business of the samurai," he wrote, "consists in reflecting on his own station in life, in discharging loyal service to his master if he has one, in deepening his fidelity in associations with friends, and, with due consideration of his own position, in devoting himself to duty above all."

According to Soko, the samurai's duty had two aspects, the martial and the social: "Outwardly he stands in physical readiness for any call to service and inwardly he strives to fulfill the Way of the lord and subject, friend and friend, father and son, older and younger brother, and husband and wife. Within his heart he keeps to the ways of peace, but without he keeps his weapons ready for use."[26]

Though the Tokugawa samurai was encouraged to follow the Confucian norms as friend, father, son, husband, and older or younger brother, his primary duty was found in the relationship between lord and subject. Devoted to service rather than self-interest, the true samurai was always ready to sacrifice his life, either for his lord or the for sake of righteousness.

The readiness of the samurai to die for his lord—or even to commit seppuku without question at the word of his lord—became a measure of his devotion to his duty. "Bushido, I have found out, lies in dying," went the opening lines of the *Hegakure*. "When confronted with two alternatives, life and death, one is to choose death without hesitation. . . . This is the essence of Bushido. If, through being prepared for death every morning and evening, the samurai expects death at any moment, Bushido will become his own, whereby he will be able to serve the lord all his life through and through without a blunder."[27]

The conscientious Tokugawa samurai had to be careful, however, not to let his readiness to die interfere with his regular duties to his lord. The samurai must not spend all day pondering death like the recluse, warned Daidoji, the author of another popular Tokugawa handbook on Bushido, for he "must on the contrary be constantly busy with his affairs both public and private."[28] The various codes of the samurai which appeared during the Tokugawa period thus exhorted the samurai-administrator not to be lazy or idle. The ideal samurai was rigidly self-controlled and stoic in adversity—if he was hungry, it was said, he would not complain but would contentedly pick his teeth with a toothpick. He avoided luxury, went to bed early, rose early, and was satisfied with simple clothes and fare. He used words sparingly. Since he lived on a fixed rice stipend, he had to live within his means. The samurai "will be very careful how he spends every penny," wrote Daidoji, but he would not be stingy, "since he spends freely where it is necessary."[29]

In this way, the Confucian writers on Bushido put forth the samurai as the exemplary Confucian warrior-administrator, a man devoted to duty, loyal, austere, temperate, self-disciplined, serene, sincere, and magnanimous, as well as courageous, discerning, and firm, and possessed of a knowledge both of the Chinese classics and the traditional martial arts—a model for all, an example whose devotion to duty would make him the respected teacher of all three classes of society.

△△ X △△

But what, in fact, did he have to teach? The model samurai of the Confucians could not solve the underlying problem: "the contradiction inherent in the existence of a numerous privileged military class throughout two hundred years of peace."[30] There were five hundred thousand of them, plus their dependents and servants, more than ten percent of the population. They could not own land (except for the *daimyo* and other high-ranking lords) or farm; they could not trade; they could not wage war; and because of the Seclusion Act they could not even gather wealth in the time-honored ways of warriors, by piracy or foreign conquest.

The amount of rice land was still fixed, and the moral example of the samurai, salutary though it may have been, did little to help the economy. In fact, many samurai were reduced to borrowing money from the despised merchants who had gradually grown in power and influence. By the beginning of the nineteenth century, some samurai stipends were cut in half. The upper-level samurai reacted by becoming more corrupt. Some samurai married the daughters of merchants; some even sold their swords. Many simply sank into debt and brooding resentment.

Whether or how the Tokugawa shoguns—or any other group of samurai—would have been able to deal with these internal problems is a moot point. For the first time since the passage of the Seclusion Act in the sixteenth century, Japan's isolation was being tested by Russian, British, and French warships. The emperor ordered the shogun to reject the barbarians, but by 1854, when Admiral Perry's black ships appeared, the Tokugawas decided that the best they could manage was to avoid war—they had seen what the British had done to the

Chinese in the Opium War—and open Japan to trade. The treaty was signed on the March 31, 1854.

Many samurai felt that the shogun had failed to fulfill his role as barbarian–conquering general. The most vociferous critics were young, lower-ranking samurai, from the outer provinces which had fought against Ieyasu Tokugawa two hundred and fifty years earlier. They were influenced by the Mito school, which followed Fujita Yukoku, a samurai-scholar who had gone back to the original Confucian texts. Fujita argued that while the lower had a duty to obey the higher, the higher also had a duty to perform his heaven-appointed task: to benefit the people he ruled. The shogun, he said, had been appointed by the emperor, who had been the absolute and highest authority since the beginning of Japan—but the shogun only could be said to truly "revere the emperor" when he stabilized the people's livelihood and protected the country. Clearly the Tokugawa shoguns had not fulfilled their duty. They had acted only to benefit themselves.

The Mito school's immediate program was expressed in the slogan "Revere the emperor, expel the barbarian." But the Mito school's long-range goal was even more ambitious. Japan, it was said, had a divine mission to found a world empire under the Imperial House. In order to expel the barbarians and prepare Japan for her destined role, the Mito school called on young samurai to awaken to their true task: devoting themselves to "real learning" instead of "empty learning" which involved nothing more than the analysis of classical Chinese texts. They must cultivate thrift, diligence, and martial discipline. Samurai must, in short, unite learning and martial training.

In 1854, Yoshida Shoin, a young samurai influenced by the Bushido of Yamaga Soko and the ideas of the Mito school, attempted to stow away on one of Perry's ships. Yoshida's pursuit of "real learning" had led him to study Sun Tzu, and he hoped to travel to the West to gather intelligence about the enemy, as Sun Tzu advised. Yoshida was promptly arrested, imprisoned for violating the Seclusion Act, and then confined to his native Choshu.

Yoshida taught at a school which became a center for new ideas. He and his followers sought to become fully acquainted with conditions all over the world. They pursued the "ancient studies" of the Mito historians, whose reading of the old Japanese texts led them to assert that the emperor was the legitimate and sacred ruler of Japan and that the shogun was a usurper. They read the banned neo-Confucian writings of the Chinese warrior-scholar Wang-Yang Ming, who taught the primacy of individual illumination and the unity of action and knowledge with the motto, "Knowledge without action is not knowledge at all."

Arguing that neither the shogun nor the high-ranking feudal lords and Tokugawa samurai could be depended on to save Japan, Yoshida called for "an uprising of grass-roots heroes." Hoping to spark such an uprising, he entered into a plot to assassinate the shogun's emissary who had gone to Kyoto to secure the emperor's signature for yet another treaty with the United States. But this plan, too, misfired, and Yoshida was once more imprisoned. This time he was sentenced to death.

Yoshida had been quite aware that his plan might cost him his life. "From the beginning of the year to the end, day and night, morning and evening, in action and repose, in speech and in silence, the warrior must keep death constantly before him and have ever in mind that the one death should not be suffered in vain," he wrote in prison. His main point, he said, was "to revere the emperor and expel the barbarian—may my death inspire at least one or two men of steadfast will to rise up and uphold this principle after my death."[31]

The young hero was only thirty when his head fell to the sword of the shogun's executor. His farewell poem—

> That such an act
> Would have such a result
> I knew well enough.
> What made me do it anyhow
> Was the spirit of Yamato.[32]

—inspired a whole generation of young samurai who would, in fact, rise up and overthrow the Tokugawas and expel the barbarians. His body was taken from the execution ground by two of his students, Ito, who would become prime minister, and Yamagata, the future founder of the citizen army.

In 1860, a party of Mito samurai cut down Lord Ia, the shogun's regent, in retaliation for the death of Yoshida and other patriots beheaded by the Tokugawas. Ronin—masterless samurai—roamed the streets, attacking foreigners. The secretary to the U.S. Legation was killed in Yedo, the British Legation was attacked. In 1862, an Englishman was murdered. The British, unable to obtain the reparations they demanded, shelled the town of Kageshima in Satsuma. On June 24, 1863, the day the emperor had ordered the expulsion of all foreigners, samurai from the Choshu clan opened fire on an American ship. The Choshu batteries were easily destroyed and the defenders scattered by the landing of a French force. In 1865 the Tokugawa samurai marched against the Choshu clan, only to suffer a humiliating defeat. Finally, in 1867, samurai from Satsuma and Choshu occupied the shogun's palace in Kyoto.

The Tokugawa shogunate had come to an end, but the new government of the restored young Emperor Meiji—he was fifteen at the time—remained in the hands of samurai, most of whom were very young men from the outer provinces of Satsuma and Choshu. They were all, in fact, products of Bushido. The clans of the outer provinces had continued to practice the martial arts in their clan schools. They had also received a good classical Chinese Confucian education. Thanks to the Mito school, they had also studied ancient Japanese texts and had a certain amount of foreign learning.

If the Tokugawa shogun fell—at least in part—because of the contradictions inherent in a peaceful samurai, then it must also be said that the Meiji Restoration rose out of samurai as well. Japan was the only Asian country to successfully resist Western imperialism and industrialize by her own efforts. No doubt there are many reasons for this. But the Japanese historian Sakata Yoshio is probably right when he cites the existence of the samurai as an intellectual and ruling class "as the most fundamental factor" in Japan's successful and unique modernization.[33]

Realizing that feudalism would no longer work, the Meiji samurai reformers found themselves presiding over the dismantling of their own class. In 1869, they convinced the very clans that had gained the most by the restoration—including Satsuma and Choshu—to voluntarily relinquish their fiefs to the imperial government for the sake of national unity, which was essential for Japan to successfully compete with foreign countries. In return, the imperial government granted the *daimyos* half of their old revenues; many of them invested in banking and commerce or went into politics.

A strong national government, however, would mean not only the end of feudalism but also the destruction of the samurai as a separate class. So the government's reforms had to move slowly, for it still had no army of its own and depended on the support of the samurai. Samurai were "allowed" to stop wearing their swords and to cut their topknots, and "requested" to accept government bonds in place of their stipends.

Perhaps the most far-reaching change was the formation of a national army in 1870. The founder, Yamagata Aritomo, was a Choshu samurai and a former student of Yoshida Shoin. Most of the army's officers were samurai, but with the beginning of conscription, the army was soon made up primarily of villagers and farmers—the "grass-roots heroes" Yoshida had called for. The samurai's military monopoly was broken.

The final straw came when the government issued an Edict Prohibiting the Wearing of Swords for all samurai, with the exception of police and military. A petition to the Imperial government from a Kyushu samurai expressed a widely shared shock and dismay. He wrote:

> In my view, the bearing of swords is a custom that characterized our Land of Jimmu even in the ancient era of the gods. It is intimately bound up with the origins of our nation, it enhances the dignity of the Imperial Throne, solemnizes the rites of our gods, banishes the spirits of evil, puts down disorders. The sword, therefore, not only maintains the tranquillity of the nation but also guards the safety of the individual citizen. Indeed, the one thing essential to this most martial nation that reveres the gods, the one thing never to be put aside even for an instant is the sword. How, then, could those upon whom is laid the burden of fashioning and promulgating a national policy that honors the gods and strengthens our land be so forgetful of the sword?[34]

How indeed? Many of the samurai who had fought against the shogun now felt that instead of creating a Japan strong enough to save the country from the West, they were turning Japan into a Western country.

In Kumamoto, in the province of Higo, about 170 members of the League of the Divine Wind dressed in the armor and helmets of medieval samurai and launched a reckless night attack on government barracks. Wielding only swords and halberds, they killed or wounded three hundred soldiers before they were beaten back by reinforcements armed with rifles. The survivors retreated to the mountains, where eighty-four of them committed seppuku, leaving a manifesto:

> Our country is the country of the gods, and for this reason it should not even for a moment be held to rank below any foreign land. But diabolical spirits now prevailing are bent on abolishing customs which

have been cherished and observed from the time of the gods, and are making our people imitate foreigners. These facts cause us the deepest sorrow. . . . Therefore the only good thing we can now do is to use our swords in the houses of officials who imitate foreigners. This alone is worthy of men of our class.[35]

Two years later, a much more serious revolt erupted in Satsuma. It was led by none other than Saigo Takemori, the popular hero of the war against the Tokugawas, and the former commander-in-chief of the Imperial Army.

Saigo took to the field with an army of forty thousand Satsuma samurai. They had some rifles, but they placed most of their faith in their swords, which they felt would be more than a match against rifles wielded by the despised commoners who made up the rank and file of the Imperial Army. But they were wrong, for the army had been drilled and trained considerably and the soldiers had a high level of morale, as well as the support of nine new battleships.

Nevertheless, much of the fighting was conducted with swords in the old samurai fashion. The Palace Guard was made up of samurai armed with swords, and a contingent of Satsuma women—The Fighting Women's Army of Kagoshima—held a bridge against a government cavalry charge. They fought with the traditional weapon of samurai women, the *naginata*, a halberdlike spear, as well as the traditional samurai sword. The war lasted for nearly six months, leaving a total of six thousand dead and ten thousand wounded.

In the end Saigo retreated with five hundred men to the summit of a hill overlooking Kagoshima Bay. Fifteen thousand government troops surrounded them. Fifty-pound guns were brought in from the ships, and bombarded the samurai day and night. Saigo and his comrades could do nothing but wait, play *go*, write poems, and drink saki. On their last night they listened to the melancholy notes of the Satsuma lute, somebody danced the *kenbu*, the ancient sword dance, and of course they wrote their death poems. At four in the morning the imperial troops began moving up the hill. Saigo was struck by a bullet in the groin. As he bowed in the direction of the Imperial Palace, one of his comrades cut off his head with one swift blow. Someone hurriedly buried it, but it was found and brought to Admiral Kawamura, bloody and clotted with dirt. The admiral, as a contemporary account tells us, "reverently washed the head with his own hands, as a mark of respect for his former friend and companion in arms during the war of the Restoration."[36]

△△ XI △△

The noble failure of Saigo and the Satsuma samurai spelled the end of the samurai as a class. But it did not spell the end of Bushido, either in Japan or in the world beyond Japan, for that matter. No longer confined to the samurai caste, the spirit of Bushido *(bushi no tamashi)* was freed to transform the lives of Japanese of all classes.

In the shock and confusion of the Meiji, a Western craze had indeed swept through Japan. Ministers wore top hats and frock coats; businessmen and politicians entertained at a perfectly reproduced Bavarian club; young men ate beef and treasured gold watches; black British-style umbrellas replaced the colorful paper ones; Smiley's *Self-Help* was a best-seller.

Clearly the pendulum had swung too far. The answer, it was thought, lay in the combination of "Western technology and Eastern ethics." But where were they to find "Eastern ethics"? Confucianism was too closely identified with the old feudal order; Buddhism was considered old-fashioned and superstitious. Shinto had been adopted as the center of the new national cult, but it was more ceremonial than ethical in nature.

The answer, provided by the young samurai leaders, was to be found in a Bushido freed of its feudal class bias. The Meiji version of Bushido asserted that it was no longer to be taken as the code of the samurai alone, but of the Japanese people. As such, it formed the basis for the Eastern (and national) ethic that would balance Western technology. "Bushido," said Yamaoka Tesshu, tutor and bodyguard to the Emperor Meiji, and a master swordsmen in the old Zen tradition, "is the proper way of life for the Japanese." It was the answer to the rampant Westernization and materialism that was engulfing the nation. "Desire for fame and wealth has replaced the desire for enlightenment," Tesshu warned. "We must look after each other without regard for our own welfare, kill selfish desires, bravely face all enemies, and keep a stainless mind—this is Bushido."[37]

Others with some experience of the West sought to promote Bushido as a kind of Japanese version of Western chivalry. In 1899, the Quaker Inazo Nitobe wrote an English book on Bushido in which he explained that "Bushido is the code of moral principals which the knights were required or instructed to observe."[38] Prime Minister Ito Hirobumi, the first Japanese to receive an education in England, argued that Bushido "provided an education which aspired to the attainment of a rustic simplicity and a self-sacrificing spirit unsurpassed in Sparta, and the aesthetic culture and intellectual refinement of Athens. Art, delicacy of sentiment, higher ideals of morality and of philosophy, as well as the highest type of valor and chivalry—all these we have tried to combine in man as he ought to be."[39]

The martial arts side of Bushido was applied to the basic institutions of the modern state. The Butokudan, the Martial Virtues Hall, was established in Kyoto in 1899, providing opportunities for some of the best classical martial artists to teach. The practice of kendo and judo, meanwhile, became popular among all classes, sometimes more as sport or exercise than as a true *do* or way. In 1911, the Ministry of Education required all middle school boys to practice either kendo or judo, while girls studied the halberdlike *naginata*.

The new grassroots citizen army also made use of Bushido. Martial artists no longer supported by their clans made a living as instructors for both army and police. Yamagata Aritomo, chief of staff of the armed forces, saw the army as a way to "transform the commoner into a samurai." Yamagata, who was both a poet and skilled spear fighter, had much to do with the moderate tone of the Imperial Precepts to Soldiers and Sailors, promulgated in 1882. The precepts cautioned against the traditional reckless samurai bravery that took no heed of consequences. "To be incited by mere impetuosity to violent action cannot be called true valor," cautioned the emperor. "The soldier and sailor should have sound discrimination of right and wrong. . . . Those who thus appreciate true valor should in their daily intercourse set gentleness first. . . . If you affect valor and act with violence, the world will in the end detest you and look upon you as wild beasts."[40]

The Meiji combination of Western technology and Eastern ethics proved remarkably effective. In 1895, the Japanese won a war with China. By 1905, the Meiji men had so successfully "enriched the country and strengthened the army" that the Japanese defeated the Russians at Port Arthur. Fighting with a combination of Western technology and organization (learned from the Prussians) and samurai spirit, the Japanese shocked the world by defeating a major Western power. They had been led by a former samurai, Admiral Nogi, who later demonstrated the persistence of one of the most archaic samurai customs, *junshi*, by following his lord, the Emperor Meiji, into death at midnight on October 5, 1912; in true samurai fashion, the admiral was joined by his wife, who respectfully waited for her husband to finish before plunging the dagger through her throat.

◮ X I I ◮

That same year a party made up largely of veterans of the Russo-Japanese War arrived in the northern island of Hokkaido. The government had been concerned that the Russians might try to occupy the island; the pioneers hoped to begin a farming and fishing commune.

The party was led by a veteran of the Russo-Japanese War by the name of Morihei Ueshiba. A sensitive and powerful man, Ueshiba had demonstrated an early interest in the spiritual world, in particular in esoteric Shinto and Shingon Buddhism. When his concerned father suggested that his son take up the martial arts to strengthen his frail body, Ueshiba had thrown himself into the project with characteristic determination. In 1901, after graduating at a young age from an abacus school, he had opened a stationery store in Tokyo and studied the New Shadow school of swordsmanship, as well as jujitsu. He continued his martial arts training after he enlisted in the army, winning distinction in the new martial art of bayonet fighting.

Ueshiba had been in Hokkaido less than a year when he heard that Sokaku Takeda, one of the last of the old-style samurai, was teaching at a nearby inn. Takeda was the heir of the *wata oyomi* or secret teachings of the Daito Ryu school of the Aizu clan. After the restoration, he had wandered around the country like the old-time samurai martial arts masters, challenging all comers. On one occasion, when he was attacked by a gang of laborers, he had cut down seven men with his sword. He had never settled down long enough to establish his own dojo (or training hall), but he was still in demand as a teacher for the police and military. In fact, it was an assignment as police instructor that had brought him to the wild frontier district of Hokkaido.

Ueshiba became Sokaku's student in the traditional way. Building a dojo for his *sensei* (teacher) on the farm commune, he cooked his meals and brewed his tea, cleaned his house, massaged his feet, and heated the evening bath.

Ueshiba received a teaching certificate in Daito Ryu aiki-jutsu from Sokaku in 1915. But he was not satisfied. Sokaku was fearless in a fight, yet he lived in fear of the spirits of the men he had killed. He kept a pair of sharpened chopsticks by his side in his home, afraid of ambush. To make sure that none of his many enemies poisoned him, he maintained the old samurai custom of not eating or drinking anything—not even a cup of tea—unless he, or Ueshiba, prepared it. Whenever he left his house he carried a ready dagger and a walking stick which concealed a razor.

Ueshiba wondered if the problem lay in Sokaku's character, or in the nature of *budo* (like Bushido, the way of the warrior, though with more emphasis on the martial arts aspect). After all, no matter how hard one trained, there was always somebody who could train harder; no matter how skilled one became, there was always somebody with more skill; and no matter how sensitive one made one's mind, there was always someone whose mind was more sensitive. Thus there was no real security in *budo*—victory through violence led only to more violence.

But the dilemma went even deeper. Recounting this pivotal crisis, one of Ueshiba's last close students, Mitsugi Saotome, writes:

> The personal ego which all the *ryu* [martial arts schools] tried to conquer still managed to survive, cunningly taking the form of loyalty and honor. So concerned with transcending individual ego, there was a failure to recognize the selfishness and overdevelopment of group ego, and the righteous ego, and the ego of no ego. Looking upon the evolution of *bujutsu* into *budo*, O Sensei saw that although a higher consciousness was struggling to evolve, the work was not finished. It had just begun.[41]

In 1925 Ueshiba's father became seriously ill. Leaving his house and the dojo in Hokkaido to Sokaku, Ueshiba set out to see his father. On the way, however, he stopped off in the village of Ayabe to investigate Omoto-kyo, one of the new religions that had sprung up in the new Japan. An eclectic mix of Shinto and shamanism, Omoto-kyo was originally based on the channeled writings of an illiterate peasant woman; it was now led by a charismatic artist, healer, and spiritual teacher by the name of Onisaburo Deguchi, who believed it was his mission to bring about a new age to the troubled world.

Intrigued by Deguchi, Ueshiba moved to Ayabe, took up farming, and threw himself into the spiritual disciplines of *chinkon-kishin*, a revived form of an archaic Shinto meditation, as well as *koto-dama*—word-spirit—a spiritual exercise based on the sounds of the universe. Deguchi enlisted Ueshiba as his personal bodyguard and encouraged him to open a dojo at Ayabe to teach martial arts to the young men of the Omoto-kyo community.

In 1924 Ueshiba accompanied Deguchi to Inner Mongolia, which he hoped would serve as the center for a new world order that would unify the world's religions and races. It was during this ill-fated expedition that Ueshiba felt he had finally begun to penetrate the true meaning of the martial ways. Traveling with members of the Inner

Mongolian Army, the Omoto-kyo group was ambushed in a mountain pass by Chinese Nationalist troops. Trapped and unable to move, with bullets coming at him from all directions, Ueshiba prepared himself for death—only to find that

> when I concentrated my vision . . . I could see pebbles of white light flashing just before the bullets. I avoided them by twisting and turning my body, and they barely missed me. This happened repeatedly with barely time to breathe, but suddenly I had an insight into the essence of budo. I saw clearly that the movements in martial arts come alive when the center of *ki* [energy-breath] is concentrated in one's mind and body and that the calmer I became, the clearer my mind became. I could intuitively see the thoughts, including the violent intentions, of the other.[42]

Ueshiba's newfound spiritual sight saved his life, but it did not save the mission. The Japanese were arrested by Chinese army troops, their Mongolian allies taken out and executed one by one. The Japanese were shackled and taken out to be executed as well, but at the last minute they were handed over to the Japanese consul.

Back in Ayabe, Ueshiba threw himself into an extensive training program, concentrating on *sojutsu,* the art of the spear, instructing his students to attack him with live blades. Retreating into the mountains, he dedicated himself to ascetic Shinto rites, fasting, praying, and meditating under a sacred waterfall. The culmination of his spiritual search came in the spring of 1925, when Ueshiba was forty-two.

A naval officer and teacher of swordsmanship had come to ask to study with Ueshiba. Kisshomaru, Ueshiba's son, recounts:

> Then during a conversation, they happened to disagree over a trifle matter. Tempers rose. They agreed to have a fight. The officer dashed forward to strike him, swinging his wooden sword. But as the Master dodged his sword very easily each time, the officer finally sat down without having once touched him. The Master says he felt the opponent's movements before they were actually executed in the same way as during the time in Mongolia.
>
> He took a rest after this game and went over to a nearby garden in which there was a persimmon tree. As he was wiping off the perspiration from his face, he was greatly overcome with a feeling which he had never experienced previously. He could neither walk nor sit. He was just rooted on the ground in great astonishment.[43]

Such moments—or nonmoments—of spiritual illumination are notoriously difficult to communicate. Ueshiba himself gave the following account:

> Then in the spring of 1925, if I remember correctly, when I was taking a walk in the garden by myself, I felt that the universe suddenly quaked, and that a golden spirit sprang up from the ground, veiled my body, and changed my body into a golden one.
>
> At the same time my mind and body became light. I was able to understand the whisperings of the birds, and was clearly aware of the mind of God, the Creator of this universe.
>
> At that moment I was enlightened: the source of *budo* is God's love—the spirit of loving protection for all beings. Endless tears of joy streamed down my cheeks.[44]

Ueshiba's spiritual breakthrough was reflected by a marked improvement in his martial skill. Ueshiba's aiki-jutsu, as he now started to call his art, was based on a deep realization of the identity of the individual *ki* (*ch'i,* in Chinese) with the *ki* of the universe. This insight and emphasis on *ki* is in agreement with the classical Taoist martial arts built on the development of *ch'i* and the principle that the soft, yielding yin is superior to the hard or yang.

But aiki-jutsu differed fundamentally from t'ai chi or jujitsu. Where jujitsu taught, "When pushed, pull back; when pulled, push forward," aiki-jutsu taught, "When pushed pivot and go around; when pulled, enter while circling." Becoming one with the opponent by entering fearlessly and directly into his attack, Ueshiba took a defensive initiative—called *go-no-sen*—in which he blended with and joined the attacker's energy, moving always in the spiraling circular swirling movements of the universe itself.

The movements—circular and centered—gave Ueshiba's art the look, and indeed the feel, of a dance in which the attacker was sucked into a spinning center, only to be thrown outward, or brought inevitably and helplessly to the ground in a jujitsulike pin. The attacker was defeated by his own aggression. If he got thrown or pinned, it was only the universe reflecting his aggression back to him.

As Ueshiba developed his art, word of his skill spread. A demonstration at the home of Admiral Takashita led to requests for lessons from members of the Imperial Household Agency, as well as army and navy officers, leading businessmen, and government officials. No one could touch him. As Kenji Tomiki, who practiced judo, said, "I faced virtually every outstanding *judo* and *jujutsu* man in my career, but not one of them could hold a candle to Morihei. He was far and above the best, likely the most gifted master of all time." When Jigaro Kano, the founder of the popular new way of judo, watched him in action, he said, "This is the ideal *budo*—true judo."[45]

In 1931 Ueshiba opened the Kobukan Dojo in Tokyo and began teaching a select group; prospective students needed two letters of recommendation, as well as Ueshiba's personal permission. Those who qualified tended to be serious martial artists whom Ueshiba drove mercilessly. Aikido was primarily a weaponless art, but he included training in sword, spear, and bayonet fighting. At the height of his physical powers, Ueshiba's aiki-budo of this period was, in the words of biographer John Stevens, "hard-style, aggressive *budo* characterized by razor-sharp execution of the techniques and muscular strength." The training was so severe and intense that the dojo was called "the hell dojo."[46]

During the twenties and thirties a dedicated group of ultranationalist right-wing militarists gained control of both the army and the government. Under the slogan "War is the father of creation and the mother of culture," they embarked on a course of imperialism abroad and repression and assassination at home. In 1935, the police moved against the followers of Deguchi burning buildings and books. Deguchi himself went to prison, charged with lèse-majesté and rebellion. Ueshiba was questioned by the police a number of times, but his contacts in high places—as well as the classes he was now teaching at the Naval Academy, the Military Staff College, and the Military Police Academy—protected him for the time being.

As the country moved toward war, the code of Bushido was once more reinterpreted. According to the Ministry of Education, Bushido, which had "shed itself of an outdated feudalism" during the Meiji period, was now said to be "the Way of loyalty and patriotism" in which "loyalty means reverence to the emperor . . . and to follow him implicitly."[47] Young soldiers were taught that the samurai spirit would make them invincible in battle. The infamous Rape of Nanking in 1938 gave the cautionary words of the Imperial Precepts a prophetic ring: "If you affect valor and act with violence, the world will in the end detest you and look upon you as wild beasts."[48]

In December of 1941 the Japanese general staff struck the American fleet at Pearl Harbor. In 1942, as part of its general mobilization, the government ordered all schools of *bujutsu* and *budo* to join the Greater Japan Martial Virtue Association. Ueshiba took the occasion to proclaim his art as aikido—the way of harmony—thus emphasizing its distinct nature as a spiritual *do* or way, separate and distinct from other forms.

With the beginning of World War II, he left the Tokyo dojo in the care of his young son and senior disciples, gave up all his teaching posts, and moved to a rustic country retreat in Iwama. Though he officially resigned for reasons of ill health, he confided his misgivings to his son:

> The military is dominated by reckless fools ignorant of statesmanship and religious ideals who slaughter innocent citizens indiscriminately and destroy everything in their path. They act in total contradiction to God's will, and they will surely come to a sorry end. True *budo* is to nourish life and foster peace, love, and respect, not to blast the world to pieces with weapons.
>
> The Way of Budo is to put new life into the original universal life force which gives birth to all things. Harmony, love and courtesy are essential to true Budo, but the people who are in power these days are only interested in playing with weapons. They misrepresent Budo as a tool for power struggles, violence and destruction, and they want to use me toward this end. I'm tired of this stupidity. I have no intention of allowing myself to become their tool. I see no other way but to go into retreat.[49]

During his retreat at Iwama, Ueshiba developed the ideal *take-muso budo*, a *budo* which integreted martial training (*take*) with *muso*, the protective life force. Believing in the union of *budo* and farming, he cleared six and half hectares and began to cultivate the land. He built a small outdoor dojo, so that he could be closer to the *ki* of nature in his practice; and finally, he constructed an Aiki Shrine to the spirit of *ai-ki*, dedicated to the forty-two guardian deities of the universe. And so he waited, farming, meditating, practicing.

◮◮ XIII ◮◮

Ivan Morris has noted how often the actions of the sincere self-sacrificing Japanese hero have caused results exactly the opposite of those intended—how, for example, the loyalist Kusunoke's support of the emperor resulted in the strengthening of the shogun; or how Saigo's attack on the Meiji government resulted in the final destruction of the samurai as a class.

In the same way—though on an infinitely more tragic scale—it may be said that the atomic bomb which leveled Hiroshima on the afternoon of August 6, 1945, was at least partly the unforeseen result of the samurai-spirited resistance-to-the-death which the Americans had encountered in the Pacific—and which they feared they would meet if they landed in Japan.

When Ueshiba returned to Tokyo after the war, he found that Japan's new military ruler, the American shogun, Douglas MacArthur, had prohibited all martial arts (with the exception of the non-Japanese karate-do) in an attempt to destroy "the roots of militarism." Continuing his retreat in Iwama, he was joined by a few disciples who vowed to keep the flame of aikido alive.

Within two years, however, the Allied occupation forces permitted the newly formed Japanese police to use kendo and judo in their training, and in 1948 Ueshiba was granted permission by both the Allied forces and the Ministry of Education to teach aikido as "a martial way devoted to the fostering of international peace and justice."

Before the war, aikido had been limited to an elite group of highly qualified students. Now all that had changed. The power that the new bomb had released—"brighter than a thousand suns," as Oppenheimer had quoted Arjuna's terrifying vision of Vishnu—demanded nothing less than a new way of thinking.

"Modern technology has given us two choices," Ueshiba said after the war. "With its help we can realize the dream of a great global family, all the people of the earth joined together in a great world community; or we can completely destroy this earth and all of humanity with it. Aggression cannot work in the face of the new weapons, nationalism cannot work as more and more we understand the depths of the interrelationships around the globe. We must study and understand the saving truth of harmony."[50]

The new aikido that emerged from Ueshiba's war retreat was deeply spiritual. But the spiritual and social dimensions of aikido were firmly roted in the disciplined and rigorous physical training of a highly evolved martial art. "As the dynamics of spiral movement exert a physical situation, you will experience a mental revolution," Ueshiba said. "This change in your mind and heart will create a spiritual revolution. And you will be one with the universal movement."[51]

Aikido was further grounded by Ueshiba's insistence that the key to harmony was to be found in conflict. All aikido forms or katas—with a few exceptions involving the use of the wooden sword of the jo, the wooden staff—required two partners, a uke who attacked and a nage who defended. It was, after all, in the heat of conflict that harmony could be found. It was only in conflict that students could come to know and so possibly transform habitual patterns of aggression or fear. The aikidoist, therefore, did not ignore conflict or spiritualize it out of existence. By entering into the attack, by joining and blending with the attack, the attack could be redirected back into the harmony of the universe. Instead of having to choose between running away or fighting, or losing or winning, aikido offered the warrior another choice.

Dedicated to an absolute defense, the aikidoist not only defended himself, but also defended the attacker against himself. Ueshiba's aikido demonstrated on the physical plane that the way of absolute defense, a defense that defended and protected even the attacker against his own folly, was a possible and indeed remarkably effective martial art. "True victory is not defeating an enemy" said Ueshiba. "True victory gives love and changes the enemy's heart."[52]

The postwar dojo in Tokyo attracted—as all dojos do—its share of strong and ambitious young men and experienced martial artists, but it was also now open to everyone regardless of their martial prowess. It was open to women as well as men, to children as well as old people, to Westerners as well as Japanese. Practicing every technique together in pairs, taking turns as *uke* and *nage* regardless of their level of skill, aikidoists got to see and feel the world from their opponent's point of view. The *uke* attacked—and was thrown or pinned; the *nage* defended—and threw or pinned. Learning to give your partner the "gift" of a good clear attack was very important, since in all the aikido techniques the defender joined the attacker's energy. But learning to keep your center and balance and awareness while falling and rolling safely was even more important.

From the outside, aikido looked like a dance. But if it was a dance, it was a warrior's dance, a dance that embodied the movements of the universe, conflict and all, the ancient genetic choreography of attack and defense, active and passive, yin and yang, waves crashing against the rocks, death-dealing and life-giving. When both partners paid full attention and respected each other's level of practice, it was the dance of life. But if one partner lost attention or turned aggressive or tried to show off, the result could be a bruised arm, a wrenched shoulder, a broken nose or arm, or worse.

One of the reasons so many different kinds of people could practice aikido with each other was Ueshiba's insistence that aikido was above all a *do*, a spiritual way, and not a sport in which physical skill and superior technique brought recognition through competition. Though some aikidoists argued that competition was necessary to keep people interested or to develop the art, Ueshiba insisted that this would destroy its spiritual essence, just as he felt it had destroyed or diluted the spiritual basis of judo and karate-do. There would be no aikido contests, competitions, or tournaments.

Instead aikido spread throughout the world and achieved what the Japanese call "internationalization" (an estimated five hundred thousand practitioners as of 1985) by means of demonstrations. During one of these, Ueshiba, by then in his late seventies, showed very clearly—as can be seen on a handful of films—how easily and effortlessly a frail old man in harmony with himself and with nature could throw five or six men who rushed to attack all at once.

"Regardless of how quickly an opponent attacks or how slowly I respond, I cannot be defeated," Ueshiba explained. "It is not that my techniques are faster than those of my opponent. It has nothing to do with speed or slowness. I am victorious right from the start. As soon as the thought of attack crosses my opponent's mind, he shatters the harmony of the universe and is instantly defeated regardless of how quickly he attacks."[53]

There are some who consider aikido to be the evolutionary culmination of the way of the warrior. Certainly a case can be made that the samurai, isolated for so many centuries on their island and relatively uncontaminated by outside invasions or influences, provide a unique chance to study the evolution of the warrior. Japan, we might say, is the Galapagos of the warrior.

In any case, Ueshiba's aikido comes close, in both principle and practice, to solving the dilemma or riddle of the warrior. What the new *budo* of the way of harmony demonstrates is that it is the warrior, not the sword, who is death-dealing or life-bestowing. The choice is ours. "True budo is the working of love in the universe," as Ueshiba said shortly before he died full of life at the age of eighty. "It is the protector of all living things."

A GOOD DAY
TO DIE

Crazy Horse
and the Sioux Warrior

One does not sell the earth upon which the people walk.
—Crazy Horse

Curly was lying deep in the earth, in a pit an eagle hunter had dug long ago. He lay naked except for his blanket, stones under his back and pebbles between his toes to keep him awake. He had not eaten or taken water. During the day the hot sun burned down on him; sometimes he was pelted with cold rain. At night the stars wheeled in the patch of black sky above him.

He had come here for a *Hanblecheyapi*—crying for a vision—after seeing the white soldiers outside of Fort Laramie kill the old Chief Conquering Bear, all because a visiting Miniconjou had shot an old skinny cow that had wandered into the camp, stumbling into tepees and cooking fires. The soldiers couldn't understand that Conquering Bear had no power to turn the Miniconjou over to them, and so a hotheaded Irish lieutenant by the name of Gratten took thirty-eight men and two howitzers to the Indian camp. Conquering Bear once again explained that he couldn't deliver the man, and offered to let the cow's owner have any two horses from his herd. Gratten replied by giving the order to fire, and Conquering Bear fell, wounded in nine places. The Sioux defended their camp, and within minutes all thirty-eight soldiers were dead.

The warriors could have taken the fort easily enough. But that was not the way they fought. They did not take advantage of their victory. Instead, they acted as if the soldiers were Crow—though Crow would never have been stupid enough to walk right into a Sioux camp—and they rode off in their separate directions.

Curly was just thirteen, and he wasn't sure that what had happened was the same as a fight with the Crow, and so he had turned his pony to the hills, to cry to Wakan Tanka, the Great Mysterious, for the vision that every Sioux warrior hoped would bring him face-to-face with his destiny—and which would also bring him the power and protection that would help him in battle. Wakan Tanka might send it to him as an eagle, or a coyote, or a spirit, or in a dream or a song . . . or nothing might happen, and then he might try again. But whatever it was, it was his path.

Curly lay there for three days, without drink or food, and though he prayed as hard as he could to Wakan Tanka, nothing happened. A vision brought many things. It could tell a man—or woman—what his road in life was to be—if he were a warrior; or a "contrary," a *heyoka* or clown who did everything opposite, riding his horse backward into battle, handling hot stones with his bare hands in the sweat lodge; or even a *winta,* a man who dressed in women's clothes and did women's things; or a medicine man. Whatever it was, it had to be followed. There was no higher authority than a vision, for it connected a man with the power of Wakan Tanka.

This power often came in the form of animals. The Sioux and other Native Americans did not look upon animals in a purely utilitarian way, nor did they consider them inferior or soulless. Rather, animals were *wakan* or spirit messengers, instructors, helpers. Animals gave warriors power. A vision of a bear, for example, might bring wisdom, for the bear could not be hurt by other animals and knew how to find herbs to heal himself; the wolf brought craft and intelligence; eagle, hawk, and owl brought courage and speed in war; raven and magpie could advise about future events; spider had great spiritual wisdom; butterfly imparted agility. But visions could come in any form; sometimes they came in or through stones, thunder, or wind.

But none of these things had come to Curly. He thought at first it might be because he wasn't yet worthy. Then he thought it might be because he had gone off by himself without making the proper preparations, without first asking a holy man like his father for guidance, without smoking the pipe, without purifying himself in the sweat lodge of the stone people, without making the tobacco offerings, and all the other things he didn't know, though he had prayed: "Wakan Tanka, maker of Sun, Moon, Star, Earth, Water, and all things thrown upon the earth and under the water, including the human on the land of the earth, help me to gain vision and power to serve and defend the people of my tribe."[1]

On the third day, he rose on shaky legs, feeling like a newborn colt or buffalo calf, and started down the hill to the stream where he had tethered his pony. Then he fainted or fell asleep about halfway down the hill, for that was where he saw the man on horseback ride out of the lake. The horse was floating like a feather changing colors in the light. The rider wore plain leggings and a plain shirt. His face was unpainted. He wore a single feather in his long brown hair, and a smooth pebble tied behind his ear. The rider told him, though he did not speak, that he should never wear a warbonnet or tie up his pony's tail, for the pony needed it to switch away flies and jump streams. He said that Curly should not paint his pony before going into battle, but should pass some dust over it in lines and streaks, and then over himself, and then he wouldn't be killed. But he should never take anything for himself.

While he was telling Curly all this, he seemed to float through bullets and arrows, which disappeared before hitting him. Then sometimes horse and rider were held back by people, his own people, coming up behind him, but he twisted out of their grasp and rode on. And then a great storm came up and the Thunders gave him his power, as lightning zigzagged on the man's cheek and a few hailstones painted his body. When the storm faded, the people grabbed him from behind again, without letting go, and a hawk screamed in the sky.[2]

◭◭ I I ◭◭

The *hamiliquipi* was one of the Seven Sacred Ways White Buffalo Woman had brought to the Lakota Sioux. Every Sioux knew the story. Two warriors had been out hunting on the Great Plains when they saw a beautiful young maiden dressed in buckskin walking toward them. As she drew closer, one of the warriors wanted to take her. The other warrior held back; there was something about her. She beckoned the warrior with lust in his heart to come to her. As he approached, a great cloud wrapped around them. When the cloud lifted, White Buffalo Woman was standing there. The warrior who had gone to her was nothing more than a pile of bones bleaching in the tall grass.

White Buffalo Woman gave the second warrior—who had approached her with respect, as a woman should be approached—the sacred pipe. It was to be the connection between the people and the Great Mysterious, the conduit between heaven and earth. The tradition, as recounted by John Lame Deer, is that White Buffalo Woman said, "With this holy pipe you will walk like a living prayer, your feet resting upon the grandmother, the pipe stem reaching all the way up into the sky to the grandfather, your body linking the Sacred Beneath with the Sacred Above."[3] She also explained the other rites, the Sun Dance, and the soul-keeping, which taught how to help the dead spirits, as well as reaffirming the older rites of the *inipi* (sweat purification) and crying-for-vision. She told him to bring them to the people and to keep them properly so that the people would survive and continue.

△△ I I I △△

The Sioux came from the east, most recently the woodlands of Minnesota, where they farmed, growing corn and squash, hunting small game and occasionally sending a party out to the buffalo across the Missouri. Their only domestic animal was the dog. They had moved West to the Great Plains around 1776, the same time that the new American government declared independence.

With this move the Sioux, too, achieved a kind of independence— an independence that depended, however, on the buffalo and the horse. No longer bound to their farms, they were free to roam like the endless herds of buffalo whose flesh, skin, and bones provided nearly all their needs.

Nineteenth century anthropologists (and most twentieth century anthropologists as well) take it for granted that humans "progress" from hunting and gathering to agriculture. But the Sioux, had any anthropologists asked them, would not have agreed. As far as they were concerned, the life they led as hunters of buffalo was far superior to the life they had led as farmers. A hunter mounted on one of the swift, tough ponies they had found on the plains could easily kill enough buffalo to feed himself and his family in one good hunt; and when the tribe hunted together, as they usually did, the hunters could kill enough to feed and clothe the tribe during the long winters. And they could trade their surplus with the Indians who still farmed.

The men spent much of their ample free time pursuing the path of war, playing in the dangerous game of battle. Good hunters were respected, but true honor and prestige were won in the game of war. These honors were carefully graded. The highest honors went to the warrior who exposed himself to the most danger, usually by counting the first coup (or blow; the word was taken from French trappers) by touching an enemy, either with hand, bow, whip, or a special coup stick. A warrior who struck the first coup was entitled to wear an upright eagle feather, the warrior who struck the second coup wore a horizontal feather, the third painted hands on his horse.

Horses were also an important part of the Plains war game (or "complex," as some anthropologists called it). In a sense, horses could be said to be the object of war—horses were wealth for the Sioux, but here again the way in which a horse was captured mattered most. The greatest honor went to those who were brave and stealthy enough to steal horses by sneaking into the enemy camp. It was considered a great feat if they managed to get away without being seen or heard, but it was also a fine opportunity for a chase and a fight if they were discovered and pursued.

Warfare might thus be considered a game in which the counters were coups and horses. Participation was purely voluntary (as it must be in a game), and there was a beginning and end. In truth, then, the Sioux did not fight wars but battles. The point was to gain honors and horses, not to take land or occupy another country (though their raids did serve to keep other tribes from encroaching too deeply on their hunting grounds).

Of course it was, like most war games, a deadly game. Warriors were wounded and killed, and the scalps of the bravest enemy dead were taken. But there were limits. When the warriors had proven their worth, it was not uncommon for someone to say, "It is enough," and they would head for home. A good war leader was one who could bring his warriors back alive. A loss of one or two men was acceptable; any more, and the raid was considered a disaster.

When the warriors returned they were greeted by the whole village. If the raid was successful there was feasting and dancing. The warriors gave away some of the horses they had captured or stolen and were encouraged to recount their deeds. The scalps were tied to a pole and displayed in a dance by the women in the village. In the victory dance the celebration of the individual warrior's prowess became a celebration of the tribe's courage and prowess; the individual's demonstration of superiority confirmed the superiority of the tribe.

Most warriors were members of various warrior societies called *akicitas*. Like so much else in the life of the plains Indians, the *akicitas* had their origins in the visions or dreams of individuals. *Akicitas* had civil as well as military responsibilities. They were especially active during the hunt, when it was their job to make sure that no one would break ranks and take a buffalo before the whole tribe was ready. If a hunter did, the *akicitas* would break his bow or even destroy his lodge. To make sure that none of the *akicitas* usurped power or abused their authority, the societies took turns with the police function. Above all, however, the members of the *akicitas* vowed to protect the people in times of danger. Some stuck their lances in the ground before battle, vowing never to retreat. The Fox Society song went:

> *I am the kit fox*
> *I live in uncertainty*
> *If there is anything difficult*
> *If there is anything dangerous*
> *That is mine*[4]

△△ I V △△

Curly's whole childhood had prepared him to be an independent and confident hunter and warrior. The Sioux child grew up knowing he was loved and cherished. He was not weaned until he himself was ready, sometimes as late as four or five. He was never punished or struck. The Sioux could not understand why the whites hurt their own children, hitting them or pulling their ears until they cried. The Sioux taught their children by example.

Curly was close to his father, who was a holy man rather than a warrior, but he belonged more to the extended family of tribe than to his parents—all elders were grandfather or grandmother. Along with the other young boys, he trapped foxes, coyotes, and prairie dogs. When he was a little older, he spent his days out on the prairie with the horses, watching for Crow horse thieves.

Above all, he rode. The Sioux were truly at one with their ponies. "The Sioux is a cavalry soldier from the time he has intelligence enough to ride a horse or fire," General Crook noted.[5] He was accustomed to killing buffalo with bow and arrow while galloping bareback over the prairie. In battle, he could shoot from behind his pony's neck. If his horse went down, he could leap onto any available mount.

Sioux boys were expected to hunt, but they were brought up as warriors. White Bull—who rode with Crazy Horse—was told by his father:

> When you go on the warpath, look out for the enemy and do something brave. Do not make me ashamed of you. Study everything you see, look it over carefully and try to understand it. Have good-will toward all your people. Tell no lies; the man who lies is a weakling. He is a coward.
>
> Keep an even temper, and *never* be stingy with food. In that way your name will become great.[6]

Some boys snuck off on war parties as early as twelve, serving as water boys and helpers. Curly scored his first coup—and his first kill—on a raiding party against the Omaha in the summer of 1855, at the age of fifteen. He had shot one of the Omaha as he darted from one tree to another. But when he went to cut the scalp, he discovered that he had killed an Omaha woman. This in itself was not considered dishonorable, as long as the woman was killed within sight of her warriors, since warriors fought hard to protect their women. But the woman's hair reminded Curly of his sister's, and he found that he was unable to scalp her. (Years later, according to one account, he said he disapproved of the custom.) The other warriors found his reluctance funny and made up a song about it.

He was lighter skinned than most of the other Indians, with long, light brown hair, a thin face, and a sharp, aquiline nose. He was thin and spare, a little under six feet. The only decoration he ever wore was an Iroquois shell necklace. He had deep black eyes—eyes, as Short Buffalo remembered much later, "that hardly ever looked straight at a man, but they didn't miss much that was going on all the same."[7]

A year or so later, when he was sixteen, he joined a party that went all the way to the Wind River, farther than any Sioux had ever gone. By this time Curly had recounted his vision to his father, who had explained that he, Curly, was the man on the horse, and that he had to help his people by following the vision he had been given. So Curly dressed himself according to his vision. He never wore a warbonnet. He let his light brown hair hang loose, put a stone behind his ear, a red-tailed hawk's feather in his hair, zigzagged lightning on his cheek, and painted a scattering of hailstones on his body. He chewed a mixture of dried eagle heart and brain and wild aster seeds, which he wore in a medicine bag around his neck, and then he passed a sacred stone over his body and his pony. Finally he sprinkled dust from a gopher hole over himself and his horse, so that they, like the gopher, would be hidden from their enemies.

The strange-speaking Indians they found—Arapaho—were up on a high hill covered with rocks, but Curly charged straight at them, floating through the bullets, just as in his vision. He killed one warrior and then whirled to down a second who had charged him. Then, with arrows flying all around him, he dismounted to take their scalps, only to be wounded by an arrow in his leg. He managed to get away, but he remembered that his vision had warned him not to take anything for himself in battle. From then on he never took scalps.

At the victory dance, the warriors sang Curly's praises, and pushed him to sing a song of his own. But Curly was strangely reticent and modest for a young Sioux brave, and he moved back without saying anything. Unlike the other warriors, he would not sing his praises or dance his deeds, nor did he have scalps for any of the women to tie on the scalp pole and dance with. And he gave away all the horses he had captured; in fact, he gave away everything he had except for weapons, and he would become famous for his acts of generosity. No one ever went hungry when he was around.

Everybody knew he was a brave warrior, but he acted strangely. When he was fighting, he was like a warrior, one of the bravest. But when he was not fighting, he was more like a holy man, who spent his time alone and said little.

The next day, however, his father moved through the camp singing his praises, and gave him his own name, a name that had been much honored in his family. He gave the name of *Tashunka-Witko*, Crazy Horse.[8]

While Crazy Horse and the other Sioux were fighting Crow, Arapaho, and Omaha for honors and horses, a very different kind of war had already begun. On September 3, 1855, Brigadier General William S. Harney found the Brule camp of Little Thunder, a "friendly" Indian. Little Thunder and Harney talked under a white flag, while Harney waited for word that his cavalry had taken up their positions behind the camp. Then he told Little Thunder that he had come to fight, and attacked from the front with infantry. The escaping Indians ran straight into the cavalry. Out of 250 Brules, 86 were killed. Harney returned to Fort Laramie with 70 captive women and children.

As soon as he heard of the massacre, Crazy Horse rode to the destroyed camp. The lodges were still burning and the dead lay on the ground, some of them women with their dresses up over their heads, their pubic hair taken as scalps. Crazy Horse found one survivor, a young Cheyenne, Yellow Woman, lying with her dead baby beside her. Putting her on a travois, he took her back to her people on the Smokey Hill River in Kansas.

Yellow Woman was the niece of a prominent Cheyenne medicine man, Ice, who taught Crazy Horse the Cheyenne ways. Ice and another Cheyenne medicine man had a plan to beat the whites. Singing special songs, they dipped their hands into the waters of a lake and asked a warrior to fire at them point-blank. The bullets bounced off harmlessly (due, perhaps, to the small amounts of powder the Indians were using). When the whites came in force, the Cheyenne, along with Crazy Horse and some other Sioux visitors, went to the river, sang the songs, and lined up to face the soldiers, with their empty hands held out front, ready to catch the bullets.

The Cheyenne never got to try out their medicine that day. By chance, it seems, the white commander ordered a saber charge, and the Cheyenne were completely routed. Four died; the rest fled.

Harney had said that he was making war to find the "murderers" of Lieutenant Gratten. Hoping to end Harney's campaign against the Sioux, five young warriors—Red Leaf and Long Chin, brothers of Stirring Bear, who had been killed by Gratten; and Red Plume, Spotted Elk, and Spotted Tail—rode into Fort Laramie, offering themselves as sacrifices to end Harney's campaign. Since no Indians who had been sent to the white man's jail had ever returned, they wore their war clothes for burial and sang their death songs.

Crazy Horse went on to Bear Butte, an old meeting place on the edge of Paha Sapa, the sacred Black Hills, where the Sioux had called a big meeting to discuss the whites. Between five thousand and seven thousand Sioux were there, camped in one huge circle: the Oglala, Miniconjou, Sans Arc, Blackfoot, Two Kettle, and Hunkpapa—all the Seven Councils except the Brules, who had had enough of the whites and had decided to fight their old enemies, the Pawnee, instead.

The rest of the Sioux all agreed that they would not give up any more land. They would resist the whites together. The council ended with a great Sun Dance, in which many of the bravest young warriors danced. But not Crazy Horse. Once again he stayed on the side, watching, listening, keeping his thoughts to himself.

The Sun Dance was the center of the Sioux way of life, a kind of communal vision quest. The center pole, the tree of life, was a cottonwood selected by a young girl. At the top, there were two cut-out rawhide figures: a man with a large, erect penis, and a buffalo bull, representing fertility. Banners in the sacred colors—yellow for the sun, blue for the sky, green for mother earth, red for the red people, white for peace and purity, and black for night—hung from the branches of the tree, along with offerings of tobacco wrapped in cloth. The dancers' pipes were placed in front of a painted buffalo skull that was filled with sage at the head of the dance ground.

For four days, from sunrise to sundown, the warriors danced to the great drums and the songs, blowing the high, piercing notes of their eagle-bone whistles, their heads and ankles wrapped in sacred sage. For four days, the warriors neither ate nor drank, testing and demonstrating their fortitude and endurance, praying to Wakan Tanka, the Great Mysterious, holding their vow in their hearts. On the third or fourth day, those who had vowed to do it demonstrated their bravery by piercing their flesh with eagle claws or wooden pegs attached to thongs hanging from the tree or to buffalo skulls, which they dragged behind them as they danced; and then they demonstrated their generosity, gratitude, courage, and fortitude by offering their flesh—which is the only thing we may truly call our own—dancing until they pulled away and their flesh broke open in an offering and sacrifice, which might bring the wisdom of a vision.

The dance ended with the dancers blessing all who had watched with their eagle-feather fans and a great feast, and then the Seven Councils disbanded to hunt. And almost nobody noticed, except perhaps the young Crazy Horse, that nothing had really been done about the whites. There was no plan or strategy; no leaders had been selected; nobody had come up with a way for the warriors to get the guns and powder they would need—maybe one out of a hundred warriors had a gun, and maybe half of those actually worked.

But probably there was no need for any of that. Everybody knew that the Sioux were the greatest warriors, and now that they had come together and decided to fight the whites, it was enough. Did they need to become white men to fight the white men?

△△ ∨ △△

In 1856, Colonel John M. Chivington, flying the American flag, massacred a peaceful village of six hundred Cheyenne and Arapaho at Sand

Creek, Colorado. White Antelope, an unarmed seventy-five-year-old chief, had come out to meet the soldiers waving a white flag, calling out clearly in English, "Stop. Stop." But he had been cut down, too, managing somehow to sing his death song:

> *Nothing lives long*
> *Only the earth and mountains.*[9]

Chivington's men had mutilated both men and women, even cutting out the women's pubic hair as scalps, just as Harney's troops had done. Enraged, the Cheyenne and the southern Lakota led by Red Cloud and Spotted Tail led a thousand Indians against the whites.

Crazy Horse soon distinguished himself as both a daring and an effective fighter. During the 1960s, Edward and Mabell Kladecek interviewed a number of Sioux who had either known Crazy Horse themselves or heard about him from their parents.

Charles Fire Thunder's father told him that Crazy Horse always used a stone war club or tomahawk and never used a gun. When he rode into battle, "he blew on his Indian bone-whistle and circled around the white soldiers or Indian enemies from other tribes. They could take shots at him, but fail to hit him."[10]

Crazy Horse always rode to battle in front of his men. According to Joseph Black Elk, "He killed every enemy he caught by knocking them on the head. He rode the fastest pony in the country. He acted with ambition and vigor to protect and defend the people of the Sioux tribe."

"The pony of warrior chief Crazy Horse could last two days of running in the battles," Joseph Black Elk says. "On certain times during the battles he rested on top of the highest hill for his pony to take the breeze and the pony gained fresh power to run again. No enemy bullet ever hit warrior chief Crazy Horse and his horse. He gained twenty-two battles during his war trail. It is believed that the inspiration of the spiritual connected his soul, mind and physical being, when he fasted on the top of the high hill of the great plains for four days and nights where he prayed to the great spirit for vision and power to serve his tribe."[11]

His enemies, too, recognized his prowess. James Sherrod, "Government Scout, Guide for Mail and Emigrant Trains, and Indian Fighter," claimed to have fought Crazy Horse on three different occasions, "but he would never get within range of my gun when he was on the war-path." He wrote that

Crazy Horse was the only Indian I ever saw that I was really afraid of. I believe he was the best Indian General that lived. He knew every bugle call and order as well as did any of the soldiers, and that alone made him a bad customer. . . . Old Crazy Horse was the worst Indian I ever saw or knew, in every way, and it takes a smart man, whether white or any other color, to be really bad.[12]

As Crazy Horse gained experience in fighting the white soldiers, he realized that the Indians would never be able to win if they continued to fight in the old ways. Bravery alone was not enough against the superior numbers and firepower of the whites, and so Crazy Horse became a skilled strategist.

In July, Crazy Horse led decoys to lure the soldiers out of a stockade across the river from the Platte Bridge. The soldiers came out of the fort with their wagon guns and over the bridge, and began to shoot, while the decoys moved slowly away, leading them on to the gullies and washes where the warriors waited in ambush. But the young braves were still fighting for coups and their own glory, and they could not wait. The soldiers saw them and the ambush was ruined.

They finally got it right on December 21, 1866. Crazy Horse led decoys again, only this time he did so as one of the four Shirt-Wearers of the Lakotas, young warriors who had been given the great responsibility of leading the people in this time of danger, taking a vow to protect all the people, without thinking of themselves or their relatives. It was the job of the Shirt-Wearers, too, to control the wild young men who still seemed to care only for coups, scalps, and horses.

Along with the other Shirt-Wearers, Crazy Horse rode his pony out and shot at the soldiers. When they started to follow, he smacked his pony with one hand as if he were trying to get away, while holding it back with the other. It took a few tries, and he had to let the soldiers get very close, but finally he got a column of soldiers to follow him—a column led by one of the most arrogant and ambitious new officers, a lieutenant by the name of Fetterman. Fetterman had just arrived in the West, and had never fought Indians before. Nevertheless, he boasted that he could ride through the entire Sioux nation with eighty men.

Fetterman marched out of the fort with strict orders not to pursue the Indians. But he couldn't resist giving chase to Crazy Horse and the other four or five decoys, who seemed to be tantalizingly just out of reach. Sometimes Crazy Horse would dismount and check his horse's hooves with a look of disgust, as if the horse had gone lame and he had to lead it with a halter. Another time he actually sat down, built a little fire, and began to boil coffee, until bullets were kicking up dust all around him.

This time the *akicita* managed to hold the warriors back, their hands over their horses' mouths. They had learned. When Fetterman's column was deep into the hills, Crazy Horse and the other decoys rode across each other's tracks. This was the signal to attack, and the hidden warriors came streaming down on all sides, in front and in back, cutting off the soldiers' retreat. Fetterman himself put his revolver to his head. Not one of the eighty men Fetterman boasted would destroy the entire Sioux nation survived.

By 1868, the U.S. government decided it had had enough. At the Laramie Treaty Council, the Sioux got everything they wanted.

According to the Laramie Treaty, the United States agreed to create a great Sioux reservation in South Dakota west of the Missouri, including the Black Hills. The United States also agreed "that the country north of the North Platte River and east of the summits of the Big Horn Mountains shall be held and considered to be unceded Indian territory" and that "military posts now established in this territory . . . shall be abandoned, and that the road leading to them and to the Territory of Montana shall be closed."[13]

It furthermore gave the Sioux hunting rights "on any lands north of the North Platte River," and stipulated that no future treaty "would be valid unless it had been signed by three-fourths of the adult males of the tribe." The Sioux, in return, were to agree to keep the peace, not to oppose the railroads being built outside their reservation, and "not to raid white men, nor carry off women and children from settlements, nor kill and scalp white men, nor molest the military posts south of the North Platte River."

The Laramie Treaty seemed to be a clear victory for the Sioux. According to historian Stanley Vestal, it was, "in fact, unique in the history of the United States. It is the only treaty made by the United States in which nothing but peace was demanded of the other signatory."[14]

Chief Red Cloud waited until the troops actually abandoned the forts on the Powder River. When they did—marching out of Fort Smith, Fort Phil Kearny, and Fort Reno—he and the Cheyenne burned them all down. Only then did he ride into Fort Laramie with his warriors and touch his pen to paper.

In 1870, Red Cloud and Spotted Bear rode the Iron Horse to Washington. There—some say—their spirits were captured in the little box by the photographer named Mathew Brady. The white men now said that the Sioux had to move to an agency in Missouri. Red Cloud managed to get them to agree to let him have his agency on Platte, as they had promised, but he did not leave with a good feeling. He did not think the Sioux could ever win against so many whites. "When we first had this land we were strong," he said, "but now we are melting like snow on a hillside, while you are grown strong like grass."

△△ VI △△

That same year Crazy Horse and He Dog were made lance bearers of the *Kangi Yuhi* (Crow Owners' Society) and they led the celebrated fight known as "When They Chased the Crows Back to Camp." When they returned from a raiding party, they were escorted back to camp and presented with the two lances of the Oglala in a big ceremony, lances that had been with the Oglalas even before they had come to the prairies.

Crazy Horse was greatly honored. But that honor did not entitle him to live on the labor of other men, as it did in the aristocratic agricultural societies of Greece, medieval Europe, or Japan. There was no separation between hunter and warrior, and so there was no separation between the man who provided the food and the man who protected the people.

In fact, both skill in hunting and honor in battle brought responsibility rather than privilege. Hunters were granted the tongue and liver of the buffalo, but they shared the rest with those who could not hunt for themselves. It was not acquisition but generosity that was the primary economic value held by the Sioux. Crazy Horse made sure that everybody had meat, and even when he came back from a raid, he gave away his horses. True to his vision, he kept nothing for himself.

Yet Crazy Horse was still a man. He had long cared for Black Buffalo Woman, whom he had known since childhood, though she had married another man, No Water. The feeling was apparently mutual, for Black Buffalo Woman left her children in the care of friends and relatives and joined Crazy Horse. This was her right as a Sioux woman, and if No Water had been a man of strong heart, he would have let Black Buffalo Woman go where she wanted. But he did not; he came into the lodge where Crazy Horse and Black Buffalo Woman sat by the fire and said, "My friend, I have come!" and pointed a pistol at Crazy Horse. Crazy Horse went for his knife, but Little Big Man stopped him, No Water pulled the trigger, the bullet hit Crazy Horse in the jaw, and he fell.

No Water got away before anybody could stop him. Crazy Horse recovered. Fighting between Sioux was looked down upon, and murder was particularly abhorrent. Black Buffalo Woman went to her relatives and Crazy Horse made it a condition that she not be blamed or harmed for what happened. Because he had broken the vows of a Shirt-Wearer by causing dissension in the tribe, his shirt was taken away. But they never gave it to anyone else. "Everything seemed to stop right there," remembered He Dog, who had fought with Crazy Horse. "Everything began to fall to pieces. After that it seemed as if anybody who wanted could wear the shirt—it meant nothing."[15]

A few years later, Crazy Horse married Red Feather's sister, Black Shawl. When asked about this marriage, He Dog said, "All I can say is that they married much later than is usual for my people." Black Shawl was twenty-eight. Soon they had a child, a daughter, Afraid-of-Her. She died when she was two, of one of the diseases the white man brought with him. Crazy Horse had been hunting when he found out. He rode to her burial scaffold and lay down beside her, grieving without food or drink for three days. How could he fight an enemy he could not see? No one was safe from the sickness the white man brought with him.

△△ V I I △△

In 1868, the Laramie Treaty had given the Sioux complete possession of Paha Sapa, the Black Hills, where men went for a *Hanblecheyapi* and the Seven Councils gathered. But soon the sacred hills were invaded by white men made mad by the discovery of gold. Crazy Horse and the other warriors killed those they found, but the white men kept coming, and on March 17, 1874, a thousand soldiers under General George C. Custer cut the road the Sioux called the Thieves' Road though the hills. When they left, they reported that they had found gold "from the grass roots down."

President Grant at first announced his determination to keep all miners out of the land that had been ceded to the Sioux. But instead of sending troops to keep out the whites who were cutting trees, digging up the earth, and killing the game, the whites sent a committee to "treat with the Sioux Indians for the relinquishment of the Black Hills."

The commissioners dispatched runners to Crazy Horse and Sitting Bull and other "wild" Indians who had continued to live in the old way, refusing to have anything to do with the government handouts that were accepted by Red Cloud and the other agency Indians. Sitting Bull said, "I want you to go and tell the Great Father that I do not want to sell any land to the government." Then he took a bit of earth between his fingers. "Not even as much as this," he said. Crazy Horse said only that he would send Little Big Man to represent his Oglalas at the council.

Little Big Man arrived with three hundred Oglalas. They rode into the council grounds firing the rifles in the air, singing:

> *The Black Hills is my land and I love it*
> *And whoever interferes*
> *Will hear this gun.*

Then Little Big Man, naked except for his breechcloth and two pistols slung through a belt, danced his horse right up to the four commissioners who were sitting in their chairs under a tarpaulin. "I will kill the first chief who speaks for selling the Black Hills," he yelled.[16]

The commissioners decided to retreat to Fort Robinson for further meetings with twenty chiefs to make their final offer: four hundred thousand dollars a year for the mineral rights or six million dollars in fifteen installments. Speaking for the Sioux, Spotted Tail firmly rejected the offers. Returning to Washington, the commissioners recommended that since the Sioux refused to sell or lease their land, Congress should buy the Black Hills even if the Sioux refused to sell.

On December 3, 1875, the Commissioner of Indian Affairs ordered all Indians living off their reservations to report to their agencies; on February 7, the War Department authorized General Philip Sheridan to begin operations against the "hostile" Indians who refused to comply, including those led by Sitting Bull and Crazy Horse. In fact, the snow was too deep for travel even if the Sioux had wanted to comply. As it was, Sitting Bull simply said he would consider coming in during the Moon When the Grass Is Up. Crazy Horse, who was camped near the Thieves' Road in the Black Hills, simply said, "One does not sell the earth upon which the people walk."[17]

* * *

On March 17, in subzero weather, with deep snow on the ground, the famous Indian-fighter General "Three Stars" Crook sent Colonel Joseph J. Reynolds to strike a village they believed to be Crazy Horse's. In fact, it was a mixed band of Cheyenne and Oglala. Some had left the Red Cloud agency to hunt in the Powder River area; others were from Crazy Horse's village to the north.

Reynolds attacked at dawn with infantry and two cavalry columns. The warriors fought off the bluecoats while the women, children, and elders crossed the river to shelter. Then the warriors themselves took up positions in the hills, watching helplessly as Reynolds burned the entire village, including a full winter's supply of buffalo meat and robes—even though his own troops were hungry and cold. He also left two dead soldiers and possibly one wounded man behind, something the Sioux never would have done.

That night the Indians managed to follow Reynolds and steal back most of their herd, as well as a fair number of Reynolds's cattle. Then they made their way to Crazy Horse's camp. "I'm glad you are come," Crazy Horse told Two Moon, the Cheyenne chief. "We are going to fight the white man again."

The attack by Reynolds, like so many other attacks on Indians who had been willing to go into the agencies, served the opposite purpose. "I am ready to fight," Two Moon told Crazy Horse. "I have fought already. My people have been killed, my horses stolen; I am satisfied to fight."[18]

As soon as it was warmer, Crazy Horse broke camp and went north to where Sitting Bull was camped at the mouth of the Tongue River. There they were joined by Brule, Sans Arc, Blackfoot, and Cheyenne. In June, in the Moon of Making Fat, Sitting Bull's Hunkpapa held their great Sun Dance. Sitting Bull cut fifty pieces of flesh from each arm and then stood facing the sun, arms raised, for three days and nights in prayer. On the fourth day he fell, and then rose to tell what he had heard and seen. "I give you these because they have no ears," a voice had told him.[19] And then he had seen many soldiers falling into camp. Wakan Tanka had given the Sioux these soldiers because they would not listen, he said.

Crazy Horse spent most of his time away from the great camp, high up in the hills, fasting for a *Hanblecheyapi*, the vision that would show him how to beat the whites and protect his people. When "Three

Stars" Crook marched into the Rosebud Valley on March 14, Crazy Horse was ready.

This time, instead of fighting as individuals, the Indians fought together, in large groups. Instead of charging straight into the carbines of the bluecoats, the Indians attacked the weak spots on the flanks.

Unable to fight in lines as they were used to doing, the bluecoats became divided, cut off, and confused. General Crook had his horse shot out from under him. Fifty-one men were killed and wounded before Crook's army began to retreat back toward Fort Fetterman. During this battle, a Cheyenne warrior was cut off when his horse was shot out from under him. His sister, who had come along to help care for the horses, rode in front of the soldiers' line and rescued him on her horse. For this reason, the Cheyenne remember the battle as the Battle Where the Girl Saved Her Brother. The whites called it the Battle of Rosebud. It was the only battle "Three Stars" ever lost.

The Sioux watched Crook retreat. Feeling secure after their great victory, they moved west to the Little Big Horn valley, where large herds of antelope had been seen. They were surprised, therefore, when only eight days later a column of soldiers attacked from the east. But it did not take long for them to form a line and drive the attackers back.

The column was one of three divisions commanded by General George Custer. Unaware of Crook's defeat, Custer had reached the Sioux by a forced march of three days and nights. His men, many of whom had never fought before, were tired and hungry. But Custer was in a hurry. He wanted to defeat the Sioux by July 4, in time for the Democratic National Convention. He had confided to his Ree scouts that if they helped him defeat the Sioux he could be made the Great Father in Washington.

When the scouts did find the encampment, they told Custer that there were too many Sioux for him to fight alone. But he was just as sure of beating the Sioux as the Sioux were that no one would dare attack their great camp after they had beaten General "Three Stars" Crook. Custer's main concern, therefore, was that the Sioux not escape, as he was sure they would try to do, and so he split his command into three columns. Major Marcus Reno was supposed to charge the village, and Custer would cut off their escape to the north.

But it didn't work out that way. Reno stopped in his tracks at the sight of the great village, and he ordered his men to form a line instead of charging directly into the village. He was subsequently driven back. "We had Reno's men on the run across the creek when Crazy Horse rode up with his men," Short Buffalo remembered in 1930. " 'Too late! you've missed the fight!' we called out to him.

" 'Sorry to miss this fight!' he laughed. 'But there's a good fight coming over the hill.' "

Short Buffalo looked at where Crazy Horse pointed, and "saw Custer and his blue coats pouring over the hill. I thought there were a million of them."

"That's where the big fight is going to be," said Crazy Horse. "We'll not miss that one."

"He was not a bit excited; he made a joke of it," said Short Buffalo. "He wheeled and rode down the river, and a little later I saw him on his pinto pony leading his men across the river." As usual when he fought, Crazy Horse was in the lead. "He was the first man across the river."[20]

Custer had tried to cross the river, but four brave Cheyenne warriors held him off. Forced back, Custer and his column—two hundred and fifty men—did their best to fight their way to the top of a hill where they hoped to be able to hold out until they were reinforced. But Crazy Horse had already led his warriors across the river and up the hill, beating Custer to the summit he hoped to gain.

Custer's fire was heavy, and some of the warriors held back. But Crazy Horse rallied them with his war cry, "Hoka Hey!" ("It is a good day to die!"). Matthew H. King, interviewed by the Kladeceks, says that on the night before the battle Crazy Horse instructed his warriors, "You cowards lay back, the Great Spirit gave us every day a beautiful day to die in."[21]

Crazy Horse was the first to break through Custer's lines. The bluecoats fired from behind the bodies of their dead horses until the Sioux overran them. Spotted Elk later said, "I was there, and all I remembered was a big cloud of dust."

When it was over, a hundred and fifty soldiers lay dead, with Custer among them. The Sioux took their clothes and whatever ammunition they had left. Then they moved upriver, leaving Reno and his survivors dug in on their hill, making sure that no one followed them.

The great camp split up, searching for the buffalo that had given them so much before the whites came. But there were hardly any buffalo left, and the Sioux were almost out of powder. The whites, meanwhile, sent more soldiers, with more supplies. They surprised and killed American Horse at Slim Butte in the fight the Sioux called the Fight Where We Lost the Black Hills. In January, General Bearcoat Miles attacked Crazy Horse at Battle Butte, using artillery "with great effect." Even so, Crazy Horse managed to make his way to the Little Powder River.

Crazy Horse's people were starving, cold, and out of ammunition. Sitting Bull planned to go to Canada, to Grandmother's land, thinking that he would be left in peace there. But Crazy Horse was finished with running. "My friend, the soldiers are everywhere," he told Sitting Bull. "The Indians are getting scattered, so that the soldiers can capture or kill them all. This is the end. All the time these soldiers will keep hunting us down. Some day I shall be killed. Well, all right. I am going south to get mine!"[22]

After Sitting Bull went to Canada, Roman Nose, Red Bear, and Touch-the-Clouds had all surrendered. Crazy Horse was the last to come in. In May 1877, Crazy Horse accepted "Three Stars" Crook's promise that he would give Crazy Horse's Oglala Sioux a reservation on the Powder River, where they could hunt and live in peace.

Red Cloud and White Hat (Lieutenant William B. Clark) met Crazy Horse on a big flat outside Fort Robinson with two troops of cavalry. They shook hands and said they were glad to see him; everybody had come in peace. Crazy Horse spread out his blanket for Red Cloud to sit on and gave his shirt to Red Cloud; He Dog did the same for White Hat. Crazy Horse dismounted from his horse, said that now was the best time for smoking the pipe of peace. He then held out his left hand to Clark, saying, "Kola [friend], I shake with this hand because my heart is on this side; I want this peace to last forever."[23]

Crazy Horse had come in, but according to General Jesse M. Lee, the military agent in charge of the Brule Sioux at Spotted Tail Agency, he had not surrendered "with the humility of a defeated, broken-spirited chief. He was an unsubdued warrior—and he had come to make such terms as would bring peace and rest to his people. To his mind, there was no 'unconditional surrender' about it."[24] He expected, and was told he would get, his own agency on the Powder River, where there was still game. He was also told that his band would be allowed to go on a buffalo hunt in the fall.

Major John G. Burke, an officer with General Crook, witnessed the surrender. "The most perfect discipline was maintained and silence reigned from the head of the cavalcade to the the furthest travois," he wrote. "When the post was reached, the warriors began to intone a peace chant."[25] Then they turned over their firearms. There were a 117 guns, mainly Winchesters and cavalry carbines, for Crazy Horse's three hundred warriors—a ratio of only one rifle for every three warriors.

Crazy Horse camped a few miles away, on Beaver Creek, as far as he could from Fort Robinson. When word came that everybody should move over to White Butte, where they were going to hold a big council, Crazy Horse decided to stay where he was, but He Dog decided to move.

"Does this mean that you will be my enemy if I move across the creek?" He Dog asked Crazy Horse.

Crazy Horse laughed in his face. He said, "I am no white man! They are the only people that make rules for other people, that say, 'If you stay on one side of this line it is peace, but if you go on the other side I will kill you all.' I don't hold with deadlines. There is plenty of room; camp where you please."[26]

At first Crazy Horse was willing to go to Washington, but only after he had secured his agency on Beaver Creek west of the Black Hills. But the soldiers wanted him to go to Washington before they gave him the agency, and then Spotted Crow and others told him that they just wanted him to go to Washington to get him away from his people and into their power. "After a while Crazy Horse got so he thought it might be true," said He Dog. He told the officers, "I am not going there. I wanted to go, but you have changed my mind. Still deep in my heart I hold that place on Beaver Creek where I want my agency. You have my horses and my guns. I have only my tent and my will. You got me to come here and you can keep me here by force if you choose, but you cannot make me go anywhere that I refuse to go."[27]

When asked whether he would go to Washington to see the Great Father, he simply said that he "was not hunting for any Great Father; *his* father was with him, and there was no Great Father between him and the Great Spirit."[28]

When Crazy Horse came in to the agency, he had believed—or at least hoped—that he and his people would get the agency he had been promised. But once he was there he found himself caught in a web of treachery and betrayal. Spotted Tail and other agency chiefs were jealous of Crazy Horse's reputation with the younger warriors and worried that the whites would make Crazy Horse more powerful than they were, while the whites skillfully played the agency Indians and the "wild" Oglalas against each other.

General Crook now wanted Crazy Horse to ride with him against Chief Joseph and the Nez Percé. Dee Brown, in *Bury My Heart at Wounded Knee,* says that Crazy Horse was so disgusted by the Sioux who accepted Crook's offer that he planned to return with his people to the Powder River. Another story has it that Crazy Horse replied,

"We are tired of war; we came in for peace, but now that your government asks our help, we will go north and fight until there is not a Nez Percé left"—but that the interpreter deliberately mistranslated his words as "until there is not a white man left."[29] Crook set out to meet with Crazy Horse himself, but when another Indian intercepted the party and said that Crazy Horse was planning to murder Crook during their council, the general turned back.

Around this same time, five warriors who had ridden with Crazy Horse—Eagle Thunder, Black Fox, and the three Kicking Bear brothers—pierced their flesh in a Sun Dance to honor Crazy Horse. (Some say this was the last time the original Sun Dance was performed.) As usual, Crazy Horse watched quietly without taking part in the dance itself. Alfred Ribman says Crazy Horse then requested "that after his death his body be painted with red war paint and plunged into the fresh water (it did not matter where) to be restored back to life, otherwise his bones would be turned into stone and his joints into flint, but his spirit would rise."[30] Then Crazy Horse rode his pony to the peak of Beaver Mountain, where he fasted to seal his vow that he would end his war trail. Then he made his prophecy: "If anything happens to me, I will return to the Thunder Gods and from there I will look after my people with the power of the Thunder Gods."[31]

Two days later, on September 5, 1877, He Dog came to tell Crazy Horse that the soldiers were coming for him. Crazy Horse took his wife, Black Shawl, to her mother in Spotted Tail's camp. On the way there, he was stopped by Indian police now working for the soldiers. "I am Crazy Horse!" he said proudly. "Do not touch me! I am not running away."[32]

He went back to Fort Reynolds, having been promised that he would be able to "explain" his side of things. In fact, the whites had already arranged to imprison Crazy Horse on one of the Far Tortugas, and when he reached Fort Robinson, he was was told that the general could not see him until morning. Then he was escorted into the guardhouse. As soon as Crazy Horse saw the room with one small barred window and men with iron chains on their legs, he drew a knife he had managed to conceal and pushed past the guards, out the door.

Then it all happened, just as it had happened in his vision. One of his own people, Little Big Man, grabbed his hand and held it behind his back. Someone yelled, "Kill him! Kill him!" A guard thrust a bayonet into his right side and through his kidneys, and then again into his back, and Crazy Horse fell. Dr. Valentine McGillycuddy moved him to the adjutant's office, where he was joined by the seven-foot

Touch-the-Clouds and then by his father. In 1930, the doctor remembered Crazy Horse's death: "At about eleven P.M. that night in the gloomy old adjutant's office, the bugler on the parade ground wailed the lonesome call for Taps. It brought back to him the old battles; he struggled to arise and there came from his lips his old rallying cry, 'A good day to fight, a good day to die! Brave hearts.'"

Touch-the-Clouds lay his hands across Crazy Horse's chest and said, "It is well. He has looked for death and it has come."[33]

McGillycuddy's version of Crazy Horse's last words might or might not be true—no one else seems to remember them that way. But they mark, in any case, the passing of the great warrior from life to legend.

Crazy Horse's body was lashed to a travois and taken from the fort by his parents. They carried him to the camp on Beaver Creek and placed his body in a burial tree, an old elm, for a night and a day. People came and sang death songs, and at noon there was a feast. That night his father and mother took the body down and buried him secretly, probably somewhere on Beaver Mountain. And another legend promptly arose—that on cold nights the fierce "warrior's wind" that was the spirit of Crazy Horse could be heard howling over the plains.

Crazy Horse himself was a warrior of few words; he spoke with his actions. Once again, the closest thing we have to a last testament, actually the longest statement attributed to him, was bequeathed to us by Dr. McGillycuddy. It runs as follows:

> We did not ask you white men to come here. The Great Spirit gave us this country as a home. You had yours. We did not interfere with you. The Great Spirit gave us plenty of land to live on and buffalo; you are taking my land from me; you are killing off our game, so it is hard for us to live. Now you tell us to work for a living, but the Great Spirit did not make us to work, but to live by hunting. You white men can work if you want to. We do not interfere with you, and again you say, why do you not become civilized? We do not want your civilization! We would live as our fathers did, and their fathers before them.[34]

⋀⋀ V I I I ⋀⋀

This was not to be. Without warfare, there was no way for the warriors to win prestige or honor—no coups, no horses to steal, no dances, no warrior societies. Without the buffalo and other game, there was no way to live, though the government did permit a hunt—the last one, it turned out—when a herd wandered through Standing Rock and Cheyenne River in 1882. In their frustration, some Indians hunted long-horned government-issue cattle as if they were buffalo—until the Indian Bureau prohibited the practice in 1890.

Having taken everything on which the Indians' culture had been based, the government next turned to the culture itself. In 1881 Hiram Price, the Commissioner for Indian Affairs, declared that "to domesticate and civilize wild Indians is a noble work, the accomplishment of which should be a crown of glory to any nation," and set out a number of "Indian offenses." These included the holding of feasts, having more than one wife, and all the practices of medicine men. It was an offense to "purchase" a wife by leaving property at her father's door, and it was an offense to destroy property, which was a traditional expression of grief. It was also an offense to hold dances, especially and including the Sun Dance. The last Sun Dance was held on the Great Sioux Reservation in 1883. The agent who permitted the Indians to hold it was the same Dr. McGillycuddy who had treated Crazy Horse at Fort Robinson.

But it was not a simple task to keep the Sioux from dancing. In 1890, they—along with many other Native Americans—joined in a Ghost Dance, which had been revealed to a Paiute prophet, Wovoka. Wovoka taught that the Ghost Dance, which went on for four nights, would bring about the regeneration of the earth. "All Indians must dance, everywhere, keep on dancing," Wovoka said. "Pretty soon in next spring the Great Spirit will come. He will bring back all game of every kind. The game will be thick everywhere. All dead Indians will come back and live again."[35]

For the Sioux, the need for such hope had never been so great. The buffalo were gone. Their cattle had been diminished by disease, their crops had failed, there were epidemics of measles, grippe, and whooping cough. Then the government cut the rations promised by its treaties in half.

The Sioux in Pine Ridge and Rosebud danced slowly around a tree, from left to right, holding hands, while a young girl held the sacred pipe toward the west, praying for the messiah to come. They danced, without out drums or rattles or eagle-bone whistles, to the songs that came in vision to some of them. They danced for four nights, wearing the ghost shirt—hung with eagle feathers, fringed with red ocher, painted with sun, crescent moon, stars, eagle, magpie, crow, or sage hen—which would make the dancers invulnerable to the bullets of the soldiers.

The agents and other whites were convinced that the "crazy" Indians were whipping themselves up to go on the warpath. The soldiers came once again, to put a stop to the dangerous "agitation." Sitting Bull, who had returned to North Dakota from Canada, was killed when Indian police attempted to arrest him on the morning of December 15, 1890. When 370 Brule Sioux from the Rosebud Reservation sought refuge at the Pine Ridge Reservation, they were intercepted and "escorted" to Wounded Knee by soldiers from the Seventh Cavalry, the cavalry once led by Custer The Brule surrendered their weapons, but when the soldiers discovered a rifle hidden under a blanket, the soldiers—some say they were crying, "Remember Custer!"—opened fire with their Hotchkiss guns. Within minutes, perhaps a hundred warriors along with sixty soldiers were dead, while another hundred or more Brule women and children were pursued and cut down as they tried to escape to the ravine along Wounded Knee Creek.

But the vision of new life, like the spirit of Crazy Horse, could not be killed. It survived to be passed on in the songs of the Ghost Dancers:

The father will descend,
The earth will tremble.

Everybody will arise.
Stretch out your hands.

We shall live again,
We shall live again.

WP-72

THE LONE
WARRIOR

The American Mission

*We have reached a point where almost everyone
exposed to combat will, within a relatively short time,
be killed, wounded, or driven mad. . . .
In such circumstances, one can only wonder
what meaning such human qualities as
courage, endurance, and heroism still have.
–Military psychiatrist Richard A. Gabriel*

Hoofbeats thunder, shots ring out. A party of Texas Rangers pursuing
Butch Cavendish and his gang into a narrow canyon ride straight into
an ambush. In the fierce gun battle that follows, all the Rangers are
killed—except for one, who comes to, days later, in a cave. An Indian
bends over him tenderly, speaks softly:

"Me . . . Tonto."

"What happened? Where am I?"

"Other Texas Rangers—all dead. You only Ranger left. *You lone
Ranger now.*"

The Lone Ranger vows to track down the gang that killed his fellow
Rangers, including his older brother. In order to keep his identity secret
from the powerful outlaw organization, he disguises himself with a
black mask cut from his dead brother's vest. "In the Ranger's eye," the
deep voice of the announcer intones, "there was a light that must have
burned in the eyes of knights in armor, a light that through the ages

must have lifted the souls of strong men who fought for justice, for God!"[1]

The Lone Ranger, with his faithful sidekick, Tonto, and his wonder horse, Silver, track down the members of the Cavendish gang one by one. Using silver bullets, he never kills or maims, but manages to shoot the outlaws' guns out of their hands. Then he ties them up and turns them over to the proper law enforcement officials. Finally, he and Tonto capture Cavendish himself. But his work has just begun. The Lone Ranger rises above personal revenge and vows to lead the fight for law and order in the Old West.

His dead brother's wife, meanwhile, has been killed by Indians. By the time the Lone Ranger finds his brother's son—who has been raised by a kindly old woman—he has become a teenager. Taking him under his wing, as he had promised, the Lone Ranger prepares the youth for his future role in life. His parents, the Lone Ranger explains, who died fighting Indians and outlaws, "have handed down to you the right to worship as you choose, and the right to work and profit from your enterprise. They've given you a land where there is true freedom, true equality of opportunity—a nation that is governed by the people, by the laws that are best for the greatest number. Your duty, Dan, is to preserve that heritage and strengthen it. That is the duty and heritage of every American."[2]

◮◮ I I ◮◮

The Lone Ranger, who first rode the airwaves of radio station WXYZ in 1933 out of Detroit, was a composite figure, the culmination of all the mythic cowboy figures that had ridden the Great Plains in pulp novels, Wild West shows, comics, radio, and movies. He was the most perfect embodiment of the myth of the lone warrior, a uniquely American version of the heroic warrior.

This myth of the lone warrior was derived partly from the Christian heroism of the European knights, partly from the citizen militia who fought against the tyranny of royalty and inherited privilege, and partly from the frontiersmen who fought Indians to clear the land for civilization. Its purest form was the cowboy savior. The myth of the lone warrior is recent, as far as myths go, and seemingly marginal, arising as it did not in any of the great centers of world civilization, but in a remote former European colony. And yet, through American force and media technology, it has tremendous power, not just in America but in the television-linked global village.

The lone warrior is very different from the ancient mythical warrior-heroes of primitive, archaic, or ancient cultures. Unlike Joseph Campbell's monomythic hero, the lone warrior does not undergo an initiation, nor does he bring power or knowledge back to his community. Nor does he suffer the tragic necessary consequences of power, like Dumezil's dark and stormy Indo-European proto-warrior. And he has even less in common with the Japanese warrior, who suffers the nobility of failure as proof of his sincerity.

At first glance, the lone warrior seems closest to the European knight-errant, as Zane Grey, who called one of his last books *Knights of the Plains,* saw. But here, too, there are crucial differences. First of all, the lone warrior saves maidens not from dragons but from Indians (tales of captivity and rescue or escape were perhaps the first American literature). Second, his weapons are firearms: a rifle if he is a frontiersman, and the six-shooter if he is a cowboy. And finally, he rides out not on a quest but a mission.

△△ I I I △△

The myth of the lone warrior grew out of an intolerable contradiction. When the first settlers arrived in the New World, they thought they had found a new Eden, "a terrestrial paradise," as Columbus called it. Just before the Puritans disembarked in Salem in 1630, John Winthrop preached a sermon telling the settlers that the community they were about to found would be "as a City on a Hill" in which the settlers would "delight in each other," since they were "of the same body."[3]

The vast space and the teeming riches of the land and the forests would provide the opportunity for all men, along with their brave and innocent women and children, to create a life of Christian love and neighborliness. The wilderness would be tamed and turned into the Garden of the New Eden.

The only problem was that the garden was already planted with corn, beans, sweet potatoes, and tobacco, and the teeming forests were already the hunting and gathering grounds of Iroquois, Algonquin, Penobscot, Cherokee, and hundreds of other peoples. Eden had to be conquered by gunpowder. The garden was created out of the blood of the same *Indios* whom Columbus had characterized as having the "innocent qualities of Adam and Eve." The contradiction led to a reversal. The invaders became the defenders. The Indians were not innocents like Adam and Eve or even Noble Savages, as Rousseau and other Romantics cast them, but brute savages who massacred and tortured their victims.

With the founding of the Republic, the original religious vision of the settlers took a civic turn. The new Eden became both the spiritual and secular hope of the world. It was a shining beacon safely removed from the corrupt and tyrannical power of the Old World. It was that hitherto unimagined thing, a democratic Eden.

The men who had used their rifles to drive back the Indians now used those same guns to fight the tyranny of the Old World kings. They were not knights or professional soldiers, but citizen militia, Minute Men. In the new Republic, there was no warrior caste to monopolize weapons. Rather, every man was a warrior, and his home his castle.

Eden, meanwhile, had been deferred and pushed west, along with the Indians. The trail was blazed by trappers and hunters, frontiersmen like Davey Crockett and Kit Carson, men who who were, as Frederick Jackson Turner wrote in his classic paper *The Significance of the Frontier in American History,* on "the outer edge of the wave—the meeting point between savagery and civilization." These buckskin-clad men were the first truly American version of the lone warrior. Out of them came the "traits of the frontier" which Turner listed as making up the distinctly American character: "That coarseness and strength combined with acuteness and inquisitiveness; that practical, inventive turn of mind, quick to find expedients; that masterful grasp of material things, lacking in the artistic but powerful to effect great ends; that restless nervous energy; that dominant individualism, working for good and evil, and with all the buoyancy that comes with freedom."[4]

After the Civil War, the frontier opened up. Thousands of veterans, from both North and South, headed west to drive great herds of Texas longhorns to Kansas, where they could be shipped to the stockyards back East on the Union Pacific.

The work was hard, lonely, grueling, monotonous, tedious, dangerous, and ill-paid. Cowboys, as they came to be called, had to stay in the saddle all day and sometimes all night, in searing heat, driving rain, and icy blizzards. They had to be able to rope and break the horses they rode, sometimes a different one every morning. They had to head off stampedes caused by lightning or thirst. They had to capture and brand calves, pull cows out of mud, untangle steers from brush. They had to protect their herds from wolves or from Indians whose hunting grounds they passed through. "Upset our wagon in River & lost Many of our cooking utensils," George Duffield recorded in his diary during a Texas longhorn drive in 1866. "Was on my horse the whole night & it raining hard. . . . Nothing but Bread & Coffee. Hands all Growling & Swearing—everything wet & cold. Indians very troublesome. Dark days are these to me."[5]

It was during this period of the open-range drives—from 1865 to 1885—that the cowboy "Code of the West" took shape. Though he was essentially a hired hand, the cowboy (like the frontiersmen before him) insisted on his independence. He was his own man, as long as he had his horse, his rope, and his gun. If he didn't get along with his boss, he could always ride away to find work on another outfit. The West was a place of fresh starts, and it was considered rude to ask a man about his past or even his name, if he didn't volunteer it. "Rude and unlettered though he might be," wrote Ramon Adams, "and treating his companions with a rough and ready familiarity, the cowboy yet accorded his neighbor the right to live the life and go the gait which seemed most pleasing to himself. One did not intrude upon the rights of others in the cattle country, and he looked to it very promptly that no one should intrude upon his own."[6]

The unwritten cowboy code grew out of the wide-open range. Cowboys were expected to keep their word, to be courageous, uncomplaining, and hard-working. Ranchers were expected to offer strangers a meal and a place to sleep. Respectable woman were treated with Victorian courtesy.

The cowboy at the end of the trail, however, was a very different creature. Riding into town, firing his six-shooters into the air, he headed straight for saloons filled with gamblers, cheap whiskey, and working women, called "soiled doves." Since nearly everybody packed a gun, it was considered safer to shoot first when arguments about gambling, women, or matters of pride arose. These gunfights were rarely, if ever, anything like chivalrous duels. In many cases, shooting a man in the back or in the dark (as Wyatt Earp shot Billy the Kid) was not considered unfair but smart.

The cowboy thus came to be both admired and feared. "They roam about in sparsely settled villages with revolvers, pistols and knives in their belts, attacking every peaceable citizen met with," *The Las Vegas Optic* of New Mexico complained in 1881. "Now and then they take part in a dance, the sound of the music frequently being deadened by the crack of their pistols, and the hoedown only being interrupted long enough to drag out the wounded," while a year later the *Texas Livestock Journal* rhapsodized that "the cowboy is as chivalrous as the famed knights of old. Rough he may be, and it may be that he is not a master in ball room etiquette, but no set of men have loftier reverence for women and no set of men would risk more in the defense of their person or their honor."[7]

◭ IV ◭

The myth of the chivalrous cowboy was largely the creation of dime novelists and the men who served as their models. Ned Buntline, for example, made Buffalo Bill Cody famous—and soon Cody was in Chicago starring in a play based on his own character. By 1882, the one-time Indian fighter, Pony Express rider, and buffalo hunter had started his own Wild West show, which would employ his old friends, Wild Bill Hickok and Buck Henry, whom he billed as "the king of the cowboys," as well as cowgirls like sharpshooter Annie Oakley and Calamity Jane. He also hired a number of Indians, including Sitting Bull, whom some spectators booed for his part in Custer's massacre. Sitting Bull himself did not seem to mind. He sold hundreds of copies of his photograph, adopted Annie Oakley, and said that Buffalo Bill, whom he called by his Indian name, Pahaska, or Long Hair, was a sincere and genuine man. On tour in Canada, Bill repaid the compliment. "The defeat of Custer was not a massacre," he told reporters. "The Indians were being pursued by skilled fighters with orders to kill. For centuries they had been hounded from the Atlantic to the Pacific and back again. They had their wives and little ones to protect and they were fighting for their existence."[8]

Buffalo Bill Cody's Wild West Show and Congress of Rough Riders was hugely successful. A million New Yorkers jammed into Madison Square Garden to watch Buffalo Bill and his Rough Riders gallop to rescue the Deadwood coach from desperados or reenact Custer's Last Stand. In 1887, Buffalo Bill took the show to Europe, where he performed for Queen Victoria in Windsor Castle on the occasion of her Golden Jubilee. To open the show, Bill rode in carrying an American flag, which he dipped in salute. The queen and her party rose and bowed in return. "Then there arose such a genuine heart-stirring American yell as seemed to shake the sky. For the first time in history since the Declaration of Independence a sovereign of Great Britain saluted the Star-Spangled Banner."[9]

In 1902, the myth was further refined when Owen Wister, a Harvard-educated lawyer, published his book *The Virginian*. The Virginian was a mysterious outsider, first glimpsed by the narrator in a Wyoming railroad station: "Lounging there at ease against the wall was a slim young giant, more beautiful than pictures. His broad, soft hat was pushed back; a loose-knotted, dull-scarlet handkerchief sagged from his throat; and one casual thumb was hooked in the cartridge-belt that slanted across his hips."[10]

The cowboy savior rescued the narrator from a runaway horse and a rattlesnake. Then he plucked the lovely eastern schoolteacher, Molly Wood, from a stagecoach sinking in a raging river. After these preliminaries, he tracked down the gang of cattle rustlers led by the evil Trampas. When one of the rustlers turned out to be a former friend, he insisted on going ahead with the lynching. The innocent Molly objected, but a rancher explained the necessity of it. "We are in a very bad way, and we are trying to make that way a little better until civilization can reach us," he said. "And so when your ordinary citizen sees this, and sees that he has placed justice in a dead hand, he must take justice back into his own hands where it was once at the beginning of all things. Call this primitive, if you will. But so far from being a *defiance* of the law, it is an assertion of it—the fundamental assertion of self-governing men, upon whom our whole social fabric is based."[11]

When the time came for the Virginian to risk his life in a shootout against Trampas, Molly threatened to call off the marriage. But the Virginian had already given Trampas two warnings. Now duty and honor demanded that he face Trampas in the first version of the western "walkdown" duel in American literature. The Virginian won, of course, after letting Trampas draw first and shoot first, by displaying two of the main qualities of the lone warrior. "You were that cool!" as one bystander says. "That quick!"[12]

In the end, Molly relented. Unlike later, more purely lonely warriors like the Lone Ranger, the Virginian got to enjoy his girl.

The lone warrior as he appeared in Buffalo Bill's Wild West Show, *The Virginian*, and *The Lone Ranger* was the mythic American answer to the contradictions inherent in the American warrior's dilemma. The Indians who performed for Buffalo Bill reinforced the fundamental denial of the myth by demonstrating that the Indians had, in fact, been the aggressors who attacked peaceful settlers. By the time the myth had crystallized as the Lone Ranger, the Indian had become the Lone Ranger's companion and sidekick.

Unlike earlier warriors, the lone warrior's power was based on the technology of firearms from the very beginning. The ideal lone warrior, therefore, was presented as a man who triumphed by speed, superior marksmanship, and—above all—control. The Virginian was cool and self-contained, but quick when he had to be. The Lone Ranger went even further. He was so skillful that he could shoot the gun out of the bad guy's hand, or maybe just nick him in the shoulder. As the writer's guidelines for the Lone Ranger scripts put it, "The Lone Ranger never shoots to kill. When he has to use guns, he aims to maim as painlessly as possible."[13]

By using his superior marksmanship to defeat his opponent without killing him, the Lone Ranger manages to reconcile the violent vigilante and the Christian cowboy savior. As Robert Jewett and John Shelton write in *The American Monomyth*, "Just as in the later theory of nuclear deterrence, unlimited power is celebrated as the ultimate defense, because it will presumably never have to be used destructively. Magical silver missiles will keep the foe from aggression, incurring no blame on selfless redeemers. All one needs to escape the ambiguity of violent power is more power."[14]

But even more is required. As the defender of a democratic small-town Eden, the lone warrior cannot rise too far above the ordinary good citizens he has vowed to protect without contradicting the very democratic values he is defending. And so the Lone Ranger renounces all the privileges and trappings of power. The coolness and control of his gunplay becomes a moral stance. With all-American asceticism, he remains anonymous, a masked heroic everyman. He does not drink, gamble, smoke, or use profanity. He renounces wealth, vowing to use the profits from the silver mine his brother left him only to support his crusade and supply his silver bullets. He renounces women, leaving the girl he has rescued behind to presumably marry the nice, if ineffectual, man on the next ranch. He renounces, in the end, the very community he has saved. He does not stay around to see what happens once Eden has been cleansed of corruption. He may be willing to risk his life to save the community, but he is not willing to risk involvement in the day-to-day life of the community. He protects the right to vote, but he does not vote himself or get involved in local politics. Instead, he rides safely off into the sunset, invincible and invulnerable, a savior who will return only whenever evil threatens Eden again, in the eternal next episode.

$$\Lambda\!\Lambda \quad V \quad \Lambda\!\Lambda$$

Owen Wister's *The Virginian* furnished the mold from which the basic myth of the cowboy would be endlessly recast and refined. Theodore Roosevelt, the man to whom *The Virginian* was dedicated, took the cowboy and turned him into a hybrid cowboy-soldier with a new mission. Roosevelt's Rough Riders fought to expand the American frontier beyond the continental limits to Latin America and the Pacific. As far as Roosevelt was concerned, the cowboy-soldier was the defender of Anglo-Saxon civilization. The Rough Rider's mission was to be part of "the grandeur of the movement by which the English-speaking race was to spread over the world's waste space, until a fourth of the habitable globe was in its hands, and until it became the mightiest race on which the sun ever shone."[15]

Roosevelt was, as his biographer John Milton Cooper, Jr., says, "the most prominent militarist in American history." But he was also much more. His vision of the warrior included but was not limited to fighting in war. He was, in the title of an earlier biographer, "Roosevelt, the Happy Warrior."[16] He preached and lived "the doctrine of the strenuous life, the life of toil and effort, of labor and strife" with great gusto. "The worst of all fears," he concluded, "is the fear of living."[17]

Theodore Roosevelt was a pivotal figure in the formation of the American warrior. He was a naturalist, a big-game hunter, a rancher, police commissioner of New York City, and finally President. He was also a gifted historian and one of the first and most effective conservationists. If he was indeed a militarist, he was not the sort of militarist who sent other men off to die; indeed, he insisted on placing himself in the thick of battle.

As a child, young "Tweedie" Roosevelt was sickly, nervous, timid, bookish, asthmatic, and nearsighted. His father told him, "Theodore, you have mind, but you have not the body and without the help of the body the mind cannot go as far as it should. You must *make* your body."[18] He agreed: "Having become quickly and bitterly conscious that I did not have the natural prowess to hold my own, I decided that I would try to supply its place by training."[19] He lifted weights, took up boxing, wrestling, rowing, and football. He learned to use a shotgun, hiked, hunted, and rode horses.

In 1884, Roosevelt lost both his mother and his young wife. Noting that "black care rarely sits behind a rider whose pace is fast enough," he continued his training in the Badlands of the Dakota Territory. Though he owned two cattle ranches, he insisted on joining his hands on the roundups and cattle drives. He even served as a deputy sheriff, tracked down a gang of horse thieves, and decked a cowboy who had insulted him in a bar. In the end, he won the respect of the cowboys— "the rough riders of the plains, the hero of the rope and revolver,"[20] as he called them—and the admiration of his eastern friends, who noticed that he had returned from the West a changed man. "It was a fine healthy life, too," he wrote in one of the numerous articles which recounted his western adventure. "It taught a man self-reliance, hardi-hood, and the value of instant decision."[21]

When the Spanish-American War came, he was in Washington, the Assistant Secretary of the Navy. He promptly resigned his post and volunteered. "I had always felt that if there were a serious war I wished to be in a position to explain to my children why I did take part in it," he explained in his autobiography, "and not why I did not." In any case, he had spoken out publicly for the war and insisted that "when a man takes such a position, he ought to be willing to make his words good by his deeds. . . . He should pay with his body."[22]

The truth was that Roosevelt had been lusting for battle for a long time. It was the final initiation, the last test that would complete the transformation of the sickly youth into a real man.

Lieutenant Colonel Roosevelt entered the service as the organizer of the First United States Volunteer Cavalry, or Roosevelt's Rough Riders, as the press dubbed them. There were bluebloods from Har-vard, Yale, and Princeton, but mostly they were cowboys. Cowboys, Roosevelt pointed out, would make the best soldiers, since they "were intelligent and self-reliant; they possessed hardihood and endurance and physical prowess; and, above all, they had the fighting edge, the cool and resolute fighting temper."[23]

July 1, 1898, was "the great day" of Roosevelt's life. Leaping on his horse, Little Texas, waving his cowboy hat, he led the Rough Riders toward the Spanish troops dug in on San Juan Ridge and Kettle Hill. He was stopped at the forward lines by a regular army officer who said he had no orders to charge. "Then let my men through, sir," Roosevelt said. "I waved my hat, and we went up the hill with a rush," he wrote.[24] Later, he found himself leading a charge accompanied by only four men, three of whom were killed in the fight. Returning to his lines, he found that no one else had heard his command to charge, and he once again led his men to Kettle Hill. Reaching the top alone except for his orderly, he shot a Spaniard dead with a pistol salvaged from the battle-ship *The Maine.* The man went down "neatly as a jackrabbit." Roose-velt was exultant. "All men who feel any power of joy in battle," he wrote later, "know what it is like when the wolf rises in the heart."[25]

That night, he strode back and forth as cannon shells exploded all around him. To his admiring men, the lieutenant colonel seemed charmed and invulnerable. As one of the Rough Riders wrote home, "I really believe firmly now they can't kill him."[26]

The Rough Riders returned to the States after four months with nearly half their number dead from bullets, yellow fever, or malaria.

Before their final muster, they presented Roosevelt with a Remington bronze, "The Bronco-Buster," a cowboy atop a bucking horse, waving his hat. Then the Rough Riders headed into New York "with wild cowboy yells."[27] The Colonel himself rode the publicity—provided by the *Herald*'s Richard Harding Davis, Stephen Crane, and the new moving pictures from the Vitagraph company—into the governor's mansion of New York, and then into the White House. Continuing the strenuous life, he led his "Tennis Cabinet" on cross-country walks, "not turning aside for anything—for instance, swimming Rock Creek or even the Potomac if it came our way."[28] He continued boxing and wrestling, until in a boxing match a young artillery captain "cross-countered me on the eye, and the blow smashed the little blood vessels."[29]

Reluctantly he gave up boxing, only to replace it with jujitsu. His jujitsu instructor was a student of Sokaku Takeda, master of Daito-ryu jujitsu (and one of the main teachers of the future founder of aikido). The American consul to Japan, Townsend Warner, had discovered the power of the art when he insulted the diminutive Takeda on a Tokyo train. Though the consul was six feet tall, Takeda had subdued him easily with a wrist lock. Thinking (rightly, as it turned out) that the President would like to know about such an effective martial art, Townsend had arranged for one of Takeda's students to teach in Washington.[30]

Age did nothing to diminish Roosevelt's eagerness for a good fight. On April 10, 1917, at the age of fifty-eight, former President Roosevelt paid a visit on his old rival, Woodrow Wilson. Roosevelt suggested that Wilson allow him to organize a volunteer regiment against the Huns in the Great War, just as he had done twenty years earlier against the Spanish in Cuba.

Wilson, who found Roosevelt to be "a great big boy," sent the Colonel's request on to the War Department. It was politely declined. The new warfare demanded not warriors but soldiers—conscripts who obeyed regulations, not volunteers who made up their own codes. Instead of a few heroes charging up hills, the new war was about numbers and firepower. The most important virtue was obedience to orders which would send hundreds of thousands of soldiers charging out of their trenches to be mowed down by machine gun fire or felled by poison gas.

Wilson had tried to keep the United States out of it as long as he could. When he finally gave in, he did so with the hope that this war, at least, would "make the world safe for democracy." Later, it would be called "the war to end all wars." And in one sense, it may have been just that. There was no longer any glory in it. Hemingway spoke for a whole generation when he wrote, "Never think that war no matter how necessary nor how justified is not a crime. Ask the infantry and ask the dead."[31]

△△ VI △△

Still, Hemingway and many others went on to fight in the Good War, the "Crusade in Europe," as General Eisenhower called it. If ever any war was worth fighting, it seemed, it was this one. Once more the war was fought by a citizen army, personified as G.I. Joe. When it was over, the most decorated G.I. of the war, the quintessential warrior-hero, turned out to be a slight, freckle-faced, blue-eyed kid by the name of Audie Murphy. Murphy had won twenty-five medals, including five Purple Hearts, six Bronze Stars, and the Congressional Medal of Honor in three years of fighting in Europe. He was credited with killing 150 Germans.

Murphy's freckled, smiling face, with his cap set jauntily askew, appeared on the cover of *Life* magazine along with the words "Most Decorated Soldier" on July 16, 1945, the same day, as it turned out, that the atomic bomb was successfully and secretly detonated at Alamogordo, New Mexico. Like Buffalo Bill, he ended playing himself, or versions of himself, in a dramatization of his book *To Hell and Back* in 1955, and in a number of other B westerns and war pictures. He was almost always victorious and seemingly invulnerable.

But when writer Thomas Morgan sought him out in his home in North Hollywood in 1967, Murphy showed him his garage, which he had converted into a bedroom so that he could sleep there with all the lights on and a pistol by his side without disturbing his wife. He had a recurrent nightmare: "I would dream I am on a hill and all these faceless people are charging up at me." In combat, he had said, all your senses are heightened, your hearing gets very acute, but now every little sound woke him up. His doctor prescribed tranquilizers. It took him years to figure out that he had become addicted.

"I guess people don't understand about war," he said. "I go back in my mind twenty-five years, I remember thinking it was going to be a great adventure. I remember we came under artillery fire my very first day in action. That was in Sicily. And I saw a couple of guys I knew get blown up. I was very serious after that. Very serious. I wanted to take what toll of the enemy I could.

"Let me tell you," he said, "the enemy is very impersonal. The enemy is just a number of people out there in uniform trying to kill you. So all you can do is develop the mental attitude of an executioner and get on with the job."

The only trouble was that when you came back it was difficult to know how to turn it off. "That's my problem, I'll admit," he said. "To become an executioner, somebody cold and analytical, to be trained to kill, and then to come back into civilian life and be alone in the crowd—it takes an awful long time to get over it. Fear and depression come over you."

But he did not want to give the wrong impression. Like many others, he had to admit that war had its good points. Being that close to death made you feel alive. It made the world real, more vivid, more exciting. It mobilized people. It put things in perspective. It forged a deep bond, a brotherhood-in-arms, "a rapport that you'll never have again, not in our society anyway."

"It brings out the best in men," he said simply. "It's gory and it's unfortunate, but most people in combat stand a little taller."[32]

ᐃᐃ V I I ᐃᐃ

The Audie Murphy who played himself or other lone warriors in the movies was part of the legacy the sons and daughters of the men who fought in the Good War grew up with. So was John Wayne, who starred in *The Sands of Iwo Jima,* and the sailors, pilots, and the great guns firing throughout the documentary television series *Victory at Sea.*

Twenty years later, many of the young men who went to Vietnam went with these images reeling through their heads. For the most part they received their ideas of what war was like from the flickering images of movies and television. "I saw myself charging up some distant beachhead, like John Wayne in *Sands of Iwo Jima,"* novelist Philip Caputo remembers, "and then coming home a suntanned warrior with medals on my chest."[33]

The reality, as usual, was very different. War on television did not include seeing your buddy get blown to bits because he happened to sit down for a cigarette in the wrong place at the wrong time. It did not include the smell of children's flesh burning with napalm. It did not include losing an arm or a foot or ending up a quadraplegic in a motorized wheelchair.

There were attempts, as always, to shore up the debacle with the old mythology. John Wayne did his best in the movie *The Green Berets*. Operations were called "Prairie," or "Sam Houston," even "Crazy Horse." The unsecured area outside the compounds was "Indian Country." And the term "cowboy" was appropriated by the CIA to mean an operative who might be called on for special assignments like assassinations.

The cavalry, who rode helicopter gunships now, did not arrive at the last minute to save the day, though they did manage to lift the ambassador and the flag off the roof of the U.S. Embassy just in time. In the end, though, the mission was judged to be a failure. Nothing was saved; no one was redeemed.

Neither were the vets who returned home welcomed like John Wayne or Audie Murphy. There was no ceremonial reentry, no purification, no rites, no parades. Soldiers in World War II had come home slowly, on troop ships, where they had debriefed themselves. Vietnam vets might be in the middle of the jungle one day, and then forty-eight hours later find themselves stepping out of a plane and out of the army in San Francisco into an America where nobody wanted to hear about it.

As the aftershocks of the war began to take their toll, in 1971 a few men active in the organization Vietnam Veterans Against the War began meeting in informal rap groups. They talked about everything— the absurdities, horrors, and atrocities of the war, the politics of the war, the nightmares of the war, the blank lack of feeling, the drugs, Agent Orange, Delayed Stress Syndrome, what it felt like to kill and what it felt like to see killing; and they wondered why they had survived. They talked about how hard it was to reenter this country where nobody wanted to hear about what had happened. They fashioned their own rite of return from the only thing they had: the shared truth of their own experience.

They talked about the myths that led them to join up, and about the reality they had found. "Always the men came back to the John Wayne thing, sensing that it had to do with psychological matters at the core of their struggle," writes Robert Jay Lifton, the Yale psychiatrist who helped start the first rap groups.

> Around that phrase they could explore a whole constellation of masculine attitudes, encouraged or even nurtured by American culture,

and contributing to war-making: being tough (even brutal) tight-lipped, fists ready (or quick on the draw), physically powerful, hard, ruthlessly competitive; anti-artistic; a no-nonsense sexual conqueror for whom women were either inferior, inscrutable, or at best weaker creatures; and, above all, unquestionable loyalty to one's immediate (often all-male) group or one's nation to the point of being ever ready to kill or die for it.[34]

Not many men could continue to wear the mask of the lone warrior—the mask of cool, controlled, contained anonymity—in a roomful of other lone warriors spilling their guts out to each other. The "John Wayne thing," as the men called it, was judged in the harsh glare of Vietnam and found wanting. Remembering the day he had killed a Viet Cong soldier with a knife, a vet confessed, "I felt sorry," and then admitted, "I don't know why I felt sorry. John Wayne never felt sorry."[35]

The John Wayne image, as Lifton found, included

both chivalric and brutalizing images of manhood, and becomes associated with a principle of honor formed around a survivor mission of either avenging old defeats, or else perpetuating old victories and their related codes of behavior. The young man can be true to this legacy, repay the "debt of honor" he owes his father and his nation . . . only by answering his call to his war.

But with Vietnam something went wrong for that young man. *This* war at *this* time did not, psychologically speaking, work for him.[36]

If it occasionally provided the chance for someone to prove himself as a warrior-hero, it generally revealed the absurdity, brutality, and mean-inglessness of war. Since most vets came to feel that the higher purpose for which the war was supposedly being fought was a sham, dying in the war became absurd. In the absence of any higher cause or purpose, the only possible "survivor mission" became revenge—which played a large part in the massacre of civilians at My Lai.

Those vets who later opposed the war, however, had "taken on a very special survivor mission, one of extraordinary historical and psychological significance," according to Lifton. Instead of joining the traditional veterans organizations which perpetuated the glories of war, they became "antiwar warriors" and found "their survival significance in exposing precisely the meaninglessness—and the evil—of their war." That they did so not as poets or philosophers "but as an organized group of ordinary war veterans" while their war was still ongoing—this was, Lifton notes, unprecedented.[37]

The vets felt compelled to tell their tales, to bear witness to what they had seen, and to fight for an end to the war. They contemptuously flung their medals back at the White House, they occupied the Statue of Liberty, they testified at the Winter Soldier Hearings, they marched in mock search-and-destroy missions—they shouted their rage at a numbed nation. The mask of the lone warrior had been ripped off—by the lone warrior himself—and no one could replace it. "You have lied to us too long," former Marine sergeant Ron Kovic cried out from his wheelchair at a rally outside the Republican National Convention in 1972. "You have burned too many babies. You may have taken our bodies, but you haven't taken our minds."[38]

At the same time, however, Lipton found that many of the vets felt the necessity to look within and confront the inner roots of their own violence and aggression. This led naturally to the kind of explorations which so many of their contemporaries had set out during the sixties and seventies. Disillusioned with the myth of the romantic heroic warrior, they found themselves in the realm of the spiritual warrior. This post-Vietnam re-visioning of the warrior was, like the counterculture itself, wildly eclectic. It included both North American Indians, such as Crazy Horse, Geronimo, and Chief Seattle, who came to symbolize resistance to the overwhelming power of the status quo and a life lived in harmony with nature, as well as Eastern warriors, such as Arjuna, martial artists such as Ueshiba, the founder of the nonviolent martial art of aikido, and Zen-inspired samurai—all of whom battled the inner enemies of delusion, ignorance, egotism, fear, and selfishness.

The notion of the spiritual warrior was first widely popularized by the publication of Don Juan: A Yaqui Way of Knowledge by anthropologist Carlos Castaneda in 1968. Castaneda's Don Juan was a wily old Mexican Indian sorcerer-shaman who introduced the naive literal-minded young anthropologist to the warrior's "path with a heart." As Don Juan told Castaneda, "The basic difference between an ordinary man and a warrior is that a warrior takes everything as a challenge while an ordinary man takes everything as either a blessing or a curse."[39] Instead of fighting wars, Don Juan's warrior fought four enemies: fear, clarity, power, and old age.

The last of these enemies was the cruelest of all, and couldn't be defeated but only fought off. But that was enough, said Don Juan, for "the spirit of a warrior is not geared only to struggle and every struggle is a warrior's last battle on earth. Thus the outcome matters very little to him. In his last battle on earth a warrior lets his spirit flow free and clear. And as he wages his battle, knowing that his will is impeccable, a warrior laughs and laughs."[40]

Another version of the spiritual warrior arrived with the influx of Tibetan Buddhist teachers who were driven from Tibet by the Chinese Communists in 1959. They brought the tradition of Shambhala, a legendary kingdom in the Himalayas, said to be inhabited by spiritual warriors who would one day ride forth to battle against the forces of darkness and materialism. But they would not, of course, fight in the conventional way, for that would simply increase the amount of ignorance and aggression in the world. Rather, the warriors of Shambhala would fight with spiritual means.

According to Chogyam Trungpa, who developed a training program based on this tradition, the central discipline of the Shambhala warrior was meditation. In the warrior's meditation, all thoughts and feelings—whether they were good or bad, or aggressive or peaceful—were faced, acknowledged, accepted, and then let go, for to fight against aggressive or "negative thoughts" in order to be spiritual or good would only fuel further aggression. Meditation could thus be considered a nonviolent training in fearlessness. "Therefore," Trungpa said, "meditation practice is regarded as a good and in fact excellent way to overcome warfare in the world: our own warfare as well as greater warfare."[41]

Faced as we are with the ongoing reality of war, the approach of the spiritual warrior may seem little more than yet another escapist fantasy. And certainly, if the spiritual warrior does not also heed the outer realities of inequality and injustice which breed wars as well, it will be. Yet it is also true that it is the denial of our own death which gives rise to the illusion of invulnerability that is the most hidden and dangerous of our self-deceptions; and that unless we find the courage—the true warrior's courage—to face ourselves as we are rather than as we hope to be, we will never be able to extricate ourselves from the ancient, persistent riptide of war and violence.

THE WOMAN
WARRIOR

*A woman won that fight, and the men
never tell about it.*
—Pretty Shield

At first glance, the realm of the warrior is the realm of the masculine. "Primordial kinship culture gave the club or spear to the spouse with the greater muscular throwing power," as anthropologist Ali Mazrui writes. "When hunters became warriors, however, their new role took on political implications. Because men fought wars, it was they who reaffirmed the right to decide between peace and war. Such decisions required high political authority. In a sense, men became politically preeminent because they were militarily preeminent."[1] As for women—as Barbara Tuchman, for example, puts it, "Women, being child-bearers, have a primary instinct to preserve life."[2]

This is the general rule, and the conventional wisdom. But it hardly stands up to a closer look. As we have seen in nearly all our previous chapters, women warriors appear in every era and place. The first evidence of the "ferocious few," as Jean Bethke Elshtain calls them in *Women and War*, [3] appears on the walls of a cave in Eastern Spain as the so-called Diana of Valltorta, which Herman Wundt dates from the close of the ice age, and which he describes as "the confident amazon . . . busy with her weapons, helping in the search for food and playing the man in the conquest of new territory as well as any spear-flourishing warrior."[4]

The Amazons, of course, are the archetypal women warriors, at least as far as Westerners are concerned. (The word may derive from the Greek *a mozos*, without a breast; or an Armenian word meaning "moon-women," which may have referred to Asian priestesses who worshiped a moon goddess.) According to Greek legends, the Amazons rode horses, hunted, and made war. They could not marry until they had killed three enemies, and they cut off their right breast, supposedly to allow them to pull their bowstrings. Some legends identified the Amazons as "man-haters" who lived without men, or enslaved them, or killed male children in favor of daughters.

Amazons fought with the greatest Greek heroes—Heracles fought the Amazonian Queen Hippolyte for her girdle as his ninth labor; Theseus later defeated an Amazonian invasion with the help of his Amazon wife, Antieppe, who was slain in the battle against her own people; Achilles was victorious against the Amazonian Queen Penthesilea, who fought on the side of the Trojans. Alexander the Great however, accepted the invitation of Queen Thalestris, who told him that since he was the greatest of all men and she the strongest of all women, their child would "surpass all mortals."

Some have interpreted the battles between the Greek heroes and the Amazons—the Amazonomachy—as a reflection of a war between a matriarchal people and a patriarchal Indo-European invader. Others suggest these legends reflect male anxieties about the dangers of powerful women. It is probably no accident that the Amazons of legend tend to be found in the outermost limits of the known world.

And yet there is archaeological evidence that locates the Amazons of Greek legend firmly in historical reality. In the 1950s, Soviet archaeologists uncovered historical evidence for the existence of the Amazons. In a burial shaft near Odessa, they found the skeleton of woman in a grave with two iron lance blades, a quiver containing twenty arrows, and an iron-scaled suit of armor, as well as a bronze mirror, glass beads, and a Greek amphora. Similar warriors were found in Soviet Georgia and the Caucasus. All the burial shafts date from the fourth and third centuries B.C. and belong to the Sarmatian culture, a nomadic Indo-European culture which flourished around the Black Sea.

If the Sarmatian finds do reflect the historical realities behind the Amazonian legend, they suggest that the Amazons lived as equals with Sarmatian men. Before marriage they rode, hunted, and went to war. After marriage, which seems to have been monogamous, they went to war only when it was necessary.

The Amazonian tradition lived on in Europe among the descendants of the Indo-Europeans. The Romans reported that women warriors fought with the Huns, who may have been descended from the Sarmatians, and with the Celts. Plutarch describes a battle at Aquae Sextiae, in which the Romans had succeeded in chasing the Celtic warriors back to their wagons. "Here the women met them," wrote Plutarch, "holding swords and axes in their hands. With hideous shrieks of rage they tried to drive back the hunted and the hunters. . . . With bare hands the women tore away the shields of the Romans or grasped their swords, enduring mutilating wounds. Their fierce spirit remained unvanquished to the end."[5] The warrior-queen Boudicca led an uprising against the Romans, for as Tacitus noted, "Britains make no distinction of sex in their appointment of commanders." Celtic women warriors also served as teachers to men. The Irish hero Chu Chulainn studied "the warrior's art" with woman warrior Scathach so that "he could beat any hero in Europe."[6]

During the Middle Ages, women defended castles and directed sieges. Some, like Eleanor of Aquitaine, accompanied their husbands on Crusades. And Jeanne d'Arc, the most celebrated European woman warrior, heeded the voice of God and succeeded in driving the English from France when all the king's men had failed.

The best example of Amazons, however, comes from the West African kingdom of Dahomey, where an elite company of women warriors served as the king's personal bodyguards. But most of the Dahomeyan Amazons fought, like the male warriors, in the slave wars which were waged to obtain slaves who were sold to European traders. These African Amazons carried blunderblusses, muskets, and razor-knives suitable for decapitation; young girls used poisoned cane arrows and served as scouts. When Frederick Forbes, an English antislavery worker, visited Dahomey in 1850, he watched the various Amazon regiments parade before the skull-bedecked throne of the king. "When the Attapahms heard we were advancing, they ran away," said one Amazonian officer. "If we go to war, and any return not conquerors, let them die. If I retreat, my life is at the king's mercy. Whatever the town to be attacked, we will conquer, or bury ourselves in its ruins."

"War is our great friend," said another. "Without it there is no cloth, no armlets. Let us to war, conquer or die." Another said, "I long to kill an elephant to show my fidelity. But the Attapahms must be exterminated first."

The Amazons remained celibate. If any were caught breaking their vows, both they and their lovers were killed. Explorer Richard Burton thought this helped make them "savage as wounded gorillas, far more cruel than their brethren in arms." Another English explorer found "their appearance is more martial than the generality of the men; and if undertaking a campaign, I should prefer the females to the male soldiers of the country."[7] The Dahomey Amazons were finally defeated in 1892 when a French army destroyed the kingdom of Dahomey.

In the East, women were among the finest of the martial artists. In *The Woman Warrior*, Maxine Hong Kingston recounts stories she heard as a child which taught her that "we could be heroines, swordswomen. Even if she had to rage across all China, a swordswoman got even with anybody who hurt her family."[8] The Chinese fighting art of Wing Chun was founded by a woman, and a blind princess made important contributions to the Philippine art of kali. In the T'ang Dynasty poet Tu Fu praised the swordplay of the self-taught Madame Kung Sun in a poem:

> *Her swinging sword flashes like the nine falling*
> *suns shot by Yi, the legendary bowman;*
> *She moves with the force of a team of dragons*
> *driven by the gods through the sky;*
> *Her strokes and attacks are like those of terrible thunder;*
> *And when she stops, all is still as waters reflecting the*
> *clear moonlight.*[9]

In Japan, samurai women always carried a dagger, both for self-defense and seppuku. Samurai women were also trained in the use of the halberdlike *naginata*. In the Satsuma Rebellion, mounted samurai women used traditional weapons to hold off the Western-trained troops of the Meiji government. The art of naginata is still practiced as a *do* or way by many Japanese women.

Native Americans also possess a hidden history of women warriors. Among the Nootka of Vancouver Island, there was a women's warrior society, which went underground after the Europeans decimated their people. (Some of this history, as remembered by Nootka women today, has been collected by Anne Cameron in *Daughters of Copper Women.*) Recently Paula Gunn Allen collected stories about Native American women warriors. In one of these stories, the Chippewa medicine woman Pretty Shield remembered seeing Strikes-two, a sixty-year-old woman, ride out against the Lakota, who were attacking her village:

> A woman won that fight, and the men never tell about it. They do not like to hear about it, but I am going to tell you what happened. . . . I saw Strikes-two, a woman sixty years old, riding around camp on a grey horse. She carried only her root-digger, and she was singing her medicine-song as though Lakota bullets and arrows were not flying around her. I hear her say, "Now all of you sing, 'They are whipped. They are running away,' and keep singing these words until I come back."
>
> When the men and even the women began to sing as Strikes-two told them, she rode straight out at the Lakota, waving her root-digger, and singing that song. I *saw* her, I *heard* her, and my heart swelled, because she was a woman.
>
> The Lakota, afraid of her medicine, turned and ran away. The fight was won, and by a woman.[10]

◭◭ II ◭◭

In modern times, firearms have made it possible for many women to serve in the armed forces or in revolutionary guerrilla bands. Women soldiers fought bravely in the Russian army during World War II, as well as with the French and Italian resistances. Israeli women are required to serve in the army. Women fought alongside men in the revolutionary struggles in Cuba, Nicaragua, and San Salvador. Women also served in the army in revolutionary Iran, following the example of Muhammad's daughter, who was a great warrior.

In the United States, women now constitute eleven percent of the armed forces. Their participation is supposedly limited to noncombatant roles. The principal argument against using women in combat goes back to the argument about upper body strength in comparison to men. Linda Grant De Pauw of the Minerva Center points out that most of the objections to women in combat reflect the stereotype of women as victim. "It's like the image they used to have of blacks before they served with them," she says, "that they were too cowardly, too stupid or would break their weapons."[11] Others point out that physical strength hardly has anything to do with the realities of many areas of modern high-tech war. "Men aren't any better at video games than women," as one submariner remarked.[12] Others—such as anthropologist Melvin Konner—have suggested that since women tend to be calmer and steadier than men in crises, it might actually be safer for women to command and control missiles and other advanced weapons.[13] In any case, there is widespread acknowledgment that the restriction means little if anything in modern warfare. "Just because you're not in a combat unit doesn't mean you won't be in combat," admits a spokesman for the Department of Defense. "When they start lobbing SCUDs with chemical weapons, they'll be aimed at everybody." Women soldiers in the Persian Gulf did indeed take part in combat. The cultural feeling against women in combat remains strong, however. When Congress proposed to open the way for women to fly in combat, most military men continued to oppose the idea—even if a woman pilot was more qualified than her male counterpart. "I admit this doesn't make much sense," Air Force Chief of Staff Merrill McPeak told a Senate subcommittee, "but that's the way I feel about it."

△△ I I I △△

The objections to women in combat that are still with us reflect a deep male anxiety about women's power that can be traced back at least as far as the Amazon legends. Movies and television rarely show women successfully defending themselves or winning a fight against aggressors. Rather, they show women as the weak victims of male violence. The main exception, Wonder Woman, is, after all, a cartoon character.

In her article "Women and the Martial Arts," Lisa Geduldig, a kung fu student, notes that "women and girls growing up in this society are exposed to few powerful role models. They're just not typically taught to be physically strong. They're told that being strong is 'acting like a boy' or 'acting like a man.'"

But this is changing as women, too, re-vision the warrior. "Many women are unlearning and challenging the false images and myths that women should not be physically powerful, verbally assertive, nor able to protect themselves," says Geduldig. "A growing number of these women are choosing to train in the martial arts."[14]

Some of these women train in co-ed dojos. Others, however, have found that they were not welcome or taken seriously by male martial artists, or that they felt uncomfortable with the macho competitive atmosphere in some dojos.

"As a student of a feminist approach to martial arts," Geduldig says, "I am taught the art form for defensive purposes, not offensive. After all, martial arts were developed by oppressed peoples to defend themselves from attackers. They didn't go out looking to kick butt either."[15]

Women practice t'ai chi, aikido, karate, and other martial arts for the same varied reasons men do, of course, but such arts also give women a way to overcome and dispel the cultural conditioning that pictures them as weak, vulnerable, powerless victims. Lisa Geduldig, for example, was initially attracted to the spiritual aspects of the martial arts, "but I had to be convinced that learning to make a fist and throw a punch was a valuable skill. One of the first times I had to punch, my instructor pointed out to me that my shoulder was raised and pulled back so as not to deliver a fully committed blow."[16]

Being able to defend yourself has important psychological dimensions. Training not only prepares women for a possible attack but can also help them heal from past experiences of abuse, incest, and assault. "When my father or siblings would hit me, my automatic reaction was always to cower in the corner and protect my head," one woman says. "Now I know I would fight back. Training has given me the confidence to know that I would never again succumb to abuse like that."[17]

One of the key concepts for the new woman warrior is empowerment—the idea of discovering and owning one's power rather than giving it away or using it as power over another person. "Training empowers women because there's something lost when a woman is attacked," says Maria Doest, an instructor at Karate Women in Los Angeles. "Something is taken away from her, and that's the ability to defend herself, the ability to control her own life. Taking self-defense or taking martial arts gives her back that feeling of control; it puts that back in her life."[18]

At some point in their training—usually at the intermediate or brown belt levels—most martial artists begin to wonder how effective the skills learned in the dojo would be in a real street fight. Unfortunately, for women this question is more crucial than for men. At least fifteen hundred women are raped every day in the United States, and the figures are growing—in fact, rape against women is now the fastest-growing crime in the United States.

In 1978, a woman who held a black belt was attacked and raped. She went back to her karate dojo feeling that she had disgraced her school. The head of the school agreed, and ordered her to leave. One of her fellow students, a man named Matt Thomas, thought that the fault lay with the training, not the student. Like most martial arts students, she had never fought against an opponent who was not following any rules or codes. In addition, since martial artists have to pull and control their punches, she had never had the experience of fighting full-out.

Thomas left the school and spent years researching police files on rape. Combining what he learned with his experience in fourteen different martial arts, he developed a course that would teach women to defend themselves without spending years in martial arts training. Taking the role of a "model mugger," he gradually developed a protective suit consisting of a heavily padded mask, a helmet, and body armor. The costume made the model mugger look like Darth Vader, but it also allowed women to strike, kick, and gouge without holding back. In this way, women were freed to discover their own power and feel what it felt like to deliver a knockout blow to an attacker. "Model Mugging," as it is called, taught women to channel the adrenaline of fear into a powerful attack. "Basically," says Thomas, "we set up an adrenaline state under which freeze and flail responses are reconditioned. If that adrenaline state is similarly aroused in a real life attack, women's bodies respond in ways their muscles remember as being effective; they fight in a no-mind warrior state of reflex action."[19]

In thirteen years, thirty-five hundred women graduated from Model Mugging. Of these, twenty reported that they had been attacked. Three decided not to fight back. Of the seventeen who did fight back, all of them delivered knockout blows to their assailants within five seconds. Many more women have reported that the strength and confidence gained from Model Mugging allowed them to escape or avoid attack without fighting.

Like all true warrior trainings, however, Model Mugging is as much about living as fighting. Women taking the training overcome their "inner mugger," which means that they can encounter and sometimes defeat the muggers who attacked them in the past. They also, therefore, discover the fierce inner warrior that is as much a part of the feminine archetype as it is of the masculine. The recovery of this suppressed archetype is very much a part of the contemporary re-visioning of the warrior. "Many women are re-creating the roles of warrior in beautiful, loving, and inspiring ways even while they learn to be dangerous and skillful when called for," says Becca Harber, a martial artist from Spencer, New York.[20]

Seeking to discover their own warrior traditions, contemporary women are rediscovering the fierce women archetypes found among the Amazons, the Celts, and goddesses like Kali, who manifests as Mother, Protector, and Destroyer. As Durga, Kali rides to battle on a tiger, carrying a sword, noose, thunderbolt, trident, discus, and ax, radiating a peaceful golden light. "Kali's message to us today is about wholeness and change," Paulette Boudeaux writes in a special issue of *woman of power.* "Women must accept the terrible and powerful Warrior/Destroyer aspects of ourselves as we also accept and nurture the loving, mothering aspects of ourselves. As Kali's agents women have sustained love and compassion in the world and women will, with Kali's power, be the agents of change."[21]

By combining the fierceness of the ancient women warriors with the life-affirming creativity that has been traditionally associated with women, the new woman warrior has a central role to play in the contemporary re-visioning of the warrior. Women learning to defend themselves in Model Mugging and other martial arts training are finding ways to go beyond being a victim without becoming a mirror image of their victimizers. "Being empowered doesn't depend on being a victor *over* others," says Danielle Evans, an aikido black belt and chief woman instructor at Model Mugging of Monterey, California. "It has to do with feeling our own highest power from within, with making choices to be the best we can be. I believe breaking the cycle of violence in this way is the path leading to a society where we can live in peace."[22]

THE WARRIOR
AND THE
BUSINESSPERSON

Capitalism is war with the gloves off.
–Tom Stoppard

The contemporary notion that the training and strategies of the warrior could be useful in business would have puzzled both knights and the samurai. European knights, as we have seen, were aristocrats who lived off the labor of peasants and the booty of war. In Japan, merchants were ranked at the very bottom of the social order, below even the farmers and peasants, whose labor at least provided food and other necessities. As for the speculators and developers who have climbed to the pinnacle of contemporary society—they were considered usurers in Europe (usury was an activity forbidden by the Church) and dangerous parasites in feudal Japan. In fact, under the Tokugawas, the samurai were forbidden to take part in business.

As we have seen, the samurai class was abolished during the Meiji Restoration. But the samurai ethic, as Robert Bellah has shown, "became the ethic of an entire people. . . . The high evaluation of military achievements and the fulfillment of one's lord's commands became generalized beyond the warrior class into a high valuation of performance in all spheres."[1] In fact, the government encouraged former samurai to enter industry and provided technical training. The "samurai spirit"—which included leadership and initiative, as well as frugality—was carried over into the industrial sphere. It was, therefore, quite simple for Yataro Iwasaki, the samurai who founded Mitsubishi in 1870, three years after the overthrow of the Tokugawa shoguns, to adapt the samurai code of his house to his new industrial company as follows:

1. Do not be preoccupied with small matters but aim at the management of large enterprises.
2. Once you start an enterprise be sure to succeed in it.
3. Do not engage in speculative enterprises.
4. Operate all enterprises with the national interest in mind.
5. Never forget the pure spirit of public service and *makoto* ("sincerity").
6. Be hard working and frugal, and thoughtful to others.
7. Utilize proper personnel.
8. Treat your employees well.
9. Be bold in starting an enterprise but meticulous in its prosecution.[2]

The same samurai ethic which had helped Japan to industrialize after the Meiji Restoration was also crucial to its miraculous economic reconstruction after World War II. The Japanese company took the place of the clan, guaranteeing workers lifelong employment in return for absolute loyalty. Inside the company, they practiced cooperation and harmony. Salaries were low, but there were bonuses twice a year. In good years, everyone benefitted. In hard years, everyone tightened their belts. Executives and workers alike thus had a fierce dedication to the success of their company. "They came in with samurai mentality . . . absolute confidence," observed one American who had watched Japanese companies prepare to enter the hitherto American-dominated photocopier market. "I've never run into that kind of confidence. They were samurai warriors coming to do battle."[3]

Of course, there was much more to it than that. Japan had no natural resources, and only minimal farming land, which was in ruins after the war. "How successful you are depends upon how desperate you are," says Atseo Kusado of Minolta. "All Japan has been desperate and will be forever because in Japan, we have nothing. That's why we're strong."[4]

Like their samurai ancestors, therefore, the Japanese corporate warriors could leap into battle—when necessary. But they were also, like their samurai ancestors, dedicated students of strategy, particularly that of Sun Tzu, who taught, as we have seen, that the greatest generals win without fighting. In addition to golf, which they pursued with a passion, some Japanese executives practiced martial arts, especially kendo, the aggressive forward-moving modern way of the sword, which utilized bamboo swords, masks, and protective gear. But some also practiced meditation, particularly Zen. And they played go, the Taoist strategy game, instead of chess. Go was not about destroying or capturing an opponent's king or queen, but about surrounding territory; and the greatest opportunities for capturing territory are found where there is the most territory—in the empty spaces.

The Japanese invaded, then, by looking for empty spaces—for openings or weaknesses *(suki)*, for places where no one had gone. Typically, they found these in the low end of the marketplace. But they did not just introduce cheaper cars, cameras, and photocopiers; rather, by drawing on centuries of miniaturization and attention to detail—and by involving their workers in the process, through quality circles (an idea they had adapted happily from the American W. E. Deming)—they introduced better products.

But the real secret of Japan's success in the economic equivalent of war it now wages is even more fundamental: they are not in business for the same reasons the Americans are. The old samurai virtues of service and *kappu maku*—"clean poverty"—here come into play. According to *kappu maku*, it is immoral for any individual to accumulate or hoard more wealth or material possessions than he really needs. While the knights had demonstrated their nobility by ostentation and generosity the samurai displayed their nobility through thrift and simplicity.

Though this approach may be changing as Japan undergoes Westernization, it still plays an important role. "Profit making is secondary in the context of Japanese business," says Boye De Mente, a long-time observer of Japanese business. "The primary concern of a Japanese businessman is to develop a company that will grow and last, that will provide permanent jobs for his employees and himself, and to make a contribution to the welfare of the country."[5]

*   *   *

The importance of the samurai spirit and strategy to Japanese business may obscure a more fundamental underlying difference between Japanese and American cultures and therefore business: Japanese culture is based on cooperation and group loyalty; American culture is based on competition and individualism.

Both Europe and Japan had a tradition of warrior-aristocrats which ran counter to mercantilism. In America, however, the heroic man was what Robert Reich, a political economist from Harvard, has called the Triumphant Individual—"the little man who works hard, takes risks, believes in himself, and eventually earns wealth, fame, and honor."

Of course, the Triumphant Individual takes many forms, depending on the prevailing economic winds. The late nineteenth century version appeared in Horatio Alger's novels about the plucky young fellow who succeeds through hard work, a brave heart, cheerfulness, thrift, discipline, and often a lucky break, which is understood to be the reward for all his uncomplaining industry. At his height, he rises to the level of a captain of industry, either an empire builder or a robber baron. In his maturity, he becomes a philanthropist, and endower of charities, arts, libraries, which—it is understood—will give other deserving Horatio Alger heroes the chance to follow the same path.

Then there are the wheeling, dealing corporate raiders of the seventies and eighties—lean, mean, fast, smart, ruthless, who preyed on the unprotected caravans and bulging storehouses of the rich. But these are closer to pirates than warriors.

The Triumphant Individual could also follow the path of the entrepreneur, an inventor or tinkerer, like Benjamin Franklin or the Wright Brothers. "Our degree of entrepreneurial drive and the social legitimacy it enjoys have long distinguished America from other cultures," says Reich. "Generations of wide-eyed inventors and investors have kept us on the social frontier. We are born mavericks and fixers. In a world of nay-sayers and traditionalists, the American personality has stood out—cheerfully optimistic, willing to run risks, ready to try anything."[6]

In general, American businesspeople have always shared certain assumptions. They were, to begin with, all Triumphant Individuals, who assumed that the primary purpose of business was to make money, the more the better. They also brought the common American obsession with competition into business. They tended, therefore, to see themselves in competition either with other executives in their company or—if they thought in terms of their own company—with other companies fighting for the same market.

The emphasis on competition led many American businesspeople and management consultants to think of business as war. This view was strengthened by the use of military language to describe business conflicts. There were trade wars, advertising campaigns, market blitzes, corporate raids, and sales forces. Executives fought in the corporate jungle. There were even "headhunters" who specialized in recruiting executives.

The Japanese, too, of course, used martial metaphors to describe business battles. But they had a sophisticated strategic tradition behind those metaphors. The Americans tended to follow the way of war instead of the warrior. "Business is simply about winning battles in the marketplace by outmanoevring an opponent to obtain a superior profit position," Barrie G. James wrote in *Business Wargames.*

> Business has always been competitive, but now more than ever companies require strategies which truly reflect the combative nature of the marketplace. The closest analogy to current market conditions is war. . . . Companies and armies share common strategic manoeuvres in terms of deterrence, offence, defence, and alliance. . . . The resemblance between the two forms of conflict is not surprising since both companies and armies are organizationally designed for one purpose—to fight, whether in the market or on the battlefield.[7]

This "business is war" approach was reflected in the structure of American companies, which tended to mimic military organizations. They were hierarchical, with authority invested in one boss. Employees were treated more like soldiers than warriors, which is to say they were replaceable and expendable cogs in a machine—and that the employees felt little if any loyalty to the company, even at the executive level. The result was that American businesses tended to stifle the innovation and freewheeling creativity of the heroic entrepreneur which was, in fact, their greatest strength.

By the time the Americans realized what had happened, it was too late. Somehow the Japanese had managed to rise, jujitsulike, from the utter devastation and defeat of World War II and beat the Americans at their own game. They surged ahead in cars, cameras, electronics, televisions, and office copiers.

Many Americans called foul, citing "unfair competition," citing Japanese trade restrictions, or blaming the funding provided by "unfair" governmental agencies such as the Ministry for International Trade and Industry. But others realized that the battlefield had changed. The marketplace was no longer local or national, it was international and global. Just as many people realized that war was no longer an acceptable way of settling international conflicts, some businessmen began to realize that the old way of doing business was fast becoming outmoded. New times demand new solutions.

The first place to look, obviously enough, was to the Japanese, who had seemingly mastered the new conditions. This led, in turn, to the part played by the samurai in the Japanese success. So it was that a growing number of American businessmen were led to look beyond the metaphor of war to the metaphor of the warrior.

One publisher, at least, was astute enough to see the opening—and so an obscure seventeenth century manual on swordsmanship and strategy, *The Book of Five Rings*, marketed with the promise that "now the secret of Japanese success in business can be yours," became a best-seller. Minyamoto Musashi, the author of the book, would have been astounded, no doubt. Musashi was a great swordsman; indeed, he was said to have been unbeaten in more than sixty challenges. But he was hardly a "successful" man. In fact, he was a ronin, a masterless samurai, and something of an eccentric. He wore his hair long instead of in the topknot of the samurai (perhaps to hide a scabrous skin disease); he rarely bathed (in a country where everyone took a hot bath daily); and his clothes were disheveled. In addition to being a ruthless killer, he was also a poet, calligrapher, and a great *sum-i* artist. At the age of fifty, he retired to a cave to meditate and write. Hardly a likely example for a corporate warrior, either in modern-day Tokyo or Wall Street!

In any case, it was not the technical explanations of his revolutionary two-sword technique that attracted businessmen in either Japan or America. Rather, it was Musashi's claim that "the true path is such that it applies at any time and in any situation."[8]

As a warrior who had been involved in many life-and-death encounters, Musashi took a realistic no-nonsense approach that was congenial to businessmen. In order for a warrior to follow the true way, he said, "it is necessary to build an indomitable spirit and an iron will; to believe that you cannot fail in doing anything." The way of the warrior, he said, meant "having no illusions in your heart, honing your wisdom and will power, sharpening your intuitive sense and your powers of observation day by night; when the clouds of illusion have cleared away, this is understood as the true path."9

Specifically, Musashi offered nine guidelines:

1. Do not think dishonestly.
2. The Way is in the training.
3. Become acquainted with every art.
4. Know the ways of all professionals.
5. Distinguish between loss and gain in worldly matters.
6. Develop intuitive judgment and understanding for everything.
7. Perceive those things which cannot be seen.
8. Pay attention even to trifles.
9. Do nothing which is of no use.

No doubt these and other maxims could be applied to business, as well as any endeavor, as Musashi himself said. But it is unlikely that more than a handful of the hundreds of thousands who bought *The Book of Five Rings* realized that their mastery depended on training in a martial art of some kind, as well as a spiritual discipline by which one could penetrate the last of the Five Rings—The Ring of Emptiness.

Still, *The Book of Five Rings*—and the numerous books and workshops it spawned—was certainly not without effect. Some businesspeople did take up the study of martial arts and meditation. (Super Hollywood agent Mike Ovitz, for example, practices aikido every morning.) The study of strategy became respectable among the business community; three or four new translations of Sun Tzu appeared, some of them directly aimed at businesspeople. In the end, American companies began looking and acting more like Japanese companies.

By the 1980s, the way of the warrior was firmly established in the business community, along with a host of other "human potential" trainings. Aikidoist Thomas Crumm and others applied the lessons of the martial arts to business. Executives practiced exercises which introduced them to the principles of centering, relaxation, awareness, and flexibility, as well as demonstrating new approaches to dealing with conflict. Instead of competing, for example, it was possible to move away, join forces, or blend with the "opponent." Instead of playing a zero-sum game in which one person's gain depended on the other person's loss, it was possible for both players to benefit, thereby arriving at a win-win solution.

Says Robert Pater, who is a martial arts instructor and organizational management consultant:

> Balance is vital for effectiveness in both the martial arts and in managing. An idealistic visionary may be able to look ahead into the future, and keep the long-range perspective. However, his weakness is in dealing with details and completing the daily job.
>
> Then there are those without a higher purpose. People who study martial arts only to dominate others don't usually progress far. Similarly, some people in the work place are bereft of vision and can see no purpose beyond reacting to circumstances from one day to the next. Their narrow perspective prevents them from reaching beyond daily problems, and it limits what they can accomplish.
>
> Don't allow yourself to become fixed at either of these extremes. Remember your *do* and practice the details of your art everyday. Stay balanced and look ahead. Develop a mission and a set of values that you can apply in real life, that help you get the job done and then help you to continue to become something more.[10]

Warriors, as we have seen, have a mission beyond themselves. The true warrior is dedicated to something greater than personal survival and comfort. The challenge for the business warrior, or the warrior who seeks warriorship through business or work, therefore is to find a way to make business serve more than personal or even corporate interest. "Business," Robert Pater insists, "can be a *do,* a Way of Life, dedicated to developing resources, providing services, and improving the quality of living."[11]

The warrior's way as played out in business is to have the vision to see above the bottom line. A business must at least break even to survive, but it must do more than that to thrive. From the warrior's point of view, the purpose of business is not to make a killing but to make a living in the deepest sense of the word.

Accounting, keeping track of the details, is no doubt an essential part of business, as of any endeavor. ("Pay attention even to trifles," as Musashi says.) The warrior's strategy is never for the warrior's sake alone; it always refers to the largest good. It always takes others into account. The samurai were originally men who serve. The samurai-derived code of Mitsubishi urged workers "to never forget the pure spirit of public service."

The business warrior—or the martial arts manager or the executive warrior, to use two recent formulations—will be concerned with the depth and quality of the lives of everyone in the company community or clan. But the business warrior can go even further than that. The fact that business is global means that business now has a global responsibility.

Indeed, an increasing number of maverick businesspeople have recognized this new responsibility. William Norris of Control Data Corporation provides training programs and builds plants in inner-city areas; Harold Willens, a Los Angeles real estate developer, founded Business Executives for National Security, which works for nuclear disarmament; Wayne Silby founded the Clavert Investment Fund, one of the first of a number of socially responsible investment groups. And Ben & Jerry's Rainforest Crunch ice cream helps the inhabitants of the rain forest by using ingredients they provide and by contributing part of the profits to defend the rain forest against development.

But perhaps the best example of this trend—the most warriorlike—is Anita Roddick, the British founder of the hugely successful The Body Shop. After starting a single Body Shop in 1976 with a bank loan of $6,400, she and her husband have expanded to more than 600 franchises in thirty-nine countries, including more than 50 shops in the U.S. In 1990, the pretax profits on sales were $34.1 million.

The Body Shop, which sells skin and hair care products, is first of all an ecologically responsible business. The products are naturally based and not tested on animals. Wasteful packaging is kept to a minimum. Replaceable plastic bottles are provided. There is no hype or advertising. No one tried to convince customers that The Body Shop products will make them beautiful or stop the aging process.

The Body Shop employees enjoy equity participation and incentive plans. Training in The Body Shop products and uses is offered at a company-run school, but there are no courses in selling. In fact, The Body Shop employees don't sell to customers, they provide them with realistic reliable information, and only if asked. They also receive one day a month off to work on a socially useful cause with pay.

But Roddick realizes that sharing in profits and receiving "quality-of-life benefits" are not enough, either for her or for the people who work for her. There has to be something more, even in business. "The idea of business, I'd agree is not to lose money," Roddick grants. "But to focus all the time on profits, profits, profits—I'd have to say I think it's deeply boring."[12]

The Body Shop has made business come alive by linking it with education and action about social and environmental issues that matter. Referring to both employees and consumers, Roddick says, "I want them to understand that this is no dress rehearsal. You've got one life, so just lead it. And try to be remarkable." Roddick, in other words, sees business as a vehicle to engage life, to help create the "vivid peace" that author and aikido teacher George Leonard and other re-visioners of the warrior have called for. When someone pursues business with the spirit of a warrior, Roddick has shown, then business, too, can become Don Juan's "path with heart."

The most unusual aspect of The Body Shop, then, is the company's environmental and social activism, which includes an ongoing program of both employee and consumer education. "You educate people by their passions," Roddick says. "You find ways to grab their imagination. You want them to feel that they're doing something important, that they're not a lone voice, that they are the most powerful, potent people on the planet."

Most "socially responsible" businesses pursue a negative course. They merely try not to harm the environment, mistrust workers, or sell useless and dangerous products. But Roddick's brand of business warriorship is active. She believes that business has a responsibility to educate and activate. In taking up the defense of Brazil's Yanomamo Indians, for example, The Body Shop mounted fund-raising drives in the stores, produced window displays and educational videos, leaflets, and T-shirts. It also brought hundreds of employees to a demonstration at the Brazilian Embassy—and then had the demonstration broadcast via satellite to Brazil. In addition to all this, The Body Shop trucks were turned into educational broadsides, announcing in large block letters:

Custodians of the Rainforests:

THE YANOMAMO INDIANS OF BRAZIL HAVE BEEN
LIVING WITH THEIR ENVIRONMENT FOR
THOUSANDS OF YEARS LARGELY UNCONTACTED
BY THE OUTSIDE WORLD. NOW THEIR VERY
LIVES ARE IN DANGER—OVER 50,000 GOLD
MINERS ARE RANSACKING THEIR LAND; WHOLE
COMMUNITIES ARE BEING DECIMATED BY
OUTSIDE DISEASES SUCH AS FLU AND MEASLES.
THEY ARE BEING SQUEEZED OUT OF EXISTENCE.
WHY CAN'T THEY BE LEFT ALONE?
    CONTACT THE BODY SHOP . . .

In this way, Roddick has managed to turn her business into something like a sword with which both she and her employees, as well as her customers, can fight for social justice and the environment as global citizens. Says Roddick:

I believe quite passionately that there is a better way. I think you can rewrite the book on business. I think you can trade ethically; be committed to social responsibility; empower your employees without being afraid of them.

It's creating a new business paradigm. It's showing that business can have a human face, and God help us if we don't try. It's showing that empowering employees is the key to keeping them, and you empower them by creating a better educational system. It's showing that you forsake your values at the cost of forsaking your work force. It's paying attention to the aesthetics of business. It's all that. It's trying in every way you can. You may not get there, but goddammit, you try to make the journey an honorable one.[13]

BRINGING
THE WARRIOR
DOWN TO EARTH

The idea of wilderness needs no defense. It only needs defenders.
—Ed Abbey

Now we must become warrior-lovers
in the service of the Great Goddess Gaia, Mother of the Buddha.
—Gary Snyder

One of the penalties of an ecological education
is that one lives in a world of wounds.
—Aldo Leopold

In the spring of 1973 armed members of the American Indian Movement, protesting the treatment of the Sioux, proclaimed the Independent Oglala Nation and occupied the settlement of Wounded Knee on the Pine Ridge Reservation. At the end of the six-week occupation (which resulted in the deaths of two Indians; two FBI agents died in a later shootout), Leonard Crow Dog led a Ghost Dance in the snow, where the original Wounded Knee battle had taken place. A week or so later, he led a Sun Dance at his camp in the Rosebud Reservation, which was attended by many of the urban members of AIM. For most of them, it was the first Sun Dance they had ever attended, much less participated in.

The Wounded Knee Indians had been joined by a few white sympathizers. One of them, a young Canadian by the name of Paul Watson, had sneaked through police lines to serve the occupiers as a medic. At the end of the occupation, he was inducted into the Sioux as a warrior-brother by Leonard Crow Dog and Wallace Black Elk, whose grandfather, the famous medicine man Black Elk, had witnessed the original Wounded Knee battle as a young boy. As part of the initiation ceremony, Watson took part in a sweatlodge. As he lay "sweating and gasping for air inside the incredibly hot lodge," Watson was seized by a vision.

"I suddenly saw myself in a grassy, rolling field, gazing into the eyes of a wolf," he remembers. "The wolf looked at me, then into a pond, and walked away. When I told the Sioux what had happened, they gave me my Indian name: Grey Wolf Clear Water. Then I went back into the vision, and saw a buffalo standing on a ridge. It began to speak to me. And as it told me that I must protect the buffalo of the sea, an arrow came and struck it in the back. Attached to the arrow was a cord, symbolic of the harpoon."[1]

And so it came to pass. A few years later Watson found himself and a few other members of a new group called Greenpeace piloting a fleet of flimsy rubber Zodiacs between a school of whales and the explosive harpoons of Russian whalers.

△△ II △△

The movement to protect the earth went back at least a hundred years or so to John Muir, the man who had founded the conservation movement and who confided to his journal that "if a war of races should occur between the wild beasts and Lord Man, I would be tempted to sympathize with the bears."[2]

In 1849, when Muir was eleven, his family moved from Scotland to Wisconsin. An inventor of some genius, he worked in factories as a young man and studied for two years at the University of Wisconsin before an industrial accident almost blinded him. Realizing that he had no more time to lose, in his words he "bade adieu to mechanical inventions, determined to devote the rest of my life to the study of the inventions of God." Setting out on a thousand-mile walk to Florida, carrying a plant-press on his back and a notebook inscribed with his address—"John Muir, Earth-planet, Universe"—the future founder of the Sierra Club encountered alligators in the Florida swamps—"Fierce and cruel they appear to us, but beautiful in the eyes of God," he noted in his journal, and generously wished that the "honorable representatives of the great saurians of an older creation . . . be blessed now and then with a mouthful of terror-stricken man by way of dainty!"[3]

Muir took a ship to California in March 1868. In San Francisco, he stayed only long enough to ask the nearest way out of town. To the inquiry "But where do you want to go?" Muir had a simple reply: "To any place that is wild." Directed to the Oakland Ferry, Muir started walking through "a vast golden flower-bed" to the mighty Sierras.

Muir's father—and his father's fathers—had taught that Nature was dark, savage, wild, unredeemed, and that God was found only in civilization; man's task (as Genesis 21 instructed) was to have dominion over the earth. But for Muir nature was radiant with the light of God. Muir found God and nature to be one and the same. "The door to the Universe," he wrote, "is through a forest wilderness." Forced to memorize the entire New Testament and much of the Old Testament as a child, he had little use for organized religion, but he adopted the cadences and images of the Bible to sing the praises of the earth. The forests were "God's First Temples." Looking into Yosemite, he wrote that "the Valley, comprehensively seen, looks like an immense hall or temple lighted from above." And riding down an avalanche, he exulted that "this flight in what might be called a milky-way of snow stars was the most spiritual and exhilarating of all the modes of motion I have ever experienced. Elijah's flight in a chariot of fire could hardly have been more gloriously exciting."[4]

Most people thought that "the world . . . was made especially for man." But this, thought Muir, "was a presumption not supported by all the facts." Like the Taoists, Muir wondered, "Why should man value himself as more than a small part of the one great unit of creation? And what creature of all that the Lord has taken pains to make is not essential to the completeness of that unit—the cosmos? The universe would be incomplete without man," he was willing to grant, "but it would also be incomplete without the smallest transmicroscopic creature that dwells beyond our conceitful eyes and knowledge."[5]

Working at a sawmill, Muir spent as much time as he could exploring the Yosemite Valley, traveling with nothing more than a loaf of bread and some tea, sleeping on a bed made of pine boughs, collecting plants, tracing the glacier which had formed the valley, building a huge fire in the middle of a storm, clambering over rocky cliffs. Over the next ten years, Muir, the wild mountain philosopher, became something of a legend.

When Ralph Waldo Emerson visited Yosemite, Muir left a note at his hotel, inviting the famous sage of Concord "to join me in a month's worship with Nature in the high temples of the great Sierra Crown behind our holy Yosemite."[6] Emerson seemed willing enough, but deferred to his Boston traveling companions who insisted that the elderly philosopher stay put, with them, in the hotel.

Rough Rider Teddy Roosevelt was a different matter. He shook his official party to ride off alone with Muir, and the two men spent four days climbing in the backwoods. Muir chided Roosevelt for hunting; Roosevelt admitted Muir was probably right.

Muir also played host to Robert Underwood Johnson, editor of the influential eastern magazine the *Century*. Camping in Yosemite, Muir pointed out the destruction caused by the "hoofed locusts," as he called sheep, and welcomed Johnson's suggestion that Yosemite be protected in the same way as Yellowstone.

In 1890, due in large part to Muir's articles in the *Century* and Johnson's contacts in Washington, Yosemite Park became the "first preserve consciously designed to protect wilderness."[7] The next year, Johnson suggested that "a Yosemite and Yellowstone defense association" was needed to protect the two new parks. Meanwhile, professors at Berkeley and Stanford were planning an alpine club. Putting the two ideas together, Muir met with twenty-seven men in San Francisco on June 4, 1892, to form the Sierra Club, which he hoped would "do something for wildness and make the mountains glad."

Muir led the club members in outings to the mountains, but they also paid close attention to political issues concerning the defense of wilderness. "The battle we have fought, and are still fighting, for the forests is part of the eternal conflict between right and wrong and we cannot expect to see the end of it," he told club members in 1895.[8]

Indeed. In 1905, the city of San Francisco began a campaign to dam Hetch Hetchy Canyon to provide water and (though this was never said aloud) cheap hydroelectric power. Hetch Hetchy was the first of the great environmental battles. It pitted the professionals who wanted to use the forests against the amateurs who wanted to preserve them for their own sake—who believed, as Henry David Thoreau had written, "that in wilderness is the preservation of the world." The professionals were led by Gifford Pinchot, the first director of the new Forest Service, who stood for managing the forests according to the latest scientific methods, so that they would yield the "greatest good for the greatest number."

The amateurs were led by Muir, who invited his readers to "imagine yourself in Hetch Hetchy on a summer day in June, standing waist-deep in grass and flowers (as I have often stood), while the great pines sway dreamily with scarcely perceptible motion," and argued that "everybody needs beauty as well as bread, places to play in and pray in, where Nature may heal and cheer and give strength to body and soul alike." He heaped scorn on "these temple destroyers, devotees of ravaging commercialism [who] seem to have a perfect contempt for Nature, and instead of lifting their eyes to God of the mountains, lift them to the Almighty Dollar."[9]

In the end, the dam was built and Hetch Hetchy disappeared beneath the rising waters. For Muir, the defeat—as environmentalist David Brower says—"quite likely . . . instilled the huge grief that hastened his death." But the fight was not over; in fact it was only beginning. As Muir himself had noted, "Ever since the establishment of the Yosemite National Park, strife has been going around its borders and I suppose this will go on as part of the universal battle between right and wrong, however much its boundaries may be shorn, or its wild beauty destroyed."[10]

◭ III ◭

In 1935 Aldo Leopold, a graduate of the Yale Forestry School, was eating lunch with some friends on a high rimrock in New Mexico. Looking down on the turbulent river below, he saw what he first took to be a deer but turned out to be a wolf. A half dozen pups jumped out from the willows to greet her. Leopold and his companions opened fire.

"We reached the old wolf in time to watch a fierce green fire dying in her eyes," Leopold later remembered. "I realized then, and have known ever since, that there was something new to me in those eyes— something known only to her and to the mountain."[11]

The dying green fire in the wolf's eyes compelled Leopold to begin "thinking like a mountain," as he put it. As a Forester, he already had moved toward wilderness preservation, having been instrumental in getting the Forest Service to set aside 574,000 acres for wilderness in the Gila National Forest in New Mexico. But though this meant there were no hotels or roads, it did not mean an absence of cattle or protection of predators. Acting in accord with the game management principles of the Forest Service, Leopold had helped eradicate wolves and coyotes for the sake of huntable deer. He thought that "fewer wolves meant more deer, that no wolves would mean hunters' paradise. But after seeing the green fire die, I sensed that neither the wolf nor the mountain agreed with such a view."[12]

The wolf had its own life, which was a necessary part of the life of the mountain. On a wolfless mountain, the deer browsed every edible bush and seedling away until they starved of their own "too-much." With too many deer, more hunters had to be brought in, which meant cutting new roads—and then the wilderness he had worked so hard to set aside was gone.

Leopold thus began his own evolution from the utilitarian school of Pinchot to the nature-centered school of Muir and Thoreau. But where Muir was ecstatic and romantic, Leopold was spare, laconic, and scientific, holding to a flinty independence. In 1933, he began teaching at the University of Wisconsin, moving to an exhausted farm at Sand Creek which he and his family restored and reforested, planting thousands of pines every year.

Taking up the fledgling science of ecology, Leopold used the metaphor of "a round river" in which "the current is the stream of energy which flows out of the soil into plants, thence into animals, thence back into the soil in a never ending circuit of life." The land, he said, was "one organism. Its parts, like our own parts, compete with each other and co-operate with each other. The competitions are as much a part of the inner workings as the co-operations." The complexity of the land organism—which "only those who know most about it know how little we know"—was, for Leopold, "the outstanding scientific discovery of the twentieth century."[13]

An understanding of this complexity led to an extension of ethics—which Leopold saw defined, ecologically, as "a limitation on freedom of action in the struggle for existence." The first ethics had been concerned with the relation between individuals; they had then been extended to include the relations between individuals and society. The next step, the land ethic, extended beyond the boundaries of the human individual and society to include "man's relation to land and to the animals and plants which grow upon it."

According to Leopold's land ethic, "A thing is right when it tends to preserve the integrity, stability, and beauty of the biotic community. It is wrong when it tends otherwise." This "ecological conscience," said Leopold, "changes the role of *Homo sapiens* from conqueror of the land community to plain member and citizen of it."[14]

But the plain member and citizen of the biotic community was also its defender. Ecological education transformed the wilderness conquerors into what Leopold called "defenders of the wilderness"—especially against their own kind. For wilderness was especially vulnerable to humans who held a "whip-hand over nature." "Wilderness is a resource which can shrink but not grow," wrote Leopold. "Invasions can be arrested or modified in a manner to keep an area usable either for recreation, or for science or for wildlife, but the creation of new wilderness in the full sense of the word is impossible."[15]

In order to save the wilderness remnants in America, Leopold and "a militant minority of wilderness-minded citizens" founded the Wilderness Society in 1935. They were, Leopold acknowledged, fighting "a rearguard action, through which retreats are reduced to a minimum." The Washington members of the Wilderness Society were "scattered through all the conservation bureaus," so that they could sound an early warning of "new invasions." The others "must be on watch throughout the nation and vigilantly available for action."[16]

The first issue of the society's magazine, *The Living Wilderness,* declared that the society had been "born of an emergency in conservation which admits no delay. The craze is to build all the highways possible everywhere while billions more may yet be borrowed from the unlucky future." Leopold himself wrote that the existence of the Wilderness Society was "a disclaimer of the biotic arrogance of *homo americanus.* It is one of the focal points of a new attitude—an intelligent humility before man's place in nature."[17]

Leopold's journal was published posthumously as *A Sand County Almanac* in 1948. "Like winds and sunsets, wild things were taken for granted until progress began to do away with them," Leopold wrote in the foreword. "Now we face the question whether a still higher 'standard of living' is worth its cost in things natural, wild, and free. . . . The whole conflict thus boils down to a question of degree. We of the minority see a law of diminishing returns in progress; our opponents do not."[18]

For the next twenty or thirty years the battle was fought in the halls of the Congress and the chambers of the courts. The weapons were mailing lists and membership lists and lawsuits, and the leaders of the various conservation and wildlife societies—such as the Sierra Club, the Audubon Society, and the Izaak Walton League—tended to be lawyers and highly paid executives concerned with lobbying, making a broad appeal, and raising funds, while keeping the lines of communication open to the politicians and power brokers they had come increasingly to depend on.

There were impressive victories (or at least some successful rearguard actions) such as the preservation of the Dinosaur Wilderness in Colorado and the passage of the Wilderness Preservation Bill of 1964, the Endangered Species Act, and the Marine Mammals Act. But the war for the earth—to use a phrase that was increasingly being heard—was nevertheless being lost. Laws were amended, overridden, bypassed, ignored, and unenforced. Meanwhile, the earth was being pillaged, plundered, poisoned, and polluted at an ever-accelerating rate.

It was at this point that a few environmentalists began to resort to direct actions. In the early seventies, a man known only as the Fox took it upon himself to protect the Fox River through such actions as plugging industrial smokestacks and diverting liquid toxic waste from U.S. Steel into a chief executive's private office. Asked by phone if what he was doing was immoral, he responded, "No more so than if I stopped a man from beating a dog or strangling a woman." In 1971, the "Billboard Bandits" cut down road signs in Michigan with chain saws; in Oregon, a pesticide-spraying helicopter went up in flames; in Minnesota, farmers known as the "Bolt Weevils" cut down sixteen high-voltage power lines cutting across their land; and in California, Mark Dubois chained himself to a boulder on a cliff above the Stanislaus River and threw away the key, protesting the flooding of the canyon by the Army Corps of Engineers. Dubois had worked within the system for years, to no avail. "Part of my spirit dies as the reservoir fills and floods the lower Stanislaus Canyon," he wrote Colonel Donald O'Shea, the chief engineer for the project. "Frustration with the bureaucracies are what finally drove me to do it," he explained later. "And I had to make a personal statement. There are no victories in the environmental movement, only delays. Maybe this will delay the flooding for a year. And that can give time for longer-term protection."[19]

Greenpeace was by far the most visible and best known of the activist environmental groups. Greenpeace traced its beginning to October 1, 1969, the day six thousand Canadians joined about a thousand American exiles from the Vietnam War and closed the border crossing between British Columbia and Washington state in a protest against American nuclear testing on the Aleutian Island of Amchitka. In 1971, a small group attempted to stop the test by sailing into the test site. One of the crew members, Robert Hunter, had been given a pamphlet which contained a two-hundred-year-old prophecy by a Cree elder, a grandmother by the name of Eyes of Fire. Eyes of Fire had foreseen a time when

> birds would fall out of the skies, the fish would be poisoned in their streams, the deer would drop in their tracks in the forest, and the sea would be 'blackened'—all thanks to the White Man's greed and technology. At that time, the Indian people would have all but completely lost their spirit. They would find it again, and they would

begin to teach the White Man how to have reverence for Mother Earth. Together, using the symbol of the rainbow, all the races of the world would band together to spread the great Indian teaching and go forth—Warriors of the Rainbow—to bring an end to the destruction and desecration of sacred Earth.[20]

The little band of Rainbow Warriors, as they subsequently called themselves, put their lives on the line to protect whales and baby harbor seals, and the earth itself. "We were moved and shaken by the same great forces of patriotism that has always driven men," Robert Hunter remembered, "but in this case—perhaps for the first time—our loyalty lay not with a country, a religion, or a language, but with the planet itself."[21]

In 1974, Greenpeace moved to save the whales, which were being slaughtered by huge Soviet factory ships off the California coast. The Rainbow Warriors planned to stop the whalers by maneuvering their flimsy rubber Zodiac boats between the whales and the whalers' explosive harpoons. But first they had to find the whalers in the vast Pacific, which they managed to do by using a combination of radio and the *I Ching*. When they launched the first Zodiac, Paul Watson, the "lead kamikaze," was wearing a white cloth wrapped around his forehead; Robert Hunter, who accompanied him, wore a strip of red cloth which had been given to him by the Gyalwa Karmapa, a revered Tibetan Buddhist teacher, who had given the Rainbow Warriors his blessing in Vancouver. "Watson was much in disfavour with most of the Greenpeace crowd because of his impetuousness, unpredictability, and a marked tendency to brag too much," Hunter remembered, "but his reflexes were excellent, he had great courage, and he was willing to die if necessary. . . . He was a warrior, and his willingness to go with me into the valley between Leviathan and the great steel harpoon gave me strength I doubted I had on my own."[22] Watson himself attributed his fearlessness to his time with the Sioux. "They said, '*Hoka Hey*, today is a good day to die.' You might die in five minutes or five years. But if you're doing what you need to be doing your life is whole."

The Rainbow Warriors hoped that their presence would deter the whalers, but it did not. A Russian gunner fired and the harpoon with its deadly steel cable slashed out over the Zodiac, barely missing Watson and Hunter, and exploded as it smashed into the body of a whale. The whale died, but the photographs taken by American draft resister

Rex Weyler from the bouncing bow of another Zodiac bore witness to the bloody carnage, which became front-page news.

In 1977, Paul Watson led a Greenpeace campaign against the annual baby harp seal hunt on the ice floes off Labrador. Watson had come upon one of the hunters just as the hunter had driven his spiked club into the skull of a baby seal. Watson grabbed the club and threw it into the ocean, followed by the seal pelt. Then he handcuffed himself to a bale of pelts about to be winched onto a ship. Watson was hauled across the ice and lifted up against the hull of the ship. Then he was dunked repeatedly into the icy waters, until he finally broke through and fell into the ocean. Only the timely arrival of his Greenpeace friends saved him from drowning.

A few months later Watson was expelled by the Greenpeace board of directors. By throwing the hunter's club in the water, they said, he had violated Canadian law and the Greenpeace code of nonviolence, and endangered the Greenpeace Foundation's status as a charitable organization. Watson, however, felt he had not gone far enough. He continued to feel that "violence was morally wrong." But at the same time, he argued that "nonviolent action alone has seldom produced beneficial change on our planet." He solved the dilemma by formulating a code for a new group he called the Sea Shepherd Society. This code "allowed violence against property but never against life, human or otherwise." In addition, Sea Shepherd activists pledged to use no weapons, including explosives; not to resist arrest with violence if apprehended; and to be prepared to take full responsibility and to suffer the possible consequences of their actions.

Two years later Watson put his new philosophy into action. For two days the *Sea Shepherd* hunted and harried a notorious pirate whaling factory ship, the *Sierra*. Finally, on July 16, Watson rammed into the *Sierra* in a kamikaze attack, ripping an eight-foot hole in the bow. The *Sierra* limped into port and the *Sea Shepherd* was seized by Portuguese authorities. Watson managed to slip out of Portugal, but a few months later someone sank the *Sierra* by attaching a magnetic mine to her hull, six feet below the waterline; the impounded *Sea Shepherd* was also scuttled. Watson then raised funds for a *Sea Shepherd II* and pledged to "continue fighting for the whales until there are either no more whalers or no more whales."[23]

That same year, Dave Foreman left his job as a lobbyist for the Wilderness Society. Foreman was frustrated and disillusioned with the mainstream environmental groups' stand on RARE II—the Roadless Area Resource Evaluation, in which the Forest Service had recommended that the government protect a mere fifteen million acres out of a possible eighty million acres of wilderness in the National Forests, much of it land that was unsuitable for loggers and other developers in any case. All the mainstream environmental groups knew what was going on, but because they were afraid of "environmental backlash" and concerned with keeping their contacts in Washington happy, they refused to sue. "Roadless areas with critical old growth forest values were allocated for the sawmill," Foreman later wrote. "Important grizzly habitat in the northern Rockies was tossed to the oil industry and the loggers."[24]

Foreman returned to his home in Arizona. In March 1980, Foreman went on a camping trip in the Pinacate Desert in Mexico, with a few "wilderness-minded" compatriots—Howie Wolke, Wyoming representative of Friends of the Earth; Mike Roselle, an oil field worker and former yippie activist; and Bart Koehler, former Wyoming representative of the Wilderness Society. The group had chosen the spot on the recommendation of one of their favorite authors, Ed Abbey, who had published a novel called *The Monkey Wrench Gang*, which recounted the adventures of George Hayduke, Doc Sarvis, Bonnie Abzug, and Seldom Seen Smith as they burned billboards, returned roads to nature, decommissioned bulldozers and Caterpillars, and planned to crack the Glen Canyon Dam.

Sitting around a campfire in the vast desert, fueled by Pacific beer and tequila, the disenchanted and frustrated environmentalists decided that what was needed was a new radical environmental group. They adopted a clenched green fist as their symbol "to symbolize militant resistance" and took the name of Earth First!, which summed up their philosophy. They also adopted the image of their local bioregion, the American Southwest. Bearded, beer-drinking, cowboy-hatted and -booted, they barnstormed the country with a road show as "rednecks for wilderness."

Their first action went unwitnessed. On April 28, 1980, a dozen Earth First!ers packed cement, shovels and a wheelbarrow three miles up the Mineral Creek box canyon to the ruins of a ghost town in the Gila National Forest. There they erected a stone monument with a wooden plaque to "VICTORIO, Outstanding Preservationist and Great American—This monument celebrates the 100th Anniversary of the great Apache chief, Victorio's raid on the Conney mining camp. . . . Victorio strove to protect these mountains from mining and other destructive activities of the white race. The present Gila Wilderness is partly a result of his efforts. (Erected by the New Mexico Patriotic Heratige [sic] Society.)"[25]

Their second action was much more visible. On the spring equinox of 1981, five Earth First!ers circumvented security guards at the Glen Canyon Dam to unfurl a three-hundred-foot-long plastic black "crack" down the face of the massive dam. Meanwhile, Ed Abbey addressed a group of supporters in the visitors' center parking lot, telling them to "oppose, resist, and if necessary subvert" to fight the industrialization of the American West.

The first photocopied issue of the *Earth First! Journal* had appeared just a few months earlier, in November 1980, with an editorial by Foreman: "We will not make political compromises. Let the other outfits do that. Earth First! will set forth the pure, hard-line, radical position of those who believe in the Earth first." The lobbying and litigating of the mainstream groups were needed, but so were grassroots "demonstrations, confrontations, and more creative tactics and rhetoric." Looking back to the antiwar and social justice movements of the sixties, Foreman went on, "It is time to be passionate. It's time to be tough. It's time to have the courage of the civil rights workers who went to jail. It's time to fight for the earth first."

For Foreman and other Earth First! activists, John Muir's war between the bear and humans had begun. Foreman called for "a warrior society to rise up out of the Earth and throw itself in front of the juggernaut of destruction, to be antibodies against the human pox that's ravaging this precious beautiful planet."[26]

The warrior's function had begun with the biological imperative of self-defense; it had evolved into a code to include the protection of family, band, tribe, class, and nation. Foreman's call was one of the signs that the warrior's code had now evolved to include—at least for some people—the earth itself.

The warrior's code—in all its various manifestations—evolved as a result of specific historical conditions and a vision of what was important to protect. The code of the wilderness warrior is evolving now as a result of the destruction of the earth and a vision of human beings as part of the earth—"ordinary citizens of the biosphere." Instead of hunting predators, the wilderness warrior's challenge is to protect and even reintroduce wolves, coyotes, and mountain lions. Instead of fighting wars, the warrior's challenge is to create a more vivid peace—a peace which allows for the fullest possible blossoming of the millions of diverse forms of life nature has brought forth.

The first Earth First! actions followed the classical forms of active civil disobedience and nonviolence developed by Gandhi and Martin Luther King, Jr., in their struggles for independence and social justice. On October 31, 1982, Yates Petroleum broke through a fence and began drilling illegally in the Salt Creek Wilderness. On Sunday, November 7, five local environmentalists set up tents across the access road. They held a banner that said, "Rape Watt, not Wilderness, Earth First!" That night bulldozers destroyed the tents, amid glaring floodlights and cries of "Get out of the way or you'll get killed." Aired on CBS News, Dan Rather called it a "wilderness battleground."

While Yates drilled, Foreman, Howie Wolke, and Jim Taylor began driving toward Salt Creek through a snowstorm. They arrived in the early morning and started hiking across the windswept grassland and yucca flats. Defying a state restraining order, they pitched their tents across the road, along with two flags: the American flag and the "Don't Tread on Me" rattlesnake flag. Warned by the sheriff's deputies that they would be arrested if they didn't leave, they held their ground. "I don't see what you're trying to preserve," the sheriff said. "The damage has already been done."

"If we don't stop the drilling in New Mexico, the Washakie or Bob Marshall Wilderness Areas will be next," said Wolke. "We have to draw the line here."

"We're protecting a hundred other wildernesses," Foreman added. "We want the rig out of here."

While they were standing there, the sheriff received a radio message: a U.S. district judge had issued a temporary restraining order against Yates, which was later extended. "This fall has proven that courageous direct action can win where traditional methods fail and that there are many Earth lovers willing to face arrest or personal injury to save our Mother," Foreman wrote in the *Earth First! Journal*. "Had it not been for the bravery and quick action of those who physically stood for the Salt Creek Wilderness, it is likely that the Department of Interior would not have moved to secure an injunction against Yates. It was direct action—in defiance of bulldozers, oil company goons, an illegal State Court restraining order, and Chaves County sheriff's deputies— that stopped Yates Petroleum Company."[27]

Soon—in April 1983—Earth First! was blocking another wilderness road, this time in the Siskiyou National Forest near Grants Pass, Oregon, protecting 150,000 acres of ancient forests. The blockade had begun on April 25, when Mike Roselle and four others were arrested for disorderly conduct and barred from the disputed area. On May 10 five Earth First!ers, fresh from a nonviolent training session, were covered with dirt from the blade of an irate bulldozer driver. Nine days later, Mary Beth Nearing and six other Oregonians handcuffed themselves to a bulldozer, shutting down work for four and a half hours. On May 12, Foreman and Dave Willis, who was confined to a wheelchair, blocked the road with a log. Deputies winched the log away and parked fifty feet down the road. Then Les Moore arrived in a pickup truck carrying six workers. Foreman stepped in front of the truck, and Moore kept going. Foreman was knocked off his feet and grabbed the bumper. He was dragged 103 yards before the truck stopped and Moore got out. "You dirty communist bastard!" he said. "Why don't you go back to the Russia!"

"But, Les," said Foreman, who had in fact served as chairman of the New Mexico Young Americans for Freedom, "I'm a registered Republican." Then the deputies drove up, handcuffed Foreman, and arrested him for disorderly conduct.[28]

Two years later, in Oregon's Willamette National Forest, activists frustrated by the ease with which they could be removed from their road blockades took to the trees. Using eight-inch pinions, a twenty-four-year-old rock climber by the name of Mike Jakubal climbed eighty feet up a Douglas fir in the aptly named Millennium Grove, hauling a plywood platform and a week's supply of water and food up after him.

Jakubal was arrested when he made the mistake of descending to take a walk during the night, not realizing that a deputy was hiding in wait for him. But his companion, Ron Huber, managed to maintain his vigil for a full month. Huber named his Douglas fir "Yggdrasil," after the Norse tree of life that supported the world. He hung an American flag from his platform and a banner reading ECOTOPIA IS RISING. He also ran lines from his platform to surrounding trees, so that they, too, could not be cut without pulling his platform down.

Living for weeks in the canopy of the forest, Huber became a part of the tree, swaying as the wind swayed his flimsy platform along with the supple branches of the great tree. Huber's neighbors included the spotted owl, an endangered species who could only survive in the fast-disappearing ancient forests, and the red vole, who lived most of life its in the canopy, far above the forest floor.

Huber's month-long tree-sit ended when the Forest Service brought in a construction crane all the way from Portland. For several hours, he managed to evade efforts to remove him from his perch. When they finally succeeded, he watched from the back of a police car, his hands handcuffed behind him, as Yggdrasil shivered and came crashing down.

Despite the heroic efforts of Dubois, Huber, and thousands of others, the destruction continued. Watching wilderness disappear before their eyes, many wilderness warriors adapted the Code of the Eco-Warrior put forth by Ed Abbey's fictional Doc Sarvis, the ringleader of The Monkey Wrench Gang: 1. Nobody gets hurt. Nobody. Not even yourself. 2. Don't get caught. 3. If you get caught you're on your own. Pass on the costs to the enemy. Work alone, or in a small circle of trusted friends. Expect no reward. Keep fit. 4. No domestic responsibilities. If married, do not breed.

"The eco-warrior" Dr. Sarvis had said, "does not fight people, he fights the institution, the planetary Empire of Growth and Greed. . . . He does not fight humans, he fights a runaway technology, an all-devouring entity that feeds on minerals, metals, rocks, soil, on the earth itself, on the bedrock of universal being."[29]

The monkey wrench was the symbolic weapon of choice, the wilderness warrior's tomahawk, for it was not a club or gun aimed at human beings, but a tool meant to take apart other tools—the perfect symbol for those defending genetic diversity and wilderness against the machinery of industrial society.

The most widespread and effective (at least for a time) form of monkeywrenching was to drive a spike high into a tree. This did not harm the tree, but it would destroy sawmill blades—unless the timber companies heeded Earth First! warnings and did not cut. Other forms of monkeywrenching included pulling up survey stakes and "decommissioning" and disabling costly equipment such as bulldozers, skidders, and other machinery by, for example, pouring sand into their engines.

Strategic monkeywrenching, as Foreman called it, was actually a form of economic warfare. In the long run, monkeywrenchers hoped that by disabling expensive machinery, forcing companies to invest heavily in security, and increasing insurance premiums, they could make the exploitation of wilderness unprofitable. In the short run, however, monkeywrenching also functioned as an emergency rearguard action, preserving threatened wilderness while lawyers obtained injunctions or new laws were passed.

Writing in *Ecodefense: A Field Guide to Monkeywrenching*, Foreman and Bill Hayward formulated a monkeywrencher's code. "Monkeywrenching is non-violent resistance to the destruction of natural diversity and other wilderness. It is not directed toward harming human beings or other forms of life. It is aimed at inanimate machines and tools."[30]

Monkeywrenching is also individual; monkeywrenchers work best alone, or with one other person in small "affinity groups," to minimize the possibility of informers and agent provocateurs. Monkeywrenching is thus not organized or directed from a central headquarters.

Monkeywrenching is also deliberate and strategic. Monkeywrenchers pick their targets carefully. "They make sure it belongs to the proper culprit. They ask themselves what is the most vulnerable point of a wilderness-destroying project and strike there." Monkeywrenching is not "mindless, erratic vandalism."

Monkeywrenching is timely. It can be counterproductive, however, during "delicate political negotiations. . . . The Earth warrior always thinks: Will monkeywrenching help or hinder the protection of this place?" But it can also be fun. "There is a rush of excitement, a sense of accomplishment, and unparalleled camaraderie from creeping about in the night."

Still, Foreman concludes, "Monkeywrenchers are very conscious of the gravity of what they do. They are deliberate about taking such a serious step. They are thoughtful. Monkeywrenchers—although non-violent—are warriors. They are exposing themselves to possible arrest or injury. It is not a casual or flippant affair. They keep a pure heart and mind about it. They remember that they are engaged in the most moral of all actions: protecting life, defending the earth."[31]

△△ IV △△

Predictably, not everyone has agreed with this philosophy. Within the cascading radical environmental activist avalanche that was spearheaded and given voice by the Earth First! movement, some argued that destruction of property would alienate potential supporters, lead to an environmental "backlash," and bring down the armed wrath of the industrialized state. Others objected to any breaking of the law or destruction of property which was not done openly, with full acceptance of the consequences. (Gandhi, perhaps, would have sat down next to the loader he had decommissioned and waited calmly to be arrested.) The editor of the *Earth First! Journal* resigned over the question.

Poet Gary Snyder wrote prophetically that "the adversary: industrial capitalist civilization, has infinite resources for violence on its side. It has long known the technique of talking law and order while sneakily irritating, provoking and ultimately drawing a frustrated violent reaction out of whatever is needling it, and then using that bit of violent reaction as an excuse for massive retaliation. Thus Wounded Knees I and II. . . . I'm sure Earth First! is already well-infiltrated and that a provocateur from within your ranks will soon be urging some bit of sabotage that will be precisely the excuse the government needs to begin to crack down."

Snyder also pointed out that "private property is more sanctified than human life in our culture. . . . Also, any quick survey of guerilla hit-and-run attacks on materials and equipment shows that inevitably people get killed sooner or later and the ante is horribly upped. . . .

"If violence ever were an only-possible-choice," Snyder cautioned, "it would have to be undertaken with true warrior's consciousness, that is to say, the deliberate and thoughtful attitude of one who had investigated and exhausted all other possible avenues, and then turns towards violence with full, sad, precise comprehension of the cause-and-effect such an act would generate. There have been cultures where men were trained in true warrior consciousness: this is not one of them. Any talk that condones violence without understanding the warrior's path is premature indeed."[32]

The whole discussion about the proper uses and limitations of violence went back, of course, to Mohandas Gandhi—perhaps the "only man," as psychoanalyst Erik Erikson says, "who has seen *and* demonstrated an over-all alternative" to the dilemma of human aggression.[33] Gandhi's militant nonviolent warrior fought with *satyagraha*—literally, "truth-force" or, we might say, "the force of truth"—rather than with physical or technological force. In all his battles, Gandhi tried first to persuade his opponents by example, and then by his willingness to endure imprisonment, physical abuse, or even death—thus demanding the ultimate in fearlessness of the *sathyagrahi,* the nonviolent warrior.

"What do you think?" Gandhi asked. "Wherein is courage required—in blowing others to pieces from behind a cannon, or with a smiling face to approach a cannon and be blown to pieces? Who is the true warrior—he who keeps death always as a bosom friend, or he who controls the death of others? Believe me that a man devoid of courage and manhood can never be a passive resister."[34]

Gandhi's nonviolence, however, was not an absolute, but one pole of a continuum. As one of Gandhi's contemporary heirs, the Vietnamese Zen master and peace activist Thich Nhat Hanh points out, "One can never be sure that one is completely on the side of nonviolence or that the other person is completely on the side of violence. Nonviolence is a direction not a separating line. It has no boundaries."[35]

When Gandhi heard that Indian villagers, thinking they were following his instructions to be nonviolent, had run away while the police were "looting their homes and molesting their women," he said, "I hung my head in shame." He continued to hold "that nonviolence is infinitely superior to violence." But the message of nonviolence, he said, "was for those who knew how to die, not for those who were afraid of death . . . If one has not that courage, I want him to cultivate the art of killing and being killed, rather than in a cowardly manner to flee from danger."[36]

So it was that discussions on monkeywrenching, self-defense, and nonviolence filled the lively anarchic letters pages of the *Earth First! Journal.* Many activists adapted a Gandhian Peaceful Direct Action Code, vowing that: 1. Our attitude is one of openness, friendliness, and respect toward all beings we encounter. 2. We will use no violence, verbal or physical, toward any being. 3. We will not damage any property and will discourage others from doing so. 4. We will not run. 5. We will carry no weapons.[37]

Many others, however, continued to see monkeywrenching, including tree spiking, as "the wilderness defending itself." Howie Wolke, for example, supported nonviolent direct actions, but he also reminded readers that "the most basic animal instinct is to fight back under attack." And Edward Abbey endorsed the publication of *Ecodefense* by writing a "Forward!" in which he affirmed that "self-defense against attack is one of the basic laws not only of human society but of life itself, not only of human life but of all life. . . . And if the wilderness is our true home, and it is threatened with invasion, pillage and destruction—as it certainly is—then we have the right to defend that home, as we would our private rooms, by whatever means are necessary."[38]

In the end, as in the beginning, nobody in Earth First! has the inclination or the authority to tell anybody how to defend the earth. As editor John Stone wrote in 1989, Earth First! recognizes that "many are the ways to defend earth first." It is all up to the individual. Meanwhile, The *Earth First! Journal* continues to report widespread occurrences of monkeywrenching and runs a monkeywrenching advice column, "Dear Ned Ludd," named after the English saboteur who was the namesake for the anti-industrial "Luddite" movement in the eighteenth century.

The recipients of monkeywrenching, of course, have not bothered with such theoretical fine points. To them, destruction of property is destruction of the American way of life. It is "criminal" and "eco-terrorism." An anti-tree-spiking rider was attached to the omnibus drug bill in 1988. In addition, a number of states enacted laws making tree spiking a felony.

The monkeywrencher's dilemma is in many ways the old warrior's dilemma of the coevolving escalation of defense and offense. Monkey-wrenching and tree spiking started as clever defensive tactics against a seemingly superior offensive force. But the timber companies and Forest Service have responded with an even greater offensive.

The FBI, for example, spent two million dollars infiltrating Arizona Earth First! in an operation remarkably similar to the CONTROPOL operations the agency had launched against the Vietnam antiwar movement, AIM, the Black Panthers, and other groups during the sixties and seventies—just as Snyder had warned. On the moonless night of the last day of March 1989, an FBI agent who had been active in Earth First! circles for more than a year—and who some say suggested the action—led FBI and other law enforcement agents to an electrical tower leading to a pumping station of a huge water development project in the desert near Wenden, Arizona. There, in the light of a bright orange flare, fifty agents accompanied by dogs and two helicopters surprised three people with a propane torch. Two of the three were arrested immediately. But one of them somehow managed to elude the agents and make her way out into the desert.

That the person who escaped was a woman was a good example of one of the best-kept secrets of the notoriously macho Earth First! movement—which is that while most of the attention of the media and the authorities has been centered on the cigar-chomping, beer-drinking men, there have been many women wilderness warriors playing key roles in many of the actions. Earth First! women can sit in front of a bulldozer as well as any man, or hike as far or climb as high, if need be—and they can use male assumptions about women's "weakness" to their advantage.

One of the most active of women warriors is Peg Millett, a native Arizonian who was more of a "cowboy redneck" than most of the Earth First! men. She had worked as a horse trainer, fished for salmon in Alaska, fought forest fires, and tended bar. She had attended an Earth First! rendezvous in 1985, and immediately felt that she had found her people—"they knew how to party, they knew how to camp, they liked to walk around in the woods, and they're good biologists, and they didn't compromise in defense of Mother Earth."[39]

Like many Earth First!ers Millett had totemic animal guides—in her case, both were nocturnal, the raccoon and the ring-tailed cat. She dressed as a raccoon when she sat down in front of an ore truck going to a uranium mine on the rim of the Grand Canyon. But it was the ring-tailed cat who had come alive in her to guide her through the circle of flak-jacketed FBI agents, dogs, and lights to the moonless desert beyond. Like the ring-tailed cat, she found that she could see in the dark—far better, as it turned out, than the agents on the ground and in the helicopters with their infrared spotlights. She could move silently and quickly through the thickets of cactus, without getting stuck once. She could sense the humans searching for her.

She was more focused and calmer and awake than she had ever been. She was completely in her body. When the hovering helicopters caught her in their searchlights, she rolled up into a tight little ball under the chaparral bushes. She walked sixteen miles through the desert that night, without food or water, navigating by the constellation Scorpio, which happened to be her sign. She walked right through a pack of javelinas, wild desert pigs. A few old boars snorted, but they didn't stampede or attack. She howled with the coyotes and hooted with the owls. "I needed that night to think and take all the stars and animals and plants in."

When she arrived back in town, she went to a friend's house, quenched her thirst, changed her clothes, and called a lawyer. Then she went to work at her job at Planned Parenthood, which was where the authorities finally caught up with her. A year later, having spent three months in jail and waiting to go to trial, she still gathered strength from that long night's walk through all the searchlights and helicopters. "It was a great coup—in the sense that a coup doesn't hurt the other person." Of course, she hadn't deliberately walked into an enemy village, like the Plains warriors, but once surrounded, she had demonstrated her bravery and courage (and the enemy's incompetence) by walking away from the overwhelming forces hunting her, right under their noses.

While Millett was waiting for the FBI to take her in ("you take the risk and the responsibility"), other agents in Tucson were rousing Dave Foreman out of bed at gunpoint. Handcuffed and shackled, he was booked for conspiracy: the undercover agent claimed that Foreman had once given the saboteurs five hundred and forty dollars to fix the transmission on their car.

In July 1989, six months after his arrest, Foreman appeared at the tenth Earth First! Round River Rendezvous in the Jemez Mountains of New Mexico, having just been granted permission to travel. Flanked by a "Don't Tread on Me" rattlesnake flag and the Earth First! flag, he recounted how it felt to wake up one Wednesday morning in May in his house in Tucson "looking into three 357 Magnum pistols cocked, held by people wearing body armor."

"So what can I say?" he said. "I'm scared. I think a lot of you should be scared. But let's not be intimidated. Let's not be stupid. It's hard. We've got to fight intelligently. We've got to fight effectively. . . .

"How do we continue effective resistance for the earth, for life, for everything on this planet, against the destruction of the industrial state? How do we do it without alienating everybody else, without creating ourselves as targets? . . .

"And in facing this incredible challenge before us, how do we respond without becoming those people who are trying to destroy us? How do we avoid that great pitfall of revolutionaries, which is to become that which you revolt against? How do we fight tyranny without becoming tyrants, how do we fight hate without hating, how do we fight death without killing, how do we fight evil without becoming evil, how do we resist without becoming that which we resist?

"I don't know," he said. "That's what I'm thinking about. That's what I'm asking, and I hope all of you think about that too. . . .

"I don't believe in martyrs," he said. "I don't believe in tragic heroes, I don't want to be a martyr. But by God if this is a ghost dance, then I'm dancing, I'm gonna dance. I'll shut up when I'm laying in the desert with Ed Abbey."

"We don't need martyrs," a voice yelled from the Earth First!ers sitting in the gathering darkness. "We need warriors."

"That's right," said Foreman. "But warriors sometimes become martyrs. And warriors can act foolishly. We need to be smart warriors. We need to learn from what the FBI has done before, we need to respond intelligently, effectively, intransigently. We need to operate with courage, we all need to go out into the wilderness. We need to watch the moon rise, look at the stars, listen to the trees, lay in the river, draw strength from that, and carry on the fight. And if we die in the fight, so be it. We die better than we could have any other way. There's nothing else to do."[40]

And then he lifted his chin and raised his eyes to the moon and let out the famous long forlorn howling wolf cry of Earth First! which echoed back from the dark huddled shapes in the meadow—a yowl of wild lonely defiance, the sound of the green fire in the eyes of Leopold's dying wolf rising up in flames.

◣◣ V ◢◢

During the next year, Foreman spent a fair amount of time thinking about how the warrior could fight without becoming like the enemy he was fighting. He published his reflections in the *Earth First! Journal,* in an article titled "The Perils of Illegality." The conscientious law-breaker or monkeywrencher, Foreman noted, was placed "in a position of opposition to the creators, beneficiaries and enforcers of those laws, or to the owners or users of that property." It was an easy step, he wrote,

> from that to creating a dualistic world of *Us* versus *Them.* When we create such a world, our opponents become the enemy, become the *other,* become *evil* men and women instead of men and women *who commit evil.* In such a dichotomous world, they lose their humanness and we lose any compulsion to behave ethically or with consideration toward them. In such a psychological state we become true believers and any action against the enemy is justified.
>
> Resist the temptation to create an *Us* versus *Them* universe. Anger, rage, and intransigent resistence to evil are all proper, but for the sake of your own mental health and the sake of the movement, don't demonize others. Accept that we are all, to varying degrees, guilty of the destruction of the Earth.[41]

Given the complex technological nature of our society, the new wilderness warrior faces a formidable, seemingly unbeatable foe. The many-headed multinational dragon is driven by a seemingly insatiable appetite for the natural resources of the planet, spewing toxic wastes, fouling its own nest. It has behind it the awesome power of the modern industrial state.

But the enemy is not only outside; it is also within. Says John Seed, Australian founder of Rainforest Action Network,

> It's not just the habits of the timber barons and industrialists that must change, but our own too. And if we environmentalists—the ones who know and care—can't change, then how the hell can we

expect change from the rest? If we can't become the cutting edge of a real awakening, we might as well shut up and stay home.

But please, don't shut up and stay home. Find the energy to deal with our crisis where it needs to be dealt with—everywhere simultaneously. Don't project the problems "out there." We have to deal with them in here, too. It is our addictions that are, in the end, consuming fossil fuels and trees, and thus destroying the ozone layer and creating the greenhouse effect; that are causing us to crowd and poison sister species at a rate such that at least another *one million* species will be extinct by the turn of the century—as many as have become extinct in the last million years.[42]

Those who are called to enter this battle in whatever way they choose cannot win by fighting in the old way. The current battle brings the warrior full circle to face the warrior's dilemma, which turns out to be the human dilemma: the arrogance of human power and force, of conquest, has become, as Aldo Leopold saw, self-defeating. For we simply do not know enough or have the right to destroy the nature that gave us birth. We must realize that we depend on the health of the biosphere for our lives, that wilderness is intrinsically alive and valuable; we must find a way to live in harmony with the earth.

How to do this is beyond the scope of this exploration—indeed, it will be the central challenge of the next human epoch. But a new kind of warrior is clearly called for—a warrior who paradoxically recognizes that the old ways of power and conquest have now themselves become the enemy. Conquest itself must be conquered or given up. Only then will we find the strength and cunning to defend our deepest and most vulnerable nature—the fierce and tender original nature of both self and planet.

The warrior that is spoken of here is not the old warrior who depends solely on the force and power of aggression. It is not necessary to wield a weapon to test courage, not necessary to kill to face death, and not necessary to go to war to discover a heightened sense of life. But it is necessary—if one is called to the way of the warrior—to engage in some worthwhile and meaningful task.

The dilemma of the warrior without war, then, is to discover this challenge in peace—to make peace more vivid, as aikidoist George Leonard suggests. Or to live each day as if it were your last, like the samurai.

No doubt there are many ways to do this. Some risk their lives in dangerous sports such as rock climbing or hang gliding; others take an inward journey, no less precipitous and dangerous; some seek wisdom in the solitude of wilderness. And many pursue the traditional training ways of the martial arts.

But all of these, we may suggest, can be seen as nothing more or less than training for the true task of the warrior in our time: the protection of the earth itself, the very ground of being, as well as the sky of the heavens.

The idea is hardly a new one, though it now seems to be breaking out everywhere. Ninety years ago, William James, arguing that man had a naturally pugnacious nature, set out to find what he called a moral equivalent to war. He found it in the vocation of exertion in dangerous and useful occupations—mining, seafaring, rescue work—which made up the optimistic nineteenth century "war against nature."

Today we know better. For by conquering nature, we find we have conquered that which sustains our lives—since our lives are necessarily and rightfully but a strand in the vastly intricate dancing web of life and death. If we destroy that web, we destroy ourselves.

Put so simply, the problem is obvious. But the solution is not. This is the worthy challenge of the warrior today, and this the worthy opponent: greed, ignorance, and the unending, all-consuming, intoxicating addictions of power.

It is still an open question whether the human species will survive its own triumphant conquest of the planet. But there is some reason to hope we may yet learn the biological wisdom of acting with restraint and living in ecological balance. For the same reproductive drive that commands us to multiply and conquer the earth also drives us to care for and protect the successive lineages of gene-related kin that branch out with ever-expanding bio-diversity from that primordial chaos into which life was first breathed. So we move from self to friend and lover, to family, band, clan, tribe, mother- and fatherland, brotherhood, sisterhood, and the human family—until we reach kinship with life itself, whose protection and care still springs (as we come full circle) from the code of the warrior within us all.

The old warriors recited their lineages when they went into battle. So, too, the wilderness warrior may gather strength and wisdom (and learn what *not* to do) from the ancestors who have gone before, calling on wolf, mountain lion, hawk, and other great predators; on the Pleistocene hunters, who respected their prey and lived without war; on Gilgamesh, who faced his own death; Inanna, who descended fearlessly to the underworld; Achilles, who fought heroically, though fated to die; Arjuna, who asked hard questions, and fought without attachment;

Krishna, the trickster; Sakyamuni, who conquered the illusion of self; the t'ai chi masters, who joined heaven and earth; Sun Tzu, who won without fighting; the samurai, who joined brush and sword with simplicity and elegance; the knights, who protected the weak and turned battles into tournaments; Crazy Horse, who lived by his vision; Ueshiba, who became one with his opponent; and John Muir, who was on the side of the bears.

NOTES

▲▲▲ PROLOGUE ▲▲▲
THE TARGET CALLS

1. Douglas Mazonowicz, *In Search of Cave Art* (Rohnert Park, Calif.: Gallery of Prehistoric Art, 1973), n.p. Includes serialgraphs of paintings. See also Antonio Beltran, *Rock Art of the Spanish Levant* (New York: Cambridge University Press, 1982), p. 50: "We must suppose, first, that the painters were deeply versed in fighting with the bow and arrow. . . ."

▲▲▲ CHAPTER ONE ▲▲▲
THE FIRST PEOPLE

1. Raymond Dart, with Dennis Craig, *Adventures with the Missing Link* (New York: Harper & Row, 1959), p. 9.
2. Raymond Dart, "On the Predatory Transition from Ape to Man," in

Richard Leakey and Roger Lewin, *Origins* (New York: E. P. Dutton, 1977), p. 208.

3. S. E. Washburn, "The Hunter or the Hunted?" *American Anthropologist* 59, no. 4 (1957): 612–14.

4. C. K. Brain, *The Hunters or the Hunted? An Introduction to African Cave Taphonomy* (Chicago: University of Chicago Press, 1981), p. 7.

5. Nancy Tanner, *On Becoming Human* (New York: Cambridge University Press, 1981).

6. Louis Leakey, in "Son of Sparrow Hawk," *Psychology Today,* September 1972, p. 83.

7. Ervin Laszlo, *Evolution: The Grand Synthesis* (Boston: Shambhala Publications, 1988), p. 6.

8. François Bordes, *The Old Stone Age* (New York: McGraw-Hill, 1968).

9. William Laughlen, "Hunting: An Integrating Biobehavior System and Its Evolutionary Importance," in Richard Lee and Irven Devore, eds., *Man the Hunter* (Chicago: Aldine, 1968), p. 304.

10. José Ortega y Gasset, *Meditations on Hunting* (New York: Macmillan, 1986), p. 100.

11. Ibid., p. 102.

12. Carlton Coon, *The Hunting Peoples* (Boston: Little, Brown, 1971), p. 116.

13. Richard Leakey and Roger Lewin, *People of the Lake* (Garden City, N.Y.: Doubleday/Anchor Books, 1978), p. 133.

14. Margaret Mead, "Alternatives to War," in Morton Fried et al., eds., *War: The Anthropology of Armed Conflict and Aggression* (Garden City, N.Y.: Natural History Press, 1968), p. 215.

15. Marshall Sahlins, "Notes on the Original Affluent Society," in Lee and Devore, eds., *Man the Hunter,* p. 85. For the full argument see Sahlins, *Stone Age Economics* (Chicago: Aldine-Atherton, 1972).

16. Elman Service, *The Hunters* (Englewood Cliffs, N.J.: Prentice Hall, 1966), p. 60. The Eskimo song duel quoted by Service comes from E. A. Hoebel, *The Law of Primitive Man* (Cambridge, Mass.: Harvard University Press, 1959), p. 93.

17. Mervyn Meggitt, *Desert People: A Study of the Walbiri Aborigines of Central Australia* (Chicago: University of Chicago Press, 1965), pp. 245–46.

18. Colin Turnbull, *The Forest People* (New York: Simon & Schuster, 1961), p. 275.

19. Coon, *The Hunting Peoples,* p. 119.

20. Lee and Devore, eds., *Man the Hunter,* p. 3.

▲▲▲ CHAPTER TWO ▲▲▲
A DEADLY BALANCE

1. Mircea Eliade, *Patterns in Comparitive Religion* (New York: New American Library, 1974), pp. 345–46.

2. Ibid.

3. Peter Matthiessen, *Under the Mountain Wall: A Chronicle of Two Seasons in the Stone Age* (New York: Viking Press, 1962), pp. 10–17.

4. Robert Gardner and Karl G. Heider, *Gardens of War: Life and Death in the New Guinea Stone Age* (New York: Random House, 1968), p. 96.

5. Marvin Harris, "A Cultural Materialist Theory of Warfare," in Brian Ferguson, ed., *Warfare, Culture, and Environment* (Orlando, Fla.: Academic Press, 1984), p. 111.

6. Marvin Harris, *Cannibals and Kings: The Origins of Culture* (New York: Random House, 1971), p. 41.

7. Napoleon Chagnon, *Yanomamo: The Fierce People* (New York: Holt, Rinehart and Winston, 1983), pp. 83–84: "The argument began when I cautioned the protein advocates that the Yanomamo did not suffer from a protein shortage and that their warfare (and warfare in any group) was too complex to reduce to a single variable such as protein scarcity. Professor Harris argued that the Yanomamo probably were suffering from a per capita shortage of protein."

8. Ibid., p. 86.

9. Marvin Harris, "A Cultural Materialist Theory of Warfare," p. 129.

10. Chagnon, p. 213.

11. Brian Ferguson, "Studying War," in Ferguson, ed., *Warfare, Culture, and Environment,* p. 20.

12. Harris, *Cannibals and Kings,* p. 10.

13. Gilbert Herdt, *Guardians of the Flutes: Idioms of Masculinity* (New York: McGraw-Hill, 1981), p. 351.

14. K. E. Read, "Nama Cult of the New Guinea Highlands," *Oceanea,* September 1952, p. 15.

15. Ibid.

16. Walter Goldschmidt, "Personal Motivation and Institutionalized Conflict," in Mary Le Cron Foster and Robert A. Rubenstein, eds., *Peace and War: Cross-Cultural Perspectives* (New Brunswick, N.J.: Transaction Books, 1986), p. 8.

17. L. L. Langness, "Ritual, Power, and Male Domination in the New Guinea Highlands," *Ethos* 2 (1974): 180.

18. Margaret Mead, *Sex and Temperament in Three Primitive Societies* (New York: Dell, 1968), p. 265.

19. Herdt, *Guardians of the Flutes,* p. 51.

20. Lewis Cotlow, *In Search of the Primitive* (Boston: Little, Brown, 1942), p. 264.

21. Ibid., pp. 273–81.

22. Robert Renaldo, "Discussion," in Robert G. Hamerton-Kelly, ed., *Violent Origins: Walter Burkert, René Girard, and Johnathan Z. Smith on Ritual Killing and Cultural Formation* (Stanford, Calif.: Stanford University Press, 1987), pp. 245–55.

23. Ibid., p. 255.

1. James B. Pritchard, *Ancient Near Eastern Texts Relating to the Old Testament* (Princeton, N.J.: Princeton University Press, 1950), p. 65.
2. Ibid.
3. Thorkild Jacobsen, *The Treasures of Darkness: A History of Mesopotamian Religion* (New Haven, Conn.: Yale University Press, 1976), p. 172.
4. Ibid., p. 79.
5. Thorkild Jacobsen, *The Sumerian King List* (Chicago: Oriental Institute of Chicago, Assyriological Studies No. 11, University of Chicago Press, 1932), p. 73. The common Sumerian expressions previously quoted, "kingship descended from heaven" and "the people who knew not grain," also occur in this text.
6. Henri Frankfort, *Kingship and the Gods* (Chicago: University of Chicago Press, 1948), p. 239.
7. Jacob Klein, "The Royal Hymns of Shulgi King of Ur," *Transactions of the American Philosophical Society* 71, part 7 (1981): 15.
8. Ibid., p. 16.
9. Ibid., p. 14.
10. Thorkild Jacobsen, *The Treasures of Darkness,* p. 138.
11. Leo Oppenheim, *Ancient Mesopotamia: Portrait of a Dead Civilization* (Chicago: University of Chicago Press, 1977), p. 98.
12. James B. Pritchard, ed., *The Ancient Near East: A New Anthology of Texts and Pictures,* vol. II (Princeton, N.J.: Princeton University Press, 1975), p. 209.
13. Thorkild Jacobsen, *Toward the Image of Tammuz and Other Essays on Mesopotamian History and Culture* (Cambridge, Mass.: Harvard University Press, 1976), p. 44.
14. Because the Gilgamesh epic exists only in various fragmented versions in Sumerian, Akkadian, Neo-Babylonian, and other languages, I found it useful to draw from the following translations: Alexander Heidel, *The Gilgamesh Epic and Old Testament Parallels* (Chicago: The University of Chicago Press, 1949); N. K. Sanders, *The Epic of Gilgamesh* (London: Penguin Books, 1960); and E. A. Spicer, "The Epic of Gilgamesh," in James B. Pritchard, ed., *The Ancient Near East: An Anthology of Texts and Pictures,* vol. I (Princeton, N.J.: Princeton University Press, 1955). For consistency, I have used "Humbaba" for the monster-guardian of the forest, though Spicer's Akkadian version has "Humwawa" in the original.
15. Sanders, *The Epic of Gilgamesh,* p. 41.
16. Spicer, "The Epic of Gilgamesh," p. 48.
17. Sanders, *The Epic of Gilgamesh,* p. 69.
18. Heidel, *The Gilgamesh Epic and Old Testament Parallels,* p. 33.
19. Ibid., p. 35.
20. Spicer, "The Epic of Gilgamesh," p. 51.
21. Ibid.

22. Ibid., p. 55.
23. Ibid., pp. 63–64.
24. Ibid., p. 95.

▲▲▲ CHAPTER FOUR ▲▲▲
THE WARRIOR'S DILEMMA

1. My version of the Indo-European invasions closely follows the work of Marija Gimbutas, formerly professor of Slavic studies at the University of California, Los Angeles. An equally convincing approach, arguing that the Indo-Europeans settled across the land through farming, may be found in Colin Renfrew, *Archeology & Language: The Puzzle of Indo-European Origins* (New York: Cambridge University Press, 1987).
2. Marija Gimbutas, "Proto-Indo-European Culture," in G. Cordova et al., eds., *Indo-European and Indo-Europeans* (Philadelphia: University of Pennsylvania Press, 1966), p. 170.
3. Stuart Piggot, *Ancient Europe* (Chicago: Aldine, 1965), pp. 14–15.
4. Marija Gimbutas, "Primary and Secondary Homeland of the Indo-Europeans: Comments on Gamkrelidge-Ivanov Articles," *Journal of Indo-European Studies* 13, nos. 1 and 2 (Spring/Summer 1985): 186.
5. Marija Gimbutas, "Old Europe in the Fifth Millennium B.C.: The European Situation on the Arrival of the Indo-Europeans," in Edgar Polome, ed., *The Indo-Europeans in the Fourth and Fifth Millennia* (Ann Arbor, Mich.: Karoma, 1982), p. 5.
6. Ibid., p. 19.
7. Personal interview, May 16, 1989, with Marija Gimbutas, at her home in Topanga Canyon, California. During our conversation, she mused: "It is natural to accept the world was always the way it is now. That war always was. But what is the prehistory of war? What is human history? The real history is so short in comparison. For millions of years human beings were not warriors. They were mild food-gatherers and only partly hunters, and used bone marrow and not much meat. The transition was very gradual. To change from horse hunting to horse mastery you have to mount the horse—otherwise you cannot control the horse."
8. Homer, *The Iliad*, translated by Robert Fitzgerald (Garden City, N.Y.: Doubleday/Anchor Books, 1975), p. 382.
9. Tacitus, *Germania*, translated by W. Peterson (London: Loeb Classical Library, 1914), p. 325.
10. Ali Mazrui, "The Warrior Tradition and the Masculinity of War," in Ali Mazrui, ed., *The Warrior Tradition in Modern Africa* (Leiden: E. J. Brill, 1977), p. 70.
11. Mircea Eliade, *Zalmoxis: The Vanishing God* (Chicago: University of Chicago Press, 1972), p. 6.
12. I have followed Paul Shepard and Barry Sanders, *The Sacred Paw: The Bear in Nature, Myth, and Literature* (New York: Viking Penguin, 1985).

13. Jan Bremmer, "An Enigmatic Indo-European Rite: Pederasty," *Arethusa* 13, no. 2 (1980): 179. See also Georges Dumezil, *The Destiny of the Warrior* (Chicago: University of Chicago Press, 1970), p. 279.
14. Eliade, *Zalmoxis,* p. 6.
15. Georges Dumezil, *The Gods of the Ancient Northmen* (Berkeley: University of California Press, 1973), p. 36.
16. Thomas Kinsella, translator, *The Tain* (New York: Oxford University Press, 1971), pp. 91–92.
17. Dumezil, *The Destiny of the Warrior,* p. 80.
18. Ibid., pp. 106–7.
19. Joseph Campbell, *The Hero with a Thousand Faces* (Princeton, N.J.: Princeton University Press, 1949), p. 30.
20. Tacitus, *Germania,* 24, in H. R. Ellis Davidson, *Myths and Symbols in Pagan Europe* (Syracuse, N.Y.: Syracuse University Press, 1988), p. 89.
21. W. Pritchett Kendrick, *The Greek State at War,* part 2 (Berkeley: University of California Press, 1974), p. 216. For both Socrates and Philostratus.
22. Thucydides, *The Peloponnesian War,* translated by Rex Warner (London: Penguin Classics, 1954), p. 37.
23. James Redfield, *Nature and Culture in the Iliad: The Tragedy of Hector* (Chicago: University of Chicago Press, 1975), pp. 100–1.
24. Werner Jaeger, *Paideia: The Ideals of Greek Culture* (New York: Oxford University Press, 1965), p. 7.
25. Davidson, *Myths and Symbols in Pagan Europe,* p. 78.
26. Homer, *The Iliad,* p. 169.
27. Jaeger, *Paideia,* p. 7.
28. Homer, *The Iliad,* p. 145. Diomedes to Glaukus: "I have not noticed you before in battle—never before in the test that brings men honor."
29. Ibid., p. 463.
30. Ibid., p. 489.
31. Simone Weil, *The Iliad: A Poem of Force* (Wallingford, Penn.: Pendle Hill Pamphlet, 1956), p. 3.
32. Homer, *The Iliad,* p. 439.
33. Homer, *The Odyssey,* translated by Robert Fitzgerald (Garden City, N.Y.: Doubleday/Anchor Books, 1963), p. 201.
34. Moses I. Finley, *The World of Odysseus* (New York: Viking Press, 1965), p. 18.
35. Thucydides, *The Peloponnesian War,* pp. 149–50.
36. Pierre Ducrey, *Warfare in Ancient Greece* (New York: Schocken Books, 1985), p. 60.
37. W. R. Conner, "Early Greek Land Warfare as Symbolic Expression," *Past and Present* 119 (May 1988): 19.
38. Walter Burkert, *Greek Religion* (Cambridge, Mass.: Harvard University Press, 1985), p. 267.
39. Pierre Ducrey, *Warfare in Ancient Greece,* p. 64.

40. Robert L. O'Connell, *Of Arms and Men: A History of War, Weapons, and Aggression* (New York: Oxford University Press, 1989), p. 52.
41. Thucydides, *The Peloponnesian War,* p. 149.
42. Plutarch, *The Lives of the Noble Grecians and Romans,* translated by John Dryden (New York: Modern Library, n.d.): "esteemed it," p. 806; "and with his friends," p. 811.
43. John Keegan, *The Mask of Command* (New York: Viking Penguin, 1987), p. 57. Of Alexander's recklessness, Keegan notes: "But the knowledge that he was risking his skin with theirs was enough to ensure that his whole army from that moment onward, fought with an energy equal to his. Total exposure to risk was his secret of total victory." p. 90.
44. Ibid., p. 44.
45. Peter Green, *Alexander the Great* (New York: Praeger, 1970), p. 116. Many scholars consider the Gordian knot story as wholly legendary. Green cites "ancient authors" as his source for this quotation.

▲▲▲ CHAPTER FIVE ▲▲▲
THE BED OF ARROWS

1. A. L. Basham, *The Wonder That Was India* (New York: Grove Press, 1954), pp. 36–37.
2. Wendy Doniger O'Flaherty, translator, *The Rig-Veda* (London: Penguin Books, 1981), pp. 278–79.
3. R. Gordon Wasson, *Soma: Divine Mushroom of Immortality* (San Diego: Harcourt Brace Jovanovich, n.d.).
4. O'Flaherty, *The Rig-Veda,* p. 121.
5. Ibid., pp. 134–35.
6. Ibid., p. 31. The fourth *varna* (literally "color," commonly rendered as "caste"), the *sudras,* or servants, created from the giant's feet, were outcastes added after the Aryan conquest, forbidden to take part in the Vedic sacrifice.
7. Bruce Lincoln, *Myth, Cosmos, and Society: Indo-European Themes of Creation and Destruction* (Cambridge, Mass.: Harvard University Press, 1986), p. 142. "For the protection of all that had been created, the most radiant one . . . prescribed protection of the people, generosity, the patronage of sacrifice, and study, and non-involvement in (other) spheres of activity for the warrior."
8. Georges Dumezil, *The Destiny of the Warrior* (Chicago: University of Chicago Press, 1970), p. 62. *Rig-Veda* (5.35.4): "Autonomous, audacious is your spirit, slaying at a single stroke, O Indra, is your male force." Page 65: Indra's epithet, "of a thousand testicles," Dumezil notes, "surely alludes to the supervirility which every people readily attributes to its human and divine warriors. . . ."
9. O'Flaherty, *The Rig-Veda,* p. 149.
10. Willard Johnstone, *Riding the Ox Home: A History of Meditation*

(Boston: Beacon Press, 1982), p. 10: "Therefore 'yoga,' the oldest word still in use for meditation, means a skill in which one trains oneself, harnessing some previously uncontrolled forces, in order for these powers to enhance the success of some undertaking or adventure."

11. S. Radhakrishnan, *The Principal Upanishads* (London: George Allen and Unwin, 1953), pp. 623–24.

12. Geoffrey Parrinder, *The Wisdom of the Forest: Selections from the Hindu Upanishads* (New York: New Directions, 1975), pp. 73–74.

13. Ruth Cecily Katz, *Arjuna in the Mahabharata* (Columbia: University of South Carolina Press, 1989), p. 95.

14. Daman Sing Singh, *Ancient Indian Warfare: With Special Reference to the Vedic Period* (Leiden: E. J. Brill, 1965), p. 162.

15. Ibid., p. 161.

16. Ibid.

17. Ibid., p. 162.

18. James A. Aho, *Religious Mythology and the Art of War: Comparative Religious Symbolism of Military Violence* (Westport, Conn.: Greenwood Press, 1981), p. 68.

19. Ibid.

20. Basham, *The Wonder That Was India,* p. 126.

21. S. Radhakrishnan, *The Bhagavadgita* (New York: Harper & Row, 1973), pp. 89–94.

22. Ibid., pp. 98–99.

23. Ibid., pp. 108–11.

24. Ibid.: "Heroism . . . ," p. 366; "he will enjoy . . . ," p. 113.

25. Ibid., p. 125.

26. Ibid., p. 273.

27. Ibid.: "mouths . . . ," p. 277; "Whenever . . . ," p. 154–55; "I am Time . . . ," pp. 279–78.

28. J. A. B. van Buitenen, translator, *The Mahabharata* (Chicago: University of Chicago Press, 1975), p. 135.

29. Ibid., p. 138.

30. Ibid., pp. 174–75.

31. Ibid., p. 175.

32. Jaan Puhvel, *Comparative Mythology* (Baltimore: The Johns Hopkins Press, 1987), pp. 87–89.

33. J. A. B. van Buitenen, translator, *The Bhagavadgita in the Mahabharata* (Chicago: University of Chicago Press, 1981), pp. 195–196.

34. N. J. Krom, *The Life of the Buddha on the Stupa of Barabudur, According to the Lalitavistara* (Varnasi, India: Bhartiya Publishing House, 1974), pp. 162–71.

35. Irving Babbitt, translator, *The Dhammapada* (New York: New Directions, 1956), p. 53.

36. Ibid., p. 18.

37. Ibid., p. 32.

38. Robert A. F. Thurman, "Edicts of Asoka," in Fred Eppsteiner, ed., *The Path of Compassion: Writings on Socially Engaged Buddhism,* revised second edition (Berkeley, Calif.: Parallax Press, 1988), p. 111.
39. Ibid., p. 113.
40. Ibid., p. 112.
41. Ibid., p. 113.
42. Ibid., p. 119.

▲▲▲ CHAPTER SIX ▲▲▲
THE TAOIST SOLUTION

1. James Legge, translator, *The Chinese Classics,* vol. 5 (Hong Kong: Hong Kong University Press, 1970 [1872]), I, iv, 4.
2. Thomas Cleary, translator, *Mastering the Art of War: Zhuge Liang's and Liu Ji's Commentaries on the Classic by Sun Tzu* (Boston: Shambhala Publications, 1989), p. 8.
3. L. S. Yang, "Historical Notes on the Chinese World Order," in John Fairbank, ed., *The Chinese World Order* (Cambridge, Mass.: Harvard University Press, 1968), p. 24.
4. Cleary, *Mastering the Art of War,* pp. 71–72.
5. Clae Waltham, *Shu Ching, Book of History,* a modernized edition of the translation of James Legge (Chicago: Henry Regnery, 1971), p. 4. Also know as the *History Classic.*
6. Ibid., p. 21.
7. Ibid.
8. Ibid., p. 25.
9. Herrlee G. Creel, *The Birth of China: A Study of the Formative Period of Chinese Civilization* (New York: Frederick Unger, 1937), p. 21.
10. K. C. Chang, *Early Chinese Civilization: Anthropological Perspectives* (Cambridge, Mass.: Harvard University Press, 1976), p. 51.
11. Erik H. Erikson, "Pseudospeciation in the Nuclear Age," *Political Psychology* 6, no. 2 (1985): 214. "The term denotes that while man is obviously one species, he appears and continues on the scene split up into groups (from tribes to nations, from castes to classes, from religions to ideologies . . .) which provide their members with a firm sense of unique and superior human identity. . . . In times of threatening technological and political change and sudden upheaval, the idea of being the preordained foremost species tends to be reinforced by a fanatic fear and anxious hate of other pseudospecies. It then becomes a periodic and often reciprocal obsession of man that these others must be annihilated or kept 'in their places' by periodic warfare. . . ."
12. Chang, *Early Chinese Civilization,* pp. 229–30.
13. James A. Aho, *Religious Mythology and the Art of War:*

    Comparative Religious Symbolisms of Military Violence (Westport, Conn.: Greenwood Press, 1981), p. 114.

14. Arthur Waley, translator *The Book of Songs* (New York: Grove Press, 1937), p. 230.

15. Waltham, *Shu Ching, Book of History,* p. 124.

16. Cho-yun Hsu, *Ancient China in Transition: An Analysis of Social Mobility* (Stanford, Calif.: Stanford University Press, 1965), p. 21.

17. Herrlee G. Creel, *Confucius: The Man and the Myth* (New York: J. Day Co., 1949), p. 171.

18. E. G. Heath, *The Grey Goose: A History of Archery* (New York: New York Graphic Society, 1972), p. 67. "A certain mental calm is required for the best performance with bow and arrow, and the practice of archery can quickly reveal impatience or an undisciplined mental approach. It has been said archery, in her many moods, can reveal the best, and the worst, in man. Confucius, in his keen and sensitive observation of human behavior, must have recognized this delicate balance of the extreme qualities, and how a tendency one way or another could be revealed through the way of the bow."

19. Arthur Waley, translator, *The Analects of Confucius* (New York: Vintage, 1938), p. 95.

20. Herrlee G. Creel, *The Origins of Statecraft in China:* vol. 1, *The Western Chou* (Chicago: University of Chicago Press, 1970), p. 258.

21. Burton Watson, translator, *The Tso chuan: Selections from China's Oldest Narrative History* (New York: Columbia University Press, 1989), p. 86.

22. Waley, *The Analects of Confucius,* p. 189.

23. Watson, *The Tso chuan,* p. 119.

24. Ibid., p. 99.

25. Ibid., p. 194.

26. Creel, *The Origins of Statecraft in China,* p. 258.

27. Thomas Cleary, translator, "Strategies of the Warring States," in Thomas Cleary, translator, *The Art of War,* by Sun Tzu (Boston: Shambhala Publications, 1988), p. 27.

28. Herrlee G. Creel, *What Is Taoism? and Other Studies in Chinese Cultural History* (Chicago: University of Chicago Press, 1970): "in this ant . . . ," p. 31; "The Great Mass . . . ," p. 43.

29. Joseph Needham, *Science and Civilization in China:* vol. 2, *History of Scientific Thought* (Cambridge: Cambridge University Press), p. 57. The Confucian made his anthropocentric remark at a lavish banquet.

30. Creel, *What Is Taoism?,* p. 33.

31. Needham, *Science and Civilization in China,* pp. 69–70.

32. Arthur Waley, *The Way and Its Power: A Study of the Tao Te Chi and Its Place in Chinese Thought* (London: George Allen and Unwin, 1956), verse LXXVII, p. 238.

33. Needham, *Science and Civilization in China,* p. 104.

34. Waley, *The Way and Its Power,* verse XXX, p. 180.

35. Cleary, *The Art of War,* p. 5.

36. Ibid.
37. Ibid., p. 41.
38. Ibid., p. 166.
39. Samuel B. Griffith, translator, *The Art of War* by Sun Tzu (New York: Oxford University Press, 1963), pp. 113–14.
40. Cleary, *The Art of War*, p. 41.
41. Ibid., p. 146.
42. Ibid., pp. 49–50.
43. Ibid., p. 147.
44. Ibid., p. 121. Wang Hsi's comment in Griffith, p. 115; "undisturbed by events . . ." by Du Mu, in Cleary, p. 121.
45. Griffith, *The Art of War*, p. 76.
46. Ibid., p. 87.

▲▲▲ CHAPTER SEVEN ▲▲▲
EVERY OPEN HAND A SWORD

1. Ryusaki Tsunada, Wm. Theodore de Bary, and Donald Keen, eds., *Sources of Japanese Tradition* (New York: Columbia University Press, 1954), p. 234.
2. Donn Draeger and Robert Smith, *The Fighting Arts of Asia* (New York: Berkeley Medallion, 1974), p. 45.
3. Joseph Needham, *Science and Civilization in China:* vol. 2, *History of Scientific Thought* (Cambridge: Cambridge University Press, 1954), p. 145.
4. Arthur Waley, *The Way and Its Power: A Study of the Tao Te Ching and Its Place in Chinese Thought* (London: George Allen and Unwin, 1956), p. 118.
5. Ibid.
6. Arthur Waley, *Three Ways of Thought in Ancient China* (London: George Allen and Unwin, 1939), p. 75.
7. Ibid.
8. Draeger and Smith, *The Fighting Arts of Asia*, p. 46.
9. Robert W. Smith, ed., *Secrets of Shaolin Temple Boxing* (Rutland, Vt., and Tokyo: Charles E. Tuttle Co., 1964), p. 23.
10. Ibid., pp. 42–43.
11. Douglas Wile, translator, *T'ai-chi Touchstones: Yang Family Secret Transmissions* (Brooklyn: Sweet Ch'i Press, 1983), p. 99.
12. Ibid., pp. 99–100.
13. Tsung Hwa Jou, *The Tao of Tai-Chi Chuan* (Warwick, N.Y.: Tai Chi Foundation, 1981) pp. 6–8.
14. Benjamin Lo et. al., translators, *The Essence of T'ai Chi Ch'uan: The Literary Tradition* (Berkeley, Calif.: North Atlantic Books, 1985), p. 27.
15. Jou, *The Tao of Tai-Chi Chuan*, p. 111.
16. Lo et al., *The Essence of T'ai Chi Ch'uan*, pp. 21–25.
17. Ibid., p. 22.
18. Jou, *The Tao of Tai-Chi Chuan*, p. 7.

19. Ibid., p. 89.
20. Lo et al., *The Essence of T'ai Chi Ch'uan,* p. 87.
21. Wile, *T'ai-chi Touchstones,* p. 12.
22. Douglas Wile, translator, *Chen Man-Ch'ing's Advanced T'ai Chi Form Instructions* (Brooklyn, N.Y.: Sweet Ch'i Press, 1985), p. 25.
23. Jou, *The Tao of Tai-Chi Chuan,* 183–184.
24. Wile, *T'ai-chi Touchstones,* p. 100.
25. Draeger and Smith, *The Fighting Arts of Asia,* p. 38.
26. James Liu, *The Chinese Knight-Errant* (Chicago: University of Chicago Press, 1967), p. 85.
27. Ibid.
28. Thomas Cleary, translator, *Mastering the Art of War: Zhuge Liang's and Liu Ji's Commentaries on the Classic by Sun Tzu* (Boston: Shambhala Publications, 1989), p. 71.
29. Kryzysztof Gawlikowski, "The School of Strategy *(bing jia)* in the Context of Chinese Civilization," *East and West,* n.s., vol. 35, nos. 1–3 (September 1985), p. 193.
30. Ibid., p. 194.
31. Cleary, *Mastering the Art of War,* p. 62.
32. Wile, *T'ai-chi Touchstones,* pp. 85–87.

▲▲▲ CHAPTER EIGHT ▲▲▲
IN SHINING ARMOR

1. F. S. Shears, "The Chivalry of France," in Edgar Prestage, ed., *Chivalry: A Series of Studies to Illustrate Its Historical Significance and Civilizing Influence* (New York: Alfred A. Knopf, 1928), p. 59.
2. Ibid.
3. Ibid., p. 60.
4. Ibid.
5. Charles T. Davis. ed., *The Eagle, the Crescent, and the Cross: Sources of Medieval History,* vol. 1 (New York: Prentice-Hall, 1967), p. 72.
6. Ibid., p. 15.
7. W. H. Koch, *Medieval Warfare* (Englewood Cliffs, N.J.: Prentice-Hall, 1978), p. 27.
8. Marc Bloch, *Feudal Society* (London: Routledge and Kegan Paul, 1961), p. 152.
9. Prestage, ed., *Chivalry* p. 6.
10. Georges Duby, *The Making of the Christian West, 980–1100* (Geneva: Skira, 1967), p. 61.
11. Bloch, *Feudal Society,* p. 413. The Peace and Truce movements were closely related; the Peace protected certain classes and properties; the Truce forbade warfare at certain times.
12. Ibid., p. 319.
13. Richard Barber, *The Knight and Chivalry* (New York: Charles Scribner's Sons, 1970), p. 25.
14. Bloch, *Feudal Society,* pp. 318–19.

15. Francis Gies, *The Knight in History* (New York: Harper & Row, 1984), pp. 33, 21. Urban's speech is quoted from the *Historia hierosolymitana* (History of Jerusalem) by Robert the Monk.
16. Ibid., p. 33.
17. Sidney Painter, *French Chivalry: Chivalric Ideas and Practices in Medieval France* (Baltimore: Johns Hopkins University Press, 1940), p. 87.
18. Koch, *Medieval Warfare*, p. 95. See also Stephen Runciman, *A History of the Crusades*, vol. 1 ((New York: Harper & Row, 1964), pp. 286–87.
19. Gies, *The Knight in History*, pp. 107, 109.
20. H. E. J. Cowdrey, "The Genesis of the Crusades," in Thomas Patrick Murphy, ed., *The Holy War* (Columbus: Ohio State University Press, 1976), pp. 23–24.
21. Gillian Anderson and William Anderson, eds., *The Chronicles of Jean Froissart* (Carbondale: Southern Illinois University Press, 1963), p. ix.
22. Frederick Goldin, translator, *The Lyrics of the Troubadours* (Garden City, N.Y.: Doubleday/Anchor Books, 1973), p. 243.
23. Duby, *The Making of the Christian West, 980–1100*, p. 82.
24. James A. Brudage, "Holy War and the Medieval Lawyers," in Thomas Patrick Murphy, ed., *The Holy War*, p. 115.
25. Georges Duby, *The Chivalrous Society* (Berkeley: University of California Press, 1978), p. 122.
26. Painter, *French Chivalry*, p. 113.
27. Ibid.
28. Ferdinand Chalandon, *Histoire de la domination normande en Italie et en Sicile* (New York: Burt Franklin, 1960), pp. 58–94. Ms. Eve Wallace directed my attention to this source.
29. Duby, *The Chivalrous Society*, p. 122.
30. Denis de Rougemont, *Love in the Western World* (Garden City, N.Y.: Doubleday/Anchor Books, 1957), pp. 104–15. Sidney Goldfarb contributed valuable insights on Cathar aesthetics.
31. Emmanuel Le Roy Ladurie, *Montaillou: The Promised Land of Error* (New York: Random House, 1979), p. 308.
32. Ibid., pp. 22–24.
33. Joseph R. Strayer, *The Albigensian Crusades* (New York: Dial Press), preface.
34. Ibid., p. 63.
35. P. M. Matarasso, translator, *The Quest of the Holy Grail* (London: Penguin Books, 1969), pp. 275–76.
36. Ibid., p. 283.
37. Ibid., pp. 283–84.
38. Bradford B. Broughton, *Dictionary of Medieval Knighthood and Chivalry* (Westport, Conn.: Greenwood Press), pp. 94–98.
39. Anderson and Anderson, eds., *The Chronicles of Jean Froissart*, pp. 94–98.

40. Ibid.
41. A. T. Hatto, "Archery and Chivalry: A Noble Prejudice," *Modern Language Review* 35 (1940): 41.
42. Broughton, *Dictionary of Medieval Knighthood and Chivalry*, pp. 276–77.
43. Koch, *Medieval Warfare*, p. 213.
44. Noel Perrin, *Giving Up the Gun: Japan's Reversion to the Sword, 1543–1879* (Boston: Shambhala Publications, 1980), p. 59.

▲▲▲ CHAPTER NINE ▲▲▲
THE LIFE-GIVING SWORD

1. Makota Sugawara, *The Ancient Samurai* (Tokyo: East Publications, 1986), p. 29.
2. Hiroshi Kitagawa and Bruce T. Tsuchida, translators, *Tale of the Heike* (Tokyo: University of Tokyo Press, 1975), p. 269.
3. Ibid.
4. Ivan Morris, *The Nobility of Failure: Tragic Heroes in the History of Japan* (New York: Holt, Rinehart and Winston, 1975), p. 83.
5. Kitagawa and Tsuchida, *Tale of the Heike*, p. 271.
6. Robert Bellah, *Tokugawa Religion: The Values of Pre-Industrial Japan* (Boston: Beacon Press, 1970), p. 182.
7. Minoru Shinoda, *The Founding of the Kamakura Shogunate, 1180–1185* (New York: Columbia University Press, 1960), pp. 110–11.
8. Ibid., p. 280.
9. D. T. Suzuki, *Zen and Japanese Culture* (Princeton, N.J.: Princeton University Press, 1970), pp. 61–62.
10. Ibid., pp. 65–66.
11. Trevor Leggett, *The Warrior Koans: Early Zen in Japan* (London: Rider; Boston: Arkana, 1987), p. 48. See also Suzuki, *Zen and Japanese Culture*, p. 66.
12. Ibid., p. 13. See also Suzuki, *Zen and Japanese Culture*, p. 64.
13. Morris, *The Nobility of Failure*, p. 120.
14. Ibid., p. 140.
15. Ibid., p. 472
16. Suzuki, *Zen and Japanese Culture*, p. 289.
17. Ryusaki Tsunada et al., eds., *Sources of Japanese Tradition* (New York: Columbia University Press, 1954), p. 329.
18. Ibid., p. 336.
19. Noel Perrin, *Giving Up the Gun: Japan's Reversion to the Sword, 1543–1879* (Boston: Shambhala Publications, 1980), p. 35.
20. Donn Draeger, *Classical Bujutsu: The Martial Arts and Ways of Japan*, vol. 1 (New York and Tokyo: John Weatherhill, 1973), p. 50.
21. Hiroaki Sato, translator, *The Sword and the Mind* (Woodstock, N.Y.: The Overlook Press, 1986), p. 5.
22. Ibid., p. 56.
23. Makota Sugawara, *Lives of Master Swordsmen* (Tokyo: The East Publications, 1985), p. 109.

24. Sato, *The Sword and the Mind*, p. 111.
25. Ibid., p. 107.
26. Tsunada et. al., eds., *Sources of Japanese Tradition*, pp. 398–400. The quotation comes from Yamaga Soko, "The Way of the Samurai."
27. Yamamoto Tsunetomo, *The Hegakure: A Code to the Way of the Samurai*, translated by Takao Mukoh (Tokyo: The Hokuseido Press, 1980), p. 35. The title literally means "Behind the Leaves" and may refer to something hidden.
28. A. L. Sadler, *The Code of the Samurai*, p. 17.
29. Ibid., p. 51.
30. G. B. Sansom, *The Western World and Japan: A Study in the Interaction of European and Asiatic Cultures* (New York: Alfred A. Knopf, 1962), p. 234.
31. Tsunada et. al., eds., *Sources of Japanese Tradition*, p. 622.
32. Ibid., p. 618.
33. Sakata Yoshio, "The Beginning of Modernization in Japan," in Ardath W. Burks, ed., *The Modernizers: Overseas Students, Foreign Employees, and Meiji Japan* (Boulder, Colo.: Westview Press, 1985), p. 80. Sakata Yoshio is Professor Emeritus of History, Kyoto University.
34. Yukio Mishima, *Runaway Horses* (New York: Alfred A. Knopf, 1973), pp. 75–76.
35. Augustus H. Mounsey, *The Satsuma Rebellion: An Episode of Modern Japanese History* (London: John Murray, 1879), pp. 91–92.
36. Ibid., p. 216.
37. John Stevens, *The Sword of No-Sword: Life of the Master Warrior Tesshu* (Boulder, Colo.: Shambhala Publications, 1984), pp. 160–62.
38. Inazo Nitobe, *Bushido: The Warrior's Code* (Burbank, Calif.: Ohara Publications, 1975), p. 14. Originally published as *Bushido, the Soul of Japan*, in 1899. Nitobe most likely had help fashioning his High-Victorian English prose. In a preface written in Malvern, Pennsylvania, Nitobe thanks his "friend Anna C. Hartshorne for many valuable suggestions."
39. Tsunada et. al., eds., *Sources of Japanese Tradition*, p. 705.
40. Ibid.
41. Mitsugi Saotome, *Aikido and the Harmony of Nature* (Boulogne, France: SEDIREP, 1986), pp. 123–24.
42. Kisshomaru Ueshiba, *The Spirit of Aikido* (Tokyo and New York: Kodansha International, 1984), p. 38.
43. Ibid., p. 98
44. Bob Aubrey, "Aikido and the New Warrior," in Richard Heckler, ed., *Aikido and the New Warrior* (Berkeley, Calif.: North Atlantic Books, 1985), pp. 55–56.
45. John Stevens, *Abundant Peace: The Biography of Morihei Ueshiba, Founder of Aikido* (Boston: Shambhala Publications, 1987), pp. 35–36.

46. Ibid., p. 75. Stevens says that, after moving to Tokyo, Ueshiba called his art, variously, Kobukon Aiki-Budo, Ueshiba Ryu Jujutsu, Tenshin Aiki-Budo. After 1942, he settled on Aikido.
47. Tsunada et. al., eds., *Sources of Japanese Tradition*, p. 787. The quotation is from the Ministry of Education's "Fundamentals of Our National Polity."
48. Ibid., p. 707.
49. Saotome, *Aikido and the Harmony of Nature*, p. 30.
50. Ibid., p. 126.
51. Ibid., p. 189.
52. Ibid., p. 144.
53. Stevens, *Abundant Peace*, p. 112, and closing quotation, "True budo. . . ."

▲▲▲ CHAPTER TEN ▲▲▲
A GOOD DAY TO DIE

1. Edward Kladecek and and Mable Kladecek, *To Kill an Eagle: Indian Views of the Last Days of Crazy Horse* (Boulder, Colo.: Johnson Books, 1981), p. 119.
2. For the early life and vision of Crazy Horse, see Marie Sandoz, *Crazy Horse: The Strange Man of the Oglalas* (Lincoln: University of Nebraska Press, 1961), and Vinson Brown, *Hoka Hey!* (Happy Camp, Calif.: Naturegraph Publications, 1971), pp. 34–47.
3. John Erdoes, *Lame Deer: Seeker of Visions* (New York: Simon & Schuster, 1972), pp. 251–52.
4. Thomas E. Mails, *Dog Soldiers, Bear Men, and Buffalo Women: A Study of the Societies and Cults of the Plains Indians* (Englewood Cliffs, N.J.: Prentice-Hall, 1972) p. 237.
5. Patrick E. Byrnie, *Soldiers of the Plains* (New York: Minton, Bele, 1926), p. 179.
6. Stanley Vestal, *Warpath: The True Story of the Fighting Sioux Told in a Biography of Chief White Bull* (Lincoln: University of Nebraska Press, 1984), p. 8.
7. Eleanor Hinman, "Oglala Sources on the Life of Crazy Horse, Interviews Given to Eleanor H. Hinman," *Nebraska History Magazine* 57, no. 1 (Spring 1976): 43. Hinman, accompanied by Marie Sandoz, traveled to the Pine Ridge and Rosebud reservations in a Model T Ford coupe in June 1930. The interviews were deposited with the Nebraska Historical Society, and later became one of the main sources for *Crazy Horse* by Marie Sandoz.
8. According to another story, given in Byrnie, *Soldiers of the Plains*, Crazy Horse was given his name because a wild pony rode through camp at his birth. Mails, in *Dog Soldiers, Bear Men, and Buffalo Women*, p. 376, remembers John C. Neihardt's pointing out on a television program that "white men's translations of Indian names often miss the point. The Sioux word that had been interpreted as

meaning 'crazy' really meant 'enchanted,' so he was really 'Enchanted Horse.' "

9. Dee Brown, *Bury My Heart at Wounded Knee: An Indian History of the American West* (New York: Bantam, 1972), p. 87.
10. Kladecek and Kladecek, *To Kill an Eagle*, p. 119.
11. Ibid., p. 80.
12. James M. Sherrod, "Sketches from the Life of James M. Sherrod of Rawlins," *Annals of Wyoming* 4, no. 3 (1926): 342.
13. Stanley Vestal, *New Sources of Indian History* (Norman: University of Oklahoma Press, 1934), pp. 224–25.
14. Ibid., p. 219.
15. Hinman, "Oglala Sources on the Life of Crazy Horse," p. 28.
16. Brown, *Bury My Heart at Wounded Knee*, p. 270.
17. Ibid., p. 262.
18. Ibid., p. 274.
19. Stanley Vestal, *Sitting Bull: Champion of the Sioux* (Boston: Houghton Mifflin, 1932), pp. 150–51.
20. Hinman, "Oglala Sources on the Life of Crazy Horse," p. 40.
21. Kladecek and Kladecek, *To Kill an Eagle*, p. 127.
22. Vestal, *Sitting Bull*, p. 182.
23. E. A. Brininstool et. al., "Chief Crazy Horse, His Career and Death," *Nebraska History Magazine*, 12, no. 1 (January/March 1929): 42.
24. Ibid., p. 7
25. Ibid., p. 48.
26. Hinman, "Oglala Sources on the Life of Crazy Horse," p. 31.
27. Ibid., p. 32.
28. Brininstool et al., "Chief Crazy Horse," p. 11.
29. Ibid., p. 38.
30. Kladecek and Kladecek, *To Kill an Eagle*, p. 114.
31. Ibid., p. 126.
32. Brininstool et al., "Chief Crazy Horse," p. 22.
33. Ibid., p. 47.
34. Ibid., p. 42.
35. Brown, *Bury My Heart at Wounded Knee*, p. 390. For various versions of Wovoka's instructions, see *The Ghost Dance Religion and the Sioux Outbreak of 1890* by James Mooney (Chicago: The University of Chicago Press, 1965), pp. 22–23. Originally published as Part 2 of the *Fourteenth Annual Report of the Bureau of Ethnology to the Secretary of the Smithsonian Institution, 1892–93* (Washington, D.C.: Government Printing Office, 1896). Mooney's classic also contains an extensive collection of Ghost Dance songs.

▲▲▲ CHAPTER ELEVEN ▲▲▲
THE LONE WARRIOR

1. David Rothel, *Who Was That Masked Man: The Story of the Lone Ranger* (Cranbury, N.J.: Barnes, 1976), p. 55.

2. Ibid., p. 79.
3. Robert Jewett and Jack Shelton, *The American Monomyth* (New York: Doubleday/Anchor Books), p. 171. See also Roderick Nash, *Wilderness and the American Mind* (New Haven, Conn.: Yale University Press), p. 35: "The driving impulse was always to carve a garden from the wilds; to make an island of spiritual light in the surrounding darkness. . . . Paradoxically, their sanctuary and their enemy were one and the same."
4. Joe B. Frantz and Julian Choate, *The American Cowboy: The Myth and the Reality* (Norman: University of Oklahoma Press), pp. 13–14.
5. William H. Forbis, *The Cowboy* (Alexandria, Va.: Time-Life Books), p. 17.
6. David Darby, *Cowboy Culture* (New York: Alfred A. Knopf), pp. 278–79.
7. Richard W. Slatta, *Cowboys of the Americas* (New Haven, Conn.: Yale University Press, 1990). pp. 46–47.
8. Henry Blackman Sell and Victor Weybright, *Buffalo Bill and the Wild West* (New York: Oxford University Press, 1955), p. 147.
9. Ibid., p. 170.
10. Jewett and Shelton, *The American Monomyth*, p. 180.
11. Ibid., p. 181.
12. Ibid., p. 183.
13. Rothel, *Who Was That Masked Man*, p. 86.
14. Jewett and Shelton, *The American Monomyth*, p. 189.
15. John Milton Cooper, Jr., *The Warrior and the Priest: Woodrow Wilson and Theodore Roosevelt* (Cambridge, Mass.: Harvard University Press, 1983), p. 35.
16. Bradley Gilman, *Roosevelt, the Happy Warrior* (Boston: Little, Brown, 1921).
17. Theodore Roosevelt, *An Autobiography* (New York: Charles Scribner's Sons, 1924), p. 347.
18. Edmund Morris, *The Rise of Theodore Roosevelt* (New York: Coward, McCann & Geoghegan, 1979), p. 60.
19. Roosevelt, *An Autobiography*, p. 28.
20. Slatta, *Cowboys of the Americas*, p. 191.
21. Roosevelt, *An Autobiography*, p. 95.
22. Ibid., p. 123.
23. Ibid., p. 227.
24. Ibid., p. 242.
25. Morris, *The Rise of Theodore Roosevelt*, p. 654.
26. Ibid., p. 656.
27. Ibid., p. 674.
28. Roosevelt, *An Autobiography*, p. 45.
29. Ibid., p. 41.
30. Toshishiro Obata, *Samurai Akijitsu* (Thousand Oaks, Calif.: Dragon Books, 1987), p. 21.
31. David Thorne and George Butler, eds., *The New Soldier* (New York: Collier Books, 1971), p. 167.

32. Thomas Morgan, "The War Hero," *Esquire,* December 1983, pp. 597–604.
33. Mark Gerzon, *A Choice of Heroes: The Changing Face of American Manhood* (Boston: Houghton Mifflin, 1982), p. 32. The quotation is from Phil Caputo, *A Rumor of War* (New York: Holt, Rinehart and Winston, 1972).
34. Robert Jay Lifton, *Home from the War: Vietnam Veterans, Neither Victims nor Executioners* (New York: Simon & Schuster, 1973), p. 238.
35. Ibid., p. 97.
36. Ibid., p. 245.
37. Ibid., p. 69.
38. Ibid., p. 329.
39. Carlos Castenada, *Tales of Power* (New York: Simon & Schuster, 1976), p. 12.
40. Carlos Castenada, *A Separate Reality* (New York: Simon & Schuster, 1974), p. 214.
41. Chogyam Trungpa, *Shambhala: The Sacred Path of the Warrior* (Boston: Shambhala Publications, 1988), p. 41.

▲▲▲ C H A P T E R   T W E L V E ▲▲▲
THE WOMAN WARRIOR

1. Ali Mazrui, "Armed Kinsmen and the Origins of the State: An Essay in Philosophical Anthropology," in Ali Mazrui, ed., *The Warrior Tradition in Modern Africa* (Leiden: E. J. Brill, 1977), pp. 10–11.
2. Barbara Tuchman, *Practicing History: Selected Essays* (New York: Alfred A. Knopf, 1981), p. 265.
3. Jean Bethke Elshtain, *Women and War* (New York: Basic Books, 1987), pp. 171–93. Page 10: "Although the seductions of war are greatest for would-be soldiers—adolescent men wondering if they will get a chance to prove themselves—women are by no means immune to the battle call of Mars."
4. Herbert Wendt, *In Search of Adam: The Story of Man's Quest for His Earliest Ancestors* (Boston: Houghton Mifflin, 1956), p. 364.
5. Tim Newkirk, *Women Warlords* (London: Sterling, 1989), p. 81.
6. Thomas Kinsella, translator, *The Tain* (New York: Oxford University Press, 1971), p. 28.
7. Newkirk, *Women Warlords,* pp. 42–43.
8. Elshtain, *Women and War,* p. 163.
9. Donn Draeger and Robert Smith, *The Fighting Arts of Asia* (New York: Berkley Medallion, 1974), pp. 52–53.
10. Paula Gunn Allen, ed., *Spider Woman's Daughter* (New York: Fawcett Columbine, 1989), p. 33.
11. "Our Women in the Desert," *Newsweek,* September 10, 1990, p. 23.
12. Ibid.

13. Melvin Konner, "One Sex or Two," *The New York Times Book Review,* December 9, 1990, p. 27. Reviewing *Making Sex* by Thomas Laquer, Konner, a medical anthropologist, says, "There *are* facts abour sex differences. . . . I personally take these facts to mean that males are an aberration—or at best an evolutionary after-thought . . . that women are more predictable than men; and that men cannot be trusted with the command and control of advanced weapons (but could perhaps be mollified enough by rough sports to stay off the streets and battlefields)."

14. Lisa Geduldig, "Women in Martial Arts," *Whole Earth Review,* Spring 1990, p. 130.

15. Ibid., p. 131.

16. Ibid., p. 134.

17. Ibid.

18. Ibid.

19. Matt Thomas, "From the Founder," *Model Mugging News* 1 (January 1987): 3.

20. Becca Harber, "Letter to the Editor," *Yoga Journal,* January/February 1957, p. 5.

21. Paulette Boudreaux, "Kali Ma," *women of power* 3 (Winter/Spring 1986): 62.

22. Danielle Evans, "Model Mugging of Monterey," *Model Mugging News* 1 (January 1987): 5.

▲▲▲ CHAPTER THIRTEEN ▲▲▲
THE WARRIOR AND THE BUSINESSPERSON

1. Robert Bellah, *Tokugawa Religion: The Values of Pre-Industrial Japan* (Boston: Beacon Press, 1970), p. 103.

2. Ibid., p. 187. Beneath the Japanese application of strategy to business there are Chinese-Taoist roots. Kryzysztof Gawlikowski, "The School of Strategy," *East and West* 35 (September 1985): 26, quotes Bo Gui (fifth century B.C.), considered the "father of business management" by the Chinese: "I manage my business affairs as Yi Yin made strategical plans and as Sun Tzu deployed troops. If someone lacks the intelligence to manage natural changes, the courage to make quick decisions, [even] being benevolent he cannot obtain anything, [even] being powerful he cannot defend what he possesses."

3. Gary Jacobson and John Hillkirk, *Xerox: The American Samurai* (New York: Collier Books, 1986), p. 120.

4. Ibid., p. 119.

5. Boye De Mente, *The Japanese Influence in America* (Lincolnwood, Ill.: Passport Books, 1989), p. 119.

6. Robert Reich, *Tales of a New America* (New York: Times Books, 1987), p. 203.

7. James G. Barrie, *Business Wargames* (London: Penguin Books, 1985), pp. 2–3.

8. Minyamoto Musashi, *The Book of Five Rings* (New York: Bantam, 1982), p. 12. See also *A Book of Five Rings,* Victor Harris, translator (Woodstock, N.Y.: The Overlook Press, 1974), which carries the plug from George Lois in *Adweek:* "I have some advice for American businessmen who are trying to figure out why the Japanese excel in business. Buy and study a copy of Musashi's *A Book of Five Rings.*"
9. Ibid., p. 106.
10. Robert Pater, *Martial Arts and the Art of Management* (Rochester, Vt.: Destiny Books, 1988), pp. 69–70.
11. Ibid., p. 68.
12. Bo Burlingham, "This Woman Has Changed Business Forever," *Inc. Magazine,* June 1990, p. 38.
13. Ibid., pp. 47, 38.

▲▲▲ CHAPTER FOURTEEN ▲▲▲
BRINGING THE WARRIOR DOWN TO EARTH

1. Paul Watson, *Sea Shepherd: My Fight for Whales and Seals* (New York: Norton, 1982), p. 110.
2. Edwin Way Teale, *The Wilderness World of John Muir* (Boston: Houghton Mifflin, 1976), p. 122.
3. John Muir, *A Thousand Mile Walk to the Gulf* (Boston: Houghton Mifflin, 1916), pp. 98–99.
4. John Muir, *The Yosemite* (San Francisco: Sierra Club Books, 1988), p. 49.
5. Teale, *The Wilderness World of John Muir,* pp. 316–17.
6. Roderick Nash, *Wilderness and the American Mind* (New Haven, Conn.: Yale University Press), p. 126.
7. Ibid., p. 132.
8. Ibid., p. 107.
9. Muir, *The Yosemite,* pp. 192, 196–97.
10. Ibid., p. 193.
11. Aldo Leopold, *Sand County Almanac with Essays on Conservation from Round Rover* (New York: Ballantine Books, 1970), p. 138.
12. Ibid., pp. 138–39.
13. Ibid., p. 190.
14. Ibid., p. 240.
15. Ibid., p. 248.
16. Ibid., p. 279.
17. Stephen Fox, *John Muir and His Legacy* (Boston: Little, Brown, 1981), p. 211.
18. Leopold, *Sand County Almanac,* p. xvii.
19. Tim Palmer, *Stanislaus: The Struggle for a River* (Berkeley: University of California Press, 1982), p. 178.
20. Robert Hunter, *Warriors of the Rainbow: A Chronicle of the Greenpeace Movement* (New York: Holt, Rinehart and Winston, 1970), p. 28.

21. Ibid., p. 93.
22. Ibid., p. 167.
23. Watson, *Sea Shepherd*, p. 251. In 1982, the Sea Shepherd helped negotiate the end of dolphin fishing at Iki Island, Japan. Dubbed the "Samurai protector of whales" by the Tokyo *Ashahi Shimbum*, after Watson's ramming of the Japanese-owned *Sierra*, Watson wrote in *Earth First! Journal*, November 1, 1990: "As an ecological activist, I have faced the Japanese as adversaries on numerous occasions. For this reason, I have studied Japanese martial strategy, especially . . . *A Book of Five Rings*. Musashi advocated the 'twofold way of pen and sword,' which I interpret to mean that one's actions must be both effective and educational."
24. Dave Foreman, *Earth First! Journal*, November 1980.
25. Christopher Manes, *Green Rage: Radical Environmentalism and the Unmaking of Civilization* (Boston: Little, Brown, 1990), p. 84.
26. Ibid., p. 73.
27. Dave Foreman, "Rare II Suit," *Earth First! Journal*, December 22, 1983, p. 1.
28. Dave Foreman, "Run Down by Truck," *Earth First! Journal*, June 21, 1983, pp. 1–4.
29. Edward Abbey, quoted in "Response to Violence," *Earth First! Journal*, June 21, 1981, p. 6.
30. Foreman and Haywood, eds., *Ecodefense* (Tucson, Ariz.: Ned Ludd Books, 1987), p. 4.
31. Ibid., pp. 14–17.
32. Gary Snyder, "Letter to the Editor," *Earth First! Journal*, August 1, 1982.
33. Erik H. Erikson, *Gandhi's Truth: On the Origins of Militant Nonviolence* (New York: W. W. Norton, 1969), p. 33.
34. Ibid., p. 225.
35. Catherine Ingram, *In the Footsteps of Gandhi* (Berkeley, Calif.: Parallax Press, 1989), p. 108.
36. Gandhi, "Gandhi on Violence," *Earth First! Journal*, December 21, 1982, p. 6.
37. Manes, *Green Rage*, p. 169.
38. Edward Abbey, "Forward!" in Foreman and Haywood, eds., *Ecodefense* 8.
39. Personal interview with Peg Millett, Boulder, Colorado, 1990, for this and following.
40. Author's transcription of talk at tenth Earth First! Rendezvous, Butterfly Springs, Jemez National Park, New Mexico, July 1989.
41. Dave Foreman, "The Perils of Illegality," *Earth First! Journal*, November 1, 1989, p. 25.
42. John Seed, "An Immodest Proposal, *Earth First! Journal*, May 1, 1986, p. 20. See also "Beyond Anthropocentrism," in John Seed, Joanna Macy, Pat Fleming, and Arne Naess, eds., *Thinking Like a Mountain* (Philadelphia: New Society Publishers, 1988).

SELECTED
BIBLIOGRAPHY

ABBEY, EDWARD. *Hayduke Lives!* Boston: Little, Brown, 1990.
————. *The Monkey Wrench Gang.* Philadelphia: Lippincott, 1975.
AHO, JAMES A. *Religious Mythology and the Art of War: Comparative Religious Symbolisms of Military Violence.* Westport, Conn.: Greenwood Press, 1981.
BELLAH, ROBERT. *Tokugawa Religion: The Values of Pre-Industrial Japan.* Boston: Beacon Press, 1970.
BIGELOW, ROBERT. *The Dawn Warriors.* Boston: Little, Brown, 1969.
BROWN, DEE. *Bury My Heart at Wounded Knee: An Indian History of the American West.* New York: Bantam, 1972.
BURKERT, WALTER. *Homo Necans: The Anthropology of Ancient Sacrificial Ritual and Myth.* Berkeley: University of California Press, 1983.
CAMERON, ANNE. *Daughters of Copper Woman.* Vancouver, B.C.: Press Gang Publishers, 1981.
CAMPBELL, JOSEPH. *The Hero with a Thousand Faces.* Princeton, N.J.: Princeton University Press, 1949.

CANETTI, ELIAS. *Crowds and Power.* Farrar, Straus & Giroux, 1984.

CHAGNON, NAPOLEAN. *Yanomamo: The Fierce People,* third rev. ed. New York: Holt, Rinehart and Winston, 1983.

CLEARY, THOMAS, translator. *The Art of War* by Sun Tzu. Boston: Shambhala Publications, 1988.

————. *Mastering the Art of War: Zhuge Liang's and Liu Ji's Commentaries on the Classic by Sun Tzu.* Boston: Shambhala Publications, 1989.

CREEL, HERRLEE G. *The Origins of Statecraft in China:* vol. 1, *The Western Chou.* Chicago: University of Chicago Press, 1970.

DARBY, DAVID. *Cowboy Culture.* New York: Alfred A. Knopf, 1981.

DRAEGER, DONN, and ROBERT SMITH. *The Fighting Arts of Asia.* New York: Berkley Medallion, 1974.

DUBY, GEORGES. *The Chivalrous Society.* Berkeley: University of California Press, 1978.

————. *William Marshall: The Flower of Chivalry.* New York: Pantheon Books, 1985.

DUMEZIL, GEORGES. *The Destiny of the Warrior.* Chicago: University of Chicago Press, 1970.

————. *The Stakes of the Warrior.* Berkeley: University of California Press, 1983.

EGENDORFF, ARTHUR. *Healing from the War: Trauma and Transformation After Vietnam.* Boston: Shambhala Publications, 1985.

ELSHTAIN, JEAN BETHKE. *Women and War.* New York: Basic Books, 1987.

ERIKSON, ERIK H. *Gandhi's Truth: On the Origins of Militant Nonviolence.* New York: Norton, 1969.

FERGUSON, BRIAN, ed. *Warfare, Culture, and Environment.* Orlando, Fla.: Academic Press, 1984. Contains an exhaustive bibliography on the anthropology of warfare.

FOREMAN, DAVE. *Confessions of an Eco-Warrior.* New York: Harmony Books, 1991.

FOSTER, MARY LE CRON, and ROBERT A. RUBINSTEIN. *Peace and War: Cross-Cultural Perspectives.* New Brunswick, N.J.: Transaction Books, 1986.

FRANTZ, JOE B., and JULIAN CHOATE. *The American Cowboy: The Myth and the Reality.* Norman: University of Oklahoma Press, 1955.

FRIED, MORTON, M. HARRIS, and R. MURPHY, eds. *War: The Anthropology of Armed Conflict and Aggression.* Garden City, N.Y.: Natural History Press, 1968.

GABRIEL, RICHARD. *No More Heroes.* New York: Hill and Wang, 1987.

GARDNER, ROBERT, and KARL G. HEIDER. *Gardens of War: Life and Death in the New Guinea Stone Age.* New York: Random House, 1968.

GERZON, MARK. *A Choice of Heroes: The Changing Face of American Manhood.* Boston: Houghton Mifflin, 1982.

GIES, FRANCIS. *The Knight in History.* New York: Harper & Row, 1984.

GRAY, J. GLENN. *The Warriors: Reflections on Men in Battle.* New York: Harcourt Brace Jovanovich, 1959.

GRIFFITH, SAMUEL B., translator. *The Art of War* by Sun Tzu. New York: Oxford University Press, 1963.

GROSSINGER, RICHARD, and LINDY HOUGH. *Nuclear Strategy and the Code of the Warrior: Faces of Man and Shiva in the Crisis of Human Survival.* Berkeley, Calif.: North Atlantic Books, 1984.

HARRIS, MARVIN. *Cannibals and Kings: The Origins of Culture.* New York: Random House, 1971.

HECKLER, RICHARD, ed. *Aikido and the New Warrior.* Berkeley, Calif.: North Atlantic Books, 1985.

HECKLER, RICHARD STROZZI. *In Search of the Warrior Spirit.* Berkeley, Calif.: North Atlantic Books, 1990.

HERDT, GILBERT. *Guardians of the Flute: Idioms of Masculinity.* New York: McGraw-Hill, 1981.

HOMER, *The Iliad,* translated by Robert Fitzgerald. Garden City, N.Y.: Doubleday/Anchor Books, 1975.

HUNTER, ROBERT. *Warriors of the Rainbow: A Chronicle of the Greenpeace Movement.* New York: Holt, Rinehart and Winston, 1970.

INGRAM, CATHERINE. *In the Footsteps of Gandhi.* Berkeley, Calif.: Parallax Press, 1989.

JACOBSEN, THORKILD. *The Treasures of Darkness: A History of Mesopotamian Religion.* New Haven, Conn.: Yale University Press, 1976.

JEWETT, ROBERT, and JACK SHELTON. *The American Monomyth.* Garden City, N.Y.: Doubleday/Anchor Books, 1977.

JOU, TSUNG HWA. *The Tao of Tai-Chi Chuan.* Warwick, N.Y.: Tai Chi Foundation, 1981.

KEEGAN, JOHN. *The Mask of Command.* New York: Viking, 1987.

KEEN, SAM. *Faces of the Enemy: Reflections of the Hostile Imagination.* New York: Harper & Row, 1986.

KINSELLA, THOMAS, translator. *The Tain.* New York: Oxford University Press, 1971.

KITAGAWA, HIROSHI, and BRUCE T. TSUCHIDA, translators. *The Tale of the Heike.* Tokyo: University of Tokyo Press, 1975.

KOCH, H. W. *Medieval Warfare.* Englewood Cliffs, N.J.: Prentice-Hall, 1978.

LEE, RICHARD, and IRVEN DEVORE, eds. *Man the Hunter.* Chicago: Aldine, 1968.

LEGGETT, TREVOR. *The Warrior Koans: Early Zen in Japan.* London: Rider; Boston: Arkana, 1987.

LEOPOLD, ALDO. *Sand County Almanac with Essays on Conservation from Round River.* New York: Ballantine Books, 1970.

LIFTON, ROBERT JAY. *Home from the War: Vietnam Veterans, Neither Victims nor Executioners.* New York: Simon & Schuster, 1973.

LINCOLN, BRUCE. *Myth, Cosmos, and Society: Indo-European Themes of

Creation and Destruction. Cambridge, Mass.: Harvard University Press, 1986.

Lo, Benjamin, et. al., translators. *The Essence of T'ai Chi Ch'uan: The Literary Tradition.* Berkeley, Calif.: North Atlantic Books, 1985.

Mails, Thomas. *Dog Soldiers, Bear Men, and Buffalo Women: A Study of the Societies and Cults of the Plains Indians.* Englewood Cliffs, N.J.: Prentice-Hall, 1972.

Manes, Christopher. *Green Rage: Radical Environmentalism and the Unmaking of Civilization.* Boston: Little, Brown, 1990.

Matthiessen, Peter. *In the Spirit of Crazy Horse.* New York: Viking Press, 1991.

――――. *Under the Mountain Wall: A Chronicle of Two Seasons in the Stone Age.* New York: Viking Press, 1962.

Mazrui, Ali, ed. *The Warrior Tradition in Modern Africa.* Leiden: E. J. Brill, 1977.

McNeill, William H. *The Pursuit of Power: Technology, Armed Force, and Society Since A.D. 1000.* Chicago: The University of Chicago Press, 1982.

Meggitt, Mervyn. *Blood Is Their Argument: Warfare Among the Mae Enga Tribesmen of the New Guinea Highlands.* Palo Alto, Calif.: Mayfair Publishing Co., 1977.

――――. *Desert People: A Study of the Walbiri Aborigines of Central Australia.* Chicago: University of Chicago Press, 1965.

Millman, Dan. *Way of the Peaceful Warrior.* Tiburon, Calif.: H. J. Kramer, 1984.

Mishima, Yukio. *Yukio Mishima on Hegakure: The Samurai Ethic and Modern Japan.* Tokyo: Tuttle, 1978.

Miyamoto, Musashi. *A Book of Five Rings,* translated by Victor Harris. Woodstock, N.Y.: The Overlook Press, 1974.

Morris, Ivan. *The Nobility of Failure: Tragic Heroes in the History of Japan.* New York: Holt, Rinehart and Winston, 1975.

Mumford, Lewis. *The Myth of the Machine: Technics and Human Development.* New York: Harcourt Brace Jovanovich, 1966.

Murphy, Thomas Patrick, ed. *The Holy War.* Columbus: Ohio State University Press, 1976.

Nash, Roderick. *Wilderness and the American Mind.* New Haven, Conn.: Yale University Press, 1973.

Needham, Joseph. *Science and Civilization in China:* vol 2, *History of Scientific Thought.* Cambridge: Cambridge University Press, 1954.

Nettleship, M. A., R. A. Givens, and A. Nettleship, eds. *War, Its Causes and Correlates.* Chicago: Aldine, 1976.

Newkirk, Tim. *Women Warlords.* London: Sterling, 1989.

Nitobe, Inazo. *Bushido: The Warrior's Code.* Burbank, Calif.: Ohara Publications, 1975.

O'Connell, Robert L. *Of Arms and Men: A History of War, Weapons, and Aggression.* New York: Oxford University Press, 1989.

Ortega y Gasset, José. *Meditations on Hunting.* New York: Macmillan, 1986.

PAINTER, SIDNEY. *French Chivalry: Chivalric Ideas and Practices in Medieval France.* Baltimore: Johns Hopkins University Press, 1940.

PERRIN, NOEL. *Giving Up the Gun: Japan's Reversion to the Sword, 1543–1879.* Boston: Shambhala Publications, 1980.

PRITCHARD, JAMES B., ed. *The Ancient Near East: An Anthology of Texts and Pictures,* vol. I. Princeton, N.J.: Princeton University Press, 1958.

————. *The Ancient Near East: A New Anthology of Texts and Pictures,* Vol. II. Princeton, N.J.: Princeton University Press, 1975.

RADHAKRISHNAN, S. *The Bhagavadgita.* New York: Harper & Row, 1973.

RAPPAPORT, ROY A. *Pigs for the Ancestors: Ritual in the Ecology of a New Guinea People.* New Haven, Conn.: Yale University Press, 1972.

REDFIELD, JAMES. *Nature and Culture in the Iliad: The Tragedy of Hector.* Chicago: University of Chicago Press, 1975.

SADLER, A. L., translator. *The Code of the Samurai,* a translation of Daidoji Yuzan's *Budo Shoshinshu.* Rutland, Vt · Tuttle, 1988.

SANDOZ, MARIE. *Crazy Horse: The Strange Man of the Oglalas.* Lincoln: University of Nebraska Press, 1961.

SAOTOME, MITSUGI. *Aikido and the Harmony of Nature.* Boston: Shambhala Publications, 1989.

SATO, HIROAKI, translator. *The Sword and the Mind.* Woodstock, N.Y.: The Overlook Press, 1986. Contains "Family-Transmitted Book on Swordmanship" and Takuan's "Divine Record of Immovable Wisdom."

SCHMOOKLER, ANDREW BARD. *Out of Weakness: Healing the Wounds That Drive Us to War.* New York: Bantam, 1988.

————. *The Parable of the Tribes.* Berkeley: University of California Press, 1984.

STEVENS, ANTHONY. *The Roots of War: A Jungian Perspective.* New York: Paragon House, 1989.

STEVENS, JOHN. *Abundant Peace: The Biography of Morihei Ueshiba, Founder of Aikido.* Boston: Shambhala Publications, 1987.

————. *The Sword of No-Sword: Life of the Master Warrior Tesshu.* Boulder, Colo.: Shambhala Publications, 1984.

SUGAWARA, MAKOTO. *Lives of Master Swordmen.* Tokyo: The East Publications, 1985.

TEALE, EDWIN WAY. *The Wilderness World of John Muir.* Boston: Houghton Mifflin, 1976.

TRUNGPA, CHOGYAM. *Shambhala: The Sacred Path of the Warrior.* Boston: Shambhala Publications, 1988.

TSUNADA, RYUSAKI, THEODORE DE BARY, and DONALD KEEN, eds. *Sources of Japanese Tradition.* New York: Columbia University Press, 1954.

TSUNETOMO, YAMAMOTO. *The Hegakure: A Code to the Way of the Samurai,* translated by Takao Mukoh. Tokyo: The Hokuseido Press, 1980.

TURNEY-HIGH, H. H. *Primitive War: Its Practices and Concepts.* Columbia: University of South Carolina Press, 1971.

WALEY, ARTHUR. *The Way and Its Power: A Study of the Tao Te Chi and Its Place in Chinese Thought.* London: George Allen and Unwin, 1956.

WATSON, BURTON, translator. *The Tso chuan: Selections from China's Oldest Narrative.* New York: Columbia University Press, 1989.

WATSON, PAUL. *Sea Shepherd: My Fight for Whales and Seals.* New York: Norton, 1982.

WEYLER, REX. *Blood of the Land.* New York: Dutton, 1983.

WILE, DOUGLAS, translator. *Ta'i-chi Touchstones: Yang Family Secret Transmissions.* Brooklyn: Sweet Ch'i Press, 1983.

UESHIBA, KISSHOMARU. *The Spirit of Aikido.* Tokyo and New York: Kodansha International, 1984.

VESTAL, STANLEY. *New Sources of Indian History.* Norman: University of Oklahoma Press, 1934.

———. *Warpath: The True Story of the Fighting Sioux Told in a Biography of Chief White Bull.* Lincoln: University of Nebraska Press, 1984.

INDEX

Indo-European, 56–57; Neanderthal, 12–13
Burke, John G., 226
Burkert, Walter, 76
Burton, Richard, 254
Bury My Heart at Wounded Knee, Brown, 227
Bushido, 173, 179, 188–89, 192; Chinese influences, 174–76; extension of, 195–96; reinterpretation of, 201
Business: warriors and, 261–71; Japanese strategy, 318n2
Business Executives for National Security, 269
Business Wargames, James, 265
Butokudan (Martial Virtues Hall), 196

Calamity Jane, 238
Cameron, Anne, *Daughters of Copper Women*, 255
Campbell, Joseph, 66
Cannibalism, 21
Cannibals and Kings, Harris, 24–25
Capellanus, Andreas, *Art of Courtly Love*, 159
Captives, treatment of, 45, 57–58, 77, 117, 148–49, 172
Caputo, Philip, 245
Carson, Kit, 236
Castaneda, Carlos, *Don Juan: A Yaqui Way of Knowledge*, 248–49
Cataclysmic holocaust, 92
Cathars, 155–59
Catholic Church, 136, 138, 156–58, 166–67; and knights, 140–42, 151, 152; and war, 142–47
Cavalry, infantry fire and, 181
Cave bears, Neanderthals and, 62
Celtic women warriors, 253
Ceremonies of knighthood, 140–41
Chadragupta, King of India, 96
Chagnon, Napoleon, 25–27, 301n7
Chang, K. C., 103
Chang Man-Ch'ing, 126
Chang San-feng, 123–26
Chansons de geste, 134
Chaos, creation and, 91–92
Character, American, 236
Charlemagne, 134, 136–37, 138
Charles Fire Thunder (Sioux), 217
Charles Martel (Frankish king), 136
Ch'en Wei-ming, 127
Cheuh Yuan, and Shaolin boxing, 122–23
La Chevalier de la Charette, Chretien de Troyes, 159–60
Ch'iang people, sacrifice of, 104
Childe, R. Gordan, 20
Children: Neolithic, work of, 20, 21; as property of fathers, 57; Sioux, 212–13

China: Buddhist monks, 120; influence in Japan, 170, 174, 179; Japanese war with, 196; warriors, 99–117, 120–31
Chivalrous warriors, ancient Greek, 72
Chivalry, 133–67; Chinese, 106–9, 114–15
Chivington, John M., 216–17
Choshu clan, 192
Chou Dynasty, 105–6
Choukoutien, China, 10–11
Chretien de Troyes, 159–61
Christendom, fight for, 134, 142–47
Christian chivalry, 147, 153; King Arthur and, 159, 160–61
Christianity: conversions to, 135–36, 138; in Japan, 175
Ch'u, King of, 100
Chuang Tzu, 110, 111, 121
Chuan tzu (gentlemen knights), 108
Chu Chulainn, 63, 64, 253
Chu Hsu Confucianism, 184
Church, 136, 150, 156–58; and knights, 140–42, 151, 152, 166; and Viking attacks, 138; and war, 142–47
Cities, 37–40, 84
Citizen army: Greek, 74–79; Japanese, 196; modern, 244; Sumerian, 44–45
City-states, Greek, 74–79
Civil disobedience, 285
Civilization, 37; Chinese, 100–101; kingship and, 40; Taoist views, 112
Civilized warfare, 38, 44–45
Civil war, Japan, 179–92
Clark, William B. (White Hat), 226
Class, military, international, 165. *See also* Social structure
Classic writings, Chou dynasty, 106
Clavert Investment Fund, 269
Clerics, feudal, 139, 140
Clovis, conversion of, 135
Code of the West, 237
Code of warriors, 3, 34–35, 66, 71–72, 284–85; aristocratic, 68–69; Buddhist teachings and, 95–96; chivalric, 133, 148–49, 152, 163–65, 167; Chinese, 106–9; environmentalist, 287; Greek, 75–77; Indo-European, 67; Japanese Bushido, 173, 188–89; Kshatriya, 90–92; samurai, applied to business, 262; Shaolin boxing, 122–23; spiritual, 97; Sumerian, Gilgamesh and, 46–47; Taoist, 100
Cody, Buffalo Bill, 238
Cohen, Ronald, 40
Columbus, Christopher, 235
Commercialization of chivalry, 149–50
Communication, hunting and, 11
Competition, 11, 69, 72; akido and, 204–5; in American business, 265; Chinese knights and, 107

Conflict: harmony and, aikido idea, 203–4; in hunter-gatherer societies, 15; for scarce resources, 40

Confucianism, 110, 183, 184, 188–89, 195

Confucius, 106, 108, 308n18; *Analects,* 107

Conquering Bear (Sioux Chief), 207–8

Conservation movement, 274–88

Constantine, Emperor of Rome, 135–36

Constantinople, Crusaders in, 144–45

Conte del Grail, Chretien de Troyes, 160–61

Contest, battle as, 68, 69–70

Coon, Carlton, 16

Cooper, John Milton, Jr., 241

Cooperation, hunting and, 11

Corporate raiders, 264

Cotlow, Lewis, 30

Council of Charroux, 139

Council of Narbonne, 140

The Counsels of the Great Yu, 101

Courtesie, 152

Court life, Japan, 179

Courtly love, cult of, 152–56, 159–60

Cowboys, 234, 236–43

Crane, Stephen, 243

Crazy Horse (Curly), 207–31, 297, 314–15n8

Creation myths: Aryan India, 83; Japanese, 169; Neolithic, 21; Sambia, 27–28; Sumerian, 38–39

Crécy, battle of, 162, 164

Creel, H. G., 102

Crockett, Davey, 236

Crook, "Three Stars" (U.S. General), 212, 223–24, 226, 227–28

Crossbows, 113, 150, 166

Crumm, Thomas, 267

Crusades, 142–47, 150, 167; World War II as, 244–45

Cuba, women warriors, 255

Cucutenci culture, 59

Cultural differences, 264

Custer, George C., 221, 224–25

Cyrus the Younger, 76

Dahomey, women warriors, 253–54

Daidoji, 188–89

Daimyo (Japanese feudal lords), 182–83, 192

Dance, Indo-European warriors and, 67

Dani people, 19–24

Dart, Raymond, 5–8, 9

Darwin, Charles, 9

Daughters of Copper Women, Cameron, 255

Davis, Richard Harding, 243

Death, 12–13, 21, 34–35, 53, 249; Aryan warriors and, 85; Bushido and, 188; Chinese knights and, 108–9; Gilgamesh and, 50–51; heroic code and, 72–73;

kshatriyas and, 91; medieval Christians and, 144; in ritual battle, 23; samurai and, 175; Taoism and, 113, 129

Decretals of Gregory IX, 151

Deguchi, Onisaburo, 198, 201

Delphic oracles, and warfare, 75–76

De Mente, Boye, 263

Deming, W. E., 263

Demonic forces, Indian gods and, 91–92

De Pauw, Linda Grant, 255

De Rougemont, Denis, *Love in the Western World,* 154–56

The Destiny of the Warrior, Dumezil, 65

Dhammapada, 95

Dharmavijaya (Indian battle), 86–87; Asoka and, 96–97

Diana of Valltorta, 252

Dinosaur Wilderness, Colorado, 279

Disarmament of population, 181–82

Divine Record of Immovable Wisdom, Takuan, 187

Doest, Maria, 257

Dominic, Saint, and Cathars, 156

Don Juan: A Yaqui Way of Knowledge, Castaneda, 248–49

Drachenloch, Germany, stone crypt, 62

Draeger, Donn, 122, 185

Dubois, Mark, 280

Duby, Georges, 152, 154

Duels, 47; battle as, 69–70; western "walkdown," 239

Duffield, George, 236–37

Dumezil, Georges, 83: *The Destiny of the Warrior,* 65

Duryodhana, 86, 90–91

Dyeus (Indo-European god), 57

Dynasties, Chinese, 101–2

Ea (Sumerian god), 38–39

Earp, Wyatt, 237

Earth First!, 283–89, 290–94

Earth First! Journal, 284, 290, 294

Earth-witnessing mudra, 95

Ecodefense: A Field Guide to Monkeywrenching, Foreman and Hayward, 288

Ecologically responsible business, 269–71

Ecuador, Jivaro people, 30–33

Education, medieval Japan, 184

Edward, Prince of Wales (Black Prince), 149–50, 163

Edward I, King of England, 161

Edward III, King of England, 161–63, 164

Eihenjahr, 61

Eisenhower, Dwight D., 244

Eleanor of Aquitaine, 153, 159, 253

Eliade, Mircea, 21, 61–64

Elshtain, Jean Bethke, *Women and War,* 251–52

New Shade swordsmanship, 185–87
New World expectations, 235–36, 316n3
Nicaragua, women warriors, 255
Nichirin Buddhists, 175
Ninurta (Sumerian god), 43–44
Nitobe, Inazo, 195
The Nobility of Failure, Morris, 178
Noble classes: Aryan, 83; Chinese, 103, 105, 106; feudal, 138, 148, 150, 163–64; Indo-European, 67; Japanese, 170
Nobunaga, Oda, 181
Nogi (Japanese Admiral), 196
Noh drama, 179–80
Non-action, Taoist, 111
Nonviolence, 88, 282, 289–90
Nootka people, 254–55
Norris, William, 269
Northmen, 137–38
No-sword technique, 186
No Water (Sioux), 220–21
Nuclear testing, protests, 280

Oakley, Annie, 238
Odessa, Amazon burial, 252
Odysseus, 73
Oglala Sioux, independence of, 273
Old Europe society, 59–60
Old Ones (Sumerian gods), 38
Olduvai Gorge, tools from, 9
Omoto-kyo, 198–99
"On the Predatory Transition from Ape to Man," Dart, 7
108 Monk Exercises, 121
Oppenheim, Leo, 45
Oppenheimer, Robert, 89
Oracle bones, Chinese, 102
Ordene de Chivalrie, 141
Order of the Garter, 161, 164–65
Les Origines de l'Ancienne France, Flach, 139
Origin myths. *See* Creation myths
Ortega y Gasset, Jose, *Meditations on Hunting*, 12, 13
O'Shea, Donald, 280
Osteodontokeratic culture, 7
Overspecialization, 2
Ovitz, Mike, 267

Pacifism, Taoist, 112
Pai Yu-feng, 122
Paleolithic era, 10; bear cult, 62
Pan-African Conference on Prehistory, 8
Pandavas, 86, 87–92
Paris (Trojan), 72
Paris, France, Viking attacks, 137
Parsifal, 160
Pater, Robert, 268
Patriarchal society, 57, 60

Patrocles, 71
Pattern drama, Neolithic, 21
Paul, Saint, 143
Peace: Japanese arts of, 184; self-defense and, 259; warriors and, 41, 295; wilderness warriors and, 284–85
Peaceful Direct Action Code, 290
Peace of God movement, 139–40, 310n11
Pearl Harbor, Japanese attack, 201–2
Peasants, feudal, 140
Pederasty, ritual, 63
Peking man, 10–11
Penthesilea, Queen, 252
People of the Lake, Leakey, 14
People's Crusade, 144
Pericles, 74, 77
"The Perils of Illegality," Foreman, 294
Perrin, Noel, *Giving Up the Gun*, 184–85
Perry, Matthew, 189
Persian Gulf War, women and, 256
Peter the Hermit, 144, 145
Phalanx, battle formation, 76, 78
Philippines, Ilongot people, 33–35
Philip VI, King of France, 162
Philosophers, Chinese, 110–12
Philostatos, 67
PIE (proto-Indo-European) language, 56
Piggott, Stuart, 67; *Ancient Europe*, 58–59
Pilgrim's war, 142
Pinchot, Gifford, 276
Plains Indians, war games, 211–12
Plutarch, 78, 253
Politics, war and, 251
Polybius, 75–76
Poor Knights, 146–47
Population control, warfare and, 24–25
Porus, King of India, 81
Poverty, samurai virtue, 263
Power, 46–53; Lone Ranger and, 240; of women, male anxiety about, 256
Prayer Mat of Flesh, Li Yu, 130
Pre-Aryan India, 84–85
Predators, 10, 12; warriors as, 61–62
Prehistoric paintings, 1–2
Pretty Shields (Chippewa woman), 255
Priam, King of Troy, 72
Price, Hiram, 230
Primitive life, views of, 14–15
Primitive warfare, theories of, 24–27
Prisoners of war. *See* Captives
Profession, warfare as, 68
Progress, views of, 279
Protectors, warriors as, 3, 41
Proto-Indo-European (PIE) language, 56
"Proto-Shiva," 84
Prowess in battle, 70–71, 72, 100
Pseudospeciation, 104, 307n11
Puhvel, Jaan, 92
Pure Land Buddhists, 175

West, code of, 237
Weyler, Rex, 282
Whales, protection of, 281–82
White Antelope (Cheyenne chief), 217
White Buffalo Woman, 209–10
White Bull (Sioux warrior), 213
White Lotus Buddhists, 129
Wilderness, protection of, 276–79
Wilderness Preservation Bill (1964), 279
Wilderness Society, 279
Wilderness warriors, 284–89, 290–97
Wildfire, 11
Willamette National Forest, 286–87
Willens, Harold, 269
Willhibee-Willhou people, 19–24
William of Normandy, 137, 148
Willis, Dave, 286
Wilson, Woodrow, 243–44
Wing Chun, 254
Winthrop, John, 235
Wister, Owen, *The Virginian*, 238–39, 240
Wives, as property of husbands, 57
Woden, Christian knights and, 147
Wolf-coat men, 61, 62
Wolke, Howie, 283, 285, 290
Wolves, destruction of, 277–78
The Woman Warrior, Kingston, 254
Women, 9, 20, 28, 29, 57, 318n13; Aryan, 82; Cathars, 155–56; Christian chivalry and, 153; courtly love and, 156; environmentalist, 291–92; and hunting, 14, 15; and martial arts, 127–28; and war, 26–27, 317n3, 318n13; warriors, 82, 103, 153, 194, 251–59
"Women and the Martial Arts," Geduldig, 256–57
Women and War, Elshtain, 251–52
The Wonder That Was India, Basham, 87
Wonder Woman, 256

Work, 15, 20, 39; of women, 29
World War I, 243–44
World War II, 201–3, 244–45; women warriors, 255
Wounded Knee: massacre, 231; Oglala occupation, 273–74
Wovoka (Piaute), 230
Wu, King (Chou Dynasty founder), 104–5
Wundt, Herman, 252
Wu-wei (Taoist philosophy), 111

Xerold, Bishop, 138

Yamato (Japanese clan), 170
Yang Ch'eng-fu, 123, 126, 130
Yang Family Secret Transmissions, 127
Yang-Lu-chu'an, 127
Yanomamo: The Fierce People, Chagnon, 27
Yanomamo people, 25–27, 270, 301n7
Yates Petroleum, 285
Yellow Turbans, 129
Yellow Woman (Cheyenne), 215
Yoga, 85, 88–89, 306n10
Yoritomo (Minamoto leader), 173–74
Yosemite Valley, Muir and, 275–77
Yoshida Shoin, 190–91
Yoshimitsu (Ashikaga shogun), 179–80
Yoshio, Sakata, 192
Yotrimasa (samurai warrior), 173
Younger sons, medieval, 151–52
Yu (Hsia Dynasty founder), 101
Yuan Dynasty, 122, 129
Yueh, Lady of, 127–28
Yukoku, Fujita, 190

Zeami (Noh actor), 180
Zen Buddhism, 119–21, 174–76, 179, 187
Zhuge Liang, 130
Zihlman, Adrienne, 9

Rick Fields is a free-lance writer, editor, and journalist. He is the author of *How the Swans Came to the Lake: A Narrative History of Buddhism in America* and *Taking Refuge in L.A.: Life in a Vietnamese Buddhist Temple,* with the photographer Don Farber, and the principal author of *Chop Wood, Carry Water: A Guide to Spiritual Fulfillment in Everyday Life.* He lives in Boulder, Colorado.